Created and Directed by Hans Höfer

Produced and Edited by Lisa Choegyal

APA PUBLICATIONS

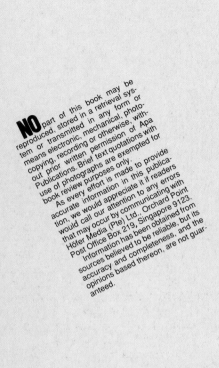
NepaL

ABOUT THIS BOOK

Welcome to *Insight Guide Nepal*. A team of experts familiar with all aspects of life in Nepal have combined, under the leadership of **Lisa Choegyal**, to produce the most authoritative and complete guide yet to the mountains and jungles of Nepal. The cultural monuments of the Kathmandu Valley are covered in detail but the book focuses on Nepal as a whole, travelling the trade trails and exploring the pilgrimage routes of the highest mountains in the world. The travel section surveys the peaks, explains the treks, and helps you enjoy the wildlife of the Terai. The diverse terrain of Nepal has something memorable to offer every visitor.

Lisa Choegyal has been a resident in Nepal since 1974 and is a Director of the Tiger Mountain group which arranges the best of adventure travel in Asia. She travels extensively throughout the country and is author of *Insight Pocket Guide: Nepal* and producer of the *Cityguide Kathmandu Valley*. In addition to editing and organising this volume, she contributed the section on festivals, Kathmandu Valley and Travel Tips, and commissioned the rest from acknowledged Nepal authorites and experts.

The Right Staff

Wendy Brewer Fleming wrote the adventure tourism, trekking, hill stations, Pokhara and river running sections as well as gave Himalayan-sized assistance in planning, advising, organising and editing. Fleming is a writer and trek leader and was for three years editor of *Nepal Traveller* magazine.

Sir Edmund Hillary, the world famous explorer and writer, contributed the first-person article on his experience with the Sherpa people. **Reinhold Messner** contributed the feature on what drives him to climb. Messner is the superstar of mountaineering who by October 1986 was the first to have scaled all the world's 8,000-meter giants.

Dr. Harka Bahadur Gurung, who wrote about geology and the Gurkhas, is one of Nepal's leading scholars and writers. Educated at the University of Edinburgh, he is a former Government minister and now has his own consultancy in Kathmandu.

The historical overview was written by **Charles Allen**, author of many books about the subcontinent, including his greatly acclaimed *Plain Tales from the Raj*. He and his brother, **Col. M.G. Allen** who wrote on fishing, were born and brought up in India.

Dor Bahadur Bista, Nepal's foremost anthropologist, contributed much of the section on the people of Nepal. **Father John K. Locke**, a Jesuit who has made a lifelong study of Hindu and Buddhist religions, wrote the piece on religion.

Charles Ramble, contributor of Natural Crossroads and the Yak and Shaman features, is a Kathmandu-based social anthropologist whose doctoral degree from Oxford University was for research conducted among Tibetan-speaking people in Nepal. He is currently Wildlife Director of Machan Wildlife Resort.

Kunda Dixit wrote the piece concerning the country's development and environmental dilemmas, Dixit is a leading Nepalese journalist based in the Philippines.

Choegyal   *Fleming*   *Allen*   *O'Connor*   *Dixit*

One of Britain's most experienced mountaineers and photographers, **Bill O'Connor** wrote the book *Trekking Peaks in Nepal*. He was the obvious person to contribute the Trekking Peak and 8,000-Meter Mountain sections and also some of his beautiful photographs.

World expert on the tiger, **Charles McDougal** has worked in Nepal since the 1960s. Wildlife Director for the Tiger Mountain group, he wrote the National Park and Jungle Safari sections. Mark Graham contributed the rare shot of the tiger in the wild.

Gisele Krauskopff, an anthropologist teaching at Paris University, worked among the unstudied Tharu people since 1975 and has published many articles and a book. She has a unique knowledge of and enthusiasm for the Nepal Terai and contributed the Tharu and Terai sections.

The features and pages involve some distinguished Nepal experts. **Elizabeth Hawley** is a journalist widely regarded as a one-woman Himalayan mountaineering institute. She is Executive Officer of Sir Edmund Hillary's Himalayan Trust and contributed the piece on Mallory and Irvine, interviewed Reinhold Messner and advised on all mountaineering aspects of the book.

David R. Shlim M.D. is medical director of the Himalayan Rescue Association and director of the CIWEC clinic in Kathmandu. His feature on problems at altitude is relevant to all trekkers. **Johan Reinhard** contributed the Shangrila legend. He has won awards for anthropology in the Himalaya and the Andes and specialises in mountain worship. **Frances Klatzel** has spent much of the last eight years in the Everest region creating the library and cultural centre at Thyangboche. **Maureen DeCoursey** wrote the page on the Gurung Hillwoman, drawn from her knowledge working for the Annapurna Conservation Area Project. **Frances Wall Higgins** introduced commercial mountain biking to Nepal and contributed a page on the subject.

Picture Perfect

Over twenty photographers combined to illustrate this book. **Galen Rowell**, the famous American climber and mountain photographer, contributed the backbone from his extensive collection. A frequent visitor to Nepal on mountaineering expeditions, he and his wife Barbara have produced works on Nepal and Tibet for National Geographic.

Less well-known names whose outstanding talent give this volume its atmosphere include **Devendra Basnet, Kevin Bubriski, Alain Evrard, Charles Gay, Thomas Laird, Craig Lovell, Gary McCue** and **Jock Montgomery**. All have lived in Nepal for months at a time and most are writers, photographers and trek leaders. They share a knowledge and passion for the country reflected in their work.

Special thanks must go to **Col. Jimmy Roberts**, founder of the trekking industry and Mountain Travel Nepal. He looked over the trekking sections and his advice, as always, was invaluable.

The late **Desmond Doig** was much missed but his Yeti feature lives on. Of great assistance were the **Ministry of Tourism, Tiger Mountain** group, **A.V. Jim Edwards, T.B. Shrestha, Manorma Mathai Moss** and **Tenzin Choegyal**.

—APA Publications

Ramble

Krauskopff

Rowell

Laird

Montgomery

CONTENTS

Roof Of The World

History, Culture & People

Playground Of The Gods

Places And Regions

Maps

TRAVEL TIPS

**For detailed Information
See Page 325**

"In a hundred ages of the gods I could not tell thee of the glories of the Himalaya."

Cradled amongst the highest mountains in the world, it is no wonder that Nepal has come to be known as the kingdom where deities mingle with mortals.

Close to a billion people revere the Himalaya as sacred. These include followers of two of the world's major religions, Buddhism and Hinduism. Nowhere on earth does a mountain range figure so prominently in the religious beliefs of such a large and diverse population. The mountains are considered the dwelling place of deities and saints, and for some they are the very embodiment of the gods themselves.

Abode of the Gods: Sherpa artists depict Mount Everest, the highest point on earth, as the goddess Miyal Langsangma, one of the Five Long-Life Sisters. Makalu embodies a fierce guardian deity and Kangchenjunga is worshipped in a ceremony in which the god so named appears as a masked dancer. Gauri Shanker is the home of Shiva and his consort Parvati, Ganesh Himal is named for the elephant-headed god and Annapurna is the goddess of plenty.

Such beliefs date back thousands of years and feature in the oldest legends and epics. Mountain worship by primitive tribes predates the established religions. It is not difficult to perceive why. Mountains influence weather and are the sources of rivers, they affect the welfare of all who live in their shadow. They unite the earth and the sky and are believed to be the guardians of the land, people and animals within their domain.

Even today a number of Himalayan peaks are still not open to climbing expeditions, preserved as holy places. Whereas mountaineers see only the physical dangers, the villagers have to worry about the long-term consequences of angering the gods. Not only can they cause accidents on the mountain but they may provoke regional catastrophes such as illness, floods and avalanches. Everest expeditions regularly make offerings and burn juniper incense to appease the goddess before attempting a climb.

The Nepalese people live close to their gods. Truth no less colourful than fiction makes Nepal one of the world's most incredible countries, a geographical wonder, an ethnological conundrum.

Diverse Heritage: None can fail to be impressed by the diversity of the land that comprises Nepal. The flat, lush plains of the lowland Terai, the Siwalik (Churia) Hills swathed in hard-wood jungles, the ochre-red farmlands of the Inner Terai, the plunging flanks of the Mahabharat range, the fertile emerald Valley of Kathmandu, the deep gorges of turbulent grey-green rivers, and layer upon layer of

Preceding pages: Tharu women from the Terai of Nepal; Sunrise over the Annapurnas; Cholatse in the Everest region of Nepal; blue pine forest below Annapurnal; magnificent Manang Valley; trekkers crossing the Thorang La pass. Left, Buddhist *lama* high in the Sherpa country of east Nepal.

foothills blued by distance. Beyond, the white Himalaya reach far above the clouds along the northern horizon. Within a single day one can fly past Everest and its neighbouring summits, pause amidst the palaces and temples of the Kathmandu Valley, then descend through the terraces of the middle hills to the plains and ride elephants through tropical jungle, inhabited with wild tigers.

This is the home of 19 million Nepalis. A rectangle 885 kilometers (553 miles) long and averaging 160 kilometers (100 miles) from north to south, Nepal bends to follow the curve of the central Himalaya. A country the size of Austria and Switzerland combined, Nepal's people, their languages and customs are as diverse as the terrain. From mountain to valley, plateau to plain, ethnic groups vary as much as the climate.

As many as 50 distinct languages and dialects have been identified and there are over 36 recognised different ethnic groups, each with their own cultural identity. The climate ranges from the nival waste of snow and ice above the alpine zone, to the humid, tropical lowland plains. The prevailing pattern of Hinduism to the south and Buddhism to the north is interwoven with Tantrism, animist rites and shamanistic practices. Both major religions co-exist in most of the country but they come together in the Kathmandu Valley to merge into a homogeneous and sophisticated civilisation.

"A Root Between Two Stones": Legends traditionally told the Nepalis all they needed to know about their origins, attributing unknown beginnings to heroes and gods. Swayambhunath was formerly a blue flame in a sacred lotus flower, floating on a pristine turquoise lake that became the Kathmandu Valley when drained by Manjushri's sword, creating present-day Chobar gorge.

Over the centuries, the history of Nepal encompasses waves of settlers who penetrated the mountain barrier from the north or the fever-infested southern jungles. A bewildering variety of people of Tibeto-Burmese and Indo-Aryan stock spread through the hills, plateaus and valleys of central Nepal. It was not uncommon for warring Himalayan principalities to invite help from an Indian or Tibetan prince, whose entourage would leave its mark on their adopted land.

Pilgrims, travellers and traders congregated, often for many months, in the clement surroundings of the Kathmandu Valley whilst waiting for passes to clear or swamps to dissipate. The genius of the indigenous Newar craftsmen was patronised by neighbouring admirers and the artisans themselves were exported along with their gilding, metalwork, woodcarving and stonework. The Chinese pagoda roof is said to have its origins and inspiration in the temple roof structures of Kathmandu.

Nepal is the world's only Hindu kingdom. It was first united by King Prithvi Narayan Shah of tiny Gorkha who subdued over 60 feuding states and principalities in the late 18th century and founded the current Shah dynasty.

<u>Left</u>, a Hindu devotee doing penance with oil lamps during a festival.

He described his new kingdom as "a root between two stones," referring to Nepal's precarious position squeezed between the vastness of Tibet and China to the north and India to the south. Such a land, precariously strategic and beset by the disadvantage of being landlocked, is truly a slender root between two massive stones. This fact is cause for as many political headaches amongst today's rulers as it was for Prithvi Narayan Shah himself. Emerging at the end of the 20th century into a new-found constitutional democracy from the confines of a formerly feudal-based tradition, foreign relations are not Nepal's only political problem today.

Roof of the World: Except for the narrow strip of Terai plain along its southern boundary and the temperate valleys spread across its middle, the country is entirely mountainous. More than a quarter of Nepal's land area is over 3,000 meters (10,000 feet) in altitude.

This stupendous mountain pedestal includes eight of the earth's fourteen 8,000 meter (26,250 feet) mountains either within or on its borders, and eight of the ten highest mountains in the world: Everest, Kangchenjunga, Lhotse, Makalu, Cho Oyu, Dhaulagiri, Manaslu and Annapurna.

The highest mountain in the world is Mount Everest, which bestrides the Nepal-Tibet border in the east of the country. It is known to Nepalis as Sagarmatha (Mother of the Universe) and in Tibet as Chomolungma (Mother Goddess). Named after George Everest, a British surveyor-general in late 19th Century India, the highest point on earth was eventually climbed on 29th May, 1953 by Sir Edmund Hillary of New Zealand and Tenzing Norgay Sherpa of India.

Some of the high passes along the northern border with Chinese Tibet remain perpetually frozen. The snow-line varies between 5,000 and 6,000 meters (16,400 feet and 19,700 feet) descending lower during winter storms. Deep river valleys incise across the range to fall rapidly to the lower valleys. The youngest range of mountains in the world is still purported by geologists to be moving and growing, a fact attested to by earthquakes and subterranean tensions.

In the last decade, age-old patterns are altering as Nepal develops mobility, communications and political awareness. Parliamentary democracy has been chosen by the people and King Birendra Bir Bikram Shah Dev may not be recognised by all as an infallible reincarnation of the Hindu god Vishnu. The younger generation of the capital, Kathmandu, may be in danger of discarding individual cultural identity in favour of a drab national unity, flavoured with Western influence.

But if the Kathmandu Valley has long been considered to be Nepal, Nepal is by no means only Kathmandu. The hills and valleys of the hinterland, beneath the protecting peaks inhabited by the Himalayan gods, will long nurture the magnificent diversity and rich heritage to be discovered in Nepal.

Right, pilgrims beneath the sacred peak of Numbur bathe in the Dudh Kunda lake, Solu Khumbu.

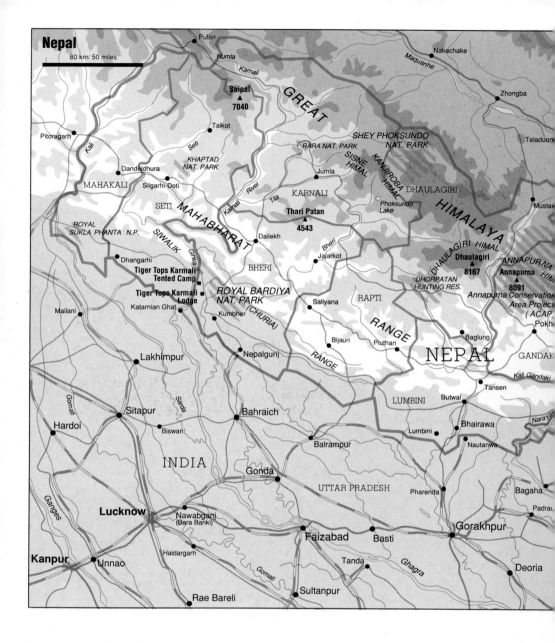

NEPAL AT A GLANCE

Area: 145,391 square kilometers (56,139 square miles), stretches 885 kilometers (553 miles) from east to west and averages 160 kilometers (100 miles) from north to south.

Terrain: Heavily mountainous. 14% of the land is cultivated, 13% is pasture, 32% is forested.

Population: About 19 million (50% under the age of 21) growing at 2.7 percent annually.

Government: Multi-party parliamentary democracy headed by His Majesty King Birendra Bir Bikram Shah Dev. The Right Honorable Giriji Prasad Koirala, leader of the Nepali Congress Party, is Prime Minister.

Capital: Kathmandu (population 500,000; Kathmandu Valley has a total population of one million).

Peoples: Tribal groups include Gurung,

Limbu, Magar, Newar, Rai, Sherpa, Tamang and Tharu, with diverse smaller groups. Major caste groups are the Brahmans and Chhetris. Large numbers of Indians and some Tibetans make their home in Nepal.

Languages: Nepali 58% (official language), Newari 3% (mainly in Kathmandu), Tibetan languages 19% (mainly in hill areas), Indian languages 20% (mainly in Terai). Nepal has over 30 languages and dozens of dialects.

Religion: Officially 90% Hindu, 8% Buddhist, 2% Islamic, but these figures are misleading and more like 25% is in reality Buddhist. Hinduism and Buddhism do overlap somewhat.

Highest Point: Mount Everest, also known as Sagarmatha and Chomolungma, the highest point on earth (8,848 meters or 29,028 feet).

Currency: Nepalese currency (about Rs 42.60 equals US$1.00)

The ancient conception of the Himalaya is one of utter immanence, the eternal home of the gods. It was an object of awe and devotion and not for men to enquire and fathom. However, a reflection on the genesis of the *shaligram* ammonite, the black fossil revered by the Hindus as an embodiment of Vishnu, leads to a geological past far beyond the age of man. The making of the ammonite fossil is related to the initial emergence of the Himalayan heights from the depths of a sea in the beginning of time.

The Collision of Continents: It was only seven decades ago that Alfred Wegener first postulated the theory of Continental Drift. The continents as we know them today were said to have broken off from a single land mass some hundreds of millions of years ago and "drifted" apart, riding on underlying plastic materials. Though discussions persist as to the actual cause and extent of the drift, modern geotechniques have reaffirmed the movement of continents, or plates, within the Theory of Plate Tectonics.

It is now largely accepted that the Himalaya were formed as a result of the collision of two large continental plates, the Indian subcontinent and Eurasia, in a process that began as early as 130 million years ago at the time when reptiles and dinosaurs roamed the earth. Having split off from a much larger southern continent called Gondwanaland – from which also came Australia, Antarctica, Africa and parts of South America – the Indian subcontinent travelled 4,400 kilometers (2,700 miles) northwards at an estimated rate of 20-25 centimeters (8-10 inches) per year and began colliding with the northern land mass, called Laurasia, approximately 50-60 million years ago.

The Tethys Sea: Studies of rock layers have been used to reconstruct the origins of the Himalaya, suggesting early periods of alternating subsidence and uplift of the earth's surface. An extensive sea existed in the region where the Himalaya now rise, stretching right across the southern margin of Eurasia wedged between Laurasia and Gondwana. The sea, known as the Tethys, came into being some 250 million years ago during the Late Palaeozoic era, when the first reptiles appeared, and dried up gradually about 40-50 million years ago, when mammals came into being. Some scientists now think that the Tethys was actually a series of seas that repeatedly subsided, were uplifted and drained away with the passing of a number of land fragments set adrift from Gondwana

which followed each other on a collision course into the northern Asian continent.

During this time, almost all of the now highly elevated areas between India and Central Asia were invaded by the Tethys Sea. Sinking and widening of the earth's surface commenced around 200 million years ago. It is believed that subsequent rising of the sub-surface brought the sea to a shallow level towards the Lower Cretaceous (110-135 million years ago).

By 40 to 65 million years ago, the bottom had risen so much as to cause the water to spill over and flood much of the surrounding land. This deluge was followed by the ulti-

Left, ammonite fossils from the ancient Tethys Sea in the Kali Gandaki valley. **Above**, glaciers and river gorges (this one in the Annapurna area) have forged the Himalaya.

mate dissolution of the Himalayan sea, as evident by the fact that all later rock types found within the Himalaya (except those in localised basins) were laid down above water.

Thus, the rising of the Tethys Sea was primarily due to the build up of marine sediments, accumulating to great thicknesses of over 4,500 meters (15,000 feet) over a period of some 200 million years. Earlier, however, during the Jurassic and late Cretaceous era (70-80 to 195 million years ago), upheavals created some minor submarine ridges and valleys, accompanied by the appearance of volcanoes and subterranean bodies of molten rock.

dormant period, coinciding with the Ice Age, when these first Himalayan chains were eroded down to form the Siwalik hills to the south. Siwalik deposits consist of coarse boulder conglomerates, 1,000 to 1,500 meters (3,000 to 5,000 feet) thick.

The fourth sequence in the uplift of the Himalaya occurred about two million years ago when older layers of rock were overthrust onto the deposits of the Siwaliks. This over-riding is well demarcated by the fault plane called the "main boundary thrust." The fifth and final upheaval ensued during the Pleistocene period, one to two million years ago, a time of much glacial activity when the progenitors of man were stirring. Its impact

The Himalaya are Born: These upheavals were the first spasms of the birth of the Himalaya, which actually took place in a series of stupendous periods of uplift punctuated by intervals of comparative quiescence. A second upheaval occurred in the Upper Eocene (38-45 million years ago), raising the primary ridges and basins of the Tethys Sea into mountain ranges with intervening shallow marshes and large river valleys. It was, however, the intense mountain-building epoch of the mid-Miocene (seven to 26 million years ago) that created the major structure of the present-day Himalaya. This third Himalayan uplift was followed by a

was felt most in the lower hills of the Himalaya where layers of rock were pushed up as much as 2,000 meters (6,000 feet).

Today's Tensions and Earthquakes: Ever since the first collision of continents, the Himalayan region has been subjected to compression, contortion, elevation and denudation. The area is still in the process of adjustment: the Indian subcontinent continues to push into Asia at a rate of about two inches (five centimeters) per year, as substantiated by the frequency of large slips along major faultlines beneath the Himalaya causing periodic earthquakes, as well as by more localized geologic events. In fact, most geologists agree that the Himalaya is still rising, noting more recent (Pliocene) over-thrusting in the foothills and a 50-degree tilt of rock layers in the western Himalaya. Kathmandu lake deposits which now dip northwards were uplifted 200 meters (600 feet) over the last 200,000 years. The present rate of uplift is difficult to tell as accurate measurements have only been made over the last hundred years.

Back to the Sea: At the same time, the Himalaya are wearing down, as all young mountains do. The monsoon rains pound at their sides, and constant freezing and thawing cracks the rocks which cause them to shed their outer layers. Although glacial

ridges in bowls and sharp rims. From its terminus, a milky stream runs thick with finely ground sediments which will eventually wash all the way down to the Ganges, returning once-submarine deposits back to the sea.

Mountain Geography: But for the narrow strip of plain along Nepal's southern border, and temperate valleys spread across its middle, the country is entirely mountainous.

The northern part of the country is characterised by towering ice and snow ranges with occasional sparse valleys. This is the Himalayan or mountain region of the country, a part of Nepal conspicuous for its extreme altitude and wild terrain. The highest ranges

fields are limited, they more than any constant force chisel away at the peaks and carve away the valleys. Season upon season of snow accumulates and is compressed into ice to depths of several hundred meters. The sheer weight shoves the glacier's lowest edge down the mountain, scraping away debris from the sides and bottom.

At the top, it scoops out a rounded valley, a cirque, which defines the mountains'

Left, Mount Everest from Kala Pattar showing the great Khumbu icefall. **Above**, wildly folded sedimentary rock high on Nuptse, photographed from 7,000 meters (24,000 feet) on Everest.

are crowned by jagged peaks. Ice-scooped basins found at lower elevations indicate a much wider glacial provenance in the past.

Mountain relief is asymmetrical, with rock strata inclined to the north, leaving steep south faces. The south-tending spurs of the main range are covered with temperate forests lower down and confine steep valleys marked with occasional waterfalls. Thunderstorms are frequent and winter frosts limit agriculture. Nevertheless, potatoes are grown to 4,000 meters (13,100 feet) and barley even higher.

North of the main range, the prospect is much more desolate with bare mountain slopes and undulating valley bottoms filled with rock debris and sparse vegetation in sheltered corners. This mountain region is a marginal area for human settlement and hence man's influence on the landscape is minimal. Summers are short, winters severe and dry with high snowfall, low temperatures and strong winds.

In the northwest of the country a fourth, trans-Himalayan range defines the boundary between Nepal and Tibet. Peaks of 6,000 to 7,000 meters (19,700 to 23,000 feet) lie about 35 kilometers (22 miles) north of the main Himalaya; their relief is less rugged, and wind-eroded landforms predominate. Here elevated *bhot* valleys – broad with open

smaller valleys make narrow, steep defiles, the larger ones have an easy gradient and a wide open character. The main north-south valleys and their upper tributary extensions make deep indentations in the middle hill topography and these low valleys have numerous old river terraces indicating changing geologic or climatic conditions at the time of alluvial deposits. Landslides and landslips are common and tributary streams, overloaded with washed-down materials, unload alluvial cones at their termini.

The mild subtropical climate and adequate rainfall have made the midland area a favourable zone for agricultural settlement. Farmers have cleared vast hillsides of trees

profiles and arid climate – are reminiscent of Tibet, particularly where the Himalayan rainshadow blocks out the monsoon rains.

Middle Hills: Below the Himalaya, running in a similar west-northwest to east-southeast direction 90 kilometers (56 miles) south of the great rise is the Mahabharat range, reaching elevations between 1,500 and 2,700 meters (4,900 and 8,900 feet). These are referred to as the sub-Himalaya.

The middle hill region, also called the *pahar*, extends between the Mahabharat and the high Himalaya. Its characteristic landforms are low hills and sinuous ridges, dissected by numerous river valleys. While the

for cultivation, spoiling the natural landscape. The typical scenery of the middle hill country is flights of terraced fields carved out of steep slopes.

The clement Kathmandu Valley falls in this belt. The moderate climate permits three harvests a year and small plantings in between. Summer maximums are about 30°C (86°F) and mean winter temperatures about 10°C (50°F). Winters are sometimes frosty, but are dry and snowless, while summer monsoons bring substantial rain. Visitors are often surprised to learn that Kathmandu's latitude – about 27°40' North – is the same as that of Florida and Kuwait, and slightly south of New Delhi.

The Lowland Landscape: The area south of the Mahabharat hills is generally known as the Terai. Despite the intervening Siwalik range, this southern region of Nepal is virtually flat, a finely graded alluvial plain overlain with silt and sand. Twenty-five to forty kilometers (15 to 25 miles) broad within the Nepalese border, the recumbent Terai is a northern extension of India's vast Ganges plain (see page 315).

The Siwalik (sometimes called the Churia) range stands out conspicuously from the swampy lowlands. They rise to heights of 750 to 1,500 meters (2,450 to 4,900 feet), higher in west Nepal corresponding to the and Mahabharat hills. These longitudinal valleys have been formed mainly by the depositions from the slopes of the enclosing Mahabharat and Siwalik ranges.

Summers are hot in the Terai and the *dun*, with temperatures often exceeding 38°C (100°F). Winters are considerably cooler, with temperatures down to 10°C (50°F). Rainfall comes primarily in the June-to-September monsoon, heaviest in the east.

The Impact of Man: Man attempts to adapt himself to the natural environment and in the process leaves his imprint on the landscape. The Terai's natural environment has considerably changed over the last decade through the agency of man. The southern strip of the

elevated Terai which stands an average of 180 meters (600 feet) above sea level in the west compared with 90 meters (300 feet) in the east. Elsewhere the Siwaliks have been much reduced in height and even appear as isolated hillocks. Their dry, immature soils support only a sparse population.

At a slightly higher elevation to the Terai plain, but with similar vegetation, lie the *dun* or Inner Terai valleys between the Siwalik

Left, a remote monastery is protected by trees in a valley sculpted with terraces in east Nepal. **Above**, ferns and leaves flourish in the summer monsoon.

Terai plain has been transformed into an extensive belt of farms and new settlers have made deep in-roads into the area by clearing forest and draining marshes.

While harsh conditions dominate in the mountain region, in the middle hill areas man has again left his mark by removing natural vegetative cover, thereby hastening soil erosion. This depletion of a critical natural resource is reflected in the increasing migration of farmers to the Terai (see page 49).

It is no wonder that the Nepalese deify the imposing mountains that divide them, and sanctify the fertile rivers that unite them.

Nepal links the south with the north by welding together the two great biogeographical realms, the Palaearctic and the Oriental. The Nepal Himalaya represents the broad band of transition between the weather patterns, and accordingly the vegetation, flora and fauna of the eastern and western Himalaya. It is a true crossroads of great natural wealth and beauty.

There is, however, an additional aspect. The country's terrain rises dramatically from only a hundred meters above sea level to the highest peaks in the world. It is this vertical axis that complicates, and to a great extent conditions, the interaction of the horizontal dimensions.

Central Himalaya: The central part of the Himalayan chain stretches for some 900 kilometers (550 miles) from the Mahakali River on Nepal's western border to the Tista River in India in the east. It can be divided into three regions, principally on the basis of vegetation types of the middle hills. Generally speaking, these subdivisions correspond to the three major river systems of Nepal: the Karnali, the Gandaki and the Kosi.

The main spine of the Great Himalayan Range is not the watershed between the Ganges and Tsangpo Rivers. This lies further north in Tibet. Consequently even those trans-Himalayan regions which fall within the political frontiers of Nepal are drained by tributaries of the Ganges.

Monsoon Rains: The monsoon begins in June and lasts for almost a quarter of the year, but its distribution of rain is not equal across Nepal. The east of the country is affected first by the wet winds from the Bay of Bengal, and thus has a longer monsoon with a considerably higher volume of water.

West Nepal lies in the hinterland of the monsoon's progress and is also under the desiccating influence of the *lhu*, the dry wind that blows across western India in the summer months. The high Himalaya themselves block the northward passage of the monsoon and much of northwest Nepal lies in the rainshadow cast by the great massifs of

Left, terraced fields of Chhomrong village in the Annapurnas.

Dhaulagiri and Annapurna.

This is in striking contrast with the Pokhara valley below, which is relatively exposed by a dip in the middle ranges to the south. Pokhara receives well over 3,000 millimeters (120 inches) of rain every year whilst Jomosom, just 65 kilometers (40 miles) to the north, gets less than 300 millimeters (12 inches).

Vegetation Zones: The east-west effects of the monsoon are cross-cut by a number of altitudinally determined climatic zones. The tropical Terai and lower Siwalik (Churia) hills extend up to about 1,000 meters (3,300 feet) and are followed by the subtropical zone from 1,000 to 2,000 meters (3,300 – 6,500 feet).

The warm temperate belt runs from 2,000 to 3,000 meters (6,500 – 10,000 feet) and is succeeded by the cool temperate or subalpine zone, which ends with the treeline at about 4,000 meters (13,000 feet).

Most of the remaining vegetation falls within the alpine belt between 4,000 and 5,000 meters (13,000 – 16,500 feet). The region above 5,500 meters (18,000 feet) is referred to as the nival or aeolian zone, euphemisms for what is effectively a wind-swept desolation of snow and ice.

The vegetation of the tropical belt remains remarkably uniform throughout the length of Nepal. The prevailing type of forest is sal, named after its dominant tree, *Shorea robusta*. This hardwood tree, much valued for its timber, grows in association with a number of other species.

These include *Lagerstroemia parviflora* which has an attractive pinkish-brown bark that falls away in flakes; *Dillenia pentagyna*, the fruits of which are favoured by villagers for making pickles; *Semecarpus anacardium*, the marking-nut tree, so called for the dark juice of the fruit which is used as ink (and also as an abortifacient).

Spatholobus roxburgii is an enormous vine which winds clockwise around its hosts – local lore has it that if you find one growing anti-clockwise, a nail hammered into it will turn to gold. There are a number of *Terminalia* species including *T. belerica*, the delicious kernel of whose fruit contains a mild narcotic. *Holarrhena antidysenterica* is used for the purpose indicated in its name in ayurvedic medicine. The milky sap of this tree is the source of its Nepali name, *dudhkare* (*dudh* means milk). Some ethnic groups bury their dead babies near the roots of this tree so they will have milk to drink in the afterworld.

Evergreens and Deciduous: The eastern and central regions of the subtropical belt are dominated by two evergreens; *Schima wallichii* and three species of *Castanopsis*. The little chestnuts of the latter are roasted with their shells and eaten by the villagers and the foliage is prized for livestock fodder. The lower forests include *Bombax ceiba*, the silk

proliferates on north facing hillsides. Interestingly, elsewhere in its distribution it is only found on south facing slopes. Chir pine resin is an important source of rosin and turpentine.

The temperate zone in eastern and central Nepal is characterised by mixed broad-leaved forest, usually on north and west slopes. It is sometimes referred to as "laurel forest" because of the abundance of *Lauraceae*. *Michelia champaca* and *Castanopsis* find their way into this belt from the lower regions together with a few tree-ferns and screw pines. Evergreen oaks (*Quercus* spp) appear at 1,200 meters (4,000 feet) and share the upper temperate forests with spe-

cotton tree, valued for the kapok yielded by the pods. *Mallotus philippinensis* is called *sindur* in Nepali after the red powder from the fruit, traditionally used before the advent of chemical dyes as the ceremonial dust in Hindu rituals.

Other trees found here become more abundant in the upper ranges: the deciduous *Engelhardtia spicata*, the *Michelia champaca*, a beautiful magnolia whose yellowish wood is valued for furniture, and the indigenous Nepalese alder (*Alnus nepalensis*).

The drier conditions of northwestern Nepal favour the growth of chir pine (*Pinus roxburghii*) in the subtropical belt where it

cies of maple as well as *Prunus*, *Magnolia* and *Osmanthus*.

Rhododendrons – The National Flower: Rhododendrons, *laligurans* in Nepali, are found from around 1,100 meters (3,600 feet). The red bloom of the imposing *Rhododendron arboreum* was declared the national flower of Nepal in 1962. The colour of the flower fades with altitude progressing through paler shades of pink until it turns entirely white at about 2,500 meters (8,200 feet). Colours of other rhododendron species range through the spectrum from white, cream and yellow to lilac and purple.

Whilst rhododendrons usually constitute

the understorey, there are regions where they grow 15 meters (50 feet) high, almost to the exclusion of other trees. The flowers are pickled by villagers but honey made from the nectar contains a natural hallucinogen, producing bizarre visual distortions.

Rhododendrons decrease in stature with altitude and dwarf species form a low carpet in certain alpine areas. Two of these, *R. cowanlum* which has purplish flowers and the lemon-yellow *R. lowndesii*, are the only two rhododendrons endemic to Nepal. People of the alpine zone value dwarf rhododendrons for incense and as a substitute for snuff. The diminutive *R. nivale*, which attains a height of just five centimeters (two

Quercus incana. Frequently occurring with the ubiquitous *Rhododendron arboreum*, it gives way at higher altitudes to mixed deciduous forests of other species of oak, the chestnut *Aesculus indica*, the maple *Acer caesium* and the walnut *Juglans regia*.

Conifers are much more in evidence in west Nepal. The low-altitude fir, *Abies pindrow*, soars up to a height of 45 meters (150 feet). In the lower parts of its range, extending from about 2,100 to 3,500 meters (7,000 – 11,500 feet), it is found with the majestic Himalayan cedar (*Cedrus deodara*) which forms magnificent forests along the Karnali. Further up is the West Himalayan spruce (*Picea smithiana*), the silver fir (*Abies*

inches), holds the altitude record for woody plants at 5,500 meters (18,000 feet).

Except for the sun-loving dwarf species, rhododendrons prefer moist habitats. They therefore thrive in eastern Nepal which boasts 30 species, whereas only five have been recorded from the Karnali basin.

Oak, Conifer and Birch: The vegetation of the temperate zone in western Nepal is generally quite different from the eastern region. The dominant species of oak in the west is

Left, crossing a monsoon-swollen stream with makeshift umbrellas. **Above**, Tharu shepherds on the overgrazed land of the Terai.

spectabilis) and the blue pine (*Pinus excelsa*). Like the blue pine, the Himalayan hemlock (*Tsuga dumosa*) is distributed throughout the subalpine region of Nepal, but the cypress (*Cupressus torulosa*), which grows between 1,800 and 3,500 meters (5,900 – 11,500 feet), occurs nowhere east of the Kali Gandaki.

Much of the treeline in Nepal is defined by birch (*Betula utilis*). Its papery bark is used by highland villagers for a number of purposes including as a ceiling material in flat-roofed Muktinath and as a natural grease-proof paper for wrapping yak-butter.

The vegetation above the treeline is divisible broadly into moist and dry alpine scrub. In addition to the dwarf rhododendrons, there are several species of juniper, two of which reach the stature of trees growing up to 10 to 15 meters (33 – 50 feet) in the moister highlands.

Those in the dry, higher elevations of central and western Nepal grow as a prostrate shrub no more than two meters (six feet) high. Other scrubland plants include shrubs such as *Hippophae*, *Spiraca*, *Berberis* and *Cotoncaster*. The arid regions of Mustang, Dolpo and Manang are dominated by thorny *Caragana* and *Lonicera* bushes.

Above all, the alpine flora makes these mountain regions worth visiting in the sum-

former, which grow in soil, are found in the temperate and subalpine zones and include the spectacular lady's slipper (*Cypripedium* spp). There are also a few saprophytic varieties, such as the tall, yellow-flowering *Galeola*, whose leaves which are not green grow beneath the humus layer of the soil. Most epiphytes (which have aerial roots) favour the subtropical and warm temperate zones. All orchids are protected by law and their export from Nepal is banned.

Another important plant is the bamboo. Twenty species occur in Nepal and are fundamental to the lifestyles of many ethnic groups. The Rai creation myth gives pride of place to bamboo as one of the first living

mer months for the amateur botanist willing to brave the heat, rain and leeches of the approach trek. Primulas (seventy species are found in the Himalaya) grow in abundance, larkspurs, fumitories, edelweiss, anemones and potentillas and a number of gentians flower into October. The ice blue Himalayan poppy is found on lower hillsides.

Orchids, Bamboo and Nettles: Whilst impossible to do justice to the whole glorious spectrum of Himalayan flora, some mention must be made of Nepal's orchids which number a staggering 319 species, in 89 genera. Orchids fall into two main groups, terrestrial and epiphytic. The majority of the

things to emerge from the womb of the goddess-creator. One survey counted 57 bamboo artifacts used in a single Rai house. Commoner items include baskets, mats, cradles, water vessels but there are also more exotic objects such as bows and arrows, rattraps, and a brush used in shaman seances.

People who have lived for countless generations on the margins of the forest have understandably come to learn how to best use its resources. A great number of species at different altitudes are valued for their fibres but none is more versatile than *Girardinia*, the Himalayan nettle.

This plant, which may reach three meters

(10 feet) in height grows best in clearings in mixed deciduous forests between 1,500 and 3,000 meters (5,000 – 10,000 feet). Its jagged leaves, which can deliver an impressive sting, are enjoyed as a vegetable when young and tender. But it is the stems, containing among the longest known plant fibres, in which the villagers are chiefly interested. Processing takes over four weeks and is carried out by women – bamboo by contrast is worked by men. The bark is stripped from the stems with their teeth and the fibres soaked, pounded, boiled and spun into a rough yarn. It is then woven on looms into a durable cloth.

Of the many other plants that are valued

for their fibres, three species of the *Thymeliaceae* family are important because of their use in paper-making. These shrubs, especially daphne, grow abundantly in oak-laurel and oak-rhododendron forests. Workers pound the plant stems with mallets to extract the pulp, then spread it over taut muslin screens to dry into sheets of coarse paper.

Medicinal Herbs, Lichens and Ferns: In a country were modern medical facilities are few, it is natural that a vast lore of medicinal

herbs should have developed. Nepal has 600 indigenous plants with recognised therapeutic properties, more than half of which occur in the subtropical zone. Some are in high demand on the international market and large quantities are exported in bulk to India, Europe and the Far East.

A number of lichens are valued as medicinal plants; some 352 species, grouped in 67 genera, have been identified in Nepal. Two species of *Parmelia* are especially in demand in India for use in spice and incense. Lichen extracts are used in perfume and some are valued for their antibiotic properties. Lichens cover a vast altitudinal range and the wealth of species found above the treeline remains practially unstudied.

Ferns, too, include a number of species (30 are listed by the Nepal Pharmaceutical Association) with medicinal properties, valued for use in respiratory ailments, intestinal worms and for the treatment of cuts and bruises. In total there are 375 species of ferns, grouped into 84 genera, although the diversity decreases as one moves westwards to the drier regions. Young shoots of several varieties are eaten as a green vegetable and may even be found on sale in the markets of Kathmandu.

Beautiful Butterflies and Multiple Moths: With such a diversity of habitats, it is not surprising that there is a vast insect fauna in Nepal. Butterflies and moths are the most conspicuous and beautiful of the entire class.

Eleven of the world's 15 families of butterflies are represented in Nepal and 614 species have been identified. This high number is due largely to the presence of both Palaearctic and Oriental species, the dividing line for which corresponds roughly to the upper limit of the temperate zone at 3,000 meters (10,000 feet). The line, of course, is somewhat blurred as there are strong fliers from both regions which shamelessly transgress the frontier by a considerable margin.

The butterfly season predictably varies as a function of altitude. Lowland species proliferate between March and November, and a few may be seen throughout the winter months. Variations occur with the monsoon, the wet season forms being distinguishable by their greater size and brighter colours.

The most spectacular butterflies of the Terai and midlands are undoubtedly the swallowtails (*Papilionidae*). The name is a misnomer as many are tailless. Other highly visible species include the tawny tigers (*Danaus* spp), close relatives of the American milkweed or monarch. They can well afford to fly unhurriedly as their orange-and-black wings warn predatory birds that their bodies contain poisons. This colour scheme has proved so successful that it is mimicked by perfectly edible species.

The swallowtail family is also represented in the opposite altitudinal extreme. The rare banded apollo (*P. acdestis*) has been found only between 5,000 and 5,500 meters (16,500 – 18,000 feet), protected from the brisk temperatures by its hairy body. The highland season is considerably shorter, last-

ing only from May to August.

Over 5,000 species of moths are found in Nepal, some of which are still to be scientifically described. The spectacular *Saturniidae* family of the atlas, moon and silk moths are represented by 20 species. These include the giant atlas moth (*Attacus atlas*), the world's largest moth with a wingspan of nearly one foot. Over 90 species (8% of the world population) have been recorded of the handsome *Sphingidae* family and include many of the world's rarest hawk moths.

One of the great pleasures of Nepal for the visitor is the profusion of butterfly and moth species, many of which have diminished in developed countries as a consequence of modern agricultural practices. For example, the swallowtail *Papilio machaon* is common in Nepal whilst in England is now confined to Norfolk's Wicken Fen. The rare Queen of Spain fritillary from the U.K. (*Issoria issaea*) is frequently encountered and there are some half-dozen species of clouded yellows (*Colias* spp), a Palaearctic genus which has extended its range down to the Terai. Not unusual in Nepal are some of the very rare British hawk moths, such as the death's head (*Acherontia* spp).

Bird Paradise: Nepal is indeed a paradise for birds with over 800 species recorded, representing 10 percent of the world's population in a tiny fraction of the land mass.

The avian wealth of the Terai is discussed in detail (see page 315) but the midlands and highlands too have a great deal to offer. Whilst altitude is the principal criterion that separates the northern Palaearctic species from the predominantly Oriental varieties of the south, the longitudinal factor is also important.

In the case of birds, however, the central division of the Nepal Himalaya seems to be a largely meaningless category. Instead, the distribution of birds points to the Kali Gandaki as a clear divide between east and west. For example, three species of titmouse (*Parus* spp) and two nuthatches (*Sitta* spp) do not occur east of the Kali Gandaki valley, which also represents the westward limit of such birds as the blood pheasant, the brown parrotbill, the golden-breasted tit babbler and the rufous-bellied shrike babbler.

The highlands offer a number of impressive residents such as the lammergeier, the golden eagle and the Himalayan griffon vulture. The last of these is common enough around the Annapurnas but is unaccountably declining in the Everest region. There is also a large range of high altitude passerines, including a number of mountain finches, rose finches, accentors and redstarts.

Mountain Mammals: The large mammals, such as the elephant, rhinoceros, gaur and tiger are restricted to the lowland Terai (see page 135) but the higher altitude parks afford protection for a number of exciting species.

Sagarmatha National Park, for example, contains the largest concentration of Himalayan tahr (*Hemitragus jemlahicus*) anywhere in the animal's wide range from Kashmir to Sikkim. The preferred altitude of this wild goat coincides with the upper haunts of the ghoral or Himalayan chamois (*Nemorhaedus goral*). This goat-antelope may be found from over 4,000 meters (13,000 feet) to as low as 900 meters (3,000 feet) where it descends to raid village crops. The ghoral and its near relative, the peculiar-looking, shy serow (*Capricornis sumatrensis*) which prefers forest habitats, are both hunted for their meat by villagers outside protected areas.

Another inveterate crop raider is the bear. There are two species in the mountains of Nepal. The Himalayan black bear (*Selanarctos thibetanus*), like the sloth bear of the

communities.

No animal has been the object of the hunters' attention as much as the musk deer (*Moschus moschiferus*), which ranges from around 2,000 to 4,500 meters (6,500 – 14,800 feet). The musk, secreted by the male in a pod under its tail, is valued in Chinese medicine, Tibetan incense and the Western perfume industry.

Although strictly protected, musk is worth several times its weight in gold and a single pod may yield over 50 grams (two ounces), providing the necessary incentive to risk the penalties.

Above the treeline, between 4,000 and 5,000 meters (13,000 – 16,500 feet), it is

Terai, has a white V-shaped bib, but ranges through the middle hills up to the limit of the forest. The brown bear (*Ursus arctos*), a Palaearctic species, is more confined to higher altitudes. Both are hunted for their gall bladders, which are in demand as ingredients for Chinese medicine. The capacity of these powerful animals to defend themselves against, and indeed to attack, incautious villagers is evident by the terrible injuries that sometimes occur in mountain

Left, Peacock Pansy butterfly (*Precis almana*).
Above, the Himalaya across the width of Nepal from the Terai plains.

often possible to see the blue sheep (*Pseudois nayaur*), locally known as a *bharal*. With exceptional luck one might glimpse their chief predator, the elusive snow leopard (*Uncia uncia*).

This elegant cat has long been persecuted for its beautiful coat, paler and thicker than that of its cousin the common leopard, and because of its penchant for domestic sheep, goats and occasionally even yaks. Its numbers are increasing in response to protection, although it has not yet reappeared in the Everest region where the last was killed in 1966. When it does return, however, it will no longer lack natural prey.

Nepal has seven national parks, three wildlife reserves and one hunting reserve all administered by the National Parks and Wildlife Conservation Department of His Majesty's Government. These 11 protected areas total 11,001 square km (4,247 square miles) and represent 8 percent of Nepal's land area.

Royal Chitwan National Park, located in the central inner-Terai region,was the kingdom's first national park. It was gazetted in 1973, with an area of 544 square km (210 square miles) and was extended in 1976

to its present size of 1,040 square km (402 square miles). This former royal hunting reserve and rhinoceros sanctuary contains abundant wildlife and is famous for its tigers.

Royal Bardiya National Park, situated in the remote and untouched far western Terai was formerly a wildlife reserve established in 1976 and extended in 1984 to its present size of 968 square km (374 square miles). It finally achieved national park status in 1988 and is comparable to Chitwan for

Above, Himalayan tahr in Sagarmatha National Park. **Right**, Rhodendron forest and primulas in east Nepal.

its richness of wildlife and tigers.

Sagarmatha National Park includes not only the peaks and valleys of the southern half of Mount Everest but also many villages of the Sherpa mountain guides. It was established in 1976 with an area of 1,243 square km (480 square miles).

Langtang National Park in the mountain region of central Nepal just south of the Tibet border was gazetted in 1976 with an area of 1,710 square km (660 square miles).

Shey Phoksundo National Park, the country's largest park and the only one in the trans-Himalayan zone, was gazetted in 1984 with an area of 3,555 square km (1,373 square miles).

Rara National Park, which includes Rara Lake and its surroundings in far west Nepal, was established in 1976 with an area of 106 square km (41 square miles).

Khaptad National Park contains one of the last examples of Nepal's middle hill forests, situated in the far west. Gazetted in 1984 with an area of 225 square km (87 square miles).

Koshi Tappu Wildlife Reserve is located on the Koshi River in the east Terai and contains the only population of wild buffaloes in Nepal. Also a sanctuary for migratory waterfowl, it was gazetted in 1976 with an area of 175 square km (68 square miles).

Parsa Wildlife Reserve, adjacent to Royal Chitwan National Park, contains Nepal's largest resident herd of wild elephants. It covers 499 square km (193 square miles) and was gazetted in 1984.

Royal Sukla Phanta Wildlife Reserve in the far western Terai contains a large population of swamp deer as well as tigers and other wildlife. It was gazetted in 1976 with an area of 155 square km (60 square miles).

Dhorpatan Hunting Reserve contains a large number of blue sheep in the western mountains and covers 1,325 square km (512 square miles). The **Annapurna Conservation Area Project** (ACAP), northwest of Pokhara, is 2,660 square km (1,027 square miles) and managed by the non-governmental King Mahendra Trust for Nature Conservation (KMTNC). An even larger region, the **Makalu-Barun National Park and Conservation Area** has recently been established in the east.

Cruising 9,000 meters (30,000 feet) above the Himalaya in a jet, the icy chaos below begins to resemble what it really is: a gigantic pile-up resulting from the head-on collision millions of years ago of two continental plates. The force of that impact squeezed out layer upon overlapping layer of rock-like toothpaste all along the impact zone.

The antecedent of what is now the Annapurna massif is a stupendous hulk soaring as high as 9,500 meters (31,000 feet) above sea level. Mount Everest's granite pyramid was the product of later upheavals. Interestingly, although the great black massif of the world's highest mountain is made of granite, the top three hundred meters (1,000 feet) is limestone which millions of years ago was lying at the bottom of the sea.

Rain storms, prototypes of present-day monsoons, soon started breaking down the southern slopes and eroding the adolescent Himalaya even as they grew. Enormous volumes of silt were washed down to the Ganges Sea which was rapidly clogged up with detritus and alluvium.

Besides putting the mountains in their geological perspective, flying above the Himalaya also gives a sense of the true scale of things. On the ground, the vertical tends to be exaggerated. From six miles high, with the earth's curvature just discernable, the mountains become no more than folds on a bedsheet. The brown expanse of the Tibetan plateau is visible below the right-hand window, just as Machhapuchhre glides by at 550 miles per hour below the wing.

The majestic south face of Annapurna looks like a living-room sofa draped in white, while Dhaulagiri stands aloof – a statue waiting to be unveiled. The foothills are humps veiled in blue haze, stacked in progressively lighter shades right up to the western horizon. To the left, the Gangetic basin stretches in an ocean-like flatness underneath a pall of dust.

Preceding pages: tourist impact – trekker with choughs at Kala Pattar with Everest behind. **Left**, Porters struggle with pipes for the hydro project at Thame. **Above**, Gurung boy in the Buri Gandaki.

It is incredible, seeing all this from one spot. This is the vantage point of the gods, who are reputed to hover over the mountains that they created. In the cockpit, where there is no other sound besides the roaring rush of wind, the flight becomes a religious experience. A brief pilgrimage to the heavens.

First Humans: It was only after the Himalaya were moulded out of the thin crust of a molten planet that the first human beings settled along the Siwalik (Churia) foothills. Echoes from the clash of continents were

still reverberating as frequent earthquakes shook the land. The power and mystery of nature, the purity and inaccessibility of distant snow peaks struck resonance with that part of the expanded human brain which had the function of pondering the spiritual.

The pre-Vedic tribes of the Indo-Gangetic plains must have been the originators of later Hindu reverence for mountains. Rivers that flowed out of the hills became fountainheads of life. Some geologists maintain that Himalayan rivers are actually older than the mountains, the relics of pre-historic river systems that carved gorges and valleys even as the mountains were rising. Sources of these rivers lie along the previous watershed of the pre-Himalayan mountains of Tibet.

The mountains were named with reverence – "Giver of Grain" (Annapurna) – and were considered symbols of deities. Their topography was vital: because of their height the mountains became monsoon traps that brought life-giving moisture to terrace farms and water to the rivers. The snow and glaciers were huge storage systems for ice which melted in spring, supplying water to downstream areas during the dry season. The lofty snows rested on the borderline between the temporal and spiritual, halfway between earth and heaven.

Most mountains became sacred. Kailas,

Guarded on the south by malarial jungles, Himalayan kingdoms became isolated but fiercely independent centres of culture.

Lying on the trade route between India and Tibet, Kathmandu thrived commercially and evolved a culture that was a rare blend of Hindu and Buddhist ways of life. Strong and belligerent Gorkha kings sent troops across the mountains to raid Lhasa, and at one point controlled the entire Himalayan arc from the borders of Kashmir to Bhutan.

Topographical reality soon imposed a limit on how far the Gorkha conquest could stretch. Generals paid the price as campaigns failed because of long supply routes across rugged inhospitable terrain.

the perfect cone reflected in the holy waters of Mansarovar, became the symbol of Shiva – the god of creation and destruction. Gauri Shankar, revered by Hindus as a manifestation of Shiva (Shankar) and his consort Parvati (Gauri), was also regarded by the Buddhist inhabitants of Rolwaling as Tseringma, one of the holy Five Long Life Sisters.

Natural Frontiers: As the population of the foothills expanded, the principalities and princedoms took natural barriers as their boundaries. The great peaks of the north became not only a frontier, but also a deterrent for invaders from Central Asia and Tibet.

Despite two wars, the British in India could not penetrate Nepal's mountain fastness. The Nepal troops, superb mountain guerillas, used hilltop forts to guard strategic passes with great effect, until the British brought in canons and started using seige tactics.

Roads and Wheels: Although the British built railroads and highways across the south Asian subcontinent, the Himalayan foothills remained as inaccessible as ever. Only a few Indian hill-resorts like Simla and Darjeeling were connected to the plains, usually with toy railways that were more fun than functional. Nepal remained for the most part roadless. The people of Pokhara, for example, saw the wheel for the first time when a DC-3 landed on a grass field in the middle of town in 1952.

Roads were enormously expensive to build, and the serpentine eternity of the Tribhuvan Raj Path from the Indian border to Kathmandu became the classical horror story of a Himalayan bus ride. But willing foreign governments were ready to build Nepal all the roads it wanted. Twisted coils of asphalt began to spread up sheer mountainsides, down the foothill slopes, along river gorges and across the midland valleys.

For anyone who knew Nepal before the roads were built, the difference is as dramatic as between the days of the covered sandy banks, up tracks carved out of the sheer cliffs at the Narayani's confluence with the Marsyangdi and Trisuli rivers, up and down the awesome vertical distances of the midhills, finally to the hilltop fortress of Gorkha, the birthplace of modern Nepal, standing boldly at the base of Himalchuli.

Today that same journey takes less than three hours. A Chinese-built hill highway has sliced through the mountains, and through time. Sleek Japanese cars chartered by tourists and smoke-belching Tata trucks zoom past heavily laden porters walking by the roadside. The road is pitifully thin, a fragile thread of asphalt stretched across a vast, precipitous mountainside. It is no won-

matic as between the days of the covered wagons and jet-age America. From the banks of the Rapti in the lush jungles of Royal Chitwan National Park, the distinctive *khukri*-shaped summit of Himalchuli is visible far on the northern horizon. Twenty years ago, it would have taken up to three weeks to walk from Chitwan to the base of that mountain. The trail traversed a perilous malarial jungle, ran along the swift-flowing Narayani river where crocodiles sunned on

Left, erosion near Ghasa in the Kali Gandaki valley. <u>Above</u>, monsoon bridge damage being repaired.

der that in the rainy season, landslides can wipe entire sections of the Nepal's highway network off the map.

A Social Upheaval: Distances not only in Nepal but all across the Himalaya have shrunk, bringing social, economic and political changes to the hinterlands. Speedier access and communications have introduced new concepts and a growing materialism from the outside world, and have also facilitated major political changes and greater interaction within.

Before the road arrived, Gorkha was a peaceful and self-contained village perched on a barren hillside west of Kathmandu. The brown brick buildings existed in harmony with the surrounding countryside. Indeed, all the materials used to build it were locally available. The market place was stocked with items people needed for their traditional lifestyles, sold by local businessmen and women.

Today Gorkha shines with the glitter of the 20th century. Corrugated roofs reflect sunlight off new buildings; the bazaar is festooned with brightly coloured plastic buckets, replacements for the traditional handtapped brass pots. Brooke Shields smiles from a computer portrait on Coca Cola ads in the town square. Roads, and the "progress" they have imposed, have made more and

imported polyester cloth, however impractical, over locally made durable weaves. Young people, swayed by magazines, television and now videos' flashy hype, are choosing short term gratifications over longer term investments in a better lifestyle such as medical care, sanitation or education.

Many say these changes were inevitable and are unstoppable. Perhaps, given time, the villagers of the Himalaya could have adjusted, differentiating the good from the bad. But it all happened overnight.

Nepal's hills are no longer carved into isolated districts that can be governed from far-off Kathmandu through the writ of centrally appointed powerful officials. After

more of Nepal's idyllic and self-content villages caricatures of distant Kowloon. The roadside vendors are migrants from the plains, the barber shaving a local official is from the Indian district of Darbhanga. Indeed not all change has come from the West.

Until very recently, there were six directions in Nepal's remote hills: north, south, east, west, up and down. The terrain kept the inhabitants of these lands isolated, but also self-sufficient, hard working and clearheaded. The construction of roads has eased the vertical and introduced unaffordable "luxury" goods in a predominantly cashless society. Villagers' now prefer the look of

centuries of autocratic and nearly-feudal rule, democracy has brought greater demands for decentralisation and a freely elected choice in leadership.

Roads have brought other benefits as well. Besides greater access to schools, hospitals, jobs and new remedial ideas, they have catalysed the physical unification of the country, a process as important as the political unification carried out by King Prithvi Narayan Shah two hundred years ago. It is not uncommon today to see traders from Dolpo and hill tribesmen from the Ganesh Himal step rather unsteadily off the bus at the terminal in Kathmandu. Dressed in their yak wool jackets and robes, they mingle in Kathmandu's urban melee with Tharu people from the plains. Nepal's ethnic diversity is as great as its extremes of altitude and climate – a variety that has endured largely because of the high ridges and valleys which isolate communities. The barriers to cultural homogenisation still exist in the hills, but are fading in the cities where it has become hard to tell a Rai man from a Gurung for their adapted Western dress.

Rural Development: "Let's split the mountains to usher in an era of progress," exhorts a patriotic song over Radio Nepal. Today, "economic development" translates as "overcoming the physical and psychological"

for their products, and impose long detours on their way to the towns to find work; children die because they cannot be taken to a health post on the other side of the river.

The child mortality rate in far-western Humla district is several times the national average. Of 1,000 children born in Humla, barely 400 live to be five years old. Most of them die of respiratory infections caused by breathing the smoke of pine wood cooking fires. In other areas of the country, contaminated water kills thousands of babies – and hundreds of adults – every year. Ironically, Western multi-national soft drinks are available in villages where there is not even safe potable water. Some experts say a tap with

barriers of the mountains." Dynamite charges rent the air as new roads are blasted, another hydroelectric project is launched or bridges are built. When rural Nepalis were asked in a survey some years ago what they wanted most – a hospital, a school, a road or electricity – the answer was: "None of the above." They wanted bridges. For them the raging torrents of fast-flowing Himalayan rivers are the most glaring obstacles to progress. The waters cut them off from markets

Left, road trouble in the Annapurna region. **Above**, community forestry poster encourages reforestation.

clean drinking water would do more for the general health of most of Nepal's districts than a fully equipped hospital.

Population Pressure: Many of the problems of health, nutrition and education are compounded by Nepal's burgeoning population. In 25 years, Nepal's 19 million population will double. Settlers of the Himalaya's the southern slopes have now far surpassed the land's capacity to sustain them. Arable land per capita has decreased from ½ hectare to less than ⅕ hectare in the last 30 years. Nepal, which is the most densely populated mountain community in the world, is faced with the formidable problems of overpopulation, falling agricultural productivity and a severely strained ecology.

Projecting these problems into the future, it is not difficult to see human misery on a massive scale. The swelling population is putting a strain on nature's capacity to regenerate. Being young and unstable, the steep flanks of Himalayan mountains are constantly crumbling because of gravity. Avalanches cut across high snow slopes, sharpening the ridges and making peaks more jagged. Monsoon rains pound the lower foothills triggering landslides and washing off the top soil. The process is called "mass-wasting" and began the moment the mountains started rising.

Denudation of the Himalayan foothills by forest cutting and overgrazing is adding to the problem. More than half of Nepal's forest cover has been slashed since 1961. Not only is wood needed for cooking, heating and construction, but vast tracts of land must be cleared to grow crops for the burgeoning number of babies. Trees stripped of their greenery for livestock fodder eventually fall to the axe, and in the meantime provide no protection to the soil from the torrential rains which lash the country in June, July and August. Without trees or grass to hold the hillsides, the soil is easily washed away. The effect of denudation is especially marked in the Siwalik hills which are made up only of boulders and sand. Once the tree cover disappears, entire hillsides in the Siwaliks can be washed off during one rainy season.

The Not-So-Fragile Mountain: Experts now discount the theory that deforestation-induced erosion of the Himalaya is the main cause of worsening floods downstream in Bangladesh and India. "Natural" erosion of the Himalaya has probably contributed most of the silt to the Ganges and the Bay of Bengal long before mankind settled in the hills. Some ecologists also refute doomsday theorists who claim that forest loss in the mountains is catastrophic, saying that deforestation is confined to the jungles of the Terai.

The intrepid inhabitants of the Himalaya have long known how to live with nature. Mountainsides sculptured with meticulously carved terraces are proof of the hill farmers' ingenuity. Hydrologically engineered terraces save the soil from washing away, and help grow food on non-irrigated

steep slopes with only a thin skin of topsoil. Since long before it became fashionable for development specialists to preach about ecological sustainability, high mountain dwellers have practised rotational grazing on the summer pastures and learned how to tap the forests' resources for food, fodder and fuel without doing permanent damage. From east to west, many communities had laws governing the use of their forests, some with forest guards and public deliberations over what penalty – *chhang* for the next festival? – the culprit should pay. In hindsight, the most disastrous single blow to Nepal's forests was the nationalisation of all forest lands in 1957, a centralist decision which dis-

solved peoples' interest in nurturing the resources and land, and instigated uncontrolled overuse to the detriment of all.

But these traditional conservation ethics are being severely tested by Nepal's swelling population. The hill farmer is driven to cultivate ever steeper, unsuitable slopes, slashing forests and shrubs to make way for the plough. Sons inherit ever-smaller plots of land, making agriculture as a sole occupation less and less viable. In some communities, a traditional land distribution system has prevented the division of land among successive generations. The Sherpas for example passed all land to the eldest son, leaving younger brothers the choice of sharing his household (and wife), making it on their own, or joining a monastery. This practice also served to keep the population down. The contemporary preference for monogamous marriages fortunately coincided with a general rise in the living conditions of Sherpas, the group which has benefitted most from mountain tourism.

Tourism: A Goose or a Golden Egg?: Many of Nepal's environmental and social concerns preceded the arrival of tourists, but the indulgent habits and cultural contrasts of an alien influx undoubtedly leave a mark on a country which was long isolated – inherently by physical barriers and later with political

blinds – from the world. Some of the effects of tourism are positive and others are not.

Tourism currently pumps more than US$60 million worth of hard currency into Nepal every year. Trekkers and mountaineers contribute more than their share, spending longer periods in the country than do other tourists. An estimated one job is created for every 7.5 tourists; again, more so for trekkers (1 per 3) supporting a labour intensive industry which provides a wider and more equitable distribution of cash in the hills where it is most

Left, Hillary school at Khumjung. **Above**, tree nursery at Sindu Palchok.

needed. That income is more likely to stay within the country than be spent outside on costly imports to furnish Western-style hotels and restaurants.

The potential is great to develop tourism-related cottage industries and food production to further stimulate the rural economies; for example setting up small scale handicraft centres in the hills and organising vegetable and meat production units to supply trekkers with fresh produce. Tourism has revived the dying arts and crafts of Bhaktapur, a city of artisans in the Kathmandu Valley and has fueled a carpet industry which rivals tourism as the country's number one generator of foreign revenue.

While tourism, directly and indirectly, brings precious foreign exchange to the national coffers, it also contributes to inflation and disrupts local markets. New-found income is making its way into mountain households accustomed to centuries of subsistence living, driving prices for basic commodities way beyond what farming families can afford. Foreigners' intended generosity, or ignorance over a fair price has the same effect; at Khumbu's Namche Saturday market, the only people buying eggs (which until recently were carried in on porters' backs out of respect for the mountain god who dislikes chickens) were lodge-owners who could pass the hefty price onto trekkers.

Like the proverbial goose that lays the golden egg, the tourism goose also fouls its nest. Not only conservation-minded planners in Nepal but a handful of trekking agents and some conscientious trekkers are worried that more hikers will mean more litter along the mountain trails. Toilet paper, cookie wrappers and non-biodegradable trash marks the over-trodden trails and campsites. Toilet facilities, if they exist at all, are often poorly maintained or dangerously near water sources. Slowly, awareness is growing into action. Projects such as the Annapurna Conservation Area Project (ACAP) are teaching the lodge-owners how to build decomposing toilets and to keep rubbish pits (see page 274). Some trekking agencies have vowed to carry out trash, but the problem remains what to do with it at roadheads or airfields.

Even the high mountains have not escaped the problems. The nearly 8,000 meter (26,250 feet) high South Col of Mount Everest is known as the "world's highest garbage dump." Discarded oxygen cylinders, stoves, boots and climbing gear are strewn about. In recent years, several clean-up crews have made a noticeable difference, but ultimately responsibility lies with the each mountaineering expedition and with the government to enforce existing regulations against litter and environmental degradation.

More serious is the fear that mountaineering and tourism will further strain the Himalaya's fragile environment. The Barun Valley in eastern Nepal and the trekkers' "highways" through Solu Khumbu and the Annapurnas are vivid examples of what uncontrolled visitor traffic can do. In the Barun, the moraines are crumbling because moun-

but accompanying porters must fend for themselves, and no one fends for the trees. Solu, where there are no tree-felling restrictions, is losing its lovely thick rhododendron forests to the construction of more and more tea houses to serve the ever-increasing number of independent trekkers. Hikers can help save the forests by bringing adequate clothing thus not relying for warmth on the lodge fireplace. Group trekkers can choose a trekking company which is environmentally conscientious, one which uses kerosene on all treks whether required by park regulations or not, and which provides warm clothing for porters on high elevation treks.

Innovative Planning: The Annapurna Con-

taineering expeditions on Mount Makalu have uprooted the dwarf junipers to burn at the base camp kitchen. The Annapurna Sanctuary's frail ecosystem is slow to recover from the tramping boots of the 10,000 trekkers who visit it every year.

The receding forests all along the Annapurna and Solu Khumbu trails are tragic reminders of the effects of indiscriminate tourism. National Park and ACAP rules now require trekkers to be self-sufficient in cooking fuel but Khumbu lodge-owners still rely on wood supplemented by yak dung to cook for hungry boarders. Trekking agencies supply kerosene for their clients' cooking needs

servation Area Project is innovative in more than one way. An entry fee collected from all visitors is used specifically on environmental protection and development activities which benefit the local inhabitants and help them accommodate trekkers in a sound manner – entrance fees from all the other national parks are absorbed into central government coffers. Villagers in the Annapurna area set up committees to manage their own forests, cultivate tree seedling nurseries, install fuel-efficient stoves in their lodges, and spread environmental awareness in community forums and in the classroom. ACAP is also helping to instill a pride in indigenous ways by training young people to lead tourists on cultural tours, and by instigating cooperation among villages where traditional ways are still at work.

The debate continues over whether the government should open more new trekking areas, such as Dolpo and Kangchenjunga which were recently de-restricted to foreign trekkers. Some say that remote regions thus far spared from the negative effects of tourism should be protected in an unspoilt state, while others argue that all mountain peoples should be entitled to share in the wealth which tourism brings. Would opening more areas lessen the litter and deterioration of overburdened areas, or should these heavily

foreign governments to facilitate irreversible change in Nepal through large scale projects such as hydro-electric generating plants. Nepal's total feasible hydropower potential is estimated at 40,000 megawatts, one of the highest per capita in the world. To date a mere 160 megawatts have been harnessed with the help of foreign governments. The main obstacle to more dams is the initial capital needed for construction.

The proposed 3,600 megawatt Chisopani plant in far west Nepal, for instance, could cost up to US$4 billion, several times the country's annual national budget. Unless Nepal can agree with neighbours about sharing the project costs in return for power and

burdened regions such as Khumbu and Annapurna be closed for several years to allow them to rejuvenate? Whatever the answers, all agree that the government and tourism industry must plan for the future so as not to spoil the object which attracts tourists here in the first place.

Hydro-Electric Potential: More ever-lasting than the fall-out of tourists' two week vacations in the Himalaya is the potential for

Left, the insidious effects of tourism – shopping above Namche. **Above left**, Khuldighar ACAP forest nursery. **Above right**, woodcutting at Tatopani.

flood-control benefits, there is little likelihood of Nepal taking on projects of that scale on its own. In the meantime, Nepal is going for medium-scale hydro-electric projects like the ones on the Marsyangdi and Arun rivers, which will meet the projected rise in power demand during the 1990s.

The social and economic problems of the Himalaya's human settlers seem fleeting and inconsequential in the grand scale of geologic time, a millisecond of historic consciousness in the limbo of drifting continents and colliding plates. But they are issues that must be dealt with, however slowly, for in the scheme of things they too took time in coming.

This awesome mountainous land was named by the ancients *Himarant* or *Himalaya*, the "Abode of Snow." Set deep in the mountains, between the Great Himalayan Range and the lower Mahabharat, was a lake. Nepalese legends speak of an island on this lake upon which grew a blue lotus containing the eternal flame of the Primordial Buddha. Manjushri, a manifestation of the Buddha, came to worship here and, to make access easier for pilgrims, he cut a passage through the Mahabharat hills and so drained the lake. A fertile valley was revealed, men settled here to farm and build cities and this became Nepal. Swayambhunath hill and its famous stupa on the summit mark the site of the original lotus island. Chobar Gorge, through which the Bagmati River drains the Kathmandu Valley, is where the Bodhisattva made his cut through the mountains.

Early Kingdoms: The first kingdoms of Nepal were confined to the Kathmandu Valley. Other centres of civilisation developed in what is now the Terai, Nepal's southern plains country. One of these was at Lumbini where in 543 B.C. was born the "Light of Asia," Prince Siddhartha Gautama, son of a local ruler, who achieved enlightenment to become the Buddha (see page 323).

Of Kathmandu Valley the Nepalese chronicles detail the rise and fall of successive dynasties of rulers: the Gopalas, the Kiratis, the Licchavis. In 637 A.D. the Chinese pilgrim, Hsuan Chuang, found its inhabitants to be of a "hard nature" but with many talents. These were the Newars, still the majority population in the Valley today. Even 1,400 years ago their artistic and mercantile skills were evident:

"The houses are of wood, painted and sculpted. The people are fond of bathing, of dramatic performances, of astrology and of blood sacrifices. Irrigation, carefully and skilfully applied, makes the soil rich. Both Buddhism and Brahmanism (Hinduism)

flourish in the main temples, which are wealthy and well supported. Commerce prospers and trade is well organised."

Already Nepal had built up profitable trading links with its powerful neighbours to the north and south, acting as middleman between two strong cultures, and in the process building up a distinctive culture of its own. This Nepalese culture came into full flower during the extended dynasty of the Malla kings. The first Malla came to power in 1200 A.D., the last was deposed in 1769. Greatest of the Malla kings was Jayasthiti Malla, who set late-14th century Nepal on the map of Asia as a prosperous, well-ordered nation. However three generations later, in 1482, the country was divided among three Malla brothers and a sister. Each became ruler of one of the four Valley towns – Kathmandu, Bhaktapur, Banepa and Lalitpur (now Patan) – and each established an independent ruling dynasty. Rivalry between these city-states led to nearly three centuries of vigorous artistic competition as the Malla kings vied to outdo each other in splendour. Newari artistry in temple and palace building, wood-carving, metal-working and scroll-painting transformed Kathmandu Valley into one of the world's richest repositories of art and architecture.

Feuding amongst themselves weakened the political supremacy of the Mallas in the region and in the surrounding hills other local rulers began to bid for power. The Muslim conquest of Northern India had driven a number of Rajput princes and their followers into the mountains. In 1559 one of these chieftains, Druvya Shah, seized the hill-fort of Gorkha, three days' march west of Kathmandu. From this stronghold his descendants gradually extended their authority over the *paharis* or hill-people of the Chaubasi Raj, the "24 Kingdoms" of central Nepal, until Prithvi Narayan Shah invaded Kathmandu Valley with his Gorkha troops. After a prolonged campaign lasting 10 years, by 1769 his conquest was complete, the Malla kings were dethroned and the Shahs became the new rulers of Nepal. His successors continued his policy of expansion after his death at the age of 52 in 1775. In effect,

Preceding pages: Chandra Shamsher Jung Bahadur Rana, ruler of Nepal in the early 20th century, flanked by his family. **Left**, King Prithvi Narayan Shah of Gorkha, founder of modern Nepal.

King Prithvi Narayan Shah laid the foundations of the present day Kingdom of Nepal.

War and Peace: Nepal then entered a period of conquest that pushed its boundaries west along the Himalaya as far as Kashmir and eastwards to Sikkim. The Nepalese next laid claim to the fertile plains to the south, where the authority of the Mogul Emperors had long been in decline. But here they came up against a rival power, the British East India Company, that was also expanding to fill the political vacuum. Diplomacy failed and in 1814 Nepal and Britain went to war. The East India Company sent four armies into the hills. Two failed to make any headway, one was repulsed and the fourth broke the main Nepal army after a hard contest.

A peace-treaty was signed in 1816 at Segauli, initiating a friendship that benefited both parties. Nepal secured her frontiers and diverted Britain's empire-building ambitions elsewhere, while the British gained a staunch ally. It was from Nepal's defeated army that volunteers came forward to form the first of the famous Gurkha regiments that to this day still serve the British Crown.

Only one feature of the "Treaty of Friendship" really irked the Nepalis: a clause requiring the Government of Nepal to accept a British Resident in Kathmandu. The Nepalis had always been fierce protectors of their independence and had never made strangers welcome, unless they came as pilgrims. Two European Jesuits had passed safely through Kathmandu in 1661 while travelling from China to India, but a party of Capuchin missionaries who followed met with disaster when it was discovered that they had come to win converts. Successive British Residents scarcely fared any better. The British Residency was deliberately sited on waste land said to be haunted by evil spirits – and its human occupants found themselves virtual prisoners with their movements, even within the Valley, severely restricted.

Nepal's self-imposed isolation from the outside world was greatly intensified when, in 1846, an army officer named Jung Bahadur Rana took advantage of a crisis meeting being held in the government armoury, known as the Kot, to massacre virtually everybody present. The king was spared, but Jung Bahadur took over the reins of power as Prime Minister and Commander-in-Chief – and ensured that after his death both posts would be inherited by a member of his own family. The Shahs remained as venerated monarchs, but it was the Ranas who ruled.

For a century the Ranas stuck to a policy of despotic self-quarantine. Writing in 1928, the journalist Percival Landon estimated that no more than 120 English and ten other Europeans had entered Kathmandu Valley before him. Of those who had entered, none had been permitted to set foot in the sur-

rounding hills except when entering or leaving Nepal, although a privileged few had been allowed to join their Rana hosts in tiger and rhinoceros shoots in the Terai. Trade links with British India were strictly controlled and what few goods were imported, chiefly to grace the palaces of the Ranas, had to be carried in on the backs of porters, since no roads were allowed to be developed.

Trade and Exploration: Only along Nepal's borders with Tibet were the local communities permitted to maintain their links with their neighbours. This border area lies north of the Great Himalayan Range and is the home of tribal groups of Tibetan stock

Left, hunts with royal invitees were popular in the early 1900s and huge "bags" of tiger and rhinoceros were recorded. **Above**, a portrait in the National Museum of Bhimsen Thapa, an early prime minister.

known collectively as Bhotia. They include the famous mountain guides of Solu Khumbu, the Sherpas, yak farmers and traders settled in the upper reaches of the Dudh Kosi in the east, who in the summer months traded into Tibet by way of the 5,716 meter (18,753 foot) Nangpa La pass. Another notable northern community is the Buddhist people of Lo or Mustang at the headwaters of the Kali Gandaki in western Nepal, who traditionally traded grain for salt across the Mustang Pass. Two other crossing points into Tibet served as traditional conduits for trade, both river passes: the Khirong La on the Trisuli River north of Kathmandu, and the Kuti La on the upper Sunkosi, the main trade

giri massif, the world's seventh highest mountain. For the next 30 years the mapmakers of the Survey of India concentrated on mapping India using a system of triangulation devised by the Surveyor-General of India, Sir George Everest. After his retirement in 1843 interest once more returned to the Himalayan barrier.

By 1852 the two great cornerstones at the far reaches of Nepal, the 8,586 meter (28,169 foot) Kangchenjunga massif in the east and Gurla Mandhata (7,728 meters, 25,355 feet) in the Nalakankar Himal in the west, had been accurately plotted, but the 800 kilometers (500 miles) of mountains and valleys between these two points lay unmapped and

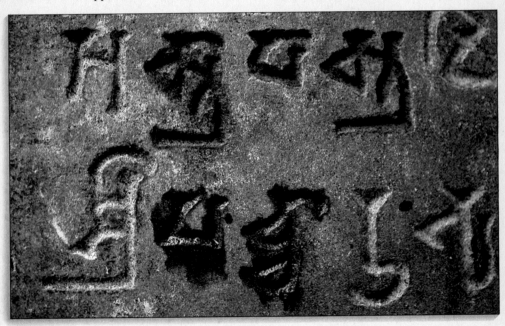

route to Lhasa and therefore the most closely guarded.

The first European to grasp the extraordinary nature of Nepal's mountains was the great geographer and map-maker James Rennell, who in 1788 observed that the highest snow peaks could be seen from the Indian plains at a distance of 240 kilometers (150 miles). When it was declared that some of the peaks might be as high as 8,000 meters (26,250 feet) there was disbelief but in 1811 a very prominent peak in west Nepal, observed from four survey stations in the Indian plains, was calculated to be 8,167 meters (26,795 feet) high. This was the Dhaula-

tantalisingly out of reach. The best that the Survey of India could do was to take theodolite bearings from the plains and compute them to produce a rough map. In 1849 bearings were taken from six different stations on a peak in east Nepal, identified only as Peak XV. Three years passed before the day when a computation clerk rushed into the office of the Surveyor-General with the news that he had "discovered the highest mountain in the world."

Everest Discovered: Once the first figure of 8,840 meters (29,002 feet) for the height of Peak XV had been verified, strenuous efforts were made to find the mountain's local name. This proved fruitless, with the unfortunate result that in 1865 Peak XV was named Mount Everest by the Survey of India. Unfortunate, because years later it was found that Everest did have a Tibetan name, Chomolungma, which has been translated variously as "Mother Goddess," "Lady Cow" or "The Mountain So High That No Bird Can Fly Over It." The official Nepalese name for Peak XV is Sagarmatha, which honours the demon-slaying King Sagar of Hindu legend and reminds the world that Nepal is a Hindu kingdom that reveres its snow-peaks as the home of the gods. The true altitude of Mount Everest, 8,848 meters (29,028 feet), was later established by im-

to Kathmandu so that Everest could be finally identified from the surrounding hills, and not until 1949 was the first climbing party permitted to enter any great distance into the country.

The Pundits: But if official visitors were forbidden to explore Nepal, what was to stop unofficial visitors from venturing in disguise? In 1863 the Survey of India hit upon the idea of using Himalayan traders to act as their surveyors. Two such men, Nain Singh and Mani Singh from Kumaon Himalaya, were the first of these explorer-spies, later known as the Pundits. They were trained for two years, given a disguise and then sent into the Himalaya with their survey instruments

proved measuring techniques, which accounts for the discrepencies in many peaks' altitudes now officially standardised by the Nepal government.

What is remarkable is that from the time of its "discovery" in 1852 Everest was to remain inviolate for another full century. Only in 1903 was an officer of the Survey of India permitted by the Rana government to come

Left, the oldest inscription in the Kathmandu Valley, dated 464 A.D., is engraved in stone at Changu Narayan. **Above**, a Malla king honors Indra in a 15th century fresco at the Palace of Bhaktapur.

hidden in secret compartments in their luggage. Lhasa was their main target but Nepal was their means of entry into Tibet. In March 1865 Nain Singh and Mani Singh crossed into Nepal and after a brief stay in Kathmandu attempted to enter Tibet by way of the Khirong La. Suspicious Nepalese customs officials detained them and searched their baggage without finding their instruments before sending them back to Kathmandu. The two then split up, Mani Singh heading west to attempt a crossing via Mustang while Nain Singh tried the Khirong La. Mani Singh failed but brought back a great deal of information about western Nepal. Nain Singh had better luck and returned to his base in India in July 1866 after an epic journey of 2,000 kilometers (1,200 miles).

These were the first of many journeys of exploration through forbidden territory made by Nain Singh, Mani Singh and their successors. The exploits of these brave men remained a closely guarded secret for some years and when accounts of their journeys were first revealed, their identities were concealed and details of their journeys withheld. The British were also anxious to preserve good relations with the Ranas, so very little was ever written about the "opening up" of Nepal by the Pundits, who would certainly have faced years of imprisonment or death

of Nepal. He first made his way eastward across the high country that drains into the Sunkosi river and up into Solu Khumbu to cross into Tibet over the Nangpa La. He then marched east for 160 kilometers (100 miles) before crossing back into Nepal by way of the Khirong La. The last section of this seven month survey – all of it paced out on foot by counted, measured steps and com-pass-bearings – took him down through the Gorkha region between Kathmandu and Pokhara.

Mountaineers and Pilgrims: Forbidden Nepal drew other trespassers besides the Pundits. The most secretive was probably an Englishman named Edmund Smyth who, as Kumaon's first Education Officer, chose

had their spying been discovered.

As a result the name of Hari Ram, code-name "M.H." or "Number 9," is hardly known today. Yet this forgotten Pundit, also a Kumaoni, quite literally did more to put Nepal on the map than any other single individual. In 1871 he made the first circuit of eastern Nepal and the Everest region in a 1,300 kilometer (800 mile) route survey. Two years later he entered western Nepal from Kumaon and traversed the northern belt as far as the Kali Gandaki gorge, with a brief foray into Tibet, then returned to follow the river down into India. Then, 14 years on, Hari Ram set out to survey the central section

Nain Singh and Mani Singh for their new profession. Smyth's chief interests lay in mountaineering, exploring and hunting rather than his work. He made two illicit journeys over the Himalayan ranges and was probably the first Westerner to "climb" in the Himalaya, following his introduction to this new sport in the Alps in 1854. He left no record of his activities but a book of reminiscences published by a retired Forest Officer in 1902 gives away at least one of his secrets. It tells us that in 1864 Smyth led a totally unauthorised expedition through the north-western corner of Nepal and over a 6,000 meter (20,000 feet) snow pass for a spot of yak hunting in Tibet.

If Smyth was the most reticent of explorers, the aptly-named Henry Savage Landor was the most boastful. This English gentleman-cad bullied his way through the same corner of west Nepal in 1897 and after being beaten up by the Tibetan authorities was thrown out again. To round off his trip, all later enlarged upon in a lurid, two-volume best-seller, *In the Forbidden Land*, Savage Landor made a record-breaking ascent of a 7,000 meter (23,400 feet) Nepalese peak Mount Api, wearing his straw boater and carrying a malacca cane. Another more worthy trespasser into Nepalese territory, the mountaineer Tom Longstaff, came that same

eller came in search of the original scriptures of Buddhism, which he believed he would find hidden in the monasteries of Nepal and Tibet. Lhasa was his goal, but beguiled by the austere charms of the upper Kali Gandaki valley, he lingered in Nepal for 15 months before moving on into Tibet. Kawaguchi's accounts of his adventures, later published as *Three Years in Tibet*, were dismissed as fiction when he returned to Japan. Nothing daunted, the monk gathered funds for a second journey, returning to Nepal in 1903. This time he came quite openly as a Japanese seeking Sanskrit texts. The Rana prime minister of the day, Chandra Shamsher, happened to be on a hunting trip in the Terai.

way six years later and was not surprised to find that Landor's 7,000 meter climb had lost some 2,000 meters (6,500 feet) over the intervening years, Landor having never reached the summit.

Others trespassed with higher motives, most notably the Japanese Zen Buddhist monk Ekai Kawaguchi, who first entered Nepal in 1899 dressed in the maroon robes of a Tibetan monk. This highly eccentric trav-

Left, victory celebrations followed the lifting of the ban on political parties, 9th April 1990. **Above**, demonstrators clashing with police on 6th April 1990 on Durbar Marg.

Kawaguchi secured an audience with him and was given permission to proceed to Kathmandu Valley – only to find himself as restricted in his movements as any British Resident. A month later he was given his scriptures and escorted back across the border. In 1905 he returned for a third and last time to Kathmandu, living for ten months at the Buddhist centre of pilgrimage at Bodhnath, under the shadow of its great stupa. He was now a well-known and much respected figure – but remained as much a prisoner of the Ranas as before.

The Doors Open: Despite the major assistance in terms of fighting men and funds given to Britain and India by Nepal during the two World Wars, it was not until the last stages of World War Two that the Ranas began to relax their grip on the country. In 1944 King Tribhuvan, who had ascended to the throne as a minor in 1911, was at last able to visit India and Europe. He initiated contacts with progressive forces outside Nepal and in November 1950 put his demands for a return to constitutional monarchy to the Rana government. He then briefly sought refuge in India before returning to bring about a "palace revolution" on 18th February 1951 that overthrew the Ranas and reestablished the Shahs as the rulers of Nepal.

A cabinet drawn from the Nepalese Con-

gress Party was formed to govern the country and for almost a decade a succession of cabinets and prime ministers came and went without providing the effective government that Nepal needed. However, this return to modern rule at last allowed Nepal to open its doors to the outside world. Desperately needed development programmes were started. Roads, schools, hospitals and much else were built and, through stages, visitors were gradually welcomed.

In 1950 a French mountaineering expedition had been granted access to western Nepal, where with strong Sherpa support it made the first ascent of Annapurna I, at 8,091 meters (26,545 feet) the highest mountain yet climbed and the first 8,000 meter (26,250 foot) peak in the world to be successfully scaled. This set the pattern for future mountaineering expeditions. In 1951 a British expedition made the first reconnaissance of Mount Everest from the Nepal side, during which the large footprints of the elusive yeti were photographed for the first time. A Swiss party followed in 1952 and, although Raymond Lambert and Tenzing Norgay Sherpa passed the 8,500 meter (28,000 feet) mark, it was left to Edmund Hillary from New Zealand and the heroic Tenzing Norgay, then on his seventh expedition to Everest, to finally conquer the world's highest mountain in May 1953 (see page 169).

King Tribhuvan died in March 1955 and was succeeded by his son King Mahendra, who in December 1960 assumed direct rule while he drew up a new constitution based on his conviction that Western-style parliamentary democracy could not work in Nepal. In its place he instituted the Panchayat system, based on the traditional Hindu model of the five (*panch*) man village council. This provided for locally elected, non-party representation and government at ward, village, district and zone levels, as well as a National Panchayat assembly to ratify decisions taken by a Council of Ministers appointed by the King. On the death of King Mahendra in 1972, his Western-educated son, His Majesty King Birendra Bir Bikram Shah Dev, inherited the throne.

The youthful King Birendra amended the constitution in 1980, following a national referendum. Maintaining the single party system, the new constitution gave more powers to the assembly, who appointed the cabinet and the Prime Minister, though only with the endorsement of the King.

Nepal remains the only Hindu monarchy in the world but since the "revolution" in April 1990 formalised in the November 1990 constitution, King Birendra is only the figurehead of a multi-party parliamentary democracy: The May 1991 general election gained a small majority for the Nepali Congress Party whose leader, Giriji Prasad Koirala, is prime minister.

Above, Nepalese soldier. **Right**, Shiva's consort at Pashupatinath.

Nepal is a veritable mosaic of over thirty different ethnic groups with their unique languages, cultures and religions who have over the centuries penetrated and settled the hills and valleys of Nepal, coming from the north and south, east and west. Despite this diversity, Nepal has a tradition of harmony rather than conflict. Society here has always been accommodating to new ideas, new values and new peoples from afar.

In this land of ethnic elements as varied as its landscape, the principles of integration and synthesis were accepted from ancient times. The earliest distinguishable races were an intermixture of Khas and Kiratis with other immigrant groups. Today, a striking example of this amalgam of north and south, of Tibeto-Burman and Indo-Aryan stocks, are the Newars of Kathmandu Valley. Patronised by the ruling nobility, the genius of Newari artisans can be seen in the temples, palaces, *bahals* (monasteries) and *chowks* (courtyards) that constitute the manmade environment of the Valley today.

The Genius of the Newars: The original Newar settlements of the Valley and beyond reflect concern for the prudent use of valuable agricultural land. Often located along ridge spines, Newari houses clustered around sites of religious significance, expanding on the basis of the individual family's structure. Villages expanded laterally along these plateaus, leaving the more fertile low-lying areas for farming. In this way, organic wastes ultimately found their way to the farms, adding valuable nutrients to the soil. The Gorkha invasion of 1768 brought a concept of nationhood into this ancient and traditional milieu. With the establishment of the capital of a united Nepal in Kathmandu, the tightly knit homogeneity of the Valley was interjected with new values. The Gorkha settlers' more independent family

structure spilled over into the traditional urban precincts.

What one sees today in Kathmandu is precisely this mixture: a medieval township that finds itself in the midst of the 20th century, a blending of the essence of old Kathmandu with the effects of latter-day migration from outside the Valley.

In a valley where there are said to be more religious monuments than houses, it is sometimes difficult to tell the difference between the divine and the worldly. A Newari house

can only be built with sacred permission, which must come prior to the foundation laying ceremony and then again after the roofing of the house. The fire-baked bricks are prepared in the Valley, though not in the old wedge-shapes which give the palaces such a distinctive air. The intricately worked wood window frames and doorways are carved as lovingly as on any temple.

The extended family is the cornerstone of Newari society and acts as both a support and a refuge. From an early age, the individual learns how to fit within the social nucleus and how to relate to the clan and caste, through respect for relatives and patron dei-

Preceding pages: Hindu boy beside a Buddhist head at Swayambhunath; enjoying a hookah in a hill village; Tharu girls from west Nepal; an ethnic mosaic of women and children watch the Indrajatra festival. **Left**, a homemade ferris wheel. **Above**, Konjo Chumbi, a Sherpa elder statesman from Khumjung village.

ties. Joint families can include three generations with 30 or more members.

The Newari *guthi* is on a higher plane than the family but symbolizes a deep aspiration to community living. These brotherhoods maintain local temple and communal services, organise feasts, festivals and processions, arrange burials, maintain family sanctuaries, care for the ailing and elderly, and even assist in the collective preparation of fields. The *guthi* provides substantial advantages to its members and is indicative of the social rank and economic potential of each family. This institution, present in the Valley since Malla times, has been both a factor of social integration and a means of perpetuating cultural

years, seven months and seven days, there is a reenactment of the *pasni*, or rice-feeding ceremony that all children go through when they are seven months old.

When death finally comes, the deceased must be taken, often in the pre-dawn hours, to the cremation *ghats* by the riverside. The sons must walk three times around their parent's corpse, carrying the butter lamp that will be placed on the face of the deceased. As the priest sets the pyre ablaze, the dead person's relatives get their heads shaved and ritually purify themselves with a bath in the sacred river. The ashes are scattered in the river which flows into the sacred Ganges.

Elsewhere in Kathmandu, life goes on – in

values and achievements.

From birth to death, special rites and celebrations mark the important events of a Newar's existence. One of the more colourful initiations is when the young girls are "married" to the god Narayan before they reach puberty, with all the symbolic rituals of a typical wedding. Although the human marriage will come later, it will technically be her second, thus ensuring that the girl will never become a widow and will also make divorce a mere formality. In a country where death comes early, age is respected and celebrated. The old are venerated, and when a relative reaches the auspicious age of 77

the streets, courtyards, temples and on the rooftops. The city is in a transition: from the tight bonds of Newari tradition and customs of the old, to the metamorphosis of the concrete reality of the jet-age present.

Watch the faces of the Nepalese people at any busy intersection in Kathmandu and you will soon discover what a fascinating melting pot of Himalayan cultures the city is. When you leave the Valley to visit outlying regions, you will find dozens of isolated pockets of distinct peoples and cultures.

The Tamang "Horse Soldiers": Outside the Valley rim, and well beyond it, live the Tamangs. Tamang is derived from "horse soldiers" in the Tibetan language, and it is supposed that they descended from Tibetan cavalry. Today, they are mostly small farmers; some work as porters and craftsmen, especially in wicker work and carpentry. Their elaborate two-story stone-and-wood houses are clustered along cobbled streets.

Tamangs are often seen in the streets of Kathmandu carrying large *doko* (baskets) by headstraps supported on their foreheads. The men and boys dress in loincloths and long, usually black tunics; in winter, they wear short-sleeved sheep-wool jackets, frequently with a *khukri* knife thrust in the waistband. They are a familiar sight carrying their hand-made, grey, beige and white

dhist religion of Tibet; but both religions have priests and deities, and variations in the rites appear to be minimal. Whereas a Buddhist walks to the left of a shrine and spins his prayer wheel clockwise, a Bon believer, a Bonpo, walks to the right and spins his prayer wheel counter-clockwise.

Like many of Nepal's peoples, the Tamangs retain *jhankris* (shamans) in addition to their *lamas* (priests). These *jhankris* conduct religious ceremonies for communal and individual well-being: their ritual procedures involve trance and possession to drive away spirits for the sick or dying, to recover lost souls, and to perform various seasonal agricultural rites, such as making sacrifices

*rhadi*s (flat-weave carpets) for sale from house to house. Women wear above-the-ankle saris of homemade cotton, and blouses adorned with ornaments and jewellery.

Tamangs are Lama Buddhists, as are most upper Himalayan peoples. They have *gompas* (monasteries) in every sizeable village. The gods, religious paintings and texts, festivals and ritual ceremonies are all of Tibetan style. Some northern peoples follow the Bon religion, generally considered the pre-Bud-

Left, boy with prayer wheels at the Golden Temple in Patan. **Above**, a Brahman bride and groom marry in traditional style in Solu Khumbu.

to ensure good crops. Not surprisingly, many of these shamanistic rites are quite similar to those once found among the peoples of Mongolia and Siberia (see page 104).

Polygamy is not uncommon in the hills, even though the government has restricted it and family economics are a limiting factor. There is an ambivalent attitude regarding sexual activities, with money as a soothing influence. If a Tamang man abducts the wife of another, for example, the new husband compensates the ex-spouse with money. Adultery is also punishable by lesser fines.

Life on the World's Edge: The high Himalayan settlements of Tibetan-speaking peo-

ples perch precariously on mountain ledges and fragile slopes. Life here is a delicate balance of hard work and social frivolity, tempered by a culture deeply founded in ancient religious tradition.

The best known of the high-mountain peoples are the Sherpas, inhabiting central and eastern hill regions of Nepal. Although the name "Sherpa" has become synonymous with "mountain guide," it is only those in the Everest region who have achieved relative prosperity through guiding mountaineering expeditions and escorting trekking groups, with their families often running small hotels and teashops in their home villages.

The southern limits of these Himalayan regions – places like Phaplu, Junbesi, Tarkeghyang and Jomosom – are sometimes thought of as attractive, even romantic, examples of high-altitude settlements. Indeed, many are. But the extreme north and other communities on higher slopes are not very comfortable or prosperous. These border settlements are few and far between; interaction with other villages requires long journeys and much of the year is spent in temporary shelters as moving with the seasons to provide grazing for their animals.

Among the inhabitants of these hardy climes are the 7,000 to 8,000 people of Mustang. They live in oasis villages on a reddish-brown rock desert, fighting a constant bitter wind to farm grains and potatoes in sheltered plots. The hard grind of daily life and subsistence survival in the high Himalaya is interrupted by seasons of feasts and festivals, marked by drinking, dancing and merry-making. Most festivals are of a religious nature and centre around the temples and monasteries, with rites conducted by *lamas* and *jhankris*. These celebrations occur on the full-moon days of May, June, July, August and November. They include the Dumje and Mani Rimdu rites of the Sherpas of Solu Khumbu; the Yartung festival of Muktinath; and the Dyokyabsi fest of Mustang (see page 113).

The Clever Thakalis: Among the most interesting northern peoples of Nepal are the Thakalis. Residing in the upper Kali Gandaki river region, astride a seam of cultures, languages, ethnic groups, climatic conditions and historic traditions that are worlds apart from one another. Over several centuries, the Thakalis have successfully integrated Lamaism and Hinduism into their own colourful faith, and have mastered the arts of trade and commerce to emerge as perhaps the most successful entrepreneurs in Nepal. Their careers began with the salt trade between Tibet and India, but today they have spread into all spheres of contemporary life – including construction, politics, business, academia, arts and literature.

The secret of this expansion is the *dighur* system. A group of friends or relatives pool a given amount of money, sometimes thousands of rupees each, and give the whole sum

every year to one among them. The recipient uses the lean as he sees fit; whether he loses or gains money is his own affair, and his only obligation is to feed the *dighur*. When everyone in the pool has taken a turn, the *dighur* is automatically dissolved. An interesting self-financing device based on mutual trust, the system does away with interest rates and presupposes stability of currency.

A good example of Thakali behavioural patterns can be seen in the village of Marpha in the shadow of the Annapurna Himal. A casual glance at this community shows a strong sense of organization, discipline, cleanliness and far-sighted vision. Marpha is

Left, women of the hills. **Above**, a Buddhist child is protected with sacred strings.

picturesquely wedged between steep sandstone cliffs on one side and a small ledge of cultivated fields overlooking the Kali Gandaki on the other. Along cobbled alleyways, whitewashed mud houses with flat roofs surround a succession of courtyards where livestock feed on fragrant juniper boughs, which the people also use to make tea. There is running water and a drainage system, an exceptional phenomenon in Nepal.

Most Thakalis are small farmers, growing barley and some potatoes. Savings are often invested in herds of yaks grazing the upper pastures. These long-haired Asiatic oxen are good providers; the females, *naks*, give milk; their cheese is sold as well as used for home

folk characterised by the high cheekbones of their northern heritage and live generally in central and western Nepal along the Kali Gandaki watershed. Farmers and herders, they cultivate maize, millet, mustard seeds and potatoes, that staple for survival in the hills. Cattle are kept and buffaloes provide meat, but sheep are of paramount importance for their wool and suitability to the middle hill grazing. Families own perhaps a dozen sheep, grouped in village flocks of 200 – 300. Four or five shepherds, accompanied by their fierce mastiff dogs, take them to the upper pastures from April to September, when the shearing is done. The flocks return to the village in October, for the important

consumption. The beasts' rough wool and hides are used in clothing, tents and pack saddles (see page 185).

People of the Middle Hills: The various peoples living in the temperate zone of Nepal's middle hills are sometimes erroneously referred to *en masse* as Gurkhas. The British and Indian armies have famed Gurkha regiments, named after the soldiers from the former Kingdom of Gorkha. But there is no single ethnic group today called Gurkha. By tradition, most Gurkha soldiers come from the Gurung, Magar, Rai, Limbu, Yakha and Sunuwar peoples of Nepal.

The Gurungs are self-sufficient hardy hill

Dasain festival when all the family gathers; then they head south for the winter, sometimes as far as the inner Terai hills. Wool is soaked and washed, but used undyed when woven in traditional patterns by Gurung women (see page 285).

Magars are quite predominant numerically. They have earned a reputation for martial qualities both within and outside of Nepal, though they are basically self-sufficient hill peasants. They grow rice, maize, millet, wheat and potatoes, depending upon the suitability of the terrain they occupy. Spread out all over western and central Nepal, from the high Himalayan valleys to the plains of the Terai, the Magars, of Tibeto-Burman stock, have adopted whatever language, culture, religion, style of dress, and even architectural style is dictated by their area of settlement.

Rai, Limbu, Yakha and Sunuwar people of the eastern hills, like Magars and Gurungs, favour military service to all other professions, mainly because soldiers return home with added prestige and income. But the majority of them stay at home and practice subsistence agriculture. They are nominally Hindu, although some have adopted Buddhism or their own animistic practices in a unique melange typical of Nepalese religion.

Brahmans and Chhetris: The ubiquitous

derstood by outsiders. It was first instigated for social expediency by the early Malla rulers to protect their regime. Most societies in the world have hierarchical systems based both on birth and pedigree as well as wealth and position, groups with whom they prefer to socialize and intermarry, and groups whom they consider different. Hinduism merely institutionalises this concept.

In Nepal, the Hindu caste system socially, occupationally and ritually defines all people by the group into which they are born. It is elaborated into a number of rules for eating, marrying, working and touching. But as strong and persuasive as this system is, Nepal is unique in the Hindu world for the

Brahmans and Chhetris, along with the occupational castes of Nepal, have also traditionally played an important role in Nepalese society. Originally from west Nepal, the majority have a preference for the temperate middle hills, although they have dispersed in all parts of the Terai.

Orthodox Hindus, they believe in a hierarchical caste structure. "Caste," a word originally brought to Nepal and the Indian subcontinent by the Portuguese, is easily misun-

Left, three Newar girls from the Kathmandu Valley. **Above**, ornate jewellery is characteristic of Tamang women.

degree to which economic, political and romantic deviations from the caste norms are accepted and incorporated into society.

Brahmans and Chhetris are, like their neighbouring ethnic groups, predominantly subsistence farmers. However, the literary and priestly tradition of the Brahmans has facilitated their taking important roles in modern Nepalese government, education and business.

Similarly, most of the ruling families, including the famous Ranas, have been drawn from the Chhetri caste. The distinguished Thakuris are also Chhetris, but they claim to have come from Rajasthan in contrast to the rest of the clan who originally migrated eastward into Nepal.

Together, the Brahmans and Chhetris have provided the *lingua franca*, Nepali, and the main cultural and legal framework for Nepal's national identity.

Peoples of the Terai: The Terai Hindus, especially the high caste peoples, are more orthodox and conservative than the hill people. Although the caste system has lost is legal support, the higher castes still control most of the region's wealth and carry considerable political clout. Movement across the India-Nepal border is unrestricted, especially for marriages and socio-economic relations, thus cementing caste ties.

Villages are clusters of 30 to 100 or more dwellings, built with bamboo walls plastered with cow dung and mud, and topped by thatched or tile roofs. Concrete walls and cement roofs are signs of wealth.

Lowland ethnic groups such as the Tharu, Danuwar, Majhi and Darai live along the northern strip of eastern Terai and throughout western Terai. Rajbansi, Satar, Dhimal and Bodo peoples live in the far eastern districts of Jhapa and Morang. Moslems are found along the central and western sections of the Terai.

Numbering about half a million people, Tharu are among the most ancient people inhabiting the Terai, and are made up of several distinct groups with different customs. The eradication of malaria in the 1950s and the land reforms of the 1960s pushed waves of hill people to settle in the Terai. Some Tharu moved away, like the Dangaura who migrated to Karnali in far west Nepal; others stayed, such as the Mahaton and Nawalpuria in the Chitwan Valley, and now live alongside other Nepalese ethnic groups.

Tharu villages are easy to recognize, being scattered and, in some cases, very picturesque clustered villages. Their spacious longhouses, with mud and latticework walls decorated with animal and fish designs, are protected from the sun by wide, sloping, grass roofs. If the means of subsistence are sufficient, these longhouses can be occupied by families of as many as 150 people. With small doorways, the huge halls inside are divided into rooms by rows of the typical Tharu silos, moulded by the women and used for grain storage (see page 143).

In most areas, their agriculture is stationary but primitive; Tharu maintain traditional irrigation systems and cultivate rice, maize, wheat and barley in the rich Terai land. They keep chickens and ducks, breed a few pigs, goats, and buffalos, and fish the big rivers by throwing jute nets. Fish, shrimps and snails are an important part of their diet, eaten daily with rice. They collect wild berries and medicinal herbs from the jungle, and occasionally hunt small animals such as porcupines or bamboo rats.

The bejewelled Tharu women usually marry early, though their life does not change much until they give birth. Their lovers must often work for their parents-in-law, sometimes for two or three years before they "earn" the right to marry. Age defines authority in the family; the old man is the overlord and the mother or elder sister rules over the female side of the household.

Living as they do in the realm of tigers, crocodiles and scorpions, Tharu venerate animistic spirits of the forest, as well as some Hindu deities. A village goddess is worshipped by each community at a small simple shrine, tended by their own priests or *gurwas*.

Above, Brahman with *tika* and topi. **Right**, cremation at Pashupatinath on the Bagmati River.

GURKHAS: BRAVEST OF THE BRAVE

Rare is the person today who has not heard of the Gurkha soldiers, the brave troops from Nepal's isolated hills who bolster the forces of the British and Indian armies. Famed for their tenacity and loyalty in warfare since the late 18th century, these *khukri*-wielding soldiers underscored their fame by playing a key role in the 1982 Falkland Islands crisis.

The original Gurkha troops were from Gorkha, the small principality in central Nepal from which Prithvi Narayan Shah conquered the Kathmandu Valley in 1769 and unified the land of Nepal. Composed largely of Thakuri, Magar and Gurung men, these forces by 1814 had swept their long *khukris* across the central Himalaya.

The first two regular Gorkhali battalions were raised in 1763. Known as the Sri Nath and Purano Gorakh, they fought together against the British in 1769, and saw separate action against Tibet and in the Anglo-Nepal war of 1814-1816. It was the Anglo-Nepal war that first thrust the legend of Gurkha bravery into Western minds.

Impressed by what they had seen, the British East India Company began recruiting Gurkhas into their service. Gurkha recruitment was not formalised by the British until 1886, but by that time, India already had eight Gurkha Rifles units. Most of the men were drawn from the Magar and Gurung tribes, but others came from the Rais, Limbus and Sunuwars of the eastern hills and from the Khasas of the west.

At first, given their past hostilities, the relationship between the British and Nepalis was uneasy. By the time of the emergence of the Rana regime in 1846 and the subsequent visit to England of Jung Bahadur Rana, there was no question of the Gurkhas' allegiance. During the Indian mutiny of 1857, the British Gurkha regiments were joined by 12,000 of Jung Bahadur's own troops, with decisive results. Over the next 50 years, the Gurkhas

fought all over south Asia, from Afghanistan to Malaya and even as far afield as African Somaliland in 1903. And when they were not fighting, they were climbing mountains. Long before the Sherpas had achieved fame as guides and mountaineers, Gurkhas were climbing many western Himalayan peaks.

In the Alps of Europe in 1894, a pair of Gurkhas named Amar Singh Thapa and Karbir Burathoki travelled 1,600 kilometers (1,000 miles) in 86 days, crossing 39 passes and scaling 21 peaks. They named a Swiss

peak Piz Gurkha after being the first to climb its 3,063 meters (10,049 feet); a nearby col was named Gurkha Pass. In 1907, Burathoki and Englishman Tom Longstaff accomplished the first major ascent of a Himalayan peak, Trisul (7,120 meters or 23,360 feet). Gurkhas were involved in five Everest expeditions between 1921 and 1937.

The World Wars: But war beckoned the Gurkhas to new destinations. With the advent of the First World War, they were called on in even greater numbers. More than 114,000 Gurkhas were called into active service in Givenchy, Ypres, Gallipolli, Palestine, Mesopotamia, Suez, Persia and

Waziristan. Another 200,000 men were mobilized in the Indian army. Two Gurkhas – Kulbir Thapa (France, 1915) and Karna Bahadur Rana (Palestine, 1918) were awarded the Victoria Cross for gallantry.

In the Second World War, Gurkha strength was expanded to 45 battalions. These soldiers saw action in Iraq, Persia, Cyprus, Tunisia, Italy, Greece, Burma, Malaya and Indonesia; ten Victoria Crosses were awarded. Two of the battalions were paratroopers.

As the tale is told today, the British were seeking volunteers in a Gurkha regiment for a risky 1,000 foot airdrop behind enemy lines. About half of the troops stepped for-

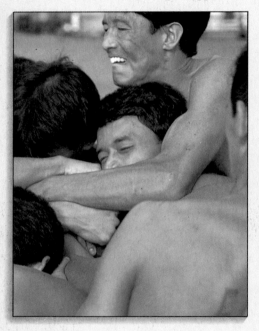

ward. The regiment leader proceeded to explain the troops' role in the drop, when a surprised voice queried: "Oh, you mean we can use parachutes?" Every remaining Gurkha promptly volunteered.

Two years after the Second World War ended, with the granting of independence to India, the Gurkha regiments were divided. Six of the ten regiments became the Indian Gurkha Rifles; the remaining four – the 2nd, 6th, 7th and 10th – remained the British Brigade of Gurkhas. In India, the troops plunged immediately into the India-Pakistan conflict over Kashmir; later came the Sino-Indian war of 1962 and further battles be-tween India and Pakistan in 1965 and 1971.

The British Brigade served in Malaya, Indonesia, Brunei and Cyprus. Another Victoria Cross, the 13th awarded to a Gurkha soldier, was presented to Lance Corporal Ram Bahadur Limbu for heroism in the face of overwhelming odds in Sarawak in 1965.

Gurkha soldiers are recruited as teenagers of 17 or 18 from their villages. There are recruiting depots at Pokhara in west Nepal and at Dharan in the east. Strict medical tests limit enlistment; those who succeed are provided with uniforms and good food, and are flown to Hong Kong for ten months of schooling and basic training. Then they have their first home leave, and their villages invariably treat them as heros.

Many Nepalese spend their entire working careers in the Gurkhas. It is a position of great status, and an important earner of foreign exchange for the country of Nepal. Only tourism in fact earns more. Gurkha salaries, pensions and related services provide a significant contribution to the economy.

Gurkhas today man posts in Hong Kong, Singapore, Brunei and Belize in Central America. But it was the South Atlantic skirmish between Britain and Argentina that brought them back into the public eye.

Perhaps the Gurkhas' ire was raised by the Argentine press, which belittled them as a cross between dwarfs and mountain goats. Perhaps the long sea voyage from the British Isles made them anxious to expend extra energy ashore; Gurkhas are notoriously bad sailors, and rely heavily on seasickness pills for travel between ports. Or perhaps the curry and rice diet which provides their daily sustenance gave them an emotional lift. Whichever, their action in the Falklands added another chapter to their legend.

Argentine troops guarding Port Stanley may have heard rumours about *khukri* decapitations of troops opposing the Gurkhas in other campaigns. For as the Gurkhas advanced on Argentine positions, the South American troops "turned and fled," according to a British newspaper report. The British Broadcasting Corporation reported that "the Argentines dropped their rifles and abandoned mortars and machine guns."

Above, celebrating after being selected as a Gurkha soldier. **Right**, physical and medical records are tested and checked.

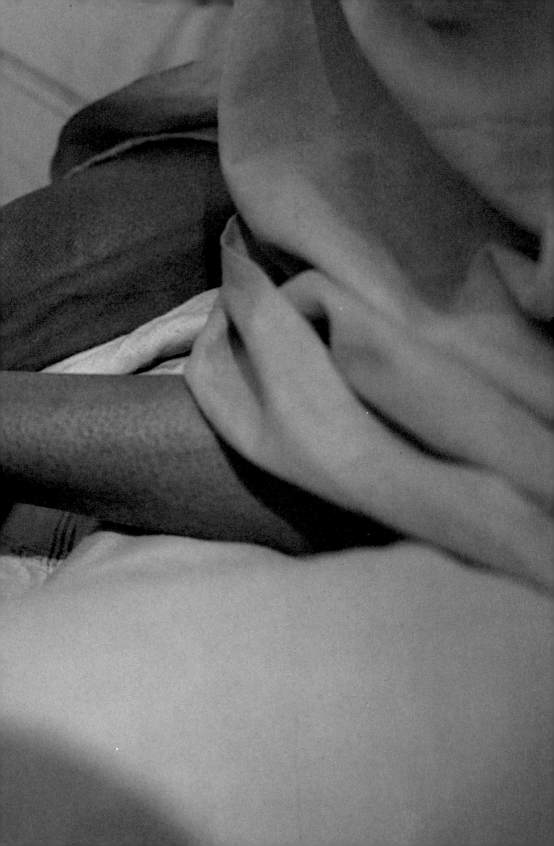

CENTRE OF THE UNIVERSE

The sacred Mount Kailas, beyond the main Himalayan range in Tibet, is regarded by millions as the spiritual centre of the universe. Worshipped by sages and celebrated by poets, this is the divine home where the gods descended to earth from heaven. Kailas and its Lake Mansarovar have for centuries captured the imagination with the classic images of creation, such as the Garden of Eden, the mountain of the Ark and the primordial ocean where creation of the cosmos began.

From this mythical centre of inspiration in the heart of Eurasia, rivers radiate in all directions; the Ob and Lena (among others) drain north through Siberia, the Hwang-Ho and Yangtze flow east to the Pacific, the Mekong to Southeast Asia, the mighty Brahmaputra, Ganges and Indus nourish the Indian subcontinent and the Oxus and Syr Darya flow west towards the Caspian.

The pristine white cone of Kailas (6,714 meters, 22,028 feet) is only visible on the clearest of days from an aircraft flying in the far west of the Nepal Himalaya. It is the object of pilgrimages by only a privileged few, due to the distance and difficulties of travel to such a remote region.

Both Hinduism and Buddhism relate to the Himalaya as a sacred source and those that live in its shadow are ever-mindful of its spiritual power – "An embodiment of the godly, fit to be worshipped" (Kalidasa, 5th century).

Daily Devotion: Every day before dawn, when sacred cows and stray dogs roam aimlessly in empty streets and when farmers are hurrying to market with their loads of vegetables or chickens, devotees of Nepal's religious cults wake up their gods in sacred temples.

As the misty rays of dawn begin to stream through the doorways, men, women and children set out for Hindu and Buddhist temples, carrying ritual offerings – *puja* – for the multiple gods of their pantheons.

They carry small copper plates piled with grains of rice, red powder and tiny yellow flower petals to scatter on the deities' images. Afterward, they mix the offerings into a paste, and apply a small amount of the mixture to their own foreheads, between the eyes: this is *tika*, a symbol of the presence of the divine.

Puja such as this is made at any and all times in Nepal, for any occasion or celebration. It is a cornerstone of Nepalese religion, inherited from the most ancient of ancestors. Offerings renew communion with the deities

most important to each individual's particular problem, caste or inclination.

Some of the devout have a special sequence of offerings, carefully arranged in a partitioned copper tray; they go from god to god for the best part of the morning. Others arrive with a couple of cups of yoghurt or *ghee*, and perhaps a few coins for the priests. Still other people may stay near their homes, contenting their deities by throwing rice, powder and petals on a particular rock or tree.

Ritual sacrifice is another foundation of Nepal's Hindu faith. Whether it is for a wedding or initiation rite or a seasonal festi-

Preceding pages: a *sadhu's* praying hands play the sacred cymbals. <u>Left</u>, Mount Kailas in Tibet. <u>Above</u>, a Hindu guru at Pashupatinath.

val for a deity, sacrifices are carried out with utter simplicity or with utmost pomp and ceremony.

The sacrifice of a chicken, goat or buffalo, always a male animal, is not only a way of slaying a beast in the presence of the divine. It also give an "unfortunate brother" a release from his imprisonment as an animal.

At the time of Nepal's biggest feast, the Dasain festival of early autumn, some 10,000 animals, mainly goats, are sacrificed in the space of a few days. More commonly, there are regular animal sacrifices at the Dakshinkali Temple in the southwest of the Valley – to the fascination of tourists crowding outside the sacrificial pits.

Religious Mainstreams: The two main spiritual currents underlying the religious practices of Nepal are Hinduism and Buddhism. It is often hard to distinguish between the two, especially since they are interwoven with the exotica of Tantrism on a background of animistic cults retained from the distant past. The result is a proliferation of cults, deities and celebrations in variations unknown elsewhere on earth.

With such diverse beliefs, religious tolerance is of the essence. In fact, proselytism is forbidden in Nepal by law – with a lengthy jail term awaiting offending parties, converter and convert.

The bulk of Kathmandu's Newars can be called Buddhist, in the sense that their family priests are Tantric Buddhist priests rather than Hindu brahmans. Such classification, however, has never prevented a villager from worshipping Tantric Hindu gods who are the village's patron deities. By becoming a follower of the Buddha, one does not cease to be a Hindu. Buddhists, in fact, regard the Hindu trinity of Brahma, Shiva and Vishnu as *avatars,* or incarnations, of the Buddha, and give the triad important places in the Buddhist cosmology. Hindus likewise revere the Buddha as an incarnation of Vishnu. It has been said that, if one asks a Newar whether he is Hindu or Buddhist, the answer will be "Yes." The question is meaningless, implying an exclusive choice which is foreign to the religious experience of Nepal's people.

The political leaders of the Kathmandu Valley have always been Hindus, but most of them have also supported development of their peoples' other faiths.

The 7th century King Narendradev, for instance, received Chinese Buddhist travellers with utmost respect. Chinese journals describe the King as a devout Buddhist who wore an emblem of the Buddha on his belt. But inscriptions left behind from Narendradev's reign insist that he regarded Shiva as his principal god.

Beginning with the time of King Jayasthiti Malla in the 14th century, growing pressure was put on Nepal's population to conform to the social structure of Hindu society. Even the Malla family deity, the goddess Taleju, was an import from South India. This trend was strengthened when the present Shah dynasty acceded to the throne over 200 years ago, adopting as its patron deity a deified Shaivite yogi, Gorakhnath.

The Rana prime ministers increased the caste differences in their century of power, enhancing the wealth and power of the ruling class. At the same time, innovation in religious arts was discouraged, with material wealth shifting to earthly "lords." Architects turned to building palaces rather than temples. The current government, however, realizes the importance of religion and promotes this cultural legacy.

The Hindu Heritage: Nepal's religions actually had their origins with the first Aryan invaders, who settled in the north of India about 1700 B.C. They recorded the *Vedas*, a collection of over 1,000 hymns defining a polytheistic religion. Out of this grew the caste-conscious Brahmanism, linking all men to the god-creator Brahma. The brahmans, or priest class, were said to have come from Brahma's mouth; the Chhetris, or warrior caste, from his arms; the Vaisyas, artisans and traders, from his thighs; and the Sudras, or serfs, from his feet.

As Brahmanism evolved into modern Hinduism, people began to feel increasingly that existence and reality were subjects too vast to be encompassed within a single set of beliefs. The Hindu religion of today, therefore, comprises many different metaphysical systems and viewpoints, some of them mutually contradictory. The individual opts for whichever belief or practice suits him and his particular inclinations the best.

Hinduism has no formal creed, no universal governing organization. Brahman priests serve as spiritual advisers to upper-caste families, but the only real authority is the ancient Vedic texts. Most important is that the individual comply with his family and social group.

Left, ritual sacrifice, a cornerstone of Hindu worship in Nepal. **Above**, applying *tika* as part of the worship in Patan's Krishna temple.

Different sects have developed a particular affinity with one or another deity – especially with Brahma "the creator," Vishnu "the preserver" and Shiva "the destroyer."

Most Nepalese Hindus regard Brahma's role as being essentially completed. Having created the world, he can now sit back astride his swan and keep out of everyday affairs. Both Vishnu and Shiva are very important in Nepal, however.

Vishnu, whose duty it is to assure the preservation of life and of the world, is traditionally considered to have visited earth as ten different *avatars*. Nepalese art pictures him as a fish, a tortoise, a boar, a lion, a dwarf, and as various men – among them

Narayan, the embodiment of universal love and knowledge; Rama, a prince; Krishna, a cowherd and charioteer; and Gautama Buddha, who corrupted the demons. The King of Nepal is also regarded as an incarnation of Vishnu.

The stories of Rama and Krishna are particularly important to Hindus. Rama is the hero of the *Ramayana*, perhaps Asia's greatest epic tale. The ideal man, Rama is brave, noble and virtuous. His beautiful wife Sita (whose legendary home is Janakpur – see page 318), is the perfect wife, loyal and devoted.

On a forest foray, Sita is captured by the

demon Rawana, who carries her off to his lair on the isle of Lanka. Rama enlists the help of the monkey people and their general, Hanuman, as well as the mythical eagle, Garuda. Together, they rescue Sita and slay Rawana. Sita proves her purity after the abduction by entering a fire and emerging unscathed. In Nepal, Hanuman and Garuda, Vishnu's vehicle, are revered.

Krishna is the central figure in the *Mahabharata* epic, particularly in that portion known as the *Bhagavad-Gita*. Nepalis love the many tales of Krishna's pranks and antics as a cowherd. It is said he once appeared to the *gopis*, the cowherd girls, in as many embodiments as there were women, and made love to each of them in the way she liked best.

But for all the devotion paid to Vishnu, it is Shiva who gets the most attention in Nepal. Those who worship Shiva do so not out of love of destruction, but because man must respect the fact that all things eventually will come to an end, and from that end will come a new beginning.

Like Vishnu, Shiva takes different forms. He is Pashupati, the lord of the beasts who guides all species in their development and serves benevolently as the tutelary god of Nepal. He is Mahadev, lord of knowledge and procreation, symbolized by the *lingum*. And he is the terrifying Tantric Bhairav, depicted with huge teeth and a necklace of skulls, intent on destroying everything he sees, including ignorance.

One of Shiva's sons, by his consort Parvati (also known as Annapurna, goddess of abundance), is the elephant-headed god, Ganesh. It is said he was born as a normal child, but had his head accidentally severed, and the elephant's head was grafted onto his neck. It is Ganesh's responsibility to decide between success and failure, to remove obstacles or create them as necessary.

The idea of "new beginnings," made manifest in the doctrine of reincarnation, is what keeps the Hindu caste system strong. Hindus believe that they must accept and act according to their station in life, no matter what it may be. Their birthright is a reward or punishment for actions – *karma* – accrued in a previous life. Their behaviour in this life will help determine their next one.

Teachings of the Buddha: Brahmanism was the dominant faith in the Indian subcontinent at the time of the emergence of Buddhism in the 6th century B.C.

The religion's founder, a Sakya prince named Siddhartha Gautama, was born about 543 B.C. (the actual date is disputed) near present-day Lumbini in Nepal's western Terai (see page 323). At the age of 29, he convinced his charioteer to take him outside the palace grounds where he lived a life of protected luxury. There, the sight of an old man, a crippled man and a corpse persuaded him to abandon his family and his lavish lifestyle for that of a wandering ascetic.

For more than five years, Gautama roamed from place to place, nearly dying of self-deprivation as he sought a solution to the

suffering he saw. He finally abandoned his asceticism, and while meditating under a *pipal* tree near Benares, India, oblivious to all distractions and temptations, he became enlightened. One must follow the Middle Way, he declared, rejecting extremes of pleasure and pain.

Now known as the Buddha, the "Enlightened One", Gautama preached a doctrine based on the "Four Noble Truths" and the "Eightfold Path." We suffer, he said, because of our attachment to people and things in a world where nothing is permanent. We can rid ourselves of desire, and do away with suffering, by living our lives with attention to right views, right intent, right speech, right conduct, right livelihood, right effort, right mindfulness and right meditation.

The "self," said the Buddha, is nothing but an illusion trapped in the endless cycle of *samsara*, or rebirth, and created by *karma*, the chain of cause and effect. By following the Buddhist doctrine, the *dharma*, he said, one can put an end to the effects of *karma*, thereby escaping *samsara* and achieving *nirvana*, which is essentially extinction of "self."

Gautama preached his doctrine for 45 years after his enlightenment, finally dying at the age of 80 and transcending to *nirvana*. Nepalis claim he may have visited the Kath-

It was Mahayana Buddhism which took hold in Nepal. One of the central beliefs of all Mahayanists is that one can achieve *nirvana* by following the example of *bodhisattvas*, or "Buddhas-to-be." These enlightened beings have, in the course of many lifetimes, acquired the knowledge and virtues necessary to attain *nirvana*, but have indefinitely delayed their transcendence to help other mortals reach a similar state of perfection.

The Buddhist emperor Ashoka of India's Mauryan dynasty made a pilgrimage to the Buddha's birthplace near Lumbini in the 3rd century B.C. He or his missionaries may have introduced some basic teachings while building stupas in the Kathmandu Valley.

mandu Valley with his disciple, Ananda, during his ministry.

In the centuries following the Buddha's life, many doctrinal disputes arose, leading to various schisms in the philosophy. Most important was the break between the Theravada or Hinayana school, which adhered more closely to the original teachings and today predominates in Southeast Asia and Sri Lanka, and the Mahayana school, which spread north and east from India.

Left, Buddhist *lama* celebrates the Tibetan New Year at Bodhnath. **Above**, guardian deity in Junbesi monastery, Solu Khumbu.

Nearly 1,000 years later, in the 7th century A.D. the Tibetan King Songtsengampo invaded the Valley and carried back a Nepalese princess as his wife. Both the Nepalese lady (later incarnated and revered as the Green Tara) and the King's Chinese consort (who became the White Tara) were Buddhists, and they persuaded him to convert to Buddhism.

Tibetan Buddhism: Since that time, Tibetan Buddhism has exerted a significant influence on Buddhist belief in Nepal. Altered in part by the earliest religion of Tibet, known as Bon, it has taken on a unique form in the world of Buddhism.

The shamanistic Bon faith, elements of which still exist today in Tibet and some remote corners of Nepal, has certain affinities with Buddhism. Bonpos (followers of Bon) claim their religion was carried from the west, possible Kashmir, by their founder, gShen-rab, who (like the Buddha) endured great hardships and meditated to achieve his spiritual knowledge. In medieval times, interchange between Bon and Buddhism led to a mutual adoption of parts of each other's pantheon under different names and guises.

The leading figure of Tibetan Buddhism – its pope, as it were – is the Dalai Lama. Every Dalai Lama is regarded as the reincarnation of his predecessor. Upon the death of a Dalai

Gelugpa, the Dalai Lama preaches free access to all teachings, including the *Kagyudpa* (Red Hats), *Nyingmapa* (Ancients) and *Salzyapa* (People of the Earth). Each of these groups has made important contributions to Tibetan Buddhist doctrine.

Tibetan Buddhism stresses the inter-relatedness of all things. Universal cosmic forces and the energies of the individual human being are one and the same, and through the faithful practice of meditation, one can learn to apply one's knowledge of these energies. This can involve an altered state of consciousness; skilled Tibetan monks are said to be able to levitate, to travel across land at the speed of the wind, and to perform other

Lama, a party of elder monks goes on a pilgrimage among Tibetan people to discover where their leader was reborn immediately following his physical death. The correct child is determined by his recognition of possessions from his previous life.

Tibetans believe that there are, at any one time, several hundred more *tulkus*, people identified in similar fashion as reincarnations of other important religious figures. These people generally go on to become leading monks themselves (see page 298).

There are four main sects of Tibetan Buddhism, most important of which is the *Gelugpa*, or Yellow Hats. Although himself a

actions which Westerners tend to relegate to the realms of the occult.

Learning proper meditation, under the guidance of a personal teacher, is the first step toward understanding the doctrine of interdependence. The most important tools of meditation are *mantra*, or sacred sound, and *mandala*, or sacred diagram. In *mantra* meditation, chanting of and concentration on certain syllables, such as *"Om mani padme hum"* is believed to intensify the spiritual power of those indoctrinated to the meaning. *Mandala* meditation requires one to visualize certain circular images to assist in orienting the self to the total universe.

Another important aspect of Tibetan Buddhism is the perception of death and dying. Accounts of pre-death and post-death experiences are an integral part of Tibet's religious archives.

Because mental and emotional states are believed to effect one's afterlife and rebirth, the dying person – accompanied by family, friends and *lamas* – meditates through the period of transition from life to death, making it easier for his spirit, or conciousness, to give up its residence in the body.

The Tantric Cults: All of Nepal's religions, whether Hindu, Buddhist or otherwise, are strongly influenced by the practices of Tantrism, a legacy of the Indian subcontinent's medieval culture. While the Moslem conquest, the British Raj and modern secularism have largely eliminated Tantrism elsewhere, it has lived on in Nepal.

Tantra is originally a Sanskrit word, referring to the basic warp of threads in weaving. Literally, Tantrism reiterates the Buddhist philosophy of the interwovenness of all things and actions.

But Tantrism, with its roots in the *Vedas* and the *Upanishads*, pre-Buddhist Brahmanistic verses, is more than that. In its medieval growth, it expanded the realm of Hindu gods, cults and rites, and added a new element to the speculative philosophy and yogic practices of the time. Within Buddhism, it created a major trend called Vajrayana, the "Path of the Thunderbolt," which reached its greatest importance in Nepal.

The *vajra*, known as the *dorje* in Tibetan Buddhism, is a main ritual object for Tantric Buddhist monks. It is a sceptre, each end of which has five digits curved in a global shape, said to represent the infinite in three dimensions. It is the symbol of the Absolute, a male instrument, and has as its female counterpart a bell or *ghanta*.

The prolific Tantric gods are represented in numerous human and animal forms, often with multiple arms, legs and heads as symbols of the omnipresence and omnipotence of the divine. Many of these deities have a terrifying appearance, like forbidding Bhairav, blood-thirsty Kali or ambivalent Shiva, who in the Tantric pantheon is both creator and destroyer. Their appearance is said to reflect man's when confronted with unknown forces.

Opposed to contemplative meditation, Tantrism substituted concrete action and direct experience. But it soon degenerated into esoteric practices, often of a sexual nature, purportedly to go beyond one's own limitation to reach perfect divine bliss.

Shaktism is such a cult, praising the *shakti*, the female counterpart of a god. Some ritual Tantric texts proclaim: "Wine, flesh, fish, women and sexual congress: these are the five-fold boons that remove all sin."

At a higher level, Tantrism is an attempt to synthesize spiritualism and materialism.

Practitioners seek to expand their mental faculties by mastering the forces of nature and achieving peace of mind. In the sexual act is seen wisdom, tranquillity and bliss, along with, of course, the mystery inherent in human union.

The image depicting sexual union is called *yab-yum*, perhaps not entirely unlike the Chinese *yin-yang*, a symbol of oneness in polarity. In several locations in the Kathmandu Valley, *yab-yum* and other erotica are carved in wooden relief on the struts of temples. The significance of these artistic expressions depends less on what they show than on who looks at them.

Left, prayer flags above Thyangboche waft prayers to the gods. **Above**, Licchavi stone statue of Vishnu at Changu Narayan.

There are few cultures in the world that lack an indigenous tradition of faith healers. While the broad outlines of Nepalese shamanism are influenced by Tibetan and Indian traditions, a great variety of local Himalayan forms has evolved paralleling the diverse ethnic groups in the country. Most of Nepal's tribal languages have their own terms for those specialists and the usual Nepali words are *jhankri* and *dhami*. The term shaman, a Siberian expression, encompasses the tremendous variety of forms.

A shaman is a man (or, less commonly, a woman) who mediates between this world and the supernatural realm of ghosts, demons, witches, ancestors and the like. His task is to restore the proper relationship between the two worlds when it has been upset. Since the commonest manifestation of imbalance is illness, the shaman is above all a healer.

Shaking and Travelling: The methods which the healers use to tackle spirits and diseases are legion. The shaman invokes one or more divinities, his familiar spirits, who enter his body and speak through him. Once possessed, the shaman falls into a trance which may involve violent shaking and wild dancing. Possession may be accompanied by dramatic demonstrations of the power temporarily bestowed by the gods: licking red-hot iron, for example, or tying swords in knots. In this case it is the gods who answer questions, make oracular statements and banish evil influences, speaking through their human medium in strange voices and even unfamiliar languages.

Another approach involves the healer achieving ecstasy – literally "standing outside." The patient has fallen ill because his soul or life force has been stolen by some malign entity, perhaps a witch, a demon, the ghost of a restless dead person or, as in certain Tibetan communities, the strange entity known as "the one who calls with the empty voice."

The shaman must leave his body and fly through the other world in search of the lost soul and bribe, cajole or force the captor into relinquishing it. Dressed in a long robe and a feather-headdress, protected by straps or

bells, ironmongery and cowries, and armed with his flat drum, the shaman negotiates the terms of his patient's recovery and will do battle with the assailants if all peaceful means fail.

The healer accompanies his performance with the recitation of a myth that may continue for many hours, revealing both his prodigious memory and his gift for storytelling. The story, which is usually sung to the accompaniment of the drum, begins with the origin of the world, and continues with the

appearance and ultimate resolution of crises between the forces of good and evil. The therapeutic power of these stories should not be underestimated: the bards of ancient Tibet, for example, were regarded as the protectors of the kingdom.

Part of the shaman's technique involves forging an identity between the myth he recites and the circumstances of the pathology with which he is faced. Through ritual performance and sheer Thespian virtuosity the shaman establishes the relevance of the myth to the everyday world; the mundane and the supernatural merge, and healing is achieved in sympathy with the narrative's resolution of the archetypal ills.

Animal sacrifice is usually a prerequisite of shamanic sessions, even in some nominally Buddhist communities who technically do not condone ritual killing. The sacrifice is an important component of the commerce between the two worlds in which the shaman is the broker. The client wants something from the spirits – the return of a stolen soul, perhaps, or simply a withdrawal of malign forces. In exchange for this concession he must send across something from the domestic sphere, such as a chicken, a goat or a pig.

The Himalayan region is a rich store of medicinal plants, and the shaman's reper-

Among the skills a shaman must learn is divination, which is essentially a magical diagnosis to establish the cause of a problem. Methods include the scrutiny of egg-yolks or the entrails of animals; the way grain moves on a lightly-tapped drumskin; the number of beads in a section of a rosary (used primarily by Buddhist shamans); scapulimancy, where the shoulder-bone of a sheep is thrown into a fire and the resulting pattern of cracks examined and interpreted; or, among the Rai people of eastern Nepal, the way in which pieces of sliced wild ginger fall on a sample of the patient's clothing.

Crossing Religious Lines: The majority of Nepal's population calls itself Hindu, fol-

toire normally includes a mastery of herbal lore. The plants are not cultivated but must be gathered from the wilderness. Pharmaceutical knowledge is only one branch of an overall familiarity with the wild and the undomesticated.

Images of the hunt also characterise many of the rituals that are performed over the course of the long shamanic nights: malign ghosts must be tracked down and brought to bay, and lost souls vigorosly recaptured like wild animals.

Left, village shaman in Helambu. **Above**, Rai shaman during the Gosainkund festival.

lowed by a strong Buddhist faction, with a small percentage of Muslims and a few Christians. Shamanism appears in both Hindu and Buddhist communities of Nepal, and parallels the activity of the priests of these religions.

The exponents of the literate religions cater to popular demand by including healing and exorcism among their other, more spiritual services; but the continuing popularity of spirit-mediums can leave little doubt that these highly revered and worshipped shamans are the acknowledged masters in the strange geography of this undiscovered country.

Of all the myths and legends of the high Himalaya of Nepal, perhaps the best known is that of the yeti or "abominable snowman."

But is it a myth? Or is there, in fact, a creature roaming the frozen wastes, preying on yaks and frightening human intruders?

Such a beast was first described to the West as a shaggy wild man by a European mercenary in Mongolia in the early 15th century. Himalayan peoples who lived in remote areas below the snow line spoke of him as anything from ape to supernatural being. To the Sikkimese, for instance, he was the spirit of the hunt: he could be seen only by the devout, and votive offerings of any kill had to be made to him.

The British tended to dismiss, as colourful legend, native sighting of strange snow creatures. In 1899, however, Major L.A. Waddell, an authority on Tibetan Buddhism, described finding mysterious footprints that "were alleged to be the trail of the hairy wild men who are believed to live among the eternal snows." In 1921, Colonel C.K. Howard-Bury, who led the reconnaissance on the north side of Everest through Tibet, saw dark figures moving across the snow and later came upon enormous footprints.

"The Abominable Snowman": Stories continued to flow from Tibet and Sikkim, and the great snowman debate was on. It was given credence by a popular British columnist who mistranslated the beast's Tibetan name – *migyu* – as "the abominable snowman." The name stuck.

Years later, when Nepal finally allowed foreigners to enter the country to climb Mount Everest, the "snowman" became fixed in the imagination of the world. The Sherpas who assisted on those early expeditions told climbers a spate of stories about the yeh-tch, or yeti. Giant footprints were seen by such well-known mountaineers as Frank Smythe, H.W. Tilman and John Hunt.

On a November afternoon in 1951, climber Eric Shipton found a clear trail of naked human-looking footprints high up in the snow of the Menlungtse Glacier. He and his companion, Sherpa Sen Tenzing, following the trail for about a mile until it disappeared in moraine. Shipton took clear and well-defined photographs of the yeti footprints; they were oval in shape, more than a foot long and very wide, with a distinctive protruding big toe. Suddenly, all those mysterious sightings, the unknown yells and whistles, the stones and branches hurled at startled travellers at night, seemed to make sense. There was something out there.

Three Types of Yeti: According to the Sherpas, the *yeh-tch* – literally "man of the rocky places" – is of three types. There is the huge, cattle-eating *dzu-tch* (or juti); it is about eight

feet tall when standing on its hind legs, but is usually on all fours, and is almost certainly the blue-bear of Tibet. There is the *thelma*, a small ape-like creature which walks on its hind legs, has long dangling arms and is covered in red or blond hair; this is probably the Assam gibbon strayed far from home. And there is the *mih-tch* (or miti), a man-sized ape, which but for its face and stomach is covered in shaggy red hair. By all ac-

Above, a priest at the Pangboche monastery displays what he claims is a yeti scalp. Some insist it is genuine. **Right**, a sherpa artist's impression of the Himalayan legend.

counts, it is an abominable creature, attacking on sight. Some say it is a man-eater.

The *mih-tch* is the true yeti for which there is no definite explanation. It is this anthropoid that is painted into monastery murals and religious scrolls. Sherpas single out the orangutan when shown photographs of known animals; fossils of long-extinct giant orangutans have been found in the Himalayan foothills. Could some have survived by taking refuge in the once-remote reaches below the snow line?

Some theorize this *mih-tch* could be a direct descendant of *Gigantopithecus*—Peking Man of one million years B.C. This ape man, they say, could have evolved in obscurity, in

inhospitable habitats.

In Search of the Yeti: Several expeditions have set out in search of the yeti. In 1954, London's *Daily Mail* fielded an impressive team of experts which, though it failed to find the yeti, returned with a bank of knowledge on the creature. Mountaineer Norman Dyhrenfurth in 1958 found footprints similar to those photographed by Shipton.

In 1960, Sir Edmund Hillary led an expedition to Shipton's yeti country, below the great peaks of Gauri Shankar and Menlungtse. The expedition was equipped with the latest scientific equipment and a signed-and-sealed order from the Nepalese

government that the yeti, if found, was on no account to be killed or kept in captivity.

Hillary's expedition procured furs alleged to be those of yetis, and found endless suspicious tracks in the snow. It also borrowed the legendary "yeti scalp," a sacred relic, from the Sherpa monastery of Khumjung. This iron-hard dome of leather and red bristles had baffled climbers and other observers for years. But when taken for examination to Chicago, Paris and London, the "scalp" was declared to be a 200-year-old artifact made from the hide of a wild Himalayan goat, the serow. Hillary's furs, meanwhile, were discovered to be those of the Tibetan blue bear. Many of the footprints were those of foxes and ravens, whose tracks had melted in the sun and had taken on grotesque sizes and shapes. Western "experts" were quick to debunk the yeti legend.

The Legend Lives On: But the yeti refuses to be killed so easily. There are two other scalps in Sherpa country, in the monasteries of Pangboche and Namche Bazaar, and a skeletal yeti hand at Pangboche. One of these scalps was examined in Europe in the early 1970s; some declared it a blatant fake but others said it was genuine.

A Sherpa girl was said to have been savaged in 1974. Several yaks' necks were broken by something that grabbed them by the horns and twisted their heads. The high whistles have been heard again. Expedition camps have been visited at night by a creature that left footprints in the snow. When members began following and photographing, something screamed at them.

Author Bruce Chatwin wrote of his discovery of tracks in the Gokyo Valley in 1983 and Reinhold Messner found traces in Tibet in 1986. Chris Bonnington led a 1988 expedition to Menlungtse, although journalists' reports of sightings and samples continued to be treated with disdain by the scientific community. Proof remains inconclusive, to say the least. There is even an irreverent though forever-to-be unconfirmed theory that Shipton's 1951 yeti footprints were an elaborate hoax.

Ape, sub-human, wild man of the snows, or demon – the myth lives on and perhaps someday the yeti will be found. It was not very long ago, after all, that China's giant panda and Africa's mountain gorilla were mere legends.

It has been observed that in Nepal every other building is a temple and every other day is a festival. With more than 50 festivals involving 120 days, celebrations are so frequent that they often overlap.

Thousands of gods and goddesses, demons and ogres, restless spirits and the family dead must be appeased and remembered. The various seasons must be honoured and there are appropriate rites for the blessing seeds to be planted and crops harvested. Some of Nepal's festivals are ancient indeed, having their origins in animism and legend. Others are more recent, the direct result of a monarch's command.

The majority are tied to one or both of the two great religions of the land, Hinduism and Buddhism. The devotees of one religion take part in the other's festivals, adapting some of the rites of the other faith to their own festivals.

The major festivals of Nepal are listed here according to the month in which they are normally held. Always check locally as dates often change due to the lunar calendar.

Magha (January and February)

The Nepali month begins with **Magha Sankranti**, an important day for ritual bathing celebrating the passing of the previous unholy month of Pousch and the promise of warmth to come. This is an important day at Devghat, north of Narayanghat.

Basant Panchami is the festival of spring and also of Saraswati, goddess of learning. The season is inaugurated before the King in Hanuman Dhoka and Saraswati's birthday is celebrated at Swayambhunath by students, artists, weavers and schoolchildren.

The shrine of Pashupatinath or the village of Sankhu are the places to be for the ceremony of **Maha Snan**, which is the holy bath given to Lord Shiva in which he is washed with milk, yoghurt, honey and *ghee* then dressed anew.

Preceding pages: Biskit festival at Bhaktapur coincides with the Nepali New Year. **Left**, the great stupa of Bodhnath is blessed at Losar, Tibetan New Year. **Above**, autumn festival in Manang.

Falgun (February and March)

One of the most beautiful celebrations of the year is **Losar** or **Tibetan New Year** when Tibetans and Sherpas feast, enjoy *lama* dances and parade on newly decorated stupas of Bodhnath and Swayambhunath.

Shivaratri, the birthday of Shiva, the Hindu god of destruction and rebirth, is one of the great festivals of the year. Thousands of townspeople, holy men and pilgrims flock to Pashupatinath for the happy celebration

and all-night vigil. *Sadhu*s, or *yogi*s, some dressed in nothing but a loin cloth carrying a metal trident, gather from throughout India and Nepal to perform rites.

The rowdy festival of colour, **Holi**, is a chaotic springtime carnival during which kids roam the streets pelting each other with water balloons and coloured powder. A day to wear your oldest clothes and have fun.

Chaitra (March and April)

The horse festival of **Ghorajatra** takes place on the Tundhikhel in Kathmandu with a display of horsemanship and gymnastics.

The same evening, the festival of **Pasa Chare** assures protection against an underground demon in a midnight procession.

Two separate festivals occur simultaneously towards the end of March. Ritual offerings are made to the goddess Durga at midday on **Chaitra Dasain**, exactly six months to the day before the great Dasain festival of September-October. **Seto Machhendranath** or **Rath** is a procession in which the deity of compassion is paraded from his temple in Asan in a towering chariot and visited by the Living Goddess.

Solu's Junbesi monastery performed exorcist rites at one of the Sherpas' greatest festivals, **Dumje**, in April.

ing of a long pole decorated with banners. Citizens of Bhaktapur play a tug-of-war to topple the pole, assuring a year of good fortune.

West of Bhaktapur in Thimi, **Bal Kumari Jatra** is celebrated at night with torchlight processions and devotees covered with vermilion powder.

Matatirtha Snan, the Nepalese Mother's Day, takes place near Thankot and is for persons whose mothers have died during the year. Living mothers are also honoured.

The birthday of the Lord Buddha, **Buddha Jayanti**, is celebrated with pilgrimages to Buddhist shrines. Bodhnath and Swayambhunath are particularly colourful.

During the full moon, **Chaitra Purnima**, Buddha's mother Mayadevi is worshipped by thousands of pilgrims in Lumbini.

One of the great Janakpur festivals, **Ram Nawami**, Ram's birthday, is also celebrated in April.

Baisakh (April and May)

Baisakh is the beginning of the Nepali New Year which concides with the week-long **Bisket Jatra** celebration in Bhaktapur. The wrathful god Bhairav and his consort, Bhadrakali, are pulled on great chariots through the streets, culminating in the rais-

Thame monastery, high in the Khumbu region of east Nepal holds its **Mani Rimdu** dance-drama festival in May during which monks enact age-old legends and evoke protector deities.

Jesth (May and June)

Sithinakha is the birthday of Kumar, the handsome warrior son of Shiva and is celebrated at Jaisedewal, south of the Kathmandu Durbar Square.

The **Ganga Deshara** festival attracts thousands of Hindu devotees to the holy Khaptad National Park in west Nepal.

Asadh (June and July)

Tulsi Bijropan is one of the most important *Ekadasis*, the eleventh day of each lunar fortnight, when no animal can be slaughtered and a day of fasting is mandatory for the religious.

Primarily a woman's ritual, the *tulsi* (basil) plant is planted in a specially chosen place within the home and then reverently worshipped.

The Khumbu Sherpas' **Dumje** celebration brings the entire community together in much gaiety and merry-making, but more important, to drive out evil forces with an elaborate liturgy and much chanting.

ensure good monsoon rainfall.

Traditionally the last day for rice planting, **Ghanta Karna** is the night of the devil, sworn enemy of Vishnu. Small boys make leafy arches and collect pennies in the street.

The birth of the popular Hindu god is celebrated at **Krishna Jayanti** in all Krishna temples. Women carrying oil lights make offerings, chant and sing as they keep vigil all night on the Krishna Mandir in Patan.

Raksha Bandhan or **Janai Purnima** is the full-moon day on which every Brahman male must renew the sacred thread worn over his shoulder and all Brahmans and Chhetris receive a thread around their wrists. Go to the Kumbeshwar temple in Patan. At Go-

Srawan (July and August)

Patan sees one of its biggest annual festivals in the summer, though the exact date varies according to astrologers. During **Bhoto Jatra** a sacred jewelled waistcoat *(bhoto)* is ritually displayed in front of the royal family. This is the culmination of **Rato Machhendranath**, the protector deity of the Valley, who is paraded through Patan for months in his huge chariot and is designed to

sainkund high in Helambu, thousands of devotees throng to bathe in the sacred lakes and make offerings, celebrating with dancing and feasting. Shamans, dressed in long white-belted robes and crowns of peacock feathers, gather at both Patan and Gosainkund to chant and perform rites of purification. This festival is also celebrated in Khaptad National Park.

Snake gods *(nags)* are widely worshipped as controllers of rainfall, earthquakes and guardians of treasure. During **Naga Panchami** prayers are said at Pashupatinath and pictures of the *nags* are displayed on every house.

<u>Left</u>, a torchlight procession at Thimi drenched with red powder. <u>Above</u>, incense is burned during Krishna Jayanti in Patan.

Late summer is the time for the important **Yartung** festival celebrated by mountain people with wild horse-racing annually at holy Muktinath, high in the Kali Gandaki valley of the Annapurna region.

Bhadra (August and September)

Musical processions of little boys dressed as holy men and stylised cows take place throughout Kathmandu during the festival of **Gaijatra**. A carnival evening follows of satire and fantastic costumes. Originally devised as a comic-relief parade to cheer the inconsolable Queen of Nepal who had lost a son to smallpox, these rituals also ease the transition of those who have died during the previous year.

The most spectacular of all the Kathmandu Valley festivals is the eight-day **Indrajatra**. Best seen from the Hanuman Dhoka, the Hindu god Indra is feted with dancing and processions. Homage is paid to the Living Goddess Kumari and she is escorted, beautifully adorned, in a special chariot. Bhairav is also honoured during this festival, the only time his great mask is exposed to the public with *chhang* (beer) pouring from his mouth to refresh revellers.

Gokarna Aunshi or **Father's Day** is celebrated with ritual bathing at the fine Mahadev temple at Gokarna for those whose fathers have died during the last year.

Teej is the most colourful women's festival, celebrated over three days of dancing, singing and bathing at Pashupatinath by women in their finest saris and jewels.

Ashwin (September and October)

The great 10-day festival of **Dasain**, also known as **Durga Puja**, is the most important Hindu festival of the whole year and normal life throughout the country comes to a standstill for up to a week. Families gather to worship the mother goddess Durga who is assuaged with offerings and animal sacrifices performed in community courtyards and in mammoth proportions in Kathmandu's Hanuman Dhoka. Entranced priests swirl and gyrate through the streets of Patan for eight nights prior to the main day, Vijaya Dasain, when each family's elder male adorns all with a red *tika* before a feast on the sacrificial meat.

Kartik (October and November)

Tihar or **Diwali**, the festival of lights is a more joyous holiday of family gatherings, feasts, gifts and offerings. Cows, dogs and crows are blessed with treats, and brothers travel for days to receive a *tika* from their sisters on **Bhai Tika**. On the fifth day **Lakshmi Puja**, the goddess of prosperity is attracted to homes by oil lamps on all windows and doors. The Newars celebrate **Mha Puja** at this time to honour the self and to mark their calendar New Year.

The yearly **Mani Rimdu** dance drama festival is held at Thyangboche monastery in the Khumbu, high on the trekking route to Everest. Monks enact Sherpa legends and evoke the protector gods with colourful masked dances. Mani Rimdu is also held during the full moon of this month at Solu's Chiwong monastery.

Reminiscent of Mani Rimdu are the dance festivals of **Dyokyabsi**, celebrated at various monasteries in the Thak Khola (upper Kali Gandaki River valley) and Mustang during October and November.

Haribodhini Ekadasi welcomes Vishnu back from his annual four month sleep in the underworld. Budhanilkantha is the culmination of celebrations after fasting devotees have concluded the long pilgrimage, singing and chanting, to the four peripheral Valley temples of Changu Narayan, Bishankhu Narayan, Sekh Narayan and Ichangu Narayan.

Marga (November and December)

Yomari Purnima is celebrated by Newars with a *mela* or fair at Panauti in December. A special cake is made out of rice flour and ritually offered to the family rice store for protection.

Poush (December and January)

HM The King's Birthday, celebrated on 28th December, is one of several public holidays decreed by the monarch.

In Janakpur in December the festival of **Biha Panchami** reenacts Ram and Sita's marriage, complete with a procession of elephants, horses and chariots.

Right, Seto Machhendra is paraded annually in a huge chariot through the streets of Kathmandu.

ADVENTURE TRAVEL

The Call of the Wild has roused a spirit of adventure in mankind from earliest times, inspiring humans to explore every corner of the earth. Contemporary Marco Polos have now turned their attention to the endless horizons of outer space; yet as recently as the 1940s one of earth's greatest natural wonders, Mount Everest, remained sequestered from all but the Nepalis who revered its preeminence but were loath to tread its sacred slopes.

Until 1949, Nepal was closed to foreign visitors; even the few who were invited by the Rana rulers were not allowed out of the Kathmandu Valley. It was the largest inhabited country yet unexplored by Europeans. The restrictions were especially disconcerting to alpinists who had climbed all of the most challenging European peaks and were eager to test their skills on the lofty summits of the Himalaya.

The first foreign explorers to enter Nepal were mountaineers and scientists. Both shared a willingness to endure the rigours of walking through rugged landscape cut off from all communication and modern amenities. There were no roads and, other than supplies carried with them, for months on end only local food and basic camping accommodations were available.

The Trekking Industry is Born: Lt. Col. Jimmy Roberts was the first to be inspired to ply a trade from the booming interest in mountain tourism. An officer in the British Indian army, Roberts was a pioneer of numerous first ascents of peaks in Nepal and Pakistan, and had organised logistical support for major Himalayan expeditions. Roberts borrowed the new sport's name from South African Boer "trekkers" and refined the camping concept from Kashmiri sheep hunting trips enjoyed by his friends in the west Himalaya. He advertised his first trek in Holiday Magazine. Three sporting middle-aged American women responded and in 1964 Nepal's trekking industry was born. Roberts called Nepal's first trekking agency, Mountain Travel Nepal, and it still flourishes today.

International news coverage of the summiting of Mount Everest and other of the great Himalayan peaks, together with frequent tales from returning mountaineers and journalists about this enchanting mountain kingdom, sparked a phenomenal growth in tourism. Between 1966 and 1970, the number of annual visitors nearly quadrupled (to 46,000), and by 1976 it had passed 100,000.

Today roughly a quarter million tourists visit Nepal each year; of these close to 50,000 are Indians who come for business, religious or shopping purposes. Of the others, over one quarter come for trekking and mountaineering, contributing a lion's share of the country's annual foreign exchange earnings. From a single trek outfitter in the mid-1960s, one hundred-plus registered trekking agencies now vie in an overly competitive market.

The same impulse which sent the

Preceding pages: Hot air balloons are an incomparable way to view Ama Dablam in the Khumbu. **Left,** trekking and camping is the only way to get deep into the mountains. **Right,** Lt. Col. Jimmy Roberts, the father of trekking.

world knocking on Nepal's door in 1949 has continued to attract mountaineers from every continent. Climbers pay large royalties and risk the loss of frozen fingers and toes – or worse – for a chance to scale the world's highest peaks. The number of mountaineers has soared to close to 1,000 some years. Expeditions wait five years or more for permission to scale a chosen mountain in a particular season. The lesser Trekking Peaks, of lower heights yet often technically demanding (see page 147) attract the amateur or self-financed mountaineer in search of a quick high.

A Boon to Hill Traders: Mountain tourism has been a boon to many of Nepal's hill economies, providing seasonal jobs to hundreds of skilled guides, thousands of subsistence farmers as porters, and a much-needed source of cash to villagers with the ingenuity to set up tourist shops and lodges.

In the 1950s, mountaineering injected the Khumbu Sherpas with an employment boost just at the time that trans-Himalayan trade with China was brought to its knees. Hill farmers, who for centuries had depended on trade as a source of supplemental income, suddenly faced tough times.

The Sherpas, living year round at elevations upward of 3,000 meters (10,000 feet), were naturally adept at scaling precipitous heights and proved a pleasure to work with. Many early foreigner – Sherpa partnerships have turned into lifetime relationships. Some children of Sherpa climbers receive educational scholarships abroad. Many of those who so diligently served the first foreign expeditions nowadays have their own trekking agencies.

With the closure of the Tibet border, the Thakali people of the upper Kali Gandaki valley in the Annapurna region faced a similar dilemma. The choice was to eke out a living in this high mountain desert, devoid of trade's supplemental income or to move to lower, more productive farmlands far from their heritage and homeland. Although some sought jobs in the mountains, many Thakalis turned their well reputed

Evening light in the Mustang district high up the Kali Gandaki valley.

traders' inns called *bhattis*, into trekkers' lodges. Today they offer the cleanest, most popular quarters on the circuit, serving some of the best food.

Tourism's Inroads: There were no roads to speak of in Nepal when the first foreigners arrived in 1949; only a short roadway extended from the Indian border railway to a few eastern foothill bazaar towns. Not even Kathmandu was linked to the outside by road. Herzog describes in the last chapter of his classic saga to Annapurna I their final walk – those with frost-bitten toes were carried – to Kathmandu to receive the King's congratulations. Early Everest explorations set out from Darjeeling; once Nepal was opened, the trek from Kathmandu to Everest Base Camp took more than a month.

Nowadays Nepal's east to west road network plus its 27 STOL (short take off and landing) mountain airstrips make the mountains much more accessible. In just a matter of two or three weeks, trekkers can reach Everest Base Camp and see much of Khumbu, or even hike around the Annapurna massif.

Tea House Trekking: The mushrooming of small lodges along popular trekking routes, many converted from homes that once served the trans-Himalayan trader, has sped tourism's inroads into certain mountain areas. During the 1970s, the peak of Kathmandu's ignominy as a drug haven, low-budget travellers began wandering into the hills unaccompanied by a Nepalese guide and staying in village tea houses, coining the phrase "tea house trekking."

The villagers caught on and built more lodges. Most are simple shelters offering wooden cots and a hot meal while others, particularly in the Annapurna and Solu Khumbu areas, are more elaborate, patterned after an alpine skier's hut with wood-panelled dining areas separate from the kitchen, private rooms and flower garden terraces. Conveniently spaced several hours to a day's hike apart, tea houses have enabled the independent trekker to travel light, with sleeping bag but without tent, food nor cooking gear.

While lodge to lodge trekking gives a taste of Nepalese home life, along with the charm can come problems. Not all lodge kitchens are hygenic and sickness out on trek can delay travellers by days, or altogether. The monotony of *dal bhaat* (rice and lentils) day after day can be tedious, as can the lack of privacy or security of dormitory living.

Camping in Style: Colonel Roberts' vision of high quality service was reminiscent of that provided by affluent early Himalayan mountaineering expeditions on their trek to base camp, of which he had much experience. Stylish tweeds and wind-up gramophones were not unknown. The last 25 years have refined professional services set by Mountain Travel Nepal. Some may feel that these pleasures are too elaborate, though there are few real complaints on this score.

Indeed, Nepal has set the standards for quality adventure travel worldwide. It is not uncommon for a group of six "members" to be accompanied by an entourage of twelve to fifteen, comprising porters, a cook and several kitchen

Sports like paragliding are still in the experimental stage in the Himalaya.

staff, two or three "Sherpas," and a chief guide called *sirdar*.

The porters carry all food needed for the trip, camp equipment including sleeping and dining tents, stools, and the members' personal belongings, and all in funnel-shaped baskets called *dokos*. Loads might weigh up to 30 kilos (66 lbs), supported by a trump line born on the carrier's forehead. Each night, camp is made by a stream or water source, often in an idyllic setting beneath the snow-crested Himalaya or overlooking a jigsaw pattern of brilliant green rice paddies.

The cook and his assistants create a variety of savoury Western and Asian concoctions over a campfire or kerosene stove. It is indeed a movable feast. Sherpas accompany individual members on the trail, and the *sirdar* (usually fluent in English) oversees the entire operation from the hiring, firing (and placating) of local porters to seeing to the clients' comfort and safety.

Many first-time trekkers, especially those used to backpacking, feel their conscience twinge upon seeing the porters, some just adolescent, male and female, bend under two or three duffel bags. But to the Nepalese, who have transported all loads on foot for centuries, such work is a chance to earn hard cash to buy household necessities or a new pair of high-tops.

The camaraderie that grows between clients and staff, despite a language barrier, is heartfelt and is one of the bonuses of trekking with an agency. At the end of a day all join in dance and song, blind to sore muscles or cold. At the trip's conclusion tearful goodbyes express more than words ever could.

Planning a Trek: First-time and many return trekkers find it easier to let the experts do all the preparatory work, and contact a trekking company either at home or in Nepal. Their assistance in arranging for permits, equipment, food and transportation, hiring reliable staff and arranging porter insurance (a government requirement) will help make the most out of limited time. In discussing a trek itinerary, make it clear how

Combination trekking, rafting and wildlife safaris to suit all budgets.

many days you wish to spend on the trail as this, along with the season and your personal interests, are the primary determinants in deciding where to go.

Treks need not be long and rigorous; they vary from several day walks on relatively easy, low-level terrain to rugged, demanding expeditions of a month or more. Do not make the mistake of thinking a short trek is necessarily easier – there are still hills and less time to get fit and into the trek rhythm. You can go virtually anywhere, except restricted zones, within the limits of your trekking permit. The following sections describe trekking areas and routes and a directory in the back gives more details.

Trekking with an agency, self-sufficient in all aspects, allows you to penetrate deep into the Himalayan wilderness, leaving behind overcrowded trails. Entry into the newly-opened Kangchenjunga and Dolpo and newly-opened trekking areas is limited to those with a registered agency who must be self-sufficient in food and fuel. Dolpo and other remote, food-poor regions simply do not have any surplus to support tea house trekkers. Having your own tent avails flexibility and a retreat from curious villagers. Health-conscious cooks prepare astonishing menus of Western and Oriental dishes which more than satiate the appetite.

The Appeal of Shangrila: What do so many trekkers find in Nepal that they cannot find hiking in their own or other foreign countries?

The early Tibetan scripts and Hindu epics tell of the wondrous Himalaya, where gods dwelt on high and mortals could find heaven-on-earth in hidden valleys. An air of mysticism indeed premeates musty monasteries and resides thick amidst a circle of gyrating, possessed shamans.

But what many travellers to Nepal find most appealing is the blissful tranquility, an affirmation of timelessness, which the outside world tries hard to ignore. In the Nepalese's simple yet arduous lives, the visitor sees a clarity of values; family strength, self-respect, purity of heart and kindness to others.

It is essential to be well equipped when trekking at altitude.

The vigilant mountains and mesmerising patterns of hard-wrought staircases of terraces massage the mind into contemplation; a moment's rest on a mountain top, an interlude by a rushing stream, the flash of a passing smile, can reveal long-cloistered moments of truth to those who listen.

The physical effort required of carrying one's body up and down this immense landscape, of paring one's daily essentials to a few, of relishing in mundane accomplishments, all invite reflection on a cluttered or distracted life back home. The rewards of trekking are unquantifiable yet immeasurable and addictive. Once is rarely enough.

Speciality Treks: A more structured approach and an educational forum appeals to some travellers and companies now combine scientific, religious and cultural study or hobbies with a trekking holiday. Tour leaders double as instructors in yoga, mountain medicine, photography, botany, birdwatching, sketching, language study and cultural interaction.

Family treks can be specially planned with a less ambitious schedule, finding time for kids' activities and extra staff to tend and carry youngsters. Pony treks are conducted out of Pokhara, for those who do not wish to or cannot walk. A group of blind trekkers recently set a world record climbing 6,654 meter (21,830 foot) Mera Peak.

A Potpourri of Adventure Sports: In the 40 years since Nepal opened its doors to the outside world, tourism has sprouted numerous new fields of adventure travel, utilising the country's full geographic range from the jungle to the mountain crests. Commercial river rafting got underway in 1976 when Himalayan River Exploration started plying the Seti and Trisuli rivers, floating visitors down to Tiger Tops in Royal Chitwan National Park. Nowadays Nepal's white-water thrills are divided among five commercially-operable rivers and attract hundreds of tourists every year (see page 129).

Enterprising kayakers occasionally shoot the rapids as well; some rafting

All terrain bicycles live up to their name and are ideally suited to the rough roads of Nepal.

124

MOUNTAIN BIKING IN NEPAL

Mountain biking is the most recent adventure sport and already its suitability to the cobweb of dirt roads that crisscross Nepal is evident. From the trading trails of the mountains to the lowland plains of the Terai, the mountain bike has proven itself the ultimate way to explore the rural countryside.

Mountain bikes were developed in the mid-1970s by a group of enthusiasts in California to handle rough, rocky trails and steep hill climbs. Old bicycles were modified with five to ten speed gears, front and rear drum brakes, motorcycle brake levers and the biggest, knobby tires they could find. These were tested and raced north of San Francisco in hills that dropped 400 meters (1,300 feet) in 2.4 kilometers (1.8 miles) averaging a 14% gradient – an ideal testing ground for the Himalaya. At the time these pioneers were having too much fun to realize their "clunkers" would become "the mountain bike" and initiate a worldwide sport.

In the mid-1980s mountain bikes were introduced to Nepal by some of the more enterprising expatriates of Kathmandu. Soon their potential was to be appreciated. Children in distant villages would run up shouting *"Gearwallas Aayo!"* – "the people of the geared bikes have come!" Thus the local Gearwalla Club was born, which soon developed into a full-fledged business.

Mountain biking is an incomparable way to explore the temples and medieval cities, the rural settlements and hill stations of the Kathmandu Valley. Some of the most interesting dirt roads connect the Valley's cultural highlights. Daily village life can be observed without the intrusion of vehicles or the constraints of travelling on foot. Beyond the Valley a mountain bike is a wonderful way to reach a trek start point, the beginning of a river trip or as a means to tour the country.

The early Gearwallas soon discovered its shortcomings, however. Mountain bikes are most inappropriate and unsuitable for mountain trekking trails, for safety and ecological reasons. Some of the main roads of Nepal, such as from Kathmandu to Pokhara, are too heavily trafficked with large trucks and noisy buses for enjoyable biking.

A more pleasant route to Pokhara on a mountain bike follows the longer, more scenic old Raj Path down to the Terai (stop off for a few nights in Royal Chitwan National Park), then takes the Siddhartha Highway up to Pokhara. Other great routes around the country include biking from Kathmandu to the Tibetan border at Kodari, Kathmandu to Jiri and Kathmandu to Dhunche, with a side trip to the ancient palace of Nuwakot. More ambitious trips go from Pokhara to Royal Bardiya National Park in the far west, or from Kathmandu to the Arun Valley in the east.

Himalayan Mountain Bikes run fully supported mountain bike trips from one day to two weeks throughout the Kathmandu Valley and beyond. If you bring your own bike, bring plenty of spare parts as none are available.

Mountain bikes are a sensitive and silent way to explore the Kathmandu Valley.

companies can arrange kayak rentals by the day. Boating on Pokhara's Phewa Lake is more restful than sporting. Row boats are readily available, with or without a rower. When the afternoon winds pick up, search out a sailboat for hire.

Spring and fall are the best seasons for sport fishing in lowland lakes and rivers. Trout-like species make the best eating and the large mahseer (see page 131) are the most fun.

In the mid-19th century, Nepal was a favored ground for big game hunters, a privilege granted only to invitees of the ruling Rana regime. The rhinos and tigers of Chitwan are now strictly protected, but highland hunters still come in search of the blue sheep, bearing a world-class prize rack, and the shaggy Himalayan *tahr*. Hunting is only permitted with a licensed guide in designated areas.

Far more popular is a wildlife viewing, tracking and photographing in the Terai jungles, a thrill which takes the mountain-engrossed tourist by surprise. Tiger Tops' world famous Jungle Lodge in the trees was the first private safari outfitter in Nepal. It flourished from a single house on stilts in 1965 to a multi-dimensional enterprise and continues to set standards in comfort and wildlife operations. The group now includes the Tiger Tops Tented Camp and Tharu Village Resort in Chitwan, and the Tiger Tops Karnali Lodge and Tented Camp in Bardiya. Tiger Tops' annual World Elephant Polo tournament pits *maharajahs* and movie stars against national park officials and corporate heads in a lumbering folly staged near the Meghauly airfield.

In total seven lodges are now licensed to lead wildlife safaris within Royal Chitwan National Park, searching for rhino, tiger and deer from atop a trained elephant; crocodiles and water fowl from canoes; wild boar and sloth bear and all of the above on foot or in vehicles. Dozens of smaller lodges operate from outside the park. Very popular is the triad of outdoor excursions featuring a planned itinerary of trekking, rafting and jungle safaries.

Exploring the Royal Chitwan National Park.

High Tech Challenges: Just as mountain climbing has become a contest of ingenuity augmented by high-tech gadgetry, the latest light-weight, tough sports equipment is finding a niche in the Himalaya. All Terrain Bicycles, better known as mountain bikes, are ideal on Nepal's labyrinth of dirt roads, whether tooling around the Kathmandu Valley amidst the temples and rice paddies or venturing farther afield. Himalayan Mountain Bikes in Kathmandu arranges rides of three to thirteen days inclusive of bikes, accommodation and meals, guides and a "sag wagon" to carry gear. Other shops in Thamel rent mountain (and one-speed Indian) bikes by the day.

The Himalaya's up-drafts and incomparable views send the imagination soaring with airborne sport opportunities. A few hot air balloons have been launched, but as yet ballooning has not taken off as a commercial venture. Similarly, hang-gliding, paravaning and gliding hold great potential.

Some mountaineers have carried light-weight wings to the tops of peaks and sailed down.

Hang-gliders can drive to the hilltops surrounding Pokhara and fly down over the gentle valley. Gliders (engineless planes) could be towed up from an airfield and merrily let loose for a spectacular personal mountain flight, should the necessary government permissions ever be granted.

Helicopter skiing in the back-country has yet to be introduced in Nepal. The slopes are generally too rocky, remote and high for commercial ski runs though a few hardy alpinists have carried in their skis and discovered some gentle enough runs in Langtang and near Jomosom.

No one visits the backcountry of Nepal without developing an awareness of the environmental issues at stake (see page 49). As visitors we marvel at the beauty and rejoice in the warm experience, but are also troubled by the Himalayan odds which face the Nepalese people as their country hurtles from medieval to modern times.

Binoculars are useful in the Terai jungles.

RIVER RAFTING

Fed by glaciers of the world's highest mountains and the snows of the Tibetan plateau, Nepal's feverish rivers provide exciting opportunities for white-water rafting and an unbeatable profile of an ever-changing landscape. On their way to India's peaceful Ganges, the melt-waters surge through Himalayan gorges, traverse rugged foothills, course between tropical forests and meander across the Terai plains – through the many faces of Nepal.

Rafting is one of the best and most thrilling ways to abandon the cities and experience the fascinating rural life of Nepal without investing the time and energy required for a long trek.

Fun and Safety: Some rafting trips let passengers partake in the paddling, leaving the steering to a professional guide. Others allow you relax and enjoy the fun while the river guide controls the boat using centre-mounted oars. Either way, rafting is a combination of intro-spective tranquility and unreserved thrills.

Many of Nepal's rivers are remote and unpredictable and a responsible river company is vital to ensuring your safety. The more reputable companies employ guides trained to international standards with years of experience on Nepal's rivers. Their training includes first aid and rescue, sanitation and environmental awareness.

Sacred Waters: The Himalayan rivers are considered sacred to the Nepalis. Ashes of the cremated dead are scattered into rivers to be eventually carried to the Ganges. The confluence of two rivers is usually revered as a holy site for ritual bathing. Water brings life, but the rivers are also feared, which explains why on the hottest days few Nepalis will be seen splashing in the water.

Thus, the first people to run Nepal's rivers were foreigners. Exalting at the opportunity to test virgin waters, early pioneers set about exploring the rivers soon after Nepal opened its borders in the early 1950s.

Sir Edmund Hillary attempted an ascent of the Sunkosi in 1968. Various rivers were kayaked and rafted by visiting adventurers, including Michael Peissel who tried to drive a hovercraft up the Kali Gandaki in 1973.

It was not until 1976 when American Al Read started systematically running and charting the rapids of the Trisuli and upper Sunkosi rivers that river-running began in earnest. Read formed Nepal's first river company, **Himalayan River Exploration** and brought in more foreign experts to train the Nepalis. H.R.E.'s first runs were down the wild stretches of the Trisuli river to Tiger Tops in Royal Chitwan National Park.

Today Nepali guides are fully capable of handling a raft with complete safety of supervising a camp staff and cooking fine meals. Many also interpret the flora and fauna of the Himalaya for guests' added appreciation.

Five Rivers: Rafting companies operate on five major rivers which are government regulated by permit.

– The **Sunkosi**, or "River of Gold,"

Left, nothing can compare with the adrenaline rush of running the remote and beautiful rivers of Nepal. **Right**, Kayakers have their crafts portered in for the first descent of the Buri Gandaki.

runs south from the turbulent Tibetan Bhote Kosi river east of Kathmandu. It is popular for one to ten day trips, the longer ones ending in far eastern Nepal.

– The **Arun**, east of Mount Everest, is perhaps the toughest river for rafting. It too rises from the Tibetan plateau and drains a region prolific in a unique flora and fauna, particularly rich in birdlife.

– The **Trisuli**, named after Shiva's trident, parallels the road from Kathmandu to Mugling before joining the Gandaki river system and becoming the Narayani River. Popular one to three day trips conclude at Royal Chitwan National Park.

–The **Seti** flows down from Pokhara to Chitwan for a combination holiday of trekking, rafting and jungle safaris.

–The **Bheri**, in far west Nepal, is the least explored and most exciting. It offers huge rapids, lovely scenery and passes through a narrow gorge before spilling onto the Terai at the Royal Bardiya National Park.

Other rivers, including the **Karnali** and **Thulo Bheri** in western Nepal and the **Tamur** in the east, may be run but only with special permission.

A Day on the River: October through mid-December and March through early May are the best times to river raft in Nepal, avoiding the very coldest time. The water temperature is generally about 6 to 10 degrees Celsius (43 to 50 degrees Fahrenheit) and the air clear and warm.

The best outfitters provide all the essentials for a safe and fun trip: life jackets, a medical box, ropes, buckets, waterproof bags and an "ammo box" for valuables, all meals and, on overnight trips, tents, sleeping bags and pads.

On longer trips time is set aside for hiking into side canyons, visiting nearby villages and swimming in the river or lazing on sandy beaches. Transportation and a government river permit fee is usually extra.

River rafting is an exceptional experience anywhere – but with Nepal's unique topography, playful people and traditional culture, it is all the more rewarding.

Camping near Chautara by the Sunkosi river.

Sport Fishing in Nepal

The river systems of Nepal are the home of a number of game fish. Most famous is the handsome mahseer family which have attracted sportsmen for centuries with their strong "take" and fine fight.

There are two species of this carp family found in Nepal; the golden mahseer (*Tor putitora*) and the silver tor mahseer (*Tor tor*). They grow up to 45 kilos (100 pounds) although the heaviest are the humpbacked mahseer (*Tor khudree*) species of South India.

Mahseer, known as sahar in Nepal, are migratory and live in the fast, rocky, snow-fed rivers of the Himalaya. In the winter they live and feed in the lowland rivers of the Terai but in March and April, as the snow melts, they move into the lower gorges. Here they feed greedily before travelling up into the headwaters to spawn during the monsoon. In October, as the rivers begin to drop and clear, the mahseer migrate down-river again.

It is during these migratory journeys that the mahseer provide prime fishing, with the best months being November and early December and mid-February to April when the rivers run clear. (Bring your own tackle.)

Fine mahseer can still be caught in the Karnali River in the far west and in the Kosi River of the east. These fish are not as common as in former times due to the huge dams, built without fish ladders, on the Kosi and Narayani rivers. The dams hinder the movement of crocodiles and dolphin and also restrain a small fish called the *chilwa* on which the mahseer feed prior to spawning.

An important factor overlooked by national planners is that the mahseer and the other migratory fish of the Himalayan rivers are a prime source of protein for the hill-peoples who fish for them by lines and nets. Fish ladders must be incorporated in future dam projects.

There are a number of other fish that can be classified as game fish. These include the bokar (or *katli*) (*Acrossocheilus hexagonolepis*) which extends from Assam into the Kosi river system.

There is the giant catfish (*Bagarius bagarius*), also known as the goonch or freshwater shark, which grows to a mammoth 150 kilos (330 pounds). Another smaller fish is the "Indian trout" (*Schizotherox richard-sonii*) known as the asla in Nepal.

The asla is not a true trout. Brown trout (*Salmo trutto*) and the rainbow trout (*Salmo gardnerii*) were both introduced into the rivers and lakes of the Indian subcontinent by the British in the late 19th century. They thrived, especially in Kashmir and Bhutan. Why are none to be found in Nepal?

Trout require water that is cold throughout the year and cannot tolerate a high level of siltation. Within Nepal the terrain drops too steeply, the rivers form at low altitudes and carry heavy silt from deforestation and agriculture.

But catching the mighty mahseer is and will remain the great challenge for the sportsman in Nepal.

Right, the mighty mahseer.

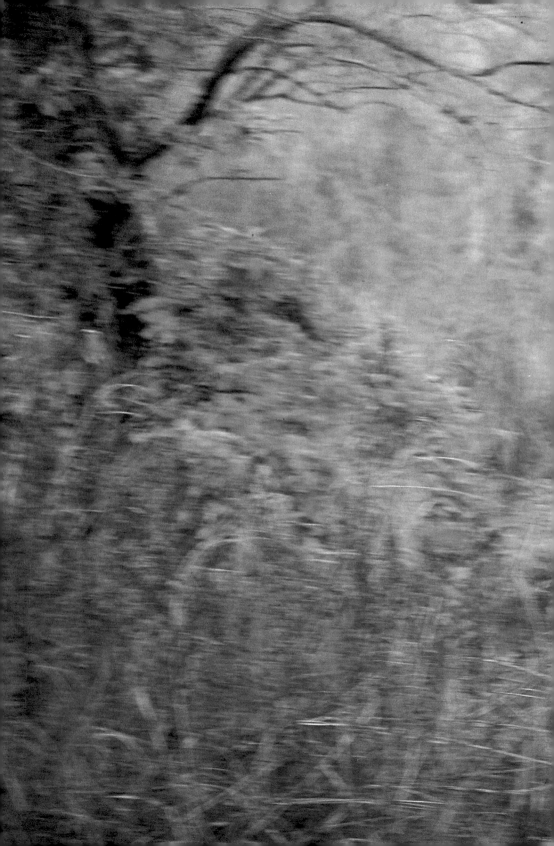

JUNGLE SAFARIS

Renowned for centuries as one of the best areas for wildlife viewing in Asia, the diverse flora and fauna of the Terai national parks attracts visitors from all over the world. Not to be compared with the wide open spaces of Africa, the intimacy of the search and discovery of Asian wildlife in its dense habitat is considered by many travellers to be equally rewarding.

Whereas yesterday's kings hunted tiger as guests of *maharajahs*, today visitors can explore these uniquely beautiful areas in similar style and considerable comfort. For those with more modest ambitions, budget possibilities abound.

Generally the best time for wildlife viewing in the Terai parks and reserves is from February to April when the thick ground cover has retreated. By March some of the summer bird migrants have arrived while many of the winter visitors have not yet left.

But some enthusiasts enjoy aspects of other seasons, and most safari outfitters remain open from October to June.

Royal Chitwan National Park: Most easy to reach, **Royal Chitwan National Park** is considered one of the richest wildlife areas in Asia and boasts the last and largest remaining areas of tall grassland habitat.

A hunting reserve of the ruling Ranas, always keen sportsmen, where every several years a great hunt would be staged during the winter months when the threat of fever was minimal. The Ranas and their guests, who included European royalty and Viceroys of India, bagged huge numbers of tigers and rhinos.

The Chitwan Valley is a lowland *dun* valley lying between the Siwalik (Churia) and Mahabharat ranges. It is drained by two major rivers, the Narayani and the Rapti. Prior to the 1950s Chitwan was only sparsely inhabited, mainly by Tharu peoples who presumably developed a resistance to the endemic malaria. After the eradication of malaria, Chitwan was cleared and cultivated and its population tripled in less than a decade.

Poaching became a problem; the rhinoceros in particular was killed for its valuable horn. In 1964 a sanctuary was declared and a large number of people were moved out and resettled. The Gaida Gusti or "Rhino Guards" attempted to patrol the park, but poaching continued. The rhino, thought to have numbered 1,000 in 1950, reached an all-time low of less than 100 individuals in the 1960s .

Only when the national park was established in 1973, with the full protection of the Royal Nepalese Army, was poaching and encroachment finally brought under control. In 1976 Royal Chitwan National Park was extended to its present size of 1,040 square kilometers (402 square miles).

Concessions were given to private jungle safari operators to build lodges within the park. The famous **Tiger Tops Jungle Lodge**, and its satellite **Tented Camp**, is the oldest, established

in 1965 predating the existence of the national park. It is renowned as one of the world's finest wildlife establishments and also as the host of the annual World Elephant Polo Championships. The adjacent **Tiger Tops Tharu Safari Resort** offers such stylish facilities as a swimming pool and riding stables in addition to wildlife activities.

Visiting Chitwan: The big animals concentrate in the dense forest and tall grasslands of the floodplain. The best way to approach them is on the back of a well trained elephant. Rhinos favour marshy ground and indeed some areas of prime habitat are only negotiable by elephant. This is also the safest way to view tiger, gaur and sloth bear.

Each of the seven lodges and tented camps which operate within the park is permitted to maintain their own stable of elephants. More recent concessions are **Gaida Wildlife Camp**, **Chitwan Jungle Lodge**, **Machan Wildlife Resort**, **Island Jungle Resort**, **Narayani Safari** and **Temple Tiger**. Outside the park at **Saurah** are a number of small hotels, the best of which is **Hotel Elephant Camp**. It is also possible to hire elephants from the Government *hatisar* (elephant camp) at Saurah.

Travelling in four-wheel drive vehicles is a rewarding way to spot deer, wild boar, rhino, sometimes gaur and occasionally tiger, leopard and sloth bear. Movement in the park is not permitted after dark.

As the road network in Chitwan is limited, it is best to combine a drive with a visit to the park headquarters, **Kasara Durbar**. There is a small museum and the Gharial Breeding Project where batches of gharial crocodile hatchlings have been raised since 1978 for restocking the Narayani.

East of Kasara is **Lame Tal**, a long ox-bow lake with spectacular birdlife and basking crocodiles. Other *tals,* such as **Devi Tal,** are good focal points for wildlife viewing. *Machans* (watchtowers) have been constructed overlooking tracts of grassland at **Sukibhar** in the west on the way to Tiger Tops and near **Dumariya** in the east.

Boarding elephants at Tiger Tops Jungle Lodge.

Peaceful boat or canoe trips down the Narayani river encounter migratory waterfowl, dolphin, marsh mugger and gharial crocodile as well as unrivalled views across the entire width of Nepal to the white Himalayan peaks.

One of Chitwan's greatest assets is the scope it offers for nature walks. For those with curiosity and perseverance, walking is the most profitable way of observing birds, studying vegetation and inspecting animal tracks. But the jungle is not without an element of danger so never go unescorted by an expert guide – visitors have been mauled by rhinos.

It is a half hour flight from Kathmandu to **Meghauly**, the grass airstrip that serves Tiger Tops. Alternatively it is a six hour drive to Chitwan from Kathmandu, via Narayanghat (Bharatpur) to Tadi Bazaar and Saurah.

Chitwan's Ecology – Fire and Flood: Nearly a quarter of the park consists of alluvial floodplain at only 150 meters (506 feet) above sea level. The remainder is low hills rising to 760 meters (2,565 feet), covered with tropical deciduous forest, dominated by the towering sal tree (*Shorea robusta*). On the highest ridges there are chir pine (*Pinus roxburghii*).

The beautiful grasslands are dominated by different species of *saccharum*, often reaching more than six meters (20 feet) in height. The grasslands are interspersed with riverine forests, featuring a mixture of shisham (*Dalbergia sisso*), khair (*Acacia catechu*), simal or kapok (*Bombax ceiba*) and bilar trees (*Trewia nudiflora*).

The grasslands periodically flood during the monsoon, when 90 percent of Chitwan's annual 2,150 millimeters (85 inches) of rain falls between June to September. This introduces a dynamic element into Chitwan's ecology, changing river courses so as to create ox-bow lakes or *tals* where wildlife concentrates.

Another factor of great importance is fire. The dying grasses have been burnt annually for centuries so that fresh shoots can appear. Now controlled by

Gaur, the largest of the world's wild cattle, descend from the hills to eat the new spring grasses.

the national park authorities, thousands of local villagers are first permitted to collect grass for thatching in January. The black, burnt areas become a mosaic of grasses in different stages of regeneration, providing tempting grazing for ungulates during the dry months.

Fire tends to preserve the grassland at the expense of the forest saplings. The "cool burn" in the sal forest does not affect the fire-resistant trees.

Diverse Animal Life: Over 50 species of mammals are found in the park, and there were more prior to the 1950s. Wild elephant (*Elephas maximus*) are now confined to a single herd of about 20, resident in the adjacent 499 square kilometer (193 square mile) Parsa Wildlife Reserve.

The greater one-horned rhinoceros (*Rhinoceros unicornis*) has made a dramatic comeback and now numbers about 400, a quarter of the world population. The preferred habitat of these primeval beasts, with their great folds of skin reminiscent of a Durer etching, is the marshy grassland where they like to wallow in the *tals*.

There are a few hundred gaur (*Bos gaurus*), the largest of the world's wild cattle, chiefly confined to the densely forested hillslopes of the Siwaliks. The best time to glimpse their sleek, dark coats is in the spring when they descend to feed on the fresh new grasses.

Four species of deer are found in the park; most numerous and gregarious is the elegant chital or spotted deer (*Axis axis*) which gather in large herds in the spring. There are also the stately sambar (*Cervus unicolor*), the stocky hog deer (*Axis porcinus*) and the barking deer (*Muntiacus muntjak*) named for its alarm call.

Wild pigs (*Sus scrofa*) are found throughout the park. There are two primates; the langur monkey (*Presbytis entellus*), with its grey coat and black face and the reddish-coloured rhesus (*Macaca mulatta*). Much of the park provides ideal habitat for the lumbering sloth bear (*Melursus ursinus*).

The Narayani river supports dwindling numbers of the freshwater

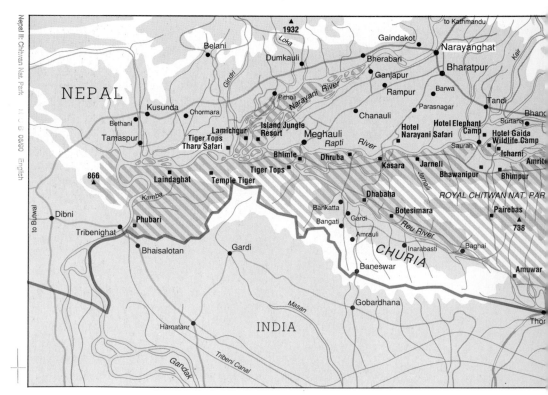

Gangetic dolphin (*Platanista gangetica*). A few wild dog (*Cuon alpinus*) course through the Chitwan in search of prey. More common are their scavenging relatives, the golden jackal (*Canis aureus*).

There is a great variety of smaller mammals including mongooses, civets, martens, honey badgers and two species of hare. There are three small cats, the jungle cat (*Felis chaus*), the fishing cat (*Felis viverrina*) and the leopard cat (*Felis bengalensis*). A number of rodents includes squirrels, flying squirrels, porcupines, bats and rats.

Tiger Tiger: Other than the rhino, Chitwan is most famous for its population of the Royal Bengal tiger (*Panthera tigris*). Containing an estimated 40 breeding adults, the total number of tigers fluctuates around 120. The park's tigers are part of a larger regional population of about 200. This includes individuals protected in the eastern Parsa Wildlife Reserve and the Valmiki Tiger Reserve in India, adjoining the southern boundary of the park, a total area of 1,875 square kilometers (724 square miles).

Chitwan's tigers prefer the floodplain where the abundance of prey species allows them to exist at comparatively high density. The most secretive and retiring of all the cats, the tiger is nocturnal and it is only a few lucky visitors who catch a glimpse of these splendid creatures.

There are not many leopards (*Panthera pardus*) in Chitwan, probably because of the intolerance of the tigers. What few there are live on the periphery of the park.

Rare Reptiles and Bountiful Birds: The gharial (*Gavialus gangeticus*) is one of two species of crocodile. It is a specialised fish-eater with an elongated snout and lives in the rivers. The marsh mugger (*Crocodylus palustris*) eats anything it can catch and lives mainly in the ox-bow lakes.

The python (*Python molurus*) is another important reptile which frequents the edges of ponds and streams. The world's largest venomous snake, the

Rhino mother and grown baby refresh themselves in the Rapti river in Chitwan.

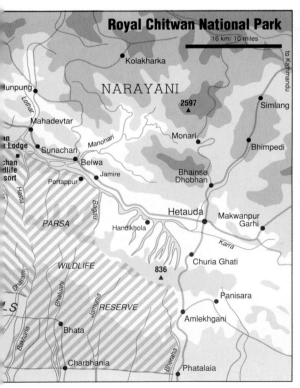

king cobra (*Ophiophagus hannah*) also lives in the park with a number of smaller, though no less poisonous cousins, kraits and vipers.

Over 450 species of birds have been counted in Chitwan, which is 38 percent of all those found in the subcontinent. Just under half of these are residents. Two of the many spectacular and endangered species found in the park are the rare Bengal florican (*Eupodotis bengalensis*) and the giant hornbill (*Buceros bicornis*).

Royal Bardiya National Park: Located in the remote and sparsely settled far west Terai is an untouched preserve for the more adventurous traveller: **Royal Bardiya National Park**.

The western region was first gazetted in 1976 as Royal Karnali Wildlife Reserve and the eastern extension was added in 1984, bringing the reserve to today's size of 968 square kilometers (374 square miles). This became Royal Bardiya National Park in 1988.

The Geruwa River, the eastern branch of the great Karnali River which diverges into two main channels and many islands, forms its western boundary. The park extends east to the Nepalgunj-Surkhet road and includes a large portion of the beautiful Babai River valley, bounded by two parallel ranges of the Siwalik hills. The northern boundary is the main crest of the Siwaliks.

Visiting Bardiya: Tiger Tops operates the only concession in Bardiya; the Karnali Lodge, set amidst the fascinating Tharu villages on the edge of the forest, and the Karnali Tented Camp on the banks of the river down-stream from Chisopani.

Visitors fly to Nepalgunj, one and a half hours from Kathmandu, where Tiger Tops arranges the three hour drive to the park. To drive all the way from Kathmandu to Bardiya takes 12 hours through memorable and scenic stretches of the Terai.

Tiger Territory: This is one of the best places in the subcontinent to see tiger in the wild and the only park where baiting is permitted on a regular basis. How-

Sunset reflected in the great Karnali river of Royal Bardiya National Park.

ever, three quarters of all the tiger viewings in Bardiya are from elephant back and many are seen from vehicles, boats and on walks.

West Nepal supports the kingdom's second largest population of this magnificent cat after Chitwan. Fifty breeding adults are distributed from Banke through Bardiya and Kailai into Kanchanpur. A few leopards live on the forest edges.

Trained elephants can be used to see tiger, rhinoceros and swamp deer in the **Manu Tappu** and **Khaura Khola** areas. However, the park has an excellent network of roads and driving is the best way to see the herds of deer that congregate on the open grassland.

There are a number of long walks, especially along the river, which are good for birdwatching and spotting deer. River trips by boat are scenically breathtaking and excellent for seeing waterfowl, gharial and marsh mugger crocodiles, smooth-coated otters and Gangetic dolphin.

Bardiya's Famous Phantas: The alluvial floodplain of the Geruwa River and its many islands are covered with tall grasses and a rich assemblage of riverine forest, though most of the park is covered with sal forest.

In 1984 1,500 inhabitants of the Babai valley were relocated onto better land outside the park. Still in the process of regeneration, the Babai valley promises to develop into one of the finest wildlife regions of the park.

Characteristic of Bardiya are the *phantas*, the short grassland meadows on the forest edge. These so facilitate wildlife viewing that they are now artificially maintained by the park management. The largest are the **Baghaura** and **Lamkhole Phantas**.

Reintroduced Rhinos and Antelope: Once endemic, the Greater One-horned rhinoceros had become extinct in Bardiya. In 1985 13 rhinos were captured in Chitwan, then the western limit of their range, and translocated to Bardiya where they are now established and breeding.

Bardiya has the same four species of

Orchids abound in the jungles of the Terai.

deer as in Chitwan but in addition has the endangered swamp deer or *barasingha* (*Cervus duvauceli*). Two species of antelope live in Bardiya; the nilgai or blue bull (*Boselaphus tragocamelus*) frequents the riverine forest. More graceful and smaller is the black buck (*Antilope cervicapra*) which once thrived on the Baghaura Phanta. Predation during the months when the grass grows tall has all but wiped them out, though there are plans to translocate some of the remaining population to the Babai valley.

No gaur exist in Bardiya but a few resident wild elephants roam the park. There are estimated to be less than ten individuals and some of the solitary bulls make their presence felt by raiding the village fields.

Despite considerable disturbance due to development in the Karnali Gorge, some crocodiles still exist – both gharial and marsh mugger species. Some 350 species of birds have been recorded in the park including such endangered species as the sarus crane (*Grus antigone*) and the silver-eared mesia (*Leiothcix argentauris*).

Royal Sukla Phanta Wildlife Reserve: Although small and remote, **Royal Sukla Phanta Wildlife Reserve** (155 square kilometers, 60 square miles) is another gem of a wildlife sanctuary, tucked into the far southwest corner of Nepal. It is well worth a visit, though the two and a half hour flights to Mahendranagar are sometimes uncertain. The tented camp concession is operated by Silent Safaris.

Sukla Phanta encompasses part of the floodplain of the Sarda River, has thick sal forests and a pretty, small lake called **Rani Tal**. The preserve has extensive open grasslands and the largest surviving population of swamp deer (*barasingha*), numbering about 2,000.

There are many deer concentrated in the open meadows and waterfowl on Rani Tal. Wildlife can best be observed from the tall *machans* or from four-wheel drive vehicles.

Koshi Tappu Wildlife Reserve: In the eastern Terai, a one hour drive from Biratnagar, is the **Koshi Tappu Wildlife Reserve** on the floodplain of the Sapta Kosi River. The reserve is bounded on the east and west by the river embankments and on the south by the barrage (dam) that forms the border with India. The reserve headquarters is at **Kusaha** but the closest hotel is in Biratnagar though temporary tented camps can sometimes be arranged..

This little-visited preserve (175 square kilometers, 68 square miles) is a haven for a superb concentration of waterfowl during the winter months. A total of 280 species of birds have been recorded, including 20 different sorts of ducks and the rare swamp partridge (*Francolinus gularis*). The migratory birds can be seen between November and March resting at the Kosi barrage and on the main channel. The trail along the east embankment provides a good vantage.

Koshi Tappu harbours the only remaining wild buffalos (*Bubalus bubalis*) in Nepal, a population of only about 100. Spotted deer, nilgai and wild pigs also occur.

Otters harass a pair of rare fish-eating gharial crocodiles.

THARU TRIBES

The original Tharu settlers of the Terai number some 600,000 people and are scattered all along the southern border of Nepal. The name Tharu is one of the few common factors uniting these "tribal" people whose cultures vary greatly. The main Tharu groups are the Kochila in the eastern Terai, Mahaton and Nawalpuria in the Chitwan valley, Dangaura in Dang and Deokhuri valleys, Katharya or Rajathya in Karnali, and Rana in the far west.

Their agrarian lifestyle remained isolated until the eradication of malaria in the 1960s, which enabled the hill-people to compete for the rich land of the Terai. Tharu live by farming and fishing, content to till land belonging to absentee landlords who mostly left them undisturbed, fearful of the lowland fevers. Occasionally aristocracy would visit for big game hunts and hire Tharu, who apparently had some immunity to malaria, to drive the elephants.

Tharu grow rice and maize during the summer rains, wheat, barley and lentils in the spring and mustard seed in the winter. They fish all year round, casting nets, damming streams or even sometimes catching fish with their bare hands. They trap small wild animals from the jungles.

From the forest they collect medicinal herbs, grasses and wood necessary for everyday life. Creepers are made into rope and marsh reeds are used to weave the colorful mats and baskets, decorated with shells, seeds and tassels, so celebrated as Tharu craft. The stately women use these to carry goods on their heads, a method practised nowhere else in Nepal.

Dangaura Tharu have best preserved their individual traditions. They live in villages of mud longhouses, with as many as 150 family members under one roof. The small entrances to the houses lead into a large central room decorated with wall paintings, nets and hanging baskets. Animals live on the right. On the left the family rooms are divided by the tall, mud grain jars providing both privacy and storage. Dangaura wear mostly white and the women are tattooed with peacock designs.

Dangaura have their own animistic religion. One interesting custom is to marry by sister exchange; that is two families exchange their daughters to marry sons. During the wedding ceremony, the newlyweds knock their heads together as a sign of union.

The Nawalpuria Tharu of Chitwan speak a similar dialect to the Dangaura and also wear mainly white. They have two-story houses and their traditional lifestyle has been much changed with the impact of roads.

In the far west the Katharya Tharu claim to be descendants of the Rajputs. Besides a distinctive short, embroidered skirt, the women's blouses are covered with silver coins and they adorn their neck and ankles with heavy silver jewellery. The Rana Tharu, are similar but live in smaller villages and decorate their houses with abstract orange and white designs set with small mirrors.

Right, elegant Tharu women of west Nepal.

TREKKING PEAKS

Apart from tentative forays by Savage Landor and Tom Longstaff, exploration of the Nepal Himalaya by Western mountaineers really began with the easing of the restrictions on foreigners in 1949. In that year a small British expedition led by Bill Tilman was allowed by the King to visit Langtang.

This tiny group roamed freely throughout Langtang. Tilman, in particular, was interested in the *cols* at the northern end of the Langtang Valley which gave access to the lofty bulk of Xixabangma in Tibet (8,046 meters, 26,398 feet), eventually the last of the 8,000 meter giants to be climbed.

Late in the season, with the monsoon approaching, Bill Tilman, Peter Lloyd and an aspiring and as yet unknown Sherpa, Tenzing Norgay, crossed the Bhote Kosi and explored the extreme southeast corner of the Ganesh Himal. During that sortie an interesting, if small, mountain was climbed called Paldor (5,928 meters, 19,450 feet). It was not only the first peak in Nepal to be scaled, but the first Trekking Peak.

What is a Trekking Peak?: Nepal, as Tilman rightly said, is a "singularly mountainous country." Despite this, relatively few peaks today are on the permitted list. Of its countless summits only 128 are officially climbable and of these 110 are classified as Expedition Peaks. This means they can only be climbed by expeditions, endorsed by their relevant Alpine Clubs, who have bought a permit and are accompanied by a liaison officer; in all a relatively complicated and expensive procedure.

In 1978, the Nepal Mountaineering Association (N.M.A.) announced that 18 Trekking Peaks were climbable without the "red tape" of a full-scale expedition. They ranged in height from 5,587 meters (18,330 feet) to 6,654 meters (21,830 feet). Apart from the payment of a small Trekking Peak fee and a proviso that attempts must be accompanied as far as base camp by Sherpa guides, these mountains can be

attempted with little formality and within a time-scale that suits an annual vacation period.

Not So Easy: Inherent in the name "Trekking Peaks" is a serious misnomer which might indicate to the uninformed that their ascent requires no further skills than the ability to walk. This is not the case. All need mountaineering experience and a knowledge of the use of ropes, ice axes and crampons.

It is true that some peaks have a high success rate with even large commercial groups – these include Island Peak, Mera, Tent Peak and Chulu Far East. However, most of these achievements can be attributed to good leadership and the use of strong Sherpas to carry loads, fix ropes and blaze the trail.

Amongst the 18 peaks are several coveted summits – such as Kusum Kanguru, Hiunchuli, Fluted Peak and Kwangde – which over the years have acquired a reputation of inaccessibility that has attracted some of the world's leading climbers. They offer technical routes of the highest standard.

Preceding pages: Island Peak (Imja Tse) is one of the most popular and beautiful of all the Trekking Peaks. **Left**, Naya Kanga, also known as Ganja La Chuli, is at the head of the Langtang Valley. **Right**, descending the Mingbo La into the Khumbu.

Where and How Much?: As might be expected, Trekking Peaks are concentrated in the Khumbu and Annapurna Himal – the most popular trekking destinations. As yet there are no trekking peaks in areas recently opened such as Dolpo, Dhaulagiri, Manaslu or Kangchenjunga.

Unlike the Expedition Peaks where permits are granted for a specific route, the Trekking Peak permit is for the mountain as a whole. This allows the adventurous mountaineer to undertake unclimbed lines. Most parties, however, will opt for established routes which naturally offer a better chance of success.

The Nepal Mountaineering Association lists Trekking Peaks in two groups. For a party of ten persons or less the Group A permit fee is US$300; for Group B, comprising the lower peaks, the permit fee is US$150. They are listed below by area.

Trekking Peaks of the Khumbu: The history of the exploration of Trekking Peaks is closely bound with the earliest

attempts on Nepal's more serious summits. The Khumbu region provided a profusion of peaks ideally suited as training acclimatisation climbs for Everest and Lhotse.

Island Peak (Imja Tse) (6,160 meters, 20,210 feet Group A)**:** This is the most popular and one of the most accessible Trekking Peaks. Dwarfed by the massive south face of Lhotse, by Baruntse and Ama Dablam, Island Peak lies between the Imja and Lhotse glaciers. From the snaking moraines near Chhukung, its south face rears up as a rocky black triangle; the end of a truncated ridge thrown down from Lhotse Shar, from which it is separated by a snowy *col* at 5,700 meters (18,700 feet).

In 1952 an expedition led by Eric Shipton followed the Imja River searching for a high route into the remote Barun gorge that cuts between Baruntse and Makalu. Near the yak pasture of Chhukung, he described an isolated mountain "resembling an island in a sea of ice." The name has stuck ever since, despite its local name, Imja Tse.

Island Peak was first climbed in 1953 by Charles Evans, Charles Wylie, Alf Gregory and Tenzing Norgay with seven Sherpas. The party comprised the then-rising stars of the climbing firmament who were preparing for the historic ascent of Everest. Their climb up the southeast flank and the south ridge, from a camp at Pareshaya Gyab, remains the normal route.

Pokalde (Dolma Ri) (5,806 meters, 19,049 feet Group B)**:** This relatively undistinguished peak is the culmination of a rocky, pinnacled ridge beyond the huge lateral moraines of Pheriche. In many ways it can be regarded as the final bony knuckle on the long fingered ridge that extends southwards from Nuptse, bounding the east bank of the Khumbu Glacier.

To the Sherpas Pokalde is immensely important. The home of major deity, it is the object of a monsoon pilgrimage during which the devout perambulate clockwise around the mountain.

The route from the east is quick and straight-forward and was probably pioneered by Sherpas to place prayer flags

Camping by moonlight in the upper Hongu valley.

on the summit. The first Western ascent was recorded in 1953 by a group from the Everest Expedition that included John Hunt, Wilfred Noyce, Tom Bourdillon and Mike Ward. They climbed the north ridge direct from the Kongma La. "A jolly ridge, in the Alpine sense," wrote Noyce later, using it as a fine viewpoint for studying the surrounding giants. Everest and Makalu rear above the clouds like two great canine teeth: "Fangs excrescent", to use Mallory's phrase, "gaunt and yellowy-brown."

Pokalde is best approached from the lodges of Lobuche and can be climbed in a day. A well-marked trail leads across the Khumbu Glacier and climbs to the pass in about three hours. The cluster of tiny lakes on the east side provide an ideal high camp.

Kongma Tse (5,849 meters, 19,190 feet Group B): Originally listed as Mehra Peak, Kongma Tse was renamed to avoid confusion with Mera Peak further south. Twinned with Pokalde, Kongma Tse rises to the north of the Kongma La. Kongma is the Sherpa name for the snow cock, a large bird which abounds in this area.

Viewed from Gorak Shep, the mountain sports fine glaciers that hang suspended above the west face. The normal route is from the lakes below the Kongma La via the south face glacier.

Lobuche East Peak (6,119 meters, 20,075 feet Group A): West of the lodges of Lobuche, the rocky east face of Lobuche Peak stands sentinel over the route to Everest Base Camp. Named after a Sherpa god, the true summit has proved an elusive goal.

The rocky outliers of the peak were first climbed by the Swiss in 1952. Subsequently numerous attempts have fallen short of the actual summit, which rises above a profound notch at the far end of a long northwest and southeast aligned ridge. It is possible the first ascent waited until April 1984 when the south ridge was climbed to the main ridge and followed over several false tops to the true summit.

The east face of the mountain, easily accessible from Lobuche village, has

High camp on Mera Peak, at 6,654 meters (21,830 feet) the highest Trekking Peak.

attracted strong teams. Jeff Lowe, a pioneer on many Trekking Peaks, has added a difficult route up an icy couloir, whilst the obvious east ridge was climbed by Todd Biblier and Catherine Freer. Both routes are difficult. A host of challenging possible lines remain.

Kwangde (6,011 meters, 19,721 feet Group A): This stunning peak is seen from Namche Bazaar where it forms a long east-west ridge bounding the Bhote Kosi. Although included in the Khumbu, Kwangde is the northern limit of the Lumding Himal.

Like most Trekking Peaks, Kwangde has several summits all of which are permissible on a single permit. The main summit, Kwangde Lho, has a formidable north face that was first climbed by Jeff Lowe and David Brearshears in 1982, setting an extreme route that required several bivouacs.

Less formidable from the north is the main, curving ridge thrown towards the Bhote Kosi from Kwangde Shar. This fine northeast ridge offers a less difficult route and was first climbed alpine style in 1978 by Lindsay Griffin and Roger Everett.

More exacting, and perhaps more interesting, is the approach to Kwangde from the south. The high, uninhabited Lumding Valley was first explored by Jimmy Roberts and Sen Tenzing in 1953. A year later American Fred Becky entered the valley, crossing the Moro La from the east before going on to discover the Lumding Tsho Teng, one of the highest lakes in the world.

From the Lumding, the south ridge of Kwangde Lho has become the normal, albeit difficult, ascent and was first climbed in 1975 by a Nepalese team.

Kusum Kanguru (6,367 meters, 20,889 feet Group A): This mountain, more than any of the other Trekking Peaks, epitomises the dilemma inherent in the name. As its Tibetan name implies, this shapely citadel of rock and ice has "three snowy summits" that have provided a difficult and adventurous challenge. Found at the southern end of Charpati Himal, Kusum Kanguru rises between the Dudh Kosi and the unin-

Porters trekking in the snow on Gosainkund.

150

habited Hinku Drangka. Rising close to Lukla, it is perhaps the easiest trekking peak to approach and hardest to climb.

Kusum Kanguru offers nothing for the incompetent and little for the merely skilful. Even by its easiest route, the east face above the Lungsamba glacier, the mountain is technically demanding. The peak has attracted the elite of the mountaineering world and boasts more routes than any other peak on the list.

Of the many climbs on its numerous faces and ridges, perhaps the most daring exploit was that of New Zealander Bill Denz who in 1981 completed a solo traverse of the mountain.

Mera Peak (6,654 meters, 21,830 feet Group A): Mera, the highest of the Trekking Peaks, forms a heavily glaciated mass between the Hinku and Hongu valleys, east of Lukla and almost due south of Everest. First climbed in 1953 by Jimmy Roberts and Sen Tenzing, it has in the last few years become one of the most frequently climbed mountains on the list. Its popularity is undoubtedly due to both its altitude and technical simplicity.

As there are no lodges in either the Hinku or Hongu valleys, parties need to be self-contained which makes it even more attractive to those in search of a mountaineering adventure.

The quickest approach is the Zatrawa La, east of Lukla. Parties approaching from Jiri can reach the mountain from the south via the Hindu Drangka and Pangkongma. The normal route of ascent is via the Mera La north of the mountain and the wide, gently sloping glaciers that fall from the summit.

Rolwaling's Trekking Peaks: The remote Rolwaling Valley remained closed to Westerners for most of the 1980s, only reopening in 1989. A high, east-west valley separated from the Khumbu by the daunting Tashi Lapcha pass, it is an untouched enclave of Sherpa culture. Explored by Shipton in 1952 when he photographed the infamous yeti footprints, it remains a kind of trekker's haven.

Ramdung (5,925 meters, 19,439 feet Group A): This is one of several appeal-

ing small peaks south of Na, best approached by crossing the Yalung La. These peaks were first climbed in 1952 by the Scottish Himalayan Expedition led by W.H. Murray.

Although not a high peak, the approach is quite long and for most parties two camps above Kyiduk will be required. A second high camp on the Ramdung glacier is usual if climbing the normal route, the north-east face from the Yalung La. In recent years several groups have favoured an approach around the west side of the mountain which eventually finds a way up the southwest flank.

Parchamo (6,187 meters, 20,298 feet Group A): This is a lovely glacier peak at the eastern end of the Rolwaling Himal, rising due south of the Tashi Lapcha. Shipton, Gregory and Evans first attempted it in 1951, following the north ridge until they were stopped by difficult terrain and lack of crampons.

Parchamo was not actually climbed until 1955, when Dennis Davis and Phil Boultbee finished off the north ridge during the Merseyside Expedition.

The Trekking Peak of Langtang and Jugal: Langtang and Jugal, being only 50 kilometers (30 miles) north of Kathmandu, are readily accessible to visitors (see page 251). A National Park since 1976, the Langtang preserves 1,710 square kilometers (660 square miles) of mountains, rivers, forest and pasture as home to some 30 species of mammal, 1,000 types of plant and over 160 recorded species of bird.

Naya Kanga (Ganja La Chuli) (5,844 meters, 19,180 feet Group B): Despite the extent of this area, Langtang and Jugal offer only one Trekking Peak. Formerly known as Ganja La Chuli, Naya Kanga is west of the Ganja La pass which separates the Langtang Valley from Helambu. The normal route climbs from the Kyangjin Gompa at the head of the Langtang Valley towards the Ganja La, and ascends the northeast face and north ridge. No record of a first ascent has been traced. Routes on the south side have been made, but these are more difficult.

Leaves and grasses on the trail.

The Trekking Peaks of Ganesh Himal:
The splendid icy pyramids of Ganesh form a stunning panorama seen from Kathmandu Valley. Set between the Buri Gandaki in the west and the Bhote Kosi in the east, they provide one of the most enjoyable Trekking Peak climbs for competent mountaineers.

Paldor (5,896 meters, 19,344 feet Group B): Paldor can be quickly approached from the Trisuli Valley and thence the Chilime Khola to Gatlang. A new road into the Mailung Khola is an intrusion but can be avoided.

Base camp is best placed at the head of the Mailung Khola from where several small peaks offer splendid training climbs. The northeast ridge, known as Tilman's Ridge, provides a fine route of ascent, as do all the ridges of this shapely peak.

Annapurna Himal Trekking Peaks: The massive barrier of lofty summits of the Annapurna Himal lie north of Pokhara, between the immense valleys of the Marsyangdi Khola in the east and the Kali Gandaki, the world's deepest valley, in the west. Home of the first 8,000 meter mountain ever to be climbed, the Annapurna massif is the focal point of two distinct groups of Trekking Peaks; those of the Annapurna Sanctuary and Manang Himal.

Annapurna Sanctuary: This vast amphitheatre of mountains is at the head of the Modi Khola. Entered through a narrow gorge between the portals of Hiunchuli and Machhapuchhre, this hidden glacial hollow is surrounded by the towering peaks of Annapurna South, Annapurna I, Khangshar Kang, Tarke Kang, Gangapurna, Annapurna III and Ghandarba Chuli. Within this circle are four Trekking Peaks.

Mardi Himal (5,587 meters, 18,330 feet Group B): Only 24 kilometers (15 miles) north of Pokhara, this lowest of the Trekking Peaks is somewhat overshadowed by the omnipotent form of the sacred Machhapuchhre. Mardi Himal forms a distinct terminal knot of *aretes* and glaciers on its southwest ridge. First identified by Basil Goodfellow in 1953, it was not climbed until

Rhododendron blossoms litter the forest during the late spring.

1961 when Jimmy Roberts reached the summit via the east flank.

Mardi Himal is seldom climbed or visited. Offering plenty of scope for new routes, it has a hidden sanctuary and unequalled views of the "fish tail" of Machhapuchhre.

Hiunchuli (6,441 meters, 21,132 feet Group A): Hiunchuli is a difficult and elusive mountain, despite its apparently accessible location. A guardian at the entrance to the Sanctuary, it looms due north of Chhomrong. All of its approaches are steep and challenging, protected by rock slabs and hanging ice.

First climbed in 1971 by an American Peace Corps Expedition, it has seen few ascents since. Scaled from the Modi gorge above Hinko Cave, the first ascent required several camps. Hiunchuli has been climbed by a circuitous route from the Sanctuary, but the mountaineering plum waiting to be picked is a direct ascent from the south.

Tent Peak (Tharpu Chuli) (5,663 meters, 18,580 feet Group B): Originally named by Jimmy Roberts for obvious reasons, this attractive peak stands opposite the lodges near the Annapurna South Base Camp on the north side of the South Annapurna glacier.

Several routes have been done on the mountain but the normal ascent route is the northwest ridge, first climbed in 1965 by Gunter Hauser and party.

Fluted Peak (Singu Chuli) (6,501 meters, 21,329 feet Group A): Fluted Peak rises north of Tent Peak and is part of the same ridgeline thrown south from Glacier Dome.

First climbed in 1957 by Wilfred Noyce and David Cox on their return from Machhapuchhre, following a route on the northeast face, the mountain has resisted most subsequent attempts. A difficult route has been established on the west face, but most of the mountain remains uncluttered by climbers' inventions and it is considered one of the most demanding.

Manang Himal: The arid landscape of Manang lies north of the Great Himalayan Range at the head of the Marsyangdi valley and was first explored by

Ice seracs on the Khumbu Glacier.

154

Tilman and Roberts in 1950. North of the Manang valley, close to the Tibetan border are a line of peaks that include the remaining three permitted summits on the Trekking Peaks list.

Pisang Peak (6,091 meters, 19,983 feet Group A): This beautiful peak is popular with trekking groups, and rises from the meadows above the interesting village of Pisang. First climbed solo by J. Wellenkamp in 1955 by the southwest face and ridge, this route remains the standard and only reported climb on the mountain, despite it having a striking west flank which presents endless possibilities.

Chulu East (Gundang) (6,584 meters, 21,601 feet Group A): This striking mountain lies due north of Ongre at the head of the Chegagji Khola, where it forms a shapely icy pyramid. It was first climbed by the German Annapurna Expedition in 1955 whose members included Wellenkamp, Biller and Lobbichler. Details of their route are not available, although it seems likely that they climbed the south ridge.

The northeast ridge, however, running up from the head of the Phu Khola, provides a splendid route of moderate difficulty. It was first climbed by Isherwood and Noble in 1979. Due east of this summit is another, smaller peak often climbed by mistake for Chulu East – it could accurately be termed Chulu Far East.

Chulu West (6,419 meters, 21,560 feet Group A): Northwest of Chulu East along the main crest of the Manang Himal and clearly visible to the southeast of the Thorong La pass, is the elegant summit of Chulu West.

Most westerly of a cluster of peaks, there is in fact a higher peak to the south east of Chulu West, which can be called Chulu Central (6,429 meters, 21,505 feet). Both can be climbed on the same permit.

Chulu West was first climbed in 1978 by Larry Zaroff and Peter Lev with Sherpas Ang Zangmo and Lhakpa Nuru by a route on the northwest ridge – a climb involving some technical rock climbing and the use of fixed ropes.

Mani **stone still life amidst the snow.**

QUEST FOR SHANGRILA

One of the best known stories of modern times is that of Shangrila. The book *Lost Horizon* was published only a little over fifty years ago, but its account of a mystical kingdom hidden beyond the Himalaya became so popular that movies were made about it, and the name Shangrila is now widely recognised throughout the world. The appeal of Shangrila continues to this day, and it is easy to understand why. It is difficult, indeed, not to be attracted to the idea of a clement paradise, set amidst snow-capped mountains, where the people are happy and protected from the strife of the outside world.

Few Westerners are aware that the story of Shangrila is based upon a tradition dating back millennia and still held among the people of Tibet and bordering regions. The hidden kingdom of Shambhala almost exactly fits the conception of Shangrila and figures prominently in Tibetan Buddhist beliefs. However, Shambhala is thought to lie far north of Tibet, whereas the similar tradition, that of the *beyuls* (the hidden lands or valleys) are scattered throughout the Himalaya.

The *beyuls* are believed to have been made by Padmasambhava, the Indian Buddhist credited with being the first to establish Buddhism in Tibet. He became deified and is attributed with many miraculous works. To provide refuges for persecuted Buddhists in Tibet, he created these blessed hidden lands, each consisting of forested and fertile valleys surrounded by high mountains, within which crops and herds prosper.

The *beyuls* do not lack for riches: gold, silver and precious stones, sacred texts, books of profound teachings and powerful ritual implements are hidden in them. People living in these *beyuls* are free from illness and hard work and are able to more easily approach true enlightenment. "The hidden land will increase your lifespan, merit and wealth, and all those born in it will be liberated from the endless cycle of rebirths," said Padmasambhava in a text to the *beyul* of Helambu, which is north of Kathmandu.

More than twenty *beyuls* have been referred to in Tibetan Buddhist literature, and many more have been labelled as such by the local inhabitants. Ancient texts called *lamyig* (guidebooks), exist describing at least half a dozen of them. These texts are believed to have been hidden by Padmasambhava in the 8th century, and discovered later, in the 14th and 15th centuries.

Only certain persons, several of whom were prophesied by Padmasambhava, were destined to find the *beyul* guidebooks. However, these "text discoverers" were often not the ones meant to find the hidden lands. The texts describe the kind of persons capable of reaching the *beyuls*, signs as to the auspicious time to begin the search, the routes to be taken, various rituals to be performed at specific places during the journey, and what will be seen once the travellers have arrived.

The route descriptions mix known place names with vague geographical features, causing serious problems with identification. For example, one mountain on the way to Helambu is described as looking like a "mother holding a baby on her lap." And there are stringent requirements, with unpleasant consequences if not carried out. In the text to a *beyul* located behind Manaslu, at one place, "If you do not make an offering to the stone that looks like a lying dog, you will vomit and have diarrhoea."

Such difficulties make it no easy task to ensure that all the text's instructions have been fulfilled and the *beyuls* correctly located. Furthermore, there are three levels of a *beyul* which can be seen, depending on the level of awareness attained by the searchers. The inner and secret valleys are said to be visible and accessible only to advanced practitioners of the Buddhist doctrine, and only they will receive the full benefits of the *beyul*.

Nonetheless, approximate locations of some of the hidden valleys can be worked out and local traditions help to

Left, this distinctive Sherpa painting shows Thyangboche Monastery and a yeti climbing the high mountains.

pinpoint them more precisely. Thus we know that one of the most famous *beyuls*, Pema-ko, is located near the mountain Namche Barwa where the Brahmaputra River bends to the south before entering Assam from Tibet. Another famous *beyul* is in Sikkim, believed to be near Kangchenjunga.

Texts and traditions place several *beyuls* in Nepal. One of the best known of these is Khembalung, located east of Mount Chamlang south of Makalu. Indeed, the Sherpa name for Makalu is Sura-rakya, a major protector deity of Khembalung. The most important of the pre-Buddhist deities were mountain gods, and they are believed to have been defeated by Padmasambhava and converted into protectors of Buddhism. Situated at the base, or in the laps as it were, of these ancient and powerful deities, the *beyuls* are not only protected by their natural surroundings but by the mountain gods as well.

At Khembalung Sherpas living in the area will show power places, one of the most prominent being a cave, where the results of magical feats performed by Padmasambhava are supposedly visible. Such sacred sites often become the goals of pilgrimages, and in Khembalung huts have been built for those wishing to take advantage of the heightened effectiveness of meditation in the *beyul*. "If Tantric practitioners stay there, they will obtain all realizations and great power," said Padmasambhava about Khembalung. The pilgrimage itself is thought to gain one considerable merit – the water has great purifying power and the white clay at the mouth of the cave is considered a potent medicine.

Thus for ordinary people the *beyuls* are not just unattainable mystical lands. Although realising they will not experience all that is promised in the texts, many persons nonetheless consider they benefit greatly from pilgrimages to these sacred valleys. Several cases are recorded of entire villages abandoning their goods and setting out in search of a *beyul*. Often they find nothing but hardship, with those surviving the jour-

A *thangka* portraying Padmasambhava, the creator of the *beyuls* or hidden valleys of Shangrila.

neys having to turn back. According to some Sherpas, their fathers originally came to the Khumbu and settled there because it was a *beyul*.

The hidden lands, whether "real" or not, thus served as true refuges for those escaping political and economic pressures. The historical context in which the *beyul* texts were "discovered" should also not be ignored. They were found at a time of considerable political instability, exacerbated by rivalries between different schools of Tibetan Buddhism. The isolated, forested valleys of the Nepal Himalaya provided real havens, the "natural fortresses" of the texts, for those in need of peace – and land.

Both *lamas* and texts warn that misfortune will befall those looking for *beyuls* before the right time has come. Opinions vary amongst *lamas* as to the interpretation of the signs described in the texts and one recent controversy concerns the Chinese invasion of Tibet in 1959. "During the decline of Buddhism, the soldiers of Hor (the land bordering Tibet to the north) will come to the centre of the country and destroy the Tibetans. This is the time the *beyul* can be found." Is this the time to be looking for *beyuls*? Some believe so, although only the most learned will get beyond the outer levels of the *beyul*, whilst others feel the signs were missed and the *beyuls* already closed. The difficulties involve the interpretation of the signs, fulfilling the demanding religious requirements and following the confusing route descriptions. The physical obstacles may well be the easiest problems to overcome.

We may never know if we have entered a "real" *beyul* or not, but in Nepal we can find some of the most spectacular mountain scenery and plenty of picturesque and fertile valleys. We also find a fascinating culture of great antiquity – and the complex roots of the legend of Shangrila. Perhaps the sacred texts are correct: We will see and experience the hidden valleys only in direct proportion to the degree of awareness we bring to them.

The Thyangboche Rinpoche officiates at a cremation, using the *dorje* and bell.

NEPAL'S 8,000-METER MOUNTAINS

The shattering force of the tectonic collision which formed the Himalaya of Nepal gave birth to eight of the world's fourteen 8,000 meter (26,250 feet) mountains and eight of the ten highest mountains in the world. These huge mountain masses range eastwards from Dhaulagiri to form a natural frontier with Nepal's neighbours.

Everest and Cho Oyu border with Tibet whilst Kangchenjunga shares its multi-summited crest with the Indian state of Sikkim. These eight great mountains, above all others, captivate the world's attention and attract its most ambitious mountaineers.

The history of the ascents of the 8,000 meter mountains by teams from an increasing number of developed and emerging nations reflects the importance today of "sporting" success. As exacting yardsticks of national and personal achievement, the highest

peaks have become the ultimate playground for the mountaineering elite.

The development of climbing in the Himalaya mirrors the evolution of Alpine exploration in Europe. Initially expeditions sought to reach summits by the easiest or most obvious routes. Once the virgin summits were scaled, those at the cutting-edge of mountaineering looked towards more difficult routes on steeper ridges and faces.

The major difference was that the effort, cost and size were escalated for Himalayan expeditions. Vast armies of climbers, porters and Sherpas marched towards base camp to lay siege to the mountain which often lasted for months.

For the select few, Himalayan endeavour is taken to the very limits of endurance in solo, turbo-charged, record breaking climbs. The Himalaya has seen an increasing number of wild performances – flying in balloons or hanggliding and ski descents. No mountain illustrates this inventiveness better than Everest.

Despite predictions for a future of multi-ascents and even faster descents, in reality this approach to Himalayan climbing will remain the preserve of the extreme few. In the meantime the majority of mountaineers are confined to the traditional approach utilising fixed camps, fixed ropes, "tinned" air and the help of Sherpas.

The Golden Decade: By 1950 the door to Nepal's mountains was open and the world's climbers were quick to take up the challenge. The mountains are listed chronologically according to their first ascents.

Annapurna I (8,091 meters, 26,545 feet) tenth highest: Annapurna I was the first 8,000 meter mountain to be climbed when, in 1950, a strong French expedition, led by Maurice Herzog, reached the summit by the north face. Having failed to find a way up Dhaulagiri, they had turned their attention to Annapurna I.

The team included such notable Chamonix guides as Gaston Rebuffat, Lionel Terray and Louis Lachenal. Lachenal and Herzog reached the sum-

Preceding pages: Sherpa guide with Everest in his eyes. Left, offerings are made to the goddess of Everest during the 1976 American Everest Expedition.

mit, but deteriorating weather and a series of mishaps almost turned success into disaster. Herzog suffered severe frostbite during an epic descent resulting in amputations during the walk out and train journey to India.

But their success heralded the beginning of the Golden Decade of Nepal's 8,000 meter mountains.

Everest (8,848 meters, 29,028 feet) Highest Point on Earth: The "Mother of the Universe" is known as Sagarmatha in Nepal and Chomolungma (Mother Goddess) in Tibet. Everest had occupied the efforts of British mountaineers over several decades, although always from the north and without success. The closing of Tibet coincided fortuitously with Nepal's opening and efforts were renewed to find a way to the top from the south side.

The leading lights of British mountaineering were soon probing the corrugated foothills east of Kathmandu to find a suitable approach to the Khumbu. The ubiquitous Bill Tilman and American Charles Houston traced a way to the foot of the Khumbu icefall in 1950 and a year later Eric Shipton's team went through the icefall to reach the Western *Cwm*.

The British, however, were not alone in their endeavour and all but lost the great prize when in 1952 a Swiss expedition came close to success.

The following spring an expedition led by Colonel John Hunt renewed the British assault on Everest. This was a strong expedition gathered from the finest mountaineers of Britain and New Zealand. On the first summit bid Charles Evans and Tom Bourdillon reached the South Summit, laying open the way to the top. Two days later on 29th May, 1953 Edmund Hillary and Tenzing Norgay were the first people to stand on the summit of the highest mountain in the world.

They brought to a close what Norman Dyhrenfurth called "an Edwardian quest for the poles of the earth" and made an auspicious start to the new Elizabethan age as the news reached London for the coronation of Queen

A sight to behold: Manaslu and Himachuli peaks.

Elizabeth II.

Cho Oyu (8,201 meters, 26,906 feet) sixth highest: Cho Oyu rises 32 kilometers (20 miles) west of Everest, the "Goddess of Turquoise" was the third of Nepal's 8,000 meter peaks to be climbed.

The first reconnaissance took place in 1951, followed a year later by the British Cho Oyu expedition led by Eric Shipton. Once again this was a powerful team including many who were to take part in the first ascent of Everest. From the Nangpa La, the traditional yak trade route to Tibet, a route was found that looked feasible though the north flank was "out of bounds" in Tibet.

In 1954 Viennese author, Dr Herbert Tichy, put together an expedition which proved the exception to the rule that 8,000 meter mountains needed large-scale expeditions. With only two European companions he organised a lightweight party very much in keeping with the "small is beautiful" philosophy expounded by Tilman and Shipton. Accompanied by half a dozen Sherpas they left Namche Bazaar for the Nangpa La in late September.

Finding a way through the icefall they established a high camp but a storm drove them down and left Tichy with frostbitten hands. In the meantime two members of a Swiss/French expedition to Gauri Shankar arrived at base camp, hoping to "poach" Cho Oyu. Though not fully recuperated, the Austrians were driven back onto the mountain and an epic ascent followed. Unable to use his damaged hands, Tichy had to be helped over the rock band, but at 3.00 p.m. on 19th October, 1954 the summit was reached by Tichy, Sepp Joechler and Pasang Dawa Lama.

To quote Tichy: "... feeling a sense of complete harmony such as we had never known before, an almost unearthly sense of joy – worth far more than a few frozen fingers."

Kangchenjunga (8,586 meters, 28,169 feet) third highest: Visible in the distant mists from Darjeeling and with access from Sikkim, the history of Kangchenjunga, like that of Everest, goes

Cho Oyu, first scaled in 1954.

back far beyond the opening of Nepal. This multi-peaked mountain, four of which are over 8,000 meters, was the best documented of all, having been attempted as early as 1905. The third highest mountain is vast; some 13 kilometers (eight miles) in length by eight kilometers (five miles) broad.

After an optimistic British reconnaissance in 1954, the Alpine Club and Royal Geographical Society of London dispatched an expedition the following spring led by Charles Evans. The particularly strong team included George Band, Joe Brown, John Jackson and Tony Streather.

The daunting south face of Lhotse, for a long time considered impossible to ascend, was climbed for the first time in 1990 by Tomo Cesen of Yugoslavia.

After a hard struggle, plagued by avalanches and not without mishap – a young Sherpa died after falling into a crevasse – Band and Brown left for the summit, using artificial oxygen, on 25th May, 1955. They had chosen a route on the southwest face and having gained the main ridge, the top lay beyond a tower of grey-green rock. Joe Brown, acclaimed as the finest rock climber of his generation, overcame this obstacle

to reach the easy slope leading to the summit. Next day, two teammates followed in their footsteps.

The four climbers kept a promise made to the Sikkimese not to stand on the sacred summit of the highest point so, although credited with the first ascent, Kangchenjunga remained the Untrodden Peak.

Makalu (8,463 meters, 27,766 feet) fifth highest: Makalu is the highest peak between Everest and Kangchenjunga and is a mountain of exceptional beauty.

As with Annapurna I, the French have laid claim to Makalu, although American and New Zealand teams had explored the region long before them. A French reconnaissance party headed by Jean Franco visited Makalu in 1954, returning a year later with a powerful expedition consisting of the very best guides Alpinist France could muster: among them Jean Couzy, Lionel Terray, Guido Magnone and Serge Coupe. They were ably supported by a doctor, geologists, 23 Sherpas and an army of

315 porters.

Their route to Camp 5 on the Makalu La proved technically very difficult and required a large amount of fixed rope. From there, they were able to traverse easy slopes on the north side. A steep couloir led to the knife-edged ridge leading to the summit, first reached on 15th May, 1955 by Couzy and Terray. In all eight Frenchmen and one Sherpa reached the summit.

This outstandingly successful expedition was a combination of a strong, well organised and highly motivated team aided by the finest equipment and blessed with good weather providing ideal climbing conditions. This latter factor is critical to success on 8,000 meter mountains.

Manaslu (8,163 meters, 26,781 feet) eighth highest: If Europeans claim some of the giants, Manaslu is determinedly an Asian mountain. Not only was it first climbed by Japanese but a high number of Nepalese, Japanese and South Korean lives have been lost on this mountain whose name means "Soul" in Sanskrit. In two days of avalanches during the spring of 1972, in the largest death toll on any Nepalese peak, 15 men lost their lives.

The mountain itself is stunning; the highest of a cluster of glorious summits including Himalchuli and Peak 29 (Ngadi Himal), standing in splendid isolation between the Annapurnas and Ganesh Himal.

Between 1953 and 1956 the Japanese served their Himalayan apprenticeship by making several attempts on Manaslu. In 1956 the venerable 62 year old leader, Yuka Maki, approached via the Buri Gandaki. The Japanese set about climbing the northeast face, despite disputes with the local villagers. Toshio Imanishi and Sirdar Gyalzen Norbu Sherpa reached the rocky pinnacle of the summit by midday on 9th May.

Lhotse (8,516 meters, 27,940 feet) fourth highest: For a long time Lhotse had no separate identity from its dominating neighbour, Mount Everest. Even its name which means South Peak implies it is not a mountain in its own right.

Once Nepal opened it borders the error became all too clear – from the south Lhotse forms a massive mountain wall.

Although unattempted until 1953, Dyhrenfurth had identified a route to the summit from the South Col. European and American assaults did not make much impact and it was not until spring 1956 that a well-planned Swiss expedition established base camp beneath the Khumbu icefall. Poor weather hampered progress but on 18th May Swiss climbers Ernest Reiss and Fritz Luchsinger reached the summit of the world's fourth highest peak.

The daunting south face of Lhotse is ranked as "amongst the most difficult in the world." As the great Reinhold Messner wrote in 1977: "At 8,500 meters (28,000 feet) this vertical face may well be impossible."

The most recent star in the firmament of Himalayan climbing, Tomo Cesen from Yugoslavia, confounded his peers by climbing this massive wall solo in April, 1990. The 30 year old sports journalist not only climbed without fixed camps or bottled oxygen, but entirely alone, with very little fixed rope and in the amazing total elapsed time of 45 hours and 20 minutes from the bottom of the face to the summit.

Dhaulagiri I (8,167 meters, 26,795 feet) seventh highest: This spectacular peak's name means, benignly enough, the "White Mountain" but Dhaulagiri has come to be known as the mountain of storms and sorrows.

Although the first of the 8,000 meter peaks to be attempted by the French in 1950, who abandoned their bid in favour of Annapurna I, ironically it was the very last 8,000 meter peak in Nepal to be climbed.

Seven expeditions attempted Dhaulagiri, including one sponsored by President Peron of Argentina, but it was not until 1960 that a massive Swiss attempt was successful via the northeast spur. Supplied by a small glacier plane piloted by Ernst Saxer, the expedition finally ended the Golden Decade of Nepal's giants by putting four Europeans and two Sherpas on the summit on 13th May, 1960.

Mighty Makalu is the fifth tallest mountain in the world.

EVEREST DATES

The massive rock of Mount Everest, 8,848 meters (29,028 feet) above sea level, bestrides Nepal's northern border with the Tibet Autonomous Region of China. It is named Everest after a British Surveyor-General of 19th-century India, George Everest. The Nepalese know it as Sagarmatha and the Tibetans as Chomolungma.

Important landmarks in man's struggle to climb Everest:

1922 – The first attempt to scale the mountain was made by Britons from the Chinese side. Seven Sherpas from India died in an avalanche, the first fatalities recorded on Everest.

1953 – Edmund Hillary of New Zealand and Tenzing Norgay Sherpa of India became the first mountaineers to reach the summit, climbing via the southeast ridge.

1963 – Two Americans, Willi Unsoeld and Tom Hornbein, became the first climbers to ascend by one route (the west ridge and north face) and descend by another (the southeast ridge).

1965 – Nawang Gombu Sherpa of India became the first person to scale Everest twice, both times (in 1963 and 1965) by the southeast ridge.

1970 – Yuichiro Miura of Japan became the first to descend a large part of Everest on skis.

1975 – Mrs Junko Tabei of Japan became the first woman to reach the summit of Everest.

1978 – Everest was first scaled without the use of artificial oxygen by Reinhold Messner of Italy and Peter Habeler of Austria.

1979 – Ang Phu Sherpa of Nepal became the first person to scale the mountain by two different routes (southeast ridge in 1970 and the west ridge in 1979).

1979 – A West German expedition led by

Gerhad Schmatz was the first to send all of its members to the summit. The leader's wife, Hannelore Schmatz, was the first woman to die on Everest when she collapsed of exposure and exhaustion during her descent.

1980 – Leszek Cichy and Krzysztof Wielcki of Poland made the first winter ascent of Everest in February.

1980 – Messner made the first solo ascent of Everest (from the Chinese side, without bottled oxygen in August, the first ascent in summer).

1982 – Yasuo Kato of Japan became the first person to reach the summit in three different seasons (spring, autumn and winter). He died in a storm on his descent.

1985 – At age 55, American Dick Bass, became the oldest person to scale Everest.

1988 – A huge Chinese-Japanese-Nepalese group scaled the first north-south and south-north traverses simultaneously.

1988 – Marc Batard of France set a speed record in an ascent of 22.5 hours on a route already made by others up the southeast ridge.

1990 – Ang Rita Sherpa of Nepal became the first person to scale the mountain six times.

1990 – A 17 year old French student became the youngest person ever to climb Everest when he reached the summit in October with his father, Jean Noel Roche. They were also the first father and son to reach the top together.

A total of 349 persons – 335 men and 14 women – had managed to attain its summit by all routes from both the Nepal and Tibet sides by March 1992. From the Nepalese side alone, 265 men and 10 women from 26 nations had gone to the summit. 109 persons have died whilst attempting the mountain, including 43 Sherpas.

Left, **Mount Everest and <u>above</u>, Tenzing Norgay Sherpa on the summit (1953).**

BECAUSE IT IS THERE:
THE LEGEND OF MALLORY AND IRVINE

"We paused, in sheer astonishment. The sight of it banished every thought; we asked no questions and made no comment, but simply looked ..."
– by George Leigh Mallory

On 8th June, 1924 on the Tibetan side of Mount Everest, two British climbers disappeared into the mists high on this huge mountain; and thereby entered the realm of speculation and legend. They were George Leigh Mallory and Andrew Irvine.

Did they reach the summit of the world's highest mountain before they perished? Why did they not manage to return to waiting teammates below? Did one of them fall and pull the other with him? Or did they become too exhausted to descend to the shelter of their tent and so died of exposure and frostbite? No one will ever know. They were never seen again and their bodies have never been found.

Mallory at age 38 had already become a well known mountaineering figure. He had been a leading participant in the first reconnaissance ever made of Everest in 1921, and in the first attempt to scale the vast mountain the following year, both from its northern flanks in an unexplored area of Tibet. When he returned to the north side of Everest in 1924 and disappeared in the clouds on his way to the top of the world, Mallory caught the imagination of a British public demoralised by the carnage of the First World War.

Handsome, a skilled alpinist, talented writer and schoolmaster, he had become known for his pithy response to a query as to why anyone would try to climb Everest. It was he who answered with the classic: "Because it is there." Amongst fellow mountaineers, Mallory was often quoted for another remark, in which he rejected the common use of the term 'conquest' when a summit is reached. "Have we vanquished an enemy? None but ourselves."

Clad in thick tweeds and carrying such essentials as wind-up gramophones to base camp, these early attempts were very different from the high-tech, super light-weight expeditions of today. There was no communication between the climbing team and base camp; those on the mountain were on their own to do or die. Burdened by hefty metal oxygen cylinders and layer upon layer of non-waterproof clothing, climbers faced minimal odds in a ground-breaking venture that exceed all known heights. European mountaineers, well acclimatised to Mont Blanc's 4,810 meter (15,781 feet) summit, didn't know what elevations of nearly twice that would do to their bodies.

Andrew Irvine was much younger, only 22, and much less experienced but he was selected by Mallory to go with him on the push for the summit. And thus he also vanished into legend with Mallory.

"I regard Mallory as the man of Everest of all generations," says Sir Edmund Hillary, the world's best known mountaineer. "He was the man who really brought Everest to the public mind and was in a sense the inspiration for all of us who followed. He certainly was for me. If anyone deserved to get to the top, he would have. But I have no idea whether he did."

Another of the world's greatest climbers, Reinhold Messner, the only person to have scaled Everest entirely alone and the first to scale all fourteen 8,000 meter peaks, has analyzed what happened, based on his vast experience. "I'm sure they did not reach the summit. They went up towards the summit from their camp and surely climbed the first step (a rock feature at 8,535 meters 28,000 feet) but surely not the second step (a greater barrier not far above the first)."

"At the first step they were already late for getting to the summit. They arrived below the second step, and in 15 minutes they could see it was impossible for them to climb this step. They slowly went back towards their camp in the middle of the afternoon, on the way they died. Maybe one fell and pulled the other off. Maybe both fell. I don't know. Anyhow I'm sure they didn't reach the summit."

Or did they?

Right, Mallory and Irvine disappeared into the mists high on Everest in 1924, never to be seen again. These three climbers looking like dots on the West Ridge were not so unlucky.

PROBLEMS AT HIGH ALTITUDE

Will I make it up Kala Pattar (5,545 meters, 18,192 feet)? Will I make it over Thorong La (5,416 meters, 17,769 feet)? These are the questions that begin months before the trip, before you actually get on the plane, before you land in Kathmandu and look up at the giant snow peaks. Some people have never hiked in the mountains, and have no experience with feeling breathless walking up hill. Others have been to 4,000 meters (13,000 feet) or more, and wonder what an additional 1,500 meters (4,900 feet) in altitude will add to the exertion. Although these questions are valid (some people will find it too difficult to get to these heights), it is important to note that these apparently enormous heights are just at the base of the peaks in the Himalaya.

Mount Everest, the highest of all mountains on earth, is 8,848 meters (29,028 feet) above sea level. At Base Camp (5,357 meters, 17,575 feet) the amount of oxygen in each breath is half that of sea level. At the top of Everest this has shrunk to one third of sea level. The tiny amount of oxygen in each breath at that altitude was at one time thought to be inadequate to support human exertion, and that therefore the summit could not be reached without carrying and breathing supplemental oxygen. This was the feeling of many scientists prior to 1978, when Reinhold Messner and Peter Habeler set off from the base camp of Everest with no artificial oxygen and went all the way to the summit. Some people even doubted their claims when they came down, so convinced were they that it was impossible! Messner put the issue to rest two years later when he left base camp on the Tibet side of Everest all alone without oxygen, and went to the summit and back in three days.

Although there was no longer any doubt that a human could climb to the top of Everest without oxygen (and several others have done it since 1980), no measurements existed to show exactly what the environment was like on top. In 1981, the American Medical Research Expedition to Everest took gas samples and atmospheric pressure readings on the summit and found that the atmospheric pressure was slightly higher than would be predicted at a similar height away from Everest. They decided that the mass of the mountain was so large that it actually pulled the atmosphere in closer at the summit, increasing the expected atmospheric pressure, and thus making the summit

slightly "lower" for the air-breathing climber. In fact, conditions are so marginal for human existence on top that some scientists feel that in order to climb the mountain without oxygen, it has to be a relatively high barometric pressure day.

Messner himself, the first man to climb all of the earth's 14 8,000-meter peaks, speaks of the environment above 8,000 meters (26,250 feet) as the "death zone." At these heights the body cannot adjust, it can only slowly deteriorate. Thinking is slowed, and neurologic function is impaired (and remains impaired for months after descent). You inevitably lose weight, both fat and

Left, during the 1982 first ascent of Cholatse, American climber John Roskelley negotiates the final ice wall in a blizzard. Above, Himalayan Rescue Association doctors at Manang lecture trekkers in an attempt to prevent altitude problems.

muscle, and along with that you lose strength. Panting rapidly in the high dry air causes you to lose litres of fluid a day, fluid that must be painstakingly replaced by chopping ice, melting it in a stove, forcing the lukewarm result past parched and often nauseated lips, spending up to four or five hours a day replacing what has been lost by climbing. Four or five days above 8,000 meters (26,250 feet) is the most time that a human has spent at that height and survived; people have perished who have tried to stay longer, trapped by storms or delayed by injuries, their bodies never recovered. In a sense, they vanished into thin air.

Human beings evolved genetically at sea

actly the limit that a human being could go on earth without supplemental oxygen. In other words, the highest point on the planet is the highest point at which a human being could survive.

The speed at which the human body can adapt to altitude is limited by a condition know an acute mountain sickness (AMS). AMS results when you ascend to altitude faster than your body can adjust. Initially you feel headachy, nauseated and tired and the symptoms can progress to coma or fluid in the lungs. Usually this process takes several days. Dr. Charles Clarke, the British climber and physician, feels that this process may be even more accelerated at high alti-

level. Yet, the potential to adapt to even these great heights is built into our bodies. Breathing automatically accelerates and red cell production is increased to carry more oxygen. Other as yet undefined changes also facilitate carrying oxygen from the lungs to the tissues that need it. If you were deposited by helicopter at the summit of Everest, without prior acclimatisation and without artificial oxygen, you would lose consciousness within minutes, and die within hours. The fact that an acclimatised person can live and function at that height is a genetic miracle. Further mystery is added by the discovery that the summit of Everest is probably ex-

tude. Case reports suggest that a milder, more preventable form of AMS may prevail at altitudes up to 5,500 meters (18,000 feet), what Dr. Clarke calls the "mountain sickness of acclimatisation." Above that height, the syndrome sometimes strikes with devastating speed and gets worse even as the victim struggles to descend. He calls this the "mountain sickness of extreme altitude."

Climbers are always trying to walk a narrow line of strategy, between spending enough time adapting to altitude and safeguarding the route and spending as little time as possible at high altitude where the body inevitably deteriorates and the weather can be deadly. As climbers attempt to climb more quickly, minimising exposure to altitude and weather, they have succumbed to the sudden onset of severe altitude sickness.

The weather at high altitude can change abruptly. Winds can exceed 200 kilometers (125 miles) per hour and temperatures drop far below freezing. Frostbite is a constant risk but stopping to warm frozen toes or fingers can be almost impossible in precarious, exposed situations. The throat and lungs become parched and coughing becomes severe and uncontrollable. Climbers have been known to break their ribs during severe coughing spells and have had to climb down unassisted with this additional pain.

However, even these great athletes are levelled by exposure to altitudes above 8,000 meters (26,250 feet). Messner has stated that fitness no longer matters at these heights; it is just willpower and experience from there to the summit and back.

What does this mean for the Himalayan trekker? Suddenly 5,500 meters (18,000 feet) does not seem so high. If you have an interest in hiking, do it regularly and are willing to take time to adjust as you gain altitude, you have every chance of being able to comfortably gain your trekking goal. Not allowing enough time is the road to defeat in the Himalaya.

Although the air is thin, you can be quite

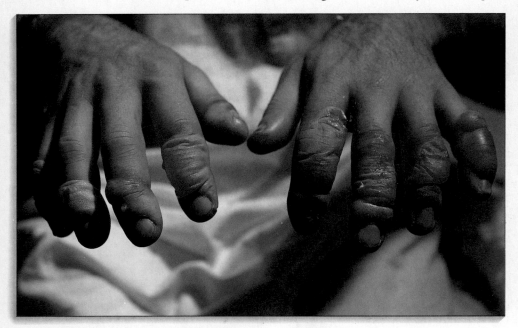

What role does physical fitness play in helping climbers at extreme altitude? Most mountaineers who have ambitions to climb high, already have some success and experience in scaling lesser peaks and have a high degree of fitness. I was impressed, when I began to meet world class mountaineers, that they had a different concept of fitness compared to ordinary people. At what I thought was the end of a hard day's climbing, these strong men and women would say, "It's not dark for half an hour yet, let's go climb ..."

Left, sick trekker is treated in the Hongu with Baruntse behind. **Above**, frostbitten fingers.

comfortable at rest at 5,500 meters (18,000 feet), only noticing the altitude when you start to walk uphill. The air is clean and dry, the sky is a deep navy blue and the surrounding walls are white and massive. These moderate heights (by Himalayan standards) should be thought of as an environment to be enjoyed and savoured, rather than a goal to be accomplished. For a few moments or a few days, you too can "vanish" into thin air, your worldly problems left far behind as your mind soars free. In the end the peaks remain, but you take your knowledge of yourself, your patience, perseverance and joy home with you.

The two best know mountaineers in the world today are New Zealander Sir Edmund Hillary and Italian Reinhold Messner.

In 1953 Hillary, a former beekeeper, became the first man to scale Mount Everest. Messner belongs to the next generation of climbers and was the first person to scale all of the worlds' fourteen giant 8,000 meter (26,250 foot) peaks.

Hillary came late to the mountains. He was 16 years old before he even saw a real mountain, and 20 when he ventured into New Zealand's rugged Southern Alps in 1939. But once his interest in mountaineering had been sparked, there was no stopping him.

He began with climbs in New Zealand before and during the Second World War. After the war, Hillary spent more and more time in the mountains, and found his way to the Himalaya in 1951.

In Nepal, Hillary met Eric Shipton, the famed British climber-explorer. Together they charted the most feasible route up Everest on the Nepalese side of the border. Hillary returned in 1953 with a British expedition, and as every schoolchild knows, he and his Sherpa companion Tenzing Norgay became the first men to ascend to the top of the world. "We knocked the bastard off," was Hillary's summary of the achievement.

As Hillary returned to climb in the Himalaya in ensuing years, he became increasingly involved in the problems of the Sherpas. They were illiterate and their health problems were acute, for there were no schools or hospitals. The organisation which Hillary founded – the Himalayan Trust – now supports 27 schools and two hospitals that he himself has taken a hand in building. He was New Zealand's ambassador to Nepal from 1985 to 1989 and now lives in New Zealand.

Hillary's adventures have not been restricted to the Himalaya. In 1957 and 1958, he led a small party in a race by tractors across the Antarctic to the South Pole. In 1977, he led a group of friends by jet-boat from the mouth of the Ganges to one of its mountain sources. As late as 1981, he was back on Everest, accompanying an American mountaineering team on an east face attempt, by way of Tibet.

Messner, born in September 1944, grew up in a village surrounded by the Dolomite mountains in the Tirol of northern Italy. Until he first ventured to the Himalaya in 1970, Messner worked as a teacher.

Messner's first attempt to conquer a Himalayan peak was successful. He and his brother Guenther, members of a German expedition to Pakistan's Nanga Parbat (8,126 meters or 26,660 feet), made history's third ascent of the mountain and the first by its Rupal face.

There are 14 of these 8,000-meter mountains on earth and Messner soon set about scaling them all. In 1972, he alone, among members of an Austrian team, gained the summit of Manaslu (8,163 meters or 26,781 feet), on a new route. In May 1978, Messner and Austrian, Peter Habeler made the first ascent of Everest without artificial oxygen. In August 1978, Messner made the first solo ascent of any 8,000-meter peak, this time on Nanga Parbat again. Messner returned to Everest in 1980 for what many consider his greatest achievement: a solo ascent of the highest mountain on earth. In four days, he climbed from Base Camp to the summit and back, without the support of fixed camps, companions or bottled oxygen.

On October 16, 1986 Messner became the first person to have scaled all fourteen 8,000-meter mountains when he made it to the summit of the world's fourth highest, Lhotse, 8,516 meters (27,940 feet), just 20 days after having been to the top of the fifth highest, Makalu, 8,463 meters (27,766 feet).

Following his success on the world's third highest, Kangchenjunga, in May 1982, he had set the autumn of 1986 as his deadline for his completing all 14, and now on schedule he had achieved this formidable goal and without ever making it easier for himself by taking bottled oxygen. He was three years ahead of his closest rival, Jerzy Kukuczka of Poland.

Preceding pages: Sir Edmund Hillary (left) and Reinhold Messner. Right, the great Sir Edmund Hillary, honoured by the Sherpa people with white silk *khatas* or scarves.

SIR EDMUND HILLARY: MY LIFE WITH SHERPAS

I first met the Sherpas in 1951 when I was a member of a four-man expedition to the Garhwal Himalaya. All of us had read great stories about the Sherpas' prowess and loyalty on expeditions in the past, and now we had the opportunity to live and work with them ourselves.

Our four Sherpas joined us from Darjeeling. We were immediately struck by their small, sinewy bodies and ready smiles. While they were not outstanding mountaineers – just middle-of-the-road, able men – we developed a warm affection for them.

By the end of that Garhwal expedition, we had successfully climbed a number of virgin peaks and learned something of the tough load-carrying ability of our Sherpas. Then two of us were invited to join the British Everest Reconnaissance to the south side of Mount Everest, led by the famous mountaineer Eric Shipton. We caught up to the British team inside a monsoon-drenched Nepal.

There I met one of the most redoubtable of all Sherpas, Sirdar Angtarkay – a cheerful, tough, brown man with tremendous vitality and strength. I admired him enormously and appreciated his kindness and friendliness. On this expedition I learned a lot about the Sherpa district of Khumbu and experienced the warm hospitality of the local inhabitants. Village elders would come out of their doors and literally drag us inside their homes, to ply us with their local raw spirits and hot tasty boiled potatoes.

First Meeting with Tenzing: In 1953 I became acquainted with a somewhat different type of Sherpa – Tenzing Norgay. Tenzing was very strong and vigorous, with a wide experience of climbing and load-carrying on many Himalayan peaks. But unlike many Sherpas, who largely climbed for the economic return produced, Tenzing had tremendous motivation to actually reach the summit of his mountains. This, combined with his physical ability, made him formidable indeed, and resulted in his reaching the summit of Everest with me on May 29, 1953.

Over the next few years, I spent much time in the mountains and in the Sherpas' homes. I learned something of their culture and religion, and built up close friendships. It was impossible not to realize how many things they lacked: education, medical care and a supply of good, clean piped water. In 1961, I first made the effort to fill some of these needs with the construction of a school at Khumjung, the first in this area. Gradually many more village schools, several hospitals, water pipelines, bridges and even airfields were built.

Meanwhile, the Sherpas were increasingly in demand for Himalayan expeditions. A wide variety of foreign expeditions kept pouring in: French, Japanese, Italian, Austrian, British, American and a dozen others. The toughness and reliability of the Sherpas and their tremendous skill at carrying loads at high altitudes made them extremely effective. And they were delightful people to work with – cheerful, hard-working, agreeable and lacking in any sense of inferiority.

"I Have Never Forgotten": I had experienced these pleasant characteristics back in 1952, when George Lowe, myself and three Sherpas made the first crossing of the Nup La pass and descended down the West Rongbuk glacier to the north side of Everest. Then the monsoon broke. The result was warm conditions, heavy snow and concealed crevasses.

We struggled back over the Nup La and plunged down the steep crevassed slopes into Nepal. There was minimal visibility and avalanches were rumbling down from every direction. I led the way down, constantly breaking through the soft snow bridges into crevasses, but always checked with a tight rope by George and the Sherpas. It seemed to go on forever and we thought we would never get out of danger.

Then we emerged onto the glacier below the icefall, still a wild and desolate place but now reasonably safe. George and I wearily started to pitch our tent but the Sherpas would have none of it. They gently sat us down on rocks, put the tents up themselves, and helped us into our warm sleeping bags. Soon we were being served tea and hot stew, and as I lay there in considerable comfort with great gusts of wind shaking the tent, I felt a tremendous sense of appreciation for the kindness and generosity of our hardy Sherpas. I have never forgotten their help on that occasion.

As the Sherpas became increasingly involved in expeditions, their exposure to mountaineering dangers grew. While foreign expedition members waited in their tents for the next thrust forward up the mountain, Sherpas were relaying loads backward and forward up the slopes. They were constantly in peril. Many died in crevasses, in avalanches and in tumbles down the mountainsides.

Trekking to New Lives: Soon there was a major change in the lives of the Sherpas. Increasing numbers of visitors were coming to Nepal and lots wanted to trek into the mountains. The Sherpas were ideal people to conduct such journeys with their energy and cheerful temperament. Whereas opportunities for rewarding employment previously had been confined to mountaineering, there

his bright eyes and ready grasp of English.

And so the lives of the Sherpas have changed. Renowned now throughout the world for their work on mountain peaks, many of them still climb as before and play a vital role in the success of great expeditions. But more are involved in trekking – in conducting visitors over the steep Nepalese countryside and up into the mountains. They have turned to other tasks too – running small hotels and tea shops, working as traders and businessmen. Some Sherpas are even politicians, pilots and wardens of national parks.

Warmth and Hospitality: If you are a friend and visit their remote homes, you will find

was now a safer road to a comfortable lifestyle. Trekking became big business.

Sherpa wives, who in the past had reluctantly accepted the mountaineering efforts of their husbands, with the potential of injury or death, now encouraged them to undertake trekking, with its similar opportunity for financial gain but a far better chance of survival. Education and the ability to speak English became of prime importance. It was easy to pick an ex-Khumjung student, with

Above, Sir Edmund Hillary building bridges in the Khumbu, one of the many projects financed by his Himalayan Trust.

that many things have not changed over the years. The warmth and hospitality remain: you will be given the place of honour beside the fire and will be plied with *chhang* (beer) and *arak* (spirits). You may indeed be presented with Tibetan tea, a traditional mixture of tea, salt and yak butter. In the background you may hear chanting from the local *gompa* – maybe prayers for the ill or the dead, or just encouragement for a good crop of potatoes. This is one of the greatest charms of the Sherpas. They introduce you so readily into their culture and religion; they ask so little from you except politeness and friendship; they laugh so easily at your jokes and their own.

REINHOLD MESSNER: WHY DOES MAN CLIMB?

For years, I have had the feeling that if I go on an expedition, nothing will happen. I am prepared, and everything is ready. But in the same moment, I have exactly the opposite knowledge – that this time, maybe, I will die. And it seems a little bit impossible, but I feel like this.

If a professional climber is going to spend his whole life doing hard things quite on the limit, the risk to die is quite high. It is almost exactly 50-50.

Of the leading climbers, 50 percent are dying on the mountain and 50 percent are surviving to die in bed. It's not that the good ones are surviving and the not-so-good ones are dying. It's a question of luck. And if somebody is climbing his whole life, he has to know that maybe he's in the 50 percent that has to die.

And each top climber who is truthful to himself knows that sometime he has had great luck, in the icefall of Everest or somewhere. A climber should know this: otherwise, he is not really aware of what he is doing.

Look back through the 100-plus years of climbing: the Matterhorn was climbed in 1865. Of the top climbers then, 50 percent died in the mountains.

And you can go all through mountaineering history. It's a miracle that Hillary and Tenzing, the two people who first reached the summit of Everest, both are alive. Normally of two summiters like them, one is dead. (Tenzing died in his bed in May 1982, at the age of 72.)

So why do people climb if the hazard is so great?

There are studies showing that in very dangerous situations, to the very limit this side of death, the body is able to make something like heroin that helps to put down all pain, to take away fear. It helps to be very concentrated, to see everything. If a man, a climber, gets this often, he has to get it again, like a man who is addicted to drugs.

The farmers in my village say that a certain man will always climb. He has to do it – he is addicted. They don't use the word "addicted" because they don't know what it is, but they say the same thing in simple words.

And there was a Swiss geologist who did a study in 1892 about the same thing. He studied maybe 80 people who fell while climbing, and they all said that after their falls they went to climb again; that with this fall, their real climbing began.

I am always surprised when relatively few people fall in the Himalaya each season. In recent years, quite a lot of the small expeditions have had accidents. I think many people know how to handle a big expedition, but it is much more dangerous if you have four members or two members only, and there is nothing between your first camp and your fifth bivouac.

I do not expect to see the number of acci-

dents in the Himalaya go down in coming years. The experienced people are getting older and will be going out of the climbing scene. The young people coming will have to learn. You can learn only with activity, and that's risky. And it will always be that way. The high peaks are high peaks, and they are not changing.

I agree with Doug Scott, the British climber, that oxygen at high altitudes is not a big help. It does give some help, but it is not a big help if you learn to acclimatise, to know

Above, Reinhold Messner, superstar of the mountains.

your body and everything about the mountains. But you need a long time to reach this point. The young climbers who are coming now say "Okay, we will do all this without oxygen." But they don't have the experience, that is the problem. Especially, to combine this with small expeditions is not so easy.

I think only the British know how to do it right. Doug Scott, Joe Tasker, Peter Boardman, they know exactly how it works, and they haven't died. They didn't succeed on K-2, but they went very high and they survived. They did Kangchenjunga on a small expedition, and they survived Everest in the winter. They know how to do it. (Editors note: Tasker and Boardman died on the northeast ridge of Everest almost as this interview was being conducted in late May, 1982.)

John Roskelley (American climber) knows how to do it; he showed that on Makalu. Then Peter Habeler and I learned to do it, and we succeeded on Everest. There is nobody else who knows how to survive at high altitudes without (artificial) oxygen.

Mountain Motives: The motivations for climbing are as different as climbers are. There are many motivations. There is also the name – I will be the first to do this and the first to do that. That's also part of climbing. Nobody speaks about it, but it's there. On the other hand, I don't think it's the most important motivation; because if someone is in a difficult situation and needs help, it breaks down.

I have found that I cannot work for a whole year without using my body and going to the limit of my abilities.

Finding out something about myself comes automatically now. In the last few years, I have got more experience in feeling my inner self and listening to it. I am quite sure that only in this way – under extreme conditions – can we go deeper into the self, as scientists are doing.

On my last expedition to Kangchenjunga (in May 1982), I found out two important things. First, I learned in dreams during the climb and afterwards – and this is true only for climbs of mountains higher than 8,000 meters – the whole dream world changes for a while.

And second, I found that you see certain things between dreaming and not dreaming, because you don't really sleep. They re-

minded me of *mandalas*; you don't see totally different pictures, but things are round and in the same form. I'm quite sure that many *lamas* have visions from high altitudes, because the *mandala* is a vision.

In the last camp near the summit, I had a very strange vision of all the human parts I am made of. It is very difficult to keep the vision, but I know that I could see a round picture with many pictures inside – not only of my body, but of my whole being. There was a lot of what my life has been, what I did these last years, like seeing my life and my body and my soul and my feelings inside a *mandala*. But I was not even sure if it was only mine or generally human, yours or anybody's, just a human being's. It was very, very strange.

So I will continue to subject myself to these extreme conditions. Maybe I have done more high-altitude expeditions than anybody else in the last ten years because I can afford it, I have the time, I am quite free. Not so many climbers are free to do it.

I have a chance to climb all of the fourteen 8,000 meter mountains in the world. I always thought that if I succeeded on Kangchenjunga, as I did, the chances would be quite good. Had I failed, I would have forgotten the idea, because I could not go back a second time to Kangchenjunga or Makalu or Lhotse.

I will never use oxygen; Kangchenjunga was the highest I had left to climb. Makalu is not so easy; I'm getting older, and it's high. Lhotse is not so difficult on the normal route. As for Dhaulagiri and Annapurna, it's no problem. They are lower, and I can always do them later.

So I am thinking about it again. But I am not in a hurry. I would be very happy if I could finish in Pakistan, finish Broad Peak and Gasherbrum II. (He was successful on both in a period of 10 days in July and August 1982.)

And then there is Cho Oyu in winter. Winter is harder and it is the only season in which I have no experience in the Himalaya. (He failed in his winter ascent of Cho Oyu in 1982.)

Cho Oyu is quite good because it's a south face, so the wind coming from the northwest should not hit us so hard. But from the technical side it is surely less difficult than Kangchenjunga.

YAKS: LIFE SUPPORT SYSTEMS

Ask people from practically anywhere in the world which animal they associate with the Himalaya and the chances are that the yak will come in a very close second after the yeti. The answer may be determined less by the prosaic concerns of pastoral economy than the aura of the mythological; but the fact is that for mountain peoples the yak beats the yeti hands-down on both counts. Not only do yaks provide food, clothing, domestic artifacts, shelter and transport, but they also occupy a far more significant place than the abominable snowman in Tibetan religious and imaginative life.

The Tibetan term for the animal is itself revealing. The word *yak* in Tibetan (but not in its more general English usage) denotes only the bull of the species while the cow is referred to as *dri* (or *nak* among some groups such as the Sherpas); the usual collective expression for yaks is *nor*. The primary meaning of *nor* is 'material wealth,' perhaps recalling the original English synonymity between "cattle" and "chattels." Yaks are movable goods par excellence.

Yaks and cattle are frequently interbred, the preferred combination being of bull cattle with cow yaks. The offspring, which are known as *dzo* (*dzomo* for the female) have certain advantages over yaks: they are more tractable when it comes to performing tasks such as ploughing. They also have a lower altitudinal range, and their milk yield is more than double that of yaks. Male crossbreeds, like mules, are always sterile, but the cows may be bred with yaks or cattle to produce generations of bovine cocktails, each with a distinct name according to the constitution of its ancestry.

A well known Nepalese folk-tale establishes a common ancestry between yaks and their more distant cousins, the buffaloes. Look at a water-buffalo: contrary to the groundward incline of the yak's neck the buffalo holds its head well up, parallel to the ground. The reason, as we might well expect,

has nothing to do with adaptation to a watery environment. Rather...Once upon a time (goes one of several variants of the tale) the yak and his brother the buffalo ran out of salt in their lowland abode. "Lend me your coat and I'll go up to the highlands and bring some down," said the yak, and off he went. But he never returned. He developed a stoop to gaze down at his homeland from his Himalayan heights, while the hairless buffalo eternally looks upward, still awaiting his brother's return.

Although the yak occupies much the same place in Tibetan life as humped Zebu cattle did in the pastoral civilization of the Indo-Aryans, the Tibetans' appreciation of their indigenous bovine never toppled over into worship. Yaks are eaten without qualms and with much relish. Killing the animals is slightly more problematic because of the Buddhist reluctance to take life, but Tibetans are nothing if not inventive. There are many cliffs off which careless animals can fall to their deaths. Yaks are not careless, but fatal errors can be encouraged. In the absence of lethal precipices, a blacksmith or some other indigent is usually willing to take on himself

Left, yaks carry double the load of a person and work with treks and expeditions. **Right**, yak caravan crosses the Kagmara pass at 5,000 meters (16,700 feet) in Dolpo.

the sin of slaughter in exchange for a portion of *digsha*, literally "sin-meat." Nothing is wasted. Even the horns are used, with the tips cut off to funnel blood and chopped entrails into the intestines as sausages. The head is often dried and eaten as a festive dish during the New Year festival, while the horns, attached by a part of the skull, may be used to adorn doorways and rooftops as a deterrent against the demons of rocks and air.

Yaks are perfectly adapted to high altitudes, and function best between 3,000 and 7,000 meters (10,000 and 20,000 feet). Originally domesticated from the *drong*, the wild ancestor, which has now become rare in Tibet in response to automatic weapons and

ately wintry conditions: they can obtain their water requirements by eating frozen snow and can dig down to eat the grass beneath, even when it is buried a yard deep. Nor are they averse to travelling. Yaks have been the main form of transport in trans-Himalayan trade, especially in the long-distance commerce in salt from the lakes of the northern plateau to southerly markets. Nepal is scored with such salt-routes, the best known being the Kali Gandaki valley, where salt was brought through Mustang to Tukche and exchanged against lowland grain.

Dairy products probably head the list of the yak's bounties. Yak-milk contains about twice as much fat as that of lowland cattle,

unchecked hunting. These animals are huge – a bull may stand up to six feet at the shoulder and weigh almost a ton. They also have a nervous temperament and very large horns, and evidently had to be bred down to more manageable proportions. The largest domestic yaks rarely exceed half a ton in weight, and most are considerably smaller.

Pastoral patterns accord with the yak's natural inclination to follow the receding snow up to the high grasslands in warmer weather and to retreat to permanent settlements (or, in the case of nomads, to lower encampments) at the onset of winter. Not that yaks are especially bothered by moder-

and has a rich, golden appearance. Fresh milk is rarely drunk but is subjected to processing. Yogurt is a favourite product. Butter is also extracted by churning the milk either in a wooden cylinder with a long-handled piston, similar to the smaller *jadong* used for mixing buttered tea. In parts of southern Tibet, the milk is churned in an earthernware vessel which is rocked to and fro on a fulcrum made from the skull of a long-horned yak or a blue sheep. The butter is consumed mainly in tea or as a lubricant for *tsampa*, but is also smeared liberally on faces and heads as protection against the desiccating atmosphere. Butter is one of the principal offerings by the faithful to monasteries, where it is used to fuel votive lamps and to make religious sculptures of sometimes exquisite complexity. The residual buttermilk is boiled and the accumulated solids skimmed off and eaten as a kind of low-fat cheese by the Sherpas. The soft cheese is often cut into cubes or squeezed through the fingers as strips and then dried. The resulting *churpi* is delicious if eaten within a few days, but beyond that (and *churpi* keeps indefinitely) the effort of consuming the the hard, dried cheese is daunting. *Churpi* should not be confused with the wheels of eminently edible yak-cheese that are sold in the Kathmandu bazaar. This is made by Tibetan refu-

hair keeps the structure waterproof. Yak-hair tents are also considerably warmer and more durable than canvas, which are quickly shredded by the terrible winter winds.

The yak's tail is an impressive bush that has long been valued in midland Nepal for such devices as royal flywhisks (these were even featured on certain coins of Kathmandu's Malla period) and healing aids for Nepalese shamans. The possessed shaman may brandish them while dancing or in some cases plunge them into boiling water before whipping the illness out of the unfortunate patient.

The soft wool beneath the hair is spun into yarn for clothing or felted to make boots.

gees according to a Swiss recipe.

The most obvious adaptation of yaks to their brisk environment is their fur, which may grow as long as two feet on their flanks, shoulders and thighs. This longer, coarser hair is used for making ropes, slings, sacks and rough blankets. It also provides the raw material for the famous black tents of the Tibetan nomads. The weave allows smoke to escape and light to enter, while the oil on the

Left, yaks and *dzos* are valued in the highlands for their milk and cheese. **Above**, impervious to cold weather, life at altitude would be impossible without yak support.

Whereas some communities shear yaks with razors, the more usual practice is simply to pull the fur out by the handful.

A recurring theme in Himalayan mythology is the identity of clans and sub-tribes based on parts of a yak's body. These myths typically relate the story of a yak-hunt after which the carcass is divided up among those present, and their future lineages subsequently named and defined according to the cut of the animal they receive.

Yaks occasionally take on a more obviously divine character when, in other myths, they descend from heaven as messengers of the gods.

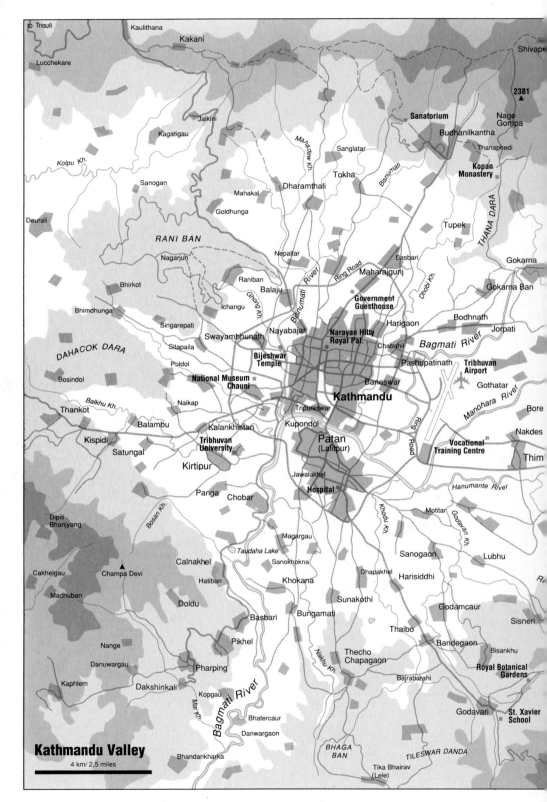

Kathmandu Valley

4 km/ 2,5 miles

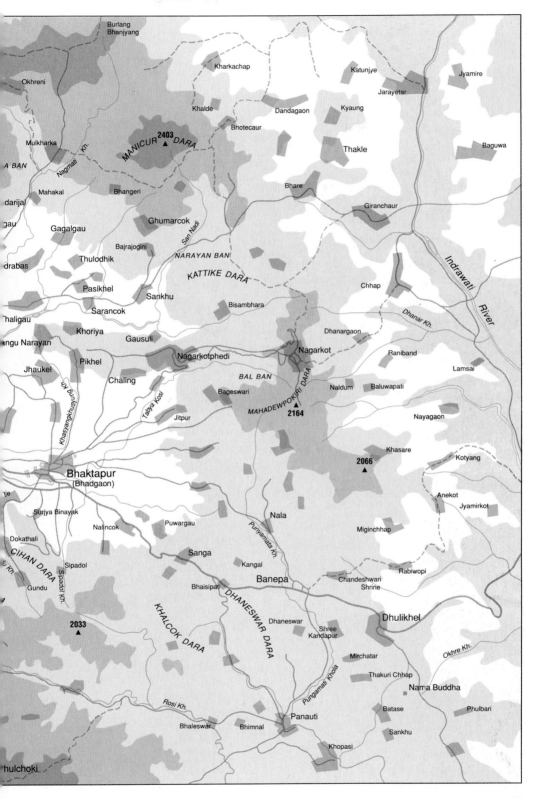

Burlang
Bhanjyang

Okhreni

Kharkachap

Katunjye

Jyamire

Jarayetar

Khalde

Dandagaon

Kyaung

Bhotecaur

MANICUR 2403 DARA

Thakle

Baguwa

A BAN

Mulkharka

Nagmati Kh.

darijal

Mahakal

Bhangeri

Bhare

gau

Gagalgau

Ghumarcok

Giranchaur

Sali Nadi

Bajrajogini

NARAYAN BAN

drabas

Thulodhik

Chhap

KATTIKE DARA

Pasikhel

Sankhu

Bisambhara

Dhanar Kh.

'haligau

Sarancok

Dhanargaon

ngu Narayan

Khoriya

Gausuli

Raniband

Indrawati River

Jhaukel

Pikhel

Nagarkotphedi

Nagarkot

Lamsai

Chaling

BAL BAN

Khasyangkhusyang Kh.

Tabya Kosi

Bageswari

MAHADEWPOKIRI DARA

Naldum

Baluwapati

Jitpur

2164

Nayagaon

Khasare

Kotyang

2066

Bhaktapur
(Bhadgaon)

Anekot

Jyamirkot

nje

Surjya Binayak

Nala

Dokathali

Nalincok

Puwargau

Miginchhap

CIHAN DARA

Sipadol

Sanga

Kangal

Rabiwopi

Kh.

Gundu

Bhaisipati

Banepa

Chandeshwari
Shrine

Dhulikhel

2033

KHALCOK DARA

DHANESWAR DARA

Dhaneswar

Shree
Kandapur

Mirchatar

Okhre Kh.

Thakuri Chhap

Nama Buddha

Pungamati Khola

Rosi Kh.

Batase

Phulbari

Bhaleswar

Bhimnal

Panauti

Sankhu

Khopasi

hulchoki

199

KATHMANDU

The founding of Kathmandu, the largest city of Nepal and the nation's capital, is estimated to have taken place during the Licchavi period, beginning about 300 A.D. Recent archaeological excavations at Harigaon indicate even earlier settlements.

However, it was during the time of the Mallas that the three great cities of the Kathmandu Valley took the shape we know today. The splendours of the Durbar Squares of the Malla city states, Kathmandu, Patan and Bhaktapur, vied for artistic ascendency. Today they form the hub of the three cities, though the urban sprawl, clamouring traffic and increasing pollution are the modern legacy.

The centre of Kathmandu old city, and indeed from whence it derives its name, is the Kasthamandap or "House of Wood." This sizeable structure was built in the 12th century at the crossroads of two important trade routes and was used originally as a community centre for trade and barter. The city developed radially, the old Royal Palace and the Durbar Square being constructed soon afterwards.

With the unification of the Valley in the 14th century by King Jayasthiti Malla, Kathmandu was selected as his capital. Considerable expansion took place from this time, with the main activity focusing on the palace complex itself, which also served as the administrative headquarters. Nevertheless, the diagonal trade route running from the Kasthamandap through Asan Tole maintained its commercial importance as indeed it still does today as a thriving and busy bazaar.

The forest of temples that comprises the Durbar Square represents a style of architecture that generally changed very little throughout the centuries. Only a trained eye can differentiate between earlier and later artistry in traditional Nepalese buildings. When damaged by age or earthquakes, temples would customarily be replaced in the same form as the old building. King Prithvi Narayan Shah, the founder of modern Nepal and the founder of the Shah dynasty which conquered the Kathmandu Valley in 1769 from his home in Gorkha, was content to enhance the magnificent Malla buildings, richly decorated with the woodcarving, metalwork and gilding that was the envy of the region.

European Influence: It was not until the mid-19th century that dramatic changes in architecture occurred, with the introduction of European neo-classical styles by the Rana rulers. The contrast with the indigenous Nepalese architecture was striking. Jung Bahadur, the founder of the Rana regime, returned in 1850 from a visit to France and Queen Victoria in England with visions of grandeur.

Ladies were encouraged to adapt their styles to Victorian fashions and anything European was admired. The sumptuous Rana palaces of Jung Bahadur and his family numbered several hundred throughout the Valley. They

Left, Swayambhunath stupa. Right, exquisite metal work decorates the *torana* above the doorway to the temple of the Living Goddess.

boasted elaborate plasterwork, imposing columns and were entirely furnished from Europe. Many still survive though in a rather tarnished condition. Taken over by the government or private organisations for offices or schools, today they are mere shadows of their former grandeur.

The culmination of this architectural vogue was the palace of **Singha Durbar**, which now houses the parliament, Prime Minister's office and several ministries. A building of gigantic proportion and size, it consisted of 17 courtyards and as many as 1,700 rooms. It was built in only 11 months in 1901. Singha Durbar was reputed to be the largest palace in Asia, based on its vast number of rooms. In 1973 much of it was damaged by a mysterious fire but several courtyards were rebuilt and the imposing, white facade restored.

Expanding Kathmandu: Under the Ranas, the suburbs of Kathmandu began to expand and the traditional Newari concept of a tightly knit city preserving every square meter of precious arable land was lost. Western-style dwellings of concrete and glass were built on the outskirts of the city.

In the last decade Kathmandu's growing pains have multiplied considerably with explosive urbanisation. Increased industry and a population that numbers over 500,000 has led to widespread, indiscriminate "infilling" that threatens to change the very character of the city. Precious rice-growing land in being lost to brick factories and private houses are built on every available terrace. Very little land within the Ring Road is left undeveloped.

Because of the markedly different styles of planning, Kathmandu is divided into two quite distinct parts. The **Tundhikhel**, the long open expanse of grassland used as the central parade ground and meeting place, separates the old medieval city to the west from the expanding eastern part with its mushrooming modern buildings. Traffic flows clockwise around the Tundhikhel. The southern end is marked by the **Martyr's Memorial** and the landmark

Singha Durbar is now the home of parliament and government ministries.

202

of **Bhimsen's Tower**. At the northern end is the **Rani Pokhari**, a tank with a small white shrine in the centre, originally built by Pratap Malla's queen in memory of their son.

Kantipath or **King's Way** continues the division. It runs north-south, parallel to the premier office street of **Durbar Marg**, at the north end of which is the modern **Narayan Hitty Royal Palace** in which the royal family lives today. Rows of flag poles bear the world's only non-rectangular flag: Nepal's flag is two superimposed red triangles with white sun and moon emblems. Durbar Marg is the main artery of the modern commercial part of town with its banks, travel agencies, airline offices and restaurants.

The street called **Lazimpat**, which is a district of embassies, becomes **Maharajgunj**, and runs due north up to the **Ring Road** which, as might be expected, circles the cities of Kathmandu and Patan.

Kathmandu still retains a rural atmosphere, even in downtown areas with

their veneer of sophistication. A small herd of goats may crowd the pavement and cows, seemingly aware of their sacred status, ruminate contentedly in the middle of the road. It is a worse offence to kill a cow in Hindu Nepal than to murder a person.

New Road: The old city of Kathmandu has remained intact through the centuries, except for **New Road**, so-called as it was rebuilt after the major earthquake of 1934. This wide street runs west from the Tundhikhel, where an arch spans the road adjacent to the Royal Nepal Airlines Building, notable for the bronze yeti sculpture bearing a tray.

Correctly called Juddha Sadak, this vital commercial axis is the paradise of the new consumer society that has flourished since Nepal was opened to the West. Electrical goods, imported clothes, videos to rent, films, drugs and jewels are all available here. Half way up on the left, shoeshine boys congregate beneath a spreading *pipal* tree. At the statue of Juddha Shamsher Rana, under whose direction the street was

Kasthaman–dap, the centre of Kathmandu, is said to have been made from a single tree trunk.

built, opposite the Crystal Hotel, a supermarket boasts the only escalator in the Valley.

The 20th century image is only skin-deep. Narrow, paved side-lanes thrust between rows of wall-to-wall traditional houses. Here there are a few dimly lit tea-shops and only the occasional concrete house to disrupt the medieval symmetry. These alleys end in squares with corner *patis*, central *chaityas* and occasional shrines.

The first lane off to the left after the statue is **Freak Street**, the famous 1960s haunt of the long-haired hippies. Today the "world-travellers" favour the more congenial and inconspicuous lake at Pokhara as their hangout, or the thriving lodges and restaurants of Thamel and Chetrapati, in the northern part of the old city. The hippies have long since gone. King Birendra's coronation in 1975 initially encouraged their departure and today's visa laws discourage dalliance.

The open brick platform at the top of New Road on the left is **Basantapur**, formerly a vegetable market and before that the home of the royal elephants. The palace looms on the right and the graceful temple silhouettes beckon visitors into the **Kathmandu Durbar Square**.

The Living Goddess: The **Kumari Bahal**, the House of the Living Goddess, is the mid-18th century stucco temple on the left with intricately carved windows. Lions flank the doorway and the woodcarving in the inner courtyard, where the *kumari* or living goddess herself may be glimpsed, is even more remarkable.

The *kumari* is considered to be the incarnation of the "virgin goddess." Stories of her origins vary, but this particular *kumari* is known as the Royal Kumari as she is worshipped by the King and to distinguish her from others in the Valley. Except for the religious festival of Indrajatra she never leaves her *bahal*, and then she is escorted in a suitably splendid procession in a flower-bedecked chariot, as her feet must not touch the ground.

The White Bhairav in Kathmandu's Durbar Square.

The living goddess is always chosen from a selection of girls four or five years of age, all belonging to the Sakya clan of Newari goldsmiths and silversmiths. The *kumari's* body must be flawless and must satisfy 32 specified, distinctive signs. After suffering a number of tests, she confirms her selection to the attendant priests by choosing the clothing and ornaments of the previous *kumari* from among a large collection of similar items. Astrologers must be assured that her horoscope is in harmony with that of the King, and then she is settled into the *bahal* which becomes her home until she reaches puberty or otherwise loses blood, as from a small wound.

When the term of the *kumari* comes to an end, the girl leaves the temple richly-endowed and free to marry. Recent *kumaris* have returned to normal lives, though there is an unhappy tradition that the ex-goddess brings bad luck to a household and also early death to her husband.

The Durbar Square: As you leave the *bahal* of the *kumari*, the **Temple of Narayan** is on your immediate left. The triple-roofed structure on a five-tiered plinth was built in 1670 and provides an excellent vantage point during festivals. On ordinary days the plinths are thronged with traders hawking their wares, farmers resting with their burdens and people chatting or simply watching and enjoying the atmosphere. There are more than 50 temples and monuments in this most historic of the three Durbar Squares, and plenty of activity.

Here in the square, and all along the bazaar that was an ancient trade route to Tibet, is the heart of old Kathmandu. Although the square will draw you eastward, reverse your direction and enjoy the most complete view of the Durbar Square from its western end. Walk into the beginning of the small street called the **Maru Tole** and here you will find the famed **Kasthamandap**, the legendary "House of Wood" which represents the very centre of the city.

One of the oldest buildings in the

Tibetan prayer wheels and artifacts for sale in the streets.

Valley it dates from the 12th century and supposedly gave Kathmandu its name. The Kasthamandap was originally a community centre, and was later turned into a temple dedicated to Gorakhnath. The god sits in the centre of the platform in a wooden enclosure. A pair of bronze lions guard the entrance and the first-floor cornice depicts Hindu epics.

Hidden behind the Kasthamandap is the small but very important golden **Ashok Binayak** shrine, known as the Maru Ganesh. There is a constant flow of worshippers here offering devotions to the obliging elephant-headed god. Particularly those departing on a journey will pay a visit to ensure a safe journey.

Returning to the square, there is a **Shiva Temple** on the left, with three roofs on a nine-step plinth. As you leave this part of the square note the **Shiva-Parvati Temple House** on the left. The deified couple, carved in wood and crudely painted with great charm, gazes benignly down from the centre window

of the upper balcony.

A statue of **King Pratap Malla** is set on a stone column at the entrance of the second part of the square. He faces the inner sanctum of his private prayer room on the third floor of the **Degu Taleju Temple** dedicated to the royal deity. Opposite the entrance to the Hanuman Dhoka Durbar stands the **Krishna Mandir**, a small octagonal temple. On the right a large wooden lattice screen hides the huge gilded face of the **Seto Bairav**, a fierce figure who is revealed only during the Indrajatra festival in August-September. At that time he is showered with rice and flowers and *chhang* (rice beer) flows out of his mouth, poured from a tank above to refresh the crowd.

Hanuman Dhoka Durbar: Straight ahead is the impressive entrance to the **Hanuman Dhoka Durbar**, the old Royal Palace and the former seat of power. It is flanked by a 1672 statue of the monkey-god Hanuman, smeared with red paste and shaded by an umbrella. The actual palace gate is colourfully painted and guarded by soldiers in the old black and white Malla uniforms. On the immediate left as you enter is the sculpture of Narsingh, an incarnation of Vishnu as a man-lion tearing apart the demon Hiranya-Kashipu.

The first courtyard is the **Nasal Chowk** where important royal ceremonies and festivals take place, including the coronations. *Nasal* means "the dancing one." The north end of the courtyard is an arched gallery with portraits of the modern Shah dynasty. In the corner are the five round roofs of the five-faced **Pancha Mukhi Hanuman**.

The Hanuman Dhoka palace is a series of 14 courtyards whose main structure was built by the Mallas though its origins are Licchavi. The superb wood-carvings for which the palace is renowned testify to their artistry. The construction began in the north with the two small courtyards built for King Pratap Malla in the 16th century, the **Mohan Chowk** and **Sundari Chowk**, and progressed south.

King Prithvi Narayan Shah renovated and added to the palace complex after

Hindu religious offerings of flower petals, sacred threads and beads.

his conquest of the Valley in 1769. He is responsible for the nine-story **Basantapur Tower** and the smaller towers of **Kirtipur**, **Lalitpur** and **Bhaktapur**. All four are set around the **Lohan Chowk** and are said to have been contributed by citizens of the towns after which they are named. There are good views if you are permitted to climb up one of the towers with the entire city spread out below, ringed with the white mountains. Admire the erotic carvings on the struts of the Basantapur Tower.

After the Ranas came to power in 1846, further changes were made and the white, stucco western wing with the neo-classical facade was added. Today this houses the museum dedicated to King Tribhuvan, the present King's grandfather who regained power from the Rana rulers in 1951. The Hanuman Dhoka Durbar was extensively restored by a UNESCO programme prior to King Birendra's splendid coronation in 1975.

The Royal Deity: Returning to the square, there are more erotic carvings on the struts of the two-tiered 17th century **Jagannath Temple**, the oldest structure in this area. Next to it is the **Gopinath Mandir** with three roofs and a three-stepped plinth.

The terrifying **Black Bhairav** relief is a masterpiece, highly admired and revered as a form of Shiva. This fierce god wears a garland of skulls, has three pairs of arms and tramples a corpse, the symbol of human ignorance. He is never without offerings of the faithful, placed in his skull bowl. The Black Bhairav is believed to punish anyone who tells lies in front of him by causing them to bleed to death.

This northeastern end of the Durbar Square is dominated by the magnificent three-tiered gilded **Taleju Temple**, built on a huge stepped platform and dedicated to the important royal deity, the goddess **Taleju Bhawani**. The walled precinct is considered so sacred that it is off-limits to all but the King and certain priests; ordinary Hindus are allowed access only once a year during

Moslem shopkeeper tends his stall in the bead market of Indrachowk.

the Durga Puja of the Dasain festival.

The Taleju Bhawani is a South Indian goddess who was brought to Nepal in the 14th century and enshrined as the ruling family's special deity. She became a symbol of legitimacy for the sovereign and shrines to her were also erected in Bhaktapur and Patan. The Kathmandu Taleju Temple was built in 1562 by King Mahendra Malla and according to legend, human sacrifices used to be performed here until the goddess became displeased with such practices. Human sacrifices were officially outlawed in Nepal in 1780.

At the northwestern end of Durbar Square is an open courtyard called the **Kot** or "armoury." It is now part of police quarters and army barracks and whilst is has little aesthetic appeal, it has great historical significance. This is the site of the terrible "Kot Massacre" in which the young army officer Jung Bahadur Rana murdered almost all the Nepal aristocracy and his political rivals, enabling him to establish the Rana regime in 1846. This regime lasted 105 years until 1951.

Bustling Bazaars: Leaving the Durbar Square, a *garuda* statue lies half buried in the street. Cast a glance at the little **Tarana Devi Mandir** hidden behind the Taleju Temple before getting swallowed up in the activity and distractions of the **Makhan Tole** bazaar. There are many temples and courtyards of interest and it is worth detouring as you explore the old bazaar areas on foot.

Indra Chowk is a junction where six streets meet and the gilded griffins rearing into the street from the first-floor shrine to **Akash Bhairav** are particularly distinctive. This area traditionally sells blankets and textiles, including the soft wool shawls known as *pashmina*. It is particularly animated and picturesque. Tucked behind an old building through a narrow entrance is the glittering magic of the *pote* **(bead) market**, where lengths of many colours can be combined as you wait.

Khel Tole, which is beyond Indra Chowk, is the oldest trading segment of the bazaar and there is constant coming-and-going of farmers, strollers, rickshaws and even cars forcing their way through the narrow lane. All manner of goods can be bought in the shops, ranging from shawls and saris to large copper pots for festivals.

White Machhendranath: Turn left at a small shrine and enter one of the most venerated shrines in the whole kingdom. The **Seto Machhendranath** is a beautiful structure standing in the middle of a monastic courtyard. Within the shrine is a form of Avalokiteshwara, known as Machhendra, the guardian deity of the Valley and the most compassionate of gods. This white *(seto)* god is pulled in a huge chariot through the streets of Kathmandu during the lively Seto Machhendra festival held annually in March-April.

The entrance to this famous temple is guarded by magnificent brass lions. Within the courtyard there is rich ornamentation and superb decoration, dating from the 17th century though with almost certainly earlier origins.

Asan Tole is the real heart of the old city. The traditional rice market and

Street vendor offers oranges from the Terai.

place to hire porters, this crossroads is thronged with people and also features several temples. Finally it emerges on Kanti Path, opposite Rani Pokhari. Beyond this fenced-in lake the solid white clock tower of the **Trichandra College** is visible, built by the Ranas. To the right is the open market and the wide expanse of the Tundhikhel.

World Travellers: To see more of the old city turn northwest from Indra Chowk. Keep north and you encounter several shrines, stupas and courtyards worth exploring. Note the "Toothache Temple" where sufferers transfer their pain by planting a nail around the tiny gilded image of **Vaisha Dev**, the god of toothache. Nearby dentists take a more worldly approach.

Nearby is the striking white Buddhist stupa of **Kathe Simbhu**, in the style of Swayambhunath. This is said to have been built as a convenience for those who are physically unable to climb up the steep steps to that hilltop shrine.

The narrow streets take on a distinctly Western air as you reach the tourist areas of **Chetrapati** and eventually **Thamel**. A more usual approach would be to drive to Thamel from **Keshar Mahal** at the top of Kanti Path or Durbar Marg. Across from the Narayan Hitty Royal Palace, the residence of the King and his family, the Keshar Mahal houses the Ministry of Education and a has a library which is open to the public and includes a fine collection of Rana hunting photographs.

Thamel and Chetrapati, favoured by world-travellers and cost-concious trekkers, features budget hotels, lodges and restaurants. Trekking equipment and *thangka* shops jostle for space with carpet and clothes stalls. This is where to rent mountain bikes or ordinary bicycles and is the "heart of the action" for those in search of a good deal.

It is a pleasant walk or bicycle ride from here to the great stupa of Swayambhunath and the **National Museum** and its neighbour, the **Natural History Museum** at Chauni, though the one-way systems preclude driving from this access.

Sacred cows mingle with traffic and children in the Kathmandu bazaar.

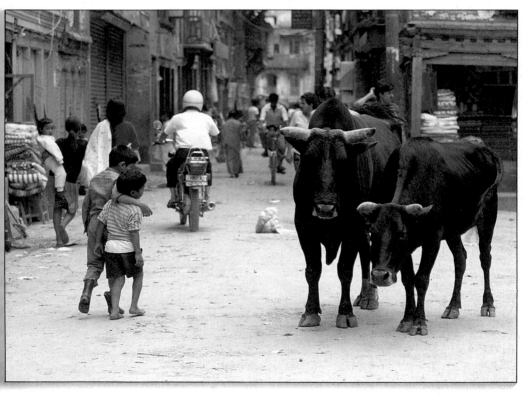

PATAN

Patan is located on a plateau above the Bagmati River south of Kathmandu. Known as the centre of fine arts and for the superb craftsmanship of its artisans, Patan is also called **Lalitpur**, "the beautiful city."

Essentially a Buddhist city, Patan is said to have been founded by Emperor Ashoka in the 3rd century B.C. although no historical proof of this exists. Four main roads radiate from the Durbar Square to the four **Ashoka stupas**, brick and grass mounds marking the boundaries of the city, more evocative for their historical relevance than their architectural interest.

Historic inscriptions establish Patan as an important town from early times. **Mangal Bazaar**, an area adjoining the Durbar Square, might have been the site of King Manadeva's palace in the 5th century. The city's great building period took place under the Mallas from the 16th to 18th centuries. Most of the monuments to be seen today were built or rebuilt at that time.

With no fewer that 136 *bahals* or courtyards and 55 major temples, Patan is really the cradle of arts and architecture of the Valley, a great centre both of the Newari Buddhist religion and of traditional arts and crafts. The Patan Durbar Square has been acclaimed as one of the finest urban streetscapes in the world.

The Royal Palace: The ancient north-south and east-west access roads divide Patan neatly into four geographic sections, which meet at the **Durbar Square** and **Royal Palace** complex. A spectacular example of Newari architecture and planning, the Royal Palace with its walled gardens on the eastern side of the square are faced by a dozen free-standing temples of various sizes and styles. Residential houses occupy the other three sides of the square.

The palace consists of three main *chowks* or courtyards which open onto the square. The most southern, smaller

The Taleju temple roof soars above other monuments.

courtyard is the **Sundari Chowk** which has in its centre a masterpiece of stone architecture and carving, the sunken royal bath called **Tusha Hiti**. Created around 1670, the walls of the bath are decorated with a double row of statuettes representing the eight Ashta Matrikas, the eight Bhairavs and the eight Nagas. Many of these are now missing. Two stone snakes or *nagas* girdle the top of the basin into which the water flows through a conch-shaped stone spout covered with gilded metal.

The three-story buildings around the *chowk* contain a corner temple, and have wonderfully carved windows and grilles. Stone images of Ganesh, Hanuman and Narsingh guard the outside of this courtyard. The central window above the entrance is of gilded metal and is flanked by two windows of carved ivory.

Krishna Jatra lights the Krishna Mandir in Patan Durbar Square.

The oldest courtyard is the central **Mul Chowk**, built in 1666 for Srinivasa Malla. The low two-story residence of the Patan royal family encloses a large courtyard with a small gilded central shrine, the **Bidya Mandir**. The **Shrine of Taleju** is guarded by two fine repousse brass images of Ganga on a tortoise and Jamuna on a mythical crocodile. On the roof over the shrine is a three-tiered square structure.

Towering over this part of the palace, in the northeast corner of the Mul Chowk is the triple-roofed octagonal tower of the **Taleju Bhawani Temple**, built in about 1666 and housing the royal deity.

Shiva and Parvati crown the much-admired **"Golden Gate"** leading to the third, northern courtyard, the **Mani Keshab Narayan Chowk**. It was completed in 1734 after 60 years of construction and has been recently extensively restored.

Between it and the central *chowk* is the temple of **Degu Talle**, the personal deity of the Malla kings. Surmounted with a four-roof tower and originally built in 1640, the kings used to perform their sacred Tantric rites here.

Krishna Mandir: Facing the Sundari Chowk is the **Krishna Temple**, a stone

shikhara-style building damaged in the 1988 earthquake. To the west is the **Bhai Dega** with a Shiva *lingum* within. To the north a huge bell hangs between two pillars and nearby is the three roofed 17th century **Hari Shankar Temple**, with its carved roof struts and elephants. Just north, a gilded statue of **King Siddhi Narsingh** prays on the top of his elegant pillar. The *shikhara* behind him dates from 1590. Beyond a small Narayan temple is probably the oldest surviving temple in the square – a two-tiered brick structure built for the god **Char Narayan** in 1565.

Opposite the northern courtyard of the palace is the remarkable **Krishna Mandir**, one of the most exquisite buildings in the Valley. It shows the influence of Moghul architecture from India and the first two stories are a series of pavilions in smooth black stone. A slender *shikhara* emerges from the top and Hindu epics are depicted in stone with explanations engraved in Newari.

The main divinity was installed in 1637 and a statue of Garuda on a high pole faces this elegant temple.

The next temple is the **Bishwa Nath Mandir**, double-roofed and profusely carved and decorated, its steps flanked by two elephants. The last temple in the row is the prosperous and highly-venerated **Bhimsen Mandir** dedicated to Bhimsen, the god of traders, and decorated in silver and gold. This brick structure was erected in the late 17th century but the marble facade dates from Rana times. At the corner of the northern *chowk* of the palace is the lotus-shaped, deeply recessed **Manga Hiti** with three lovely carved water spouts in the shape of crocodile heads.

Northern Patan: Leaving the wonders of Patan Durbar Square is a maze of fascinating small streets, rich in monuments of great interest. Patan is renowned for its *bahals*, two story Newari Buddhist monasteries and the less elaborate *bahils*. The most renowned of these is the marvellous **Kwa Bahal**, better known as the **"Golden Temple,"** just north of the Durbar Square. This is an ancient sanctuary and legend con-

Mother and child at Patan.

nects its origins with a 12th century queen.

This actively patronised monastery is a large, rectangular building with three roofs and a facade richly embossed with gilded copper. The entrance is guarded by a pair of temple lions. Within the shrine are many images and some early bronzes, and a gilded frieze depicts the life of the Buddha. The metalwork and gilding shows great detail and craftsmanship and the small central shrine is lavishly embellished.

Further north the towering **Kumbeshwar Temple** dominates this whole area of rural streets and houses. The Kumbeshwar, the Nyatapola in Bhaktapur and Panch Mukhi Hanuman in Hanuman Dhoka are the only three temples in the Valley with five roofs.

Founded in 1392, the Kumbeshwar is also the oldest existing temple in Patan. Its spacious precincts are scattered with early and rare sculptures and its struts, cornices and door frame are intricately carved. Two ponds in the courtyard are believed to be fed from the holy Go-

sainkund Lake, several days' walk north of Kathmandu Valley. Dedicated to Shiva, the Kumbeshwar is the focus of several colourful festivals. During the Janai Purnima in July-August, thousands of pilgrims pay homage to a silver and gold *lingum* that is placed in the middle of the tanks.

Southern Patan: Down a narrow street southwest of the Durbar Square, it is not hard to find the much-visited architectural masterpiece, the **Maha Bauda** or "Temple of the Thousand Buddhas." The road is well marked down a lane to the right, and curio shops line the route.

Maha Bauda stands in a cramped courtyard and is a tall *shikhara* structure entirely covered by terra-cotta plaques depicting the Buddha. The best view is from the roof terrace of an adjacent house. Built at the end of the 16th century, the monument was damaged and rebuilt after the 1934 earthquake. The spareparts "left over" from the restoration were used to construct the smaller *shikhara*. Farther south is another famous monastery, the **Uku Bahal**, with

The goddess Jamuna flanks a palace doorway.

gilded roofs and animal sculptures.

Return to the main axis and turn west to reach the three-story **Rato Machhendranath Temple**. Here is the Patan home of the popular Tantric god Avalokiteshwara in the form of the Red (*Rato*) Machhendra. Venerated as Shiva by Hindus, he is worshipped by all as the guardian of the Valley and the god of rain and plenty.

The present temple dates from 1673 and a row of prayer wheels lines the base. Under the metal roofs, the struts show the various tortures of condemned souls in hell and inside various animals on pillars face the main alter.

The Rato Machhendra is taken out of his shrine every year and paraded through the streets of Patan in a chariot for several weeks of processions during the summer months. This is Patan's biggest festival, designed to ensure good monsoon rain. It culminates in the Bhoto Jatra festival at Jawalakhel, southwest suburb of Patan, when the King presides and the sacred bejewelled waistcoat (*bhoto*) of the serpent king is displayed,

and the chariot dismantled.

However, every 12 years the huge chariot has to be dragged all the way to Bungamati (see page 234), a village six kilometers (four miles) south of Patan where the Rato Machhendra deity spends the winter months. This is a major undertaking and progress is slow over the uneven road, punctuated with prayers and offerings. Normally the deity is carried in a small palanquin to his winter quarters, a tradition dating from the late 16th century.

Jawalakhel, home of the Kathmandu **Zoo**, is one of the centres of the carpet industry and the best place to select a handmade Tibetan carpet from the many displayed in the rows of shops. Watch them being woven in the **Tibetan Refugee Camp**, three or four persons at each loom weaving traditional designs, chatting and singing. This Camp was first established in the 1960s to promote a handicraft that has now grown to become Nepal's biggest export and the largest employer in the Kathmandu Valley.

The sacred bejewelled waistcoat is displayed on the chariot of Rato Machhendra at Patan's biggest festival.

KIRTIPUR

South of Patan various roads and trails link settlements and sacred sites to the one-time capital. There is a trail to Lele via Chapagaon, a road to Pharping and Dakshinkali, and another through pretty country villages to the botanical gardens at Godavari. A lane leads east to the forgotten villages of **Sanagaon** and **Lubhu**. The history of these settlements is linked to that of Patan. Most important of them all, however, is the rocky ridgetop city of **Kirtipur**, west of the Bagmati River.

Kirtipur is a magnificent exception to the usual Newari settlements that are built on plateaus. Perched on twin hillocks and clinging to a saddle about five kilometers (three miles) southwest of Kathmandu, Kirtipur has two satellite hamlets of **Panga** and **Nagaon**, located to the south.

First established as a kind of outpost of Patan in the 12th century, it became an independent kingdom and was the last stronghold of the Mallas, only falling to King Prithvi Narayan Shah in 1769, after a prolonged and terrible seige. After the conquest it is said the vengeful Gorkha ruler had the noses and lips of all the men of the town cut off, sparing only players of wind instruments. Remains of the fortified wall and part of the original 12 gates can still be seen.

Most of the 20,000 inhabitants of Kirtipur are farmers and merchants and some go daily to office jobs in Kathmandu. The nearby campus of the **Tribhuvban University** occupies portions of Kirtipur's former farmlands. The traditional occupation of spinning and weaving produces handloom fabric for sale in Kathmandu. The thud of the looms in the houses can be heard whilst walking down the narrow streets and children offer little dolls made from ends of fabric.

Kirtipur has a neglected feeling and age and decay has gnawed at many buildings. There are still some lovely woodcarvings on the multi-storied houses of the town. The brick-built homes are set on stepped terraces linked by steep paths. A long flight of steps leads up to Kirtipur from the Valley floor and a motorable road switchbacks part way up the hill.

The southern hill is surmounted by the **Chilanchu Vihar**, a central stupa surrounded by four smaller stupas at cardinal directions. The paved area of this former monastery is often used for drying crops. The higher northern hill is inhabited by Hindus who surround the **Kvath**. The approach up stone steps is flanked by a pair of fine stone elephants and the striking patchwork of the Valley and the mountains beyond.

In the middle of Kirtipur, where the two hills meet north of the tank, stands the famous **Bagh Bhairav Temple**. This three-roofed temple is enclosed within a courtyard and contains an image of Bhairav in his tiger form. The walls of the temple are decorated with shields and swords presented by the Newari troops after Prithvi Narayan Shah's conquest.

Gilded Ganesh.

BHAKTAPUR

Bhaktapur is said to have been founded in the shape of Vishnu's conch shell by King Ananda Malla in the 9th century. In fact the ancient city, also known as **Bhadgaon**, is a double S-shape and from a distance has a beautiful skyline of temples roofs with a backdrop of white peaks.

Its southern boundary is marked by the sacred **Hanumante River**.

Bhaktapur is a former capital of the Valley and was once a flourishing city on the trade route to Tibet. It has preserved its traditional character better than the other two cities, due to its more isolated location and the greater attraction of Kathmandu when the Valley was reunified by the Gorkha invasion of 1768. Bhaktapur, with its 150,000 inhabitants, is regarded today as a classic showcase of "medieval" Nepalese town life.

Bhaktapur is also the most self-con-tained and self-sufficient of the Valley's major settlements. Its own farmers supply food from the surrounding fields and the craftsmen of the city build and decorate the houses, carve their windows and restore the temples. Its people also have maintained their original traditions and the women still wear their unique red-edged black saris, called *patasi*.

Capable Thimi: Bhaktapur is 16 kilometers (10 miles) east of Kathmandu along a pleasant tree-lined road which leads to Banepa, Dhulikhel and eventually to the Chinese border. Industrial development is beginning to line the road. A more interesting rural route takes you through the pottery village of **Sano Thimi**, also known as **Nikosera**, and famous for its terracotta work, including delightful peacock and elephant flower-pots and imaginative, moulded candlesticks and ashtrays. The significant settlement of **Thimi**, a name that derives from *chhemi* meaning "capable people," is north of the road. Thimi is also known for its colourful

Nyatapola temple of Bhaktapur towers above the skyline.

painted masks and dolls.

The approach road from Kathmandu passes a grove of pine trees on a hillock and the north side of the **Siddha Pokhari**, a water tank that used to supply the city. Follow the tarmac road through narrow medieval streets to the **Bhaktapur Durbar Square**. This part of town was originally outside the city boundaries.

The early center of Bhaktapur was the eastern square, Tachupal Tole, around the Dattatraya Temple. There are indications that the town was fortified by the mid-15th century and during the 14th to 16th centuries, when Bhaktapur was capital of the Kathmandu Valley, the center moved west to Taumadi Tole. The Durbar Square only became integrated during the reign of King Bupathindra Malla around the beginning of the 17th century.

Bhaktapur Durbar Square: Entering the Durbar Square through the royal gate, the sparseness of the temples is immediately apparent, compared to the profusion in the Durbar Squares of Kath-

mandu and Patan. The devastating 1934 earthquake destroyed many of the highly decorated buildings of all shapes and sizes that once crowded the square. Legend claims there were 99 courtyards here, though this is hard to believe. Today by contrast the brick square has a pleasant, open feeling.

On the right are a pair of very fine stone statues representing **Ugrachandi Durga** with her 18 arms, and **Bhairav** with 12. The houses on the south side of the square are used for offices. Nearby is the **Rameshwar Temple** dedicated to Shiva and a brick *shikhara*-style temple dedicated to Durga with images of Hanuman and Narsingh. The most striking feature ahead of you as you enter the square is the exquisite gilded statue of the great **King Bupathindra Malla**, seated on a tall stone pillar, surveying the glories of the beautiful square that he created.

The Royal Palace: Bupathindra Malla is facing the superb **Sun Dhoka** or "Golden Gate" leading into the royal palace, generally considered the great-

Pottery items for sale in Thimi.

est single masterpiece of art in the Valley. Created in 1753 by Jaya Ranjit Malla, it is a monument to the skill and artistry of the craftsmen who produced it. In gilded copper the door frame illustrates many divinities and the gate itself, set in glazed brickwork, is capped with a gilded roof with finials of elephants and lions.

Standing back from the Sun Dhoka, what remains of the former **Royal Palace** can be seen, though it was much damaged in the 1934 earthquake. The 18th century "Palace of 55 Windows" is on the right built of brick with carved windows. To the left is the rebuilt white Rana section of the palace which now houses the **National Art Gallery** with its fine collection of *thangkas* and artworks. The entrance is flanked by Hanuman, the monkey god, and Narsingh, the man-lion.

Walk through the spectacular Sun Dhoka into the religious and ritual courtyards of the royal palace. Pass under a couple of low doorways across small courtyards and wind your way

around to the back where the elaborately carved entrance to the **Taleju Chowk** is on the left. This is as far as non-Hindu visitors may go as the two *chowks* of the Taleju and Kumari are sacrosanct. Try and persuade the guards to allow a glimpse into the courtyard and in particular note the **Taleju Godhouse** on the southern side with its rich carving and decoration.

In the far right-hand corner is the small doorway that leads to the **Kumari Chowk**. These two courtyards can be singled out as those most endowed with rare and precious artistic masterpieces, as well as representing two of the most holy shrines to be found anywhere in the Valley.

Beyond is the **Sundari Chowk**, the ritual bathing courtyard of the Bhaktapur kings and now occupied by the police. Unlike others, this one is no longer surrounded with buildings but the tank itself has some stone divinities and is unusually large. From the centre of the tank rises a magnificent *naga* or sacred serpent.

Although not complete, the Bhaktapur palace is a place to linger awhile and contemplate the beauties contained in what must have once been the most impressive of all the Durbar Squares in the Valley.

Pavilions and Pillars: Return to the Durbar Square. Ahead is the **Chaysiln Mandap**, an octagonal pavilion destroyed by the 1934 earthquake and entirely reconstructed from 19th century drawings as a donation by Chancellor Helmut Kohl of West Germany. Note the finest woodcarving available today and the interior steel girders, ensuring a longer life than the previous building. Great effort has gone into detecting and reassembling the original woodcarvings and a small exhibition explains the task of restoration of the Chaysiln Mandap.

Turn left to the eastern plaza and pass on the left a fine stone *shikhara* **Durga Temple** with interesting animal guardians. A two-story *dharmasala*, or rest house for pilgrims, frames this corner of the main square. Today the ground floor is full of shops selling *thangkas* and

The statue of King Bupathindra Malla sits serene over the Bhaktapur Durbar Square.

puppets. To the east is an unusual Buddhist monastery called **Tadhunchen Bahal** which opens onto the street beyond.

Reorient yourself by the pillar of Bupathindra and note the big bell that was erected in the 18th century. Next to the bell, the stone *shikhara* of **Batsala Durga** is a symphony of pillars and arches with many divinities represented by stone carvings. The *shikhara* is surmounted by copper pinnacles and wind bells. A sunken stone *hiti* or water fountain is behind.

Further on is the large, two-roofed **Pashupati Temple**, one of the oldest temples in the Valley dating from the 15th century. Beyond, a narrow lane, **Taumadi Tole**, lined with inviting shops and small restaurants, leads down to the lower square.

Two Great Shrines: Taumadi Square contains two great mystical shrines. The **Nyatapola Temple** is Nepal's tallest and stands more than 30 meters (98 feet). Carved wooden columns support five roofs and form a balcony around the sanctum. The temple is balanced superbly upon five receding square plinths. The steep central stairway is flanked by huge stone guardians. Each pair of guardians is believed to have ten times the strength of the pair on the plinth immediately below them. Thus the two famous Malla wrestlers at the bottom of the stairway are ten times as strong as ordinary people and the elephants ten times as strong as the wrestlers, and so on.

Power culminates in the Nyatapola's main deity, Siddhi Lakshmi, a Tantric goddess to whom the patron-king Bupathindra Malla dedicated the temple in 1702. Exactly 108 painted wooden struts supporting the roofs show the goddess in her different forms. People gather on the brick platforms surrounding the temple, exchanging views and trading goods. The huge steps, are periodically daubed with political slogans and are a perfect platform for political meetings.

The **Kasi Bishwanath Temple** is set at right angles to the Nyatapola and is a

The steps of the Nyatapola temple are guarded by mythical animals.

perfect architectural foil to its spire-like lines. The rectangular base rests directly onto the square and its three-tiered roof gives a massive, solid appearance. Dedicated to the god Bhairav, his awesome powers also counterbalance those of the Tantric goddess, portraying the Nepalese perception of the balance of terror.

The image of Bhairav is taken out for chariot processions across the town during the Bisket festival. It is hardly a foot high, and usually rests in a niche close to the ground, protected by a brass door through which offerings are thrust into the mysterious inner space of the temple. The real entrance to the Kasi Bishwanath is from behind, through the small **Betal Temple**.

Potters and Ghats: The Nyatapola Cafe pavilion opposite the Kasi Bishwanath is a pleasant place to overlook the square and watch the constant activity. A street behind winds its way west to the **pottery market**, where hundreds of pots dry in the open square. The huge potters' wheels are spinning all day long and women pound grain as the men mould the wet clay. Ganesh, the elephant-headed patron of potters, presides from his **Jeth Ganesh Temple**, originally donated by a potter in 1646.

Streets west out of the pottery market will take you through narrow lanes to several interesting temples, courtyards and *bahals*. A lane to the south leads downhill to the **Hanumante River** and the **Ram Ghat**, one of the bathing and cremation places serving the western part of the city.

From Taumadi Square, the steep flag-stoned lane merges directly into the **Khalna Tole**. This is the processional route taken by the chariots of Bhairav and his goddess Bhadrakali during the annual Bisket festival on their way to the **Chuping Ghat**. Thousands of people gather for this most boisterous of Valley festivals, which coincides with the New Year in April with the raising of a 25 meter (82 foot) *lingum* pole, decorated with banners and streamers.

The bridge across the Hanumante River was Nepal's traditional main

Left, popular shrine at Bhaktapur. **Right**, Bhaktapur's Jamuna goddess.

route to Tibet and the east. Many small temple-complexes, shrines and *patis* line the river and it is a pleasant country walk upstream to the confluence at the **Hanuman Ghat**. Further east is the **Maheshwari Temple**, dedicated to the goddess of that name.

This is the oldest part of Bhaktapur and the narrow lanes north of here are a maze of passages, inner courtyards and old houses. This was the area most damaged in the August 1988 earthquake, when several people of Bhaktapur lost their lives.

Dattatreya Square: This part of the city is called **Tachupal Tole** and **Dattatreya Square**, with its commanding **Dattatreya Temple**, was the former centre of ancient Bhaktapur. Reminiscent of the Kasthamandap in Kathmandu, the Dattatreya Temple was originally a community centre and dates from 1427. This is the only temple in the Valley dedicated to Dattatreya, who is worshipped by followers of both Shiva and Vishnu as well as Buddhists who consider the god to be a cousin of the Lord Buddha.

At the opposite end of the square is the two-story **Bhimsen Temple**, erected in 1605 in front of a deeply recessed *hiti* or water fountain.

This square was also the headquarters of the West German Bhaktapur Development Project which supervised the restoration of the city. Their offices were in the 1763 **Pujari Math** or "Priest's House" south of the Dattatreya Temple and now a woodcarving museum. Round the corner down a narrow lane is the much-acclaimed **Peacock Window**. On the north side of the Tachupal Tole is the little **Salan Ganesh**, erected in 1654 in a lavishly decorated temple.

The road east out of the square passes the **Nava Durga Shrine**, and leaves the city to join the main road past an army encampment to the hilltop village of Nagarkot. Southwest from Dattatreya Square runs the **Golmadi Tole**, a main street with shops and houses that leads directly to the Taumadi Square and the Durbar Square.

Quiet moment during a Bhaktapur festival.

BUDDHIST STUPAS

Ancient Swayambhunath: Atop a green hillock west of Kathmandu stands the great stupa of **Swayambhunath**, a site over 2,500 years old marking the point where the legendary patriarch Manjushri discovered the lotus of the ancient Valley lake. For centuries an important centre of Buddhist learning, the painted eyes of the Buddha gaze out from all four sides of this monument.

Constructed to specific rules each with a symbolic meaning, the stupa of Swayambhunath is a model of its kind. Its dazzling white hemispherical mound represents the four elements of earth, fire, air and water. The 13 gilded rings of the spire are the 13 degrees of knowledge and represent the ladder to *nirvana*, itself symbolized by the umbrella on top. The whole is hung with multi-coloured prayer flags whose every flutter releases holy prayers. The faithful circumambulate the stupa

Preceding pages: Tamang girls at Bodhnath. Left, All-**seeing eyes. Below, Swayambhunath bedecked for a festival.**

clockwise, turning the banks of prayer wheels and even prostrating full-length in reverence.

The pilgrim's approach to the shrine is through a wooded park up a steep flight of 300 stone steps, lined with stone sculptures of animals and birds, vehicles of the gods. Cars can drive part-way up the back side of the hill and park near one of the Tibetan monasteries. Legend relates how Manjushri had his hair cut at Swayambhunath, each hair becoming a tree, and the lice becoming monkeys.

Statues of the Buddha repose in richly decorated niches at the four cardinal points of the stupa. Statues of the goddesses Ganga and Jamuna, masterpieces of Newari bronze art, guard the eternal flame in a gilded cage behind the stupa. On the surrounding terrace are many *chaityas*, small stupas, two *shikhara*-style temples and a huge *vajra* (symbolic thunderbolt). An adjacent *gompa* (Tibetan monastery) conducts daily services in the light of flickering butter lamps.

Bodhnath's Beauty: The largest stupa in Nepal is **Bodhnath**, located on flat land in the east of the Valley and encircled by pastel-painted facades of houses. The huge white dome is surmounted by penetrating red, yellow and blue painted all-seeing eyes and is set on concentric, ascending terraces in the powerful pattern of a *mandala*. Around the base of this enormous and strikingly simple stupa is a ring of 108 images of the Buddha and 147 insets containing prayer wheels.

Poles are hung with prayer flags, renewed and blessed with fragrant juniper incense at the Losar Tibetan New Year festival in February-March. As hundreds of Tibetans gather in their best clothes and jewellery, a portrait of their spiritual leader, the Dalai Lama, is processed under silk umbrellas accompanied by the growls of the long horns. Masked dancing completes the celebrations on this most happy and picturesque day in the Valley.

Bodhnath shelters the largest community of the 12,000 Tibetans who have made Nepal their home. The many new

monasteries and the *Rinpoches* who reside here have established Bodhnath as one of the most flourishing centres of Tibetan Buddhism in the world.

Chabahil and Gorakhnath: There are a number of important Buddhist pilgrimage places in and around the Valley. One of the most evocative is **Namo Buddha** near Dhulikhel and one of the most scenic is the stupa on the top of **Nagarjun**, where Buddha was believed to have preached a sermon.

The ancient stupa of **Chabahil** is at a crossroads west of Bodhnath and marks an early Licchavi settlement. It is a more primitive stupa but has some early sculptures and *chaityas*.

Near Pharping, south east of Kathmandu, is a monastery and meditation center near the **Gorakhnath Cave**, for named for an ancient sage who meditated here and whose footprints are carved in stone. It is sacred to the great Tibetan saint, Guru Padma Sambhava, who is said to have introduced Buddhism to Tibet.

VISHNU TEMPLES

A god with a thousand names, Vishnu comes in various forms or incarnations. Part of the Hindu trinity of Brahma, Vishnu and Shiva, he fooled a demon by changing from dwarf to giant and encompassed in three strides the earth, the air and the heaven.

As the god Narayan he is most often depicted lying in the cosmic ocean. As Krishna, he frolicked with the *gopis* (cowgirls).

Since the 14th century the successive rulers of Nepal have been considered incarnations of Vishnu. Every former royal palace has its Vishnu shrine and there are several more scattered throughout the Valley. None is richer in spectacular Licchavi sculpture than the hilltop temple of **Changu Narayan**.

Changu Narayan: The road access to Changu Narayan, 12 kilometers (7.5 miles) east of Kathmandu is from behind Bhaktapur. Alternatively it is a 45 minute walk up from the Sankhu road, across the Manohara River, using the old pilgrim's route; or a pleasant half-day hike along the ridge from Nagarkot on the eastern Valley rim.

The lavishly decorated two-tiered temple was rebuilt after a fire in 1702, but the earliest inscription in the Valley dated 464 A.D. testifies to the considerable talents of the Licchavi King Manadeva I, Nepal's first great historical figure.

The temple stands in a spacious courtyard, littered with priceless stone sculptures from the 4th to 9th century A.D. Licchavi period. This golden age of classical Newari art produced masterpieces that were entirely religious in character.

Note especially the lion-headed Vishnu Narsingh, dismembering the king of the demons; Vishnu with ten heads and ten arms going through the different layers of the universe; Vishnu Vikrantha, a dwarf with six arms.

Beside the stele with the oldest inscription which is set in front of temple, is an image of a Garuda, the mythical

Left, devotees bathe in the Balaju water spouts. <u>Right</u>, Vishnu, the preserver.

bird that serves as Vishnu's heavenly vehicle. Graceful statues of King Bupathindra Malla and his queen sit in a gilded cage.

Three Narayan Temples: Once a year in October-November a day's pilgrimage requires devotees to visit the four great Narayan shrines, no mean feat as they lie far apart. In addition to Changu Narayan, the other three are found in rural villages settings.

Worshippers start at **Ichangu Narayan**, an ancient site supposedly founded by King Hari Datta in the 6th century A.D. The little temple complex is in a clump of trees just beyond the village of **Ichangu**, a pleasant half-hour walk west from the Ring Road crossroads opposite Swayambhunath.

Bishankhu Narayan can be reached by a dirt track from the Godavari road beyond **Bandegaon**. Although only a twisting rock cave it is one of the most celebrated Vishnu shrines in the Valley. **Sekh Narayan** is near Pharping at the southern fringe of the Valley, set amidst sculptures and a series of pools.

Budhanilkantha and Balaju: The massive black statue of the reclining Vishnu at **Budhanilkantha** (nine kilometers, six miles north of Kathmandu) lies comfortably half submerged in the primeval ocean, resting on a bed of snakes. Nowhere else have the Licchavi sculptors translated the ancient image into stone so powerfully or so literally. Some 1,500 years ago man had apparently dragged the five-meter (16-foot) rock from outside the Valley and placed the "creator of life" in this small pond at the foot of the Shivapuri hills.

Worshippers strew the sleeping Vishnu with offerings of flower petals and rice. A forecast of death forbids the kings of Nepal from looking on Budhanilkantha's monumental sculpture, though they are permitted to see the smaller reclining Vishnu image at Balaju.

The **Balaju Vishnu** reclines in a shady garden at the foot of the Nagarjun forest. In the same park are the 22 carved stone water spouts of the **Balaju Hiti**, more than any other *hiti* in the Kathmandu Valley.

The temple of Changu Narayan.

SHIVA SHRINES

Shiva is both the Destroyer and Creator, at once the end of things and the beginning of new ones. Amongst others, he is Bhairav "The Cruel," Mahadeva "The Great God" or Pashupati "Lord of the Beasts."

Shiva is usually represented as a light-skinned man with a blue throat, five faces, four arms and three eyes. He holds a trident (the symbol of lightning), a sword, a bow and a mace topped with a skull. His vehicle, the bull, is an ancient symbol of fecundity. Together with his elephant-headed son, Ganesh, he is the most helpful god in the Valley – and also the most awesome.

Pashupatinath: Sometimes Shiva is seen as an unkempt holy man, and many of his *sadhu* followers covered with sackcloth, dust and ashes swarm to **Pashupatinath** in February-March to celebrate his birthday. Shivaratri is one of the great festivals of the Valley, attracting thousands of pilgrims to one of the four most important Shiva shrines in the entire subcontinent.

Throughout the year, Shiva is worshipped at Pashupatinath as a *lingum* (phallus) in his incarnation as the Lord Pashupati.

The great temple complex is five kilometers (three miles) east of Kathmandu. The easiest way to reach it is to walk from the Bagmati Bridge, near to the Royal Nepal Golf Club.

Entrance to the temple precinct is forbidden to non-Hindus. The best view is from the terrace on the wooded hill across the river. The large, gilded, triple-roofed temple was built in 1696 though 300 years earlier there was a structure on this site. The Bagmati River is lined with *dharmsalas* and cremation *ghats*, including a royal *ghat* reserved exclusively for members of the royal family. There is usually a cremation in progress on one of the platforms by the river. The ashes will be scattered in the river, regarded as holy as it flows into the sacred Ganges.

The Hindu temple of Pashupatinath.

There are many occasions when the faithful take ritual purificatory baths in the river. One of the most colourful is the women's festival of Teej when dressed in their finest red and gold saris hundreds of women, laughing and singing, converge on Pashupatinath.

If you continue up the hill, the path leads through the trees to the tall brick structure of the **Gorakhnath Shikhara**, flanked by the large brass trident of Shiva and surrounded by resthouses and *lingas* on a wide platform.

Down the hill on the other side is the **Guhyeshwari Temple** dedicated to Shiva's *shakti* (consort) in her manifestation as Kali. This riverside shrine is also forbidden to non-Hindus.

Gokarna Mahadev: Beyond Pashupatinath and the stupa of Bodhnath, take the road left to the important Shiva shrine, the **Gokarna Mahadev**, also on the banks of the Bagmati river in the small village of **Gokarna**.

The ochre-coloured three-roofed temple was built in 1582 and has recently been carefully restored. The fine woodcarvings are stripped to their original pure beauty and the golden roofs glisten in the sun, framed against the dark forest across the river. Irregular stone steps descend the river bank, where Shiva lies on a stone bed of cobras. In August-September at Gokarna Aunshi, or Father's Day, those whose fathers have died during the previous year must come and ritually bathe here.

Early sculptures surround this scenic shrine, but none are more beautiful than the 8th century statue of Parvati, the oldest image at Gokarna now protected by clothes inside a small shrine, set between the main temple and the road.

Tika Bhairav: A Shiva shrine of an altogether different register is located at **Tika Bhairav** near **Lele**, where Shiva is portrayed in his terrible form as Bhairav. To reach this unusual shrine, you must travel outside the Kathmandu Valley to the adjoining Lele Valley to the south. Do not look for a conventional temple. This monumental, multi-coloured fresco is an abstract closeup of Bhairav's face painted on a huge brick wall, barely sheltered by a tin roof.

Four Ganesh Temples: Ganesh, the elephant-headed god, is one of the most favoured divinities in Hinduism and is certainly the most favoured in the Kathmandu Valley. The god of good luck who casts aside obstacles is believed to be the son of Shiva and Parvati. The shrew is his vehicle and he especially likes offerings of food.

Ganesh has numerous shrines throughout the Valley but four are particularly sacred. The **Chandra Binayak** is in the middle of the village of Chabahil, 200 meters (650 feet) behind the Chabahil stupa. This small Ganesh is enshrined amidst rich brasswork and is believed to cure diseases and external bodily injuries.

The simple stone Ganesh at the **Surjya Binayak** is halfway up the foothills south of Bhaktapur. The path heads uphill and passes under a Rana gateway to the little shrine, considered able to give the power of speech to children who are slow to talk.

In a forest preserve between the villages of Bungamati and Khokana lies the **Karya Binayak**. From the road linking the hamlets, a path leads up to a beautiful clearing and the walled compound of the shrine. Here Ganesh is an elephant-shaped stone and is believed to help complete difficult tasks.

Those seeking strength of character go to worship Ganesh at **Jal Binayak**, just beyond the Chobar Gorge. A beautiful brass shrew faces the massive rock that represents Ganesh in this triple-roofed temple constructed in 1602.

Hindu Goddesses: Female Hindu deities inevitably take on ferocious, fierce and bloodthirsty appearances. The most important of these goddesses is **Maha Devi**, the dominating and sexually active *shakti* of Shiva. She can take thousands of names and incarnations. She is the black goddess Kali "the Dark One" and Durga "The Terrible of Many Names." She is forever giving birth but her stomach can never be filled and her craving for blood is insatiable. Sacri-

Left, Shiva devotees gather from all over the subcontinent to celebrate Shivaratri at Pashupatinath.

fices are characteristic of her cults of worship, particularly popular in Nepal.

Sankhu's Bajra Jogini: Hills surround the sleepy village of Sankhu, once on the trade route east to Helambu. Forests above the village hide an important temple to the Tantric goddess, **Bajra Jogini**. Follow the wide stone path north of the village and climb up the steps to the temple, flanked with smaller shrines, stupas and statues. The main structure is 17th century and has a fine golden *torana* above the door. Behind the temple there are other shrines and sculptures.

Dakshinkali: The sinister shrine of **Dakshinkali** is the most spectacular of all the Kali temples. A 45 minute drive south from Kathmandu, the main road ends here just beyond Pharping, home of yet another mysterious 17th century **Bajra Jogini Temple**.

Located in a dark valley at the confluence of two streams, Dakshinkali is renowned for its twice weekly sacrifices on Tuesdays and Saturdays. Only male animals are sacrificed in Nepal, usually buffaloes, goats, chickens or ducks. Women line up on one side and men on the other, carrying their animals to the priest who will ritually decapitate them with a *khukri* knife and bathe the black stone image of Kali in blood.

The Chandeshwari Shrine: Outside the Valley is the **Chandeshwari Shrine**, located north of the sprawling trading town of Banepa. A track leads northeast past the Adventist Hospital to the temple on the bank of a forested gorge.

Legend says that this entire valley was once crowded with wild beasts, regarded locally as demons. The temple is dedicated to Parvati, whom they called upon to slay Chand, the most fearsome of these demons. It thus became known as Chandeshwari, "The Slayer of Chand."

The main attraction is a remarkable fresco of Bhairav, painted on the western wall of the main structure. The *torana* and struts of the three-tiered temple are richly carved with the eight Astha Matrikas, or "Mother Goddesses" and eight Bhairavs.

The Gorakhnath Shikhara in the forest above Pashupatinath.

232

NATURE SITES

The hills surrounding the Kathmandu Valley provide wonderful opportunities for trekking and day walks (see page 239), and some of these viewpoints (see page 247) afford sweeping panoramas. Roads radiate to the rim of the Valley and beyond, and it is especially rewarding to combine the cultural wonders of the Kathmandu Valley, such as the more remote temples and shrines, with some of the natural sites. In a matter of minutes' walk off the beaten track you can return to the natural cycle of the seasons and the gentle rhythm of village life.

Birdwatching in the Kathmandu Valley, with its over 400 species of birds, is especially good when the migrants are arriving or departing in October and March-April. However it is worthwhile viewing them at any time of year. The wide variety of habitats and range of altitudes from the Valley floor at 1,200 meters (4,000 feet) up to the surrounding hilltops at 2,700 meters (9,000 feet) accounts for the great richness in birdlife.

Phulchoki and Godavari: One such rich birdwatching area is **Phulchoki**, the "flower-covered hill," highest on the Valley rim at 2,762 meters (9,062 feet). This triple-peaked hill is 20 kilometers (13 miles) southeast of Kathmandu and a road winds its way to the top where a small shrine has been built to the mother of the forest, **Phulchoki Mai**. Another small **Phulchoki Shrine** to her is to be found at the bottom of the hill, near the disfiguring marble quarry. Spring is a spectacular time to see the flowers – rhododendrons, orchids and daphne – and many good walks start from here (see page 239).

At the foot of Phulchoki Hill is the village of **Godavari** and **St. Xavier's School**, one of two schools in the Valley run by the Jesuits. The **Royal Botanical Garden** with its **Department of Medicinal Plants** is further on. This is a pleasant spot with its rushing streams and shady meadows and is popular for picnics. A greenhouse on the hill above has a notable collection of orchids and ferns. A quiet path leads to the **Godavari Kunda**, a spring where the sacred waters of the Godavari river pour from the mountains.

The tree-lined road running southeast to Godavari from the Ring Road passes through the pleasant country towns of **Harisiddhi**, **Thaibo** and **Bandegaon**, where the road branches to Bishankhu Narayan. The settlements of **Lubhu** and **Sanogaon** are a little further north.

South Kathmandu Valley: There is another important *kunda* in the dusty **Lele Valley**, a bumpy trip south from Kathmandu, only visited by the more intrepid tourists. Leaving the Kathmandu Valley, the track winds its way steeply downhill through intricately terraced fields and reddish-brown soil to the ancient Licchavi village of Lele. The **Saraswati Kunda** is marked by a shrine built in 1668. The Tika Bhairav fresco is nearby.

The road to Lele passes some beautiful countryside with terraced mustard

Ganesh is one of the most popular and helpful gods in the Valley.

fields and bamboo stands drenched in sunlight. Drive through the 16th century brick-built towns of **Sunakothi** and **Thecho**. At **Chapagaon** take the path east to the important Tantric temple of **Vajra Varahi**, located in a sacred grove of trees. Although built in 1665 the site is much older and various natural sculpted stones are regarded as images of Ganesh, Bhairav and the Ashta Matrikas.

The twin villages of **Bungamati** and Khokana date from the 16th century and are located south of Kathmandu down a rutty road dotted with *chaityas*, appropriate for an ancient processionary route. Bungamati is famous as the winter home of the Rato Machhendra god of Patan (see page 214) who resides every winter in a powerful, *shikhara*-style temple. Its spacious courtyard is often used for spreading grain to dry in the sun. The shrine of Karya Binayak is located between the two settlements. **Khokana** is slightly bigger than Bungamati and is known for its manufacture of mustard-oil. The oil presses can be seen at work in the village houses.

After skirting Kirtipur and the university on the right(see page 215) the road to Dakshinkali reaches one of the most celebrated natural sites of the Valley, the **Chobar Gorge**. This is where, legend tells us, the patriarch Manjushri released the waters of the lake with his mighty sword and the Chobar Hill is indeed sliced in two by the waters of the Bagmati River. Now much disfigured with a massive cement factory, this sacred spot is marked with the **Adinath Lokeshwar** temple on the top of the Chobar Hill. This 1640-built temple is decorated with household utensils.

A steel suspension bridge imported from Scotland as early as 1903 crosses the river near the Jal Binayak shrine. Just beyond the gorge is the pretty **Taudaha Lake** overgrown with water hyacinth which, according to legend, was created by Manjushri himself for the *nagas* (serpents) who were stranded when the Valley lake was drained.

There is a pleasant new resort at **Hatiban**, the Himalayan Heights Re-

Panauti, a Newar village south of Banepa, has some of the most interesting temples in the Valley and is set on the confluence of two rivers.

234

sort, with stunning views across the Valley from part way up **Champa Devi** hill which rises to the right. The road follows the twists and turns of the Bagmati River until it reaches **Pharping**, the largest village in this historic corner of the Valley, before dropping down to Dakshinkali. In the vicinity of Pharping are the Gorakhnath Cave (see page 226), Sekh Narayan (see page 228) and the 17th century Bajra Jogini temples.

North Kathmandu Valley: Driving west the old Rana ropeway which used to carry goods from Hetauda to Kathmandu crosses over the road. The police checkpoint at the village of **Thankot** checks all traffic leaving the Valley. A path branching south uphill is the old walking route to India, along which everything had to be carried into the Valley prior to the road's completion.

The "Mountain of the Moon," historic **Chandragiri**, rises behind the statue of King Tribhuvan, builder of the **Tribhuvan Raj Path**. Completed in 1956, it is still the only road out of the Kathmandu Valley to India.

The "Queen's Forest" of **Nagarjun** is a beautiful walled hill topped with a Buddhist *chaitya* (see page 226). There are two sacred caves and pheasant, deer and monkeys can be seen here. It rises above **Balaju**, the "industrial-estate" of Kathmandu where the reclining Vishnu and the 22 water spouts (see page 228) share a small park.

The road northwest to Trisuli and the fort at Nuwakot leaves the Valley near the viewpoint village of **Kakani** (2,073 meters, 6,801 feet). An old retreat of the British envoys to Nepal since the mid-19th century, a delightful Raj-style cottage at Kakani still belongs to successive British Ambassadors to Nepal.

Budhanilkantha, with its monumental reclining Vishnu and British-run boarding school, is a modest village on the north side of the Valley close by one of the earliest Licchavi settlements. It nestles at the foot of the **Shivapuri Hills** (2,732 meters, 8,963 feet), a favourite trekking and birdwatching area.

The meditation centre of Buddhist

Valley village streets are used for practical purposes such as drying grain.

teaching is the monastery at **Kopan** in a pretty hilltop setting southeast of Shivapuri, accessible by road north of Bodhnath.

Gokarna, Sankhu and Nagarkot: The entrance to the **Gokarna Safari Park**, also known as the "King's Forest," is from the south side of the walled park, past Bodhnath and the hamlet of **Jorpati**.

A favourite Saturday picnic spot with a pretty golf course, this 260 hectare (650-acre) royal forest offers facilities which include elephant rides, pony rides and a restaurant. You will see semi-wild black buck, cheetal, monkeys, tigers in a large enclosure and even a pythonina cage.

Before reaching Jorpati, the road branches north to the little village of Gokarna and the splendid Gokarna Mahadev (see page 231). This road continues north to **Sundarijal** with its century-old reservoir that still supplies parts of the Valley with water.

From the main road east past the Gokarna Safari Park you can see the

great hilltop temple of Changu Narayan (see page 226) on the right. This road ends at the ancient trading outpost village of **Sankhu**, home of the powerful Bajra Jogini temple (see page 232) but there is a good walk from here up to the village of **Nagarkot** (see page 248). The beautiful viewpoint at Nagarkot (2,099 meters, 6,886 feet) is more usually reached by road from behind Bhaktapur.

Banepa Valley and Panauti: The "Chinese Road" or **Arniko Raj Marg** skirts Bhaktapur and leaves the rim of the Kathmandu Valley at the village of **Sanga** before descending into the **Banepa Valley**. In the mushrooming and charmless trading town of **Banepa**, turn right at the Tribhuvan statue to Panauti and left to the Chandeshwari Shrine (see page 232). To the northwest a track runs through terraced rice fields to **Nala**, another former outpost of Bhaktapur.

A treasure trove of art and architecture, **Panauti** is set south of Banepa at the confluence of the **Pungamati** and **Roshi Khola Rivers**. Once an important staging post on the Tibet trade route with pre-Licchavi origins, Panauti boasts one of the only two known pre-Malla structures, the **Indreshwar Mahadev Temple**. Contemporary with the 12th century Kasthamandap and of the finest proportions with exquisite woodcarvings - especially the simple but beautiful roof struts - this important temple is now sadly decayed.

At the confluence itself is a pleasing jumble of small temples, shrines, *lingas* and a cremation *ghat*. Across the river is the 17th century **Brahmayani Temple**, a recently restored little masterpiece, with superb Newari paintings or *paubha*.

The hilltop **Dhulikhel** (see page 247) is half an hour's drive beyond Banepa. It is possible to walk or drive though only in a four wheel drive vehicle to the important Buddhist shrine of **Namo Buddha** (see page 247). The main road continues to the Chinese border and eventually to Lhasa, the Tibetan capital, provided it is not obstructed by snow or landslides.

Left, Chobar Gorge with the Jal Binayak temple. **Right**, the Bhairav mural at the Chandeshwari shrine near Banepa.

HIKES IN THE KATHMANDU VALLEY

There are many enjoyable hikes within the Kathmandu Valley that offer the rewards of wandering further afield; countryside serenity, an introduction to Nepalese hill life and dramatic mountain views. All of these walks can be done in a day or combined into two to three day mini-treks. A Schneider Valley map is helpful, as is a local guide where trails are spotty.

Day Hikes from Nagarkot: The Kath–mandu Valley is ringed with hills reaching to 2,000-2,700 meters (6,600-8,600 feet), with trails linking much of the perimeter. **Nagarkot** on the eastern rim (2,099 meters, 6,886 feet) is a good place to begin several day hikes or a longer northern rim trek. It is accessible by road and is a pleasant place to spend the night (see page 248).

A half day walk to **Changu Narayan**, an impressive temple with early stone sculptures descends westward from Nagarkot village through corn terraces and thatched-roof villages. The trail crosses the road at a sharp bend and heads along the ridge to the temple's gilded roofs. From Changu Narayan, a staircase leads down to a fork in the trail, the left one to Bhaktapur, and the right descending to rice paddies and across a stream to the Sankhu road.

A new dirt road winds down from Nagarkot to **Sankhu**. It is more fun for mountain biking or motor-cycling than walking three or four hours on a graded track. An alternative route heads north to the **Kattike Dara** ridge and curves west, descending to the Sankhu-to-Helambu trail then climbing again to the Bajra Jogini temple (see page 232) above Sankhu. A third route drops steeply from the sharp bend in the Nagarkot road to the north and reaches Sankhu across the fields.

Descending southeast from Nagarkot to **Banepa** is another pleasant excursion. The trail begins below the view tower within the military area, which is sometimes closed to the public. Two tracks lead south down through terraced fields to **Nala**, an old village with splendid temples, reaching Banepa in five to six hours.

The Northern Rim Trek: A two day hike from Nagarhot to **Shivapuri** or a day and a half to **Sundarijal** share the same trail for the first eight hours, following the dirt road then staying high on the ridge to Burlang Bhanjyang (2,438 meters, 8,000 feet) where food and lodging are available. The main Sundarijal to Helambu trail crosses here; the path south leads to **Mulkarka** and **Sundarijal**, serviced by taxis or bus.

The way to Shivapuri continues through forest along the ridge for approximately four hours, without water, before mounting the final knoll (2,732 meters, 8,963 feet) for a 360 degree view of the Himalaya and the Kathmandu Valley. Two trails descend to **Budhanilkantha**; the easterly one emerges at **Nage Gompa** and down a steep trail or a dirt road to the bottom. The other heads west and follows a main path south to the reserve office. Together the two paths make a challenging but rewarding day hike of four to five hours up and three hours down. From Nage Gompa, another trail heads down the ridge to **Kopan** monastery above Bodhnath.

The rim trek continues west to **Kakani** (2,073 meters, 6,801 feet) in eight to ten hours, almost certainly requiring a guide unless the dirt road is picked up half-way down Shivapuri. A forest ridge trail heads west, crossing the main Kathmandu to Likkhu Khola trail (a possible campsite) and continues toward two prominent hills from where Kakani's white lodge is visible. A bus to Kathmandu can be stopped on the main Trisuli road. Or the next day, descend to **Baleju** for an easy half-day hike along the hillside above the Trisuli road, southwesterly through forests and meadows using Nagarjun's white stupa as a landmark, and down to the Valley floor within an hour of Baleju. To continue on the perimeter trek, cross the paved road to Nagarjun's entry gate rather than exiting to Balaju.

Sacred Summits: The prominent

Preceding page: women wending their way through the emerald rice fields of the Kathmandu Valley. Below, views trekking in the Kathmandu Valley are rewarding and accessible.

forested hill west of Kathmandu is **Nagarjun**, also called **Jamachok**. A minimal entry fee is requested at the main gate, one kilometer up the Trisuli road from Baleju. A dirt road winds to the top (2,096 meters, 6,877 feet), while hikers can reach there in two hours on a direct footpath. At the top is a Buddhist stupa – and a superb view of Ganesh Himal, Langtang and the Kathmandu Valley. A return trail descends the southwest side of Nagarjun to Ichangu Narayan (see page 228) and reaches Kathmandu via a dirt road that joins the Ring Road behind Swayambhunath. There is no easy-to-follow Valley rim route in this area. A few Nepali phrases or a guide helps in asking the way to **Thankot** or **Kisipidi** on the Pokhara highway, approximately a day's walk from Ichangu village.

The hike to the top of **Champa Devi** (2,278 meters, 7,474 feet), the highest peak on the **Chandragiri Ridge** southwest of **Kirtipur**, affords a panoramic view of the west Kathmandu Valley backdropped by the snow-cov-ered Himalaya. Several trails lead up to the Chandragiri ridge, which roughly parallels the Kathmandu to Pokhara road as far as the **Nagdhunga Pass** where the road leaves the Valley. Before the Tribhuvan Raj Marg was completed in 1956, every visitor and all supplies came in this historic route via Thankot by foot or horse; Kathmandu's first automobiles had to be disassembled and carried in by porters.

From Thankot or Kisipidi, paths ascend to **Dipiti Bhanjyang** or Deurali Bhanjyang (2,330 meters, 7,644 feet), identifiable by the convergence of a ropeway and power lines. Here it joins the ridge trail to Champa Devi and reaches **Pharping** in two days.

Day hikes to Champa Devi also start from the Chobar road, one from beyond the lake south of the cement factory and another further on from **Pikhel**. The trails climb steeply to join at a saddle close to the top. Though the path peters out, a scramble up the rocky slope leads to a white stupa and a Hindu shrine marking the Champa Devi summit.

Mustard fields stretch towards Pharping, Kathmandu Valley.

Several return routes are possible; staying close to the ridge continuing west, a trail descends from the second saddle north to Kirtipur. From the third saddle the trail reaches Kisipidi.

The Southern Crossing: There is no main trail connecting Pharping to **Phulchoki**, the next major hill and highest on the Valley rim (2,762 meters, 9,062 feet). Village trails can be pieced together only with constant inquiries. The route descends to cross the Bagmati and passes near **Danwargaon** before crossing a 1,600 meter (5,250 foot) ridge to **Lele**, a day and a half or two's walk from Pharping. Ancient temples distinguish Lele amidst sprawling fields and dusty valley. Phulchoki lies due east, visible from atop **Tileswar Dara** ridge and reachable in a long day.

A much easier approach to Phulchoki is from **Godavari**, in the Valley's southeastern corner. Two trails lead to the top in about four hours, one climbing straight up from the temple across from the marble quarry, the other ascending more gradually along the next ridge north. Both enjoy a lovely rhododendron and oak forest and cross the motorable road half a dozen times. On top, several dish antennae overshadow a small cluster of Shiva tridents. The view from here is nothing short of breathtaking: white peaks from Himalchuli to Everest, the entire Kathmandu Valley and to the south blue crests stretching into the haze toward the Terai and India. During springtime, the hill earns its name "flower-covered hill" when it is festooned with rhododendron, orchids and clematis vines.

The last leg of the perimeter trek links Phulchoki to historic **Panauti**, south of Banepa. It is not an easy descent without a trail down the northeastern slopes of Phulchoki to the **Roshi Khola**, but once there a trail follows the stream most of the way to Panauti. The last part of the six or seven hour hike from the top is heavily travelled. From Panauti it is four hours' walk to **Dhulikhel** with its comfortable lodges, or six hours walk via a worthwhile detour to the Buddhist pilgrimage site of **Namo Buddha**.

Left, early morning at Swayambhunath. **Below**, rice paddies near Nagarkot. **Right**, a Nepalese beauty with nail clippers.

MOUNTAIN VIEWPOINTS

Vestiges of Nepal's glorious past are conveniently concentrated in the Kathmandu Valley, but sometimes their profusion is overwhelming or the urban environment distracting. To experience rustic Nepal, one must go into the countryside where the images of village life and pastoral beauty are everlasting.

Fortunately for the non-trekker, there are a number of "viewpoints" with clean and comfortable accommodations and easy day trips to interesting villages or historic and sacred sites. The sedentary *connoisseur* of fine mountain scenery can enjoy it all from the comfort of a deck-chair.

A Gilded Trade Post: A forty-minute drive along the Arniko Raj Marg east of Kathmandu reaches the town of **Dhulikhel** set on a hilltop enveloped in copper-soiled terraces. Today's truck-stop town of **Banepa**, passed en route, was once the capital of a 14th-century kingdom which boasted diplomatic relations with China's Ming emperors. Dhulikhel was an important trade-post and duty collected on gold and riches destined for the *rajas* of Kathmandu financed the elegant woodcarvings on some of its handsome buildings.

The ancient art of Newari woodcraft is kept alive at two charming resorts near Dhulikhel's outskirts. The **Himalayan Horizon Hotel** and **Dhulikhel Mountain Resort** both incorporate indigenous styles of architecture but with modern amenities of high tourist standards. From garden patios and bedroom windows, an impressive vista of the snowy central Himalaya makes an incongruous backdrop to the gentle hills and temperate climate.

Another, budget-priced lodge shares the town's main street with shops selling vegetables, cloth and hammered metal pots of all sizes.

Dhulikhel is central to a number of day excursions, beginning with an early morning 30-minute hike up to the **Bhagvati Temple** for an unforgettable sunrise over the Himalaya. Trails lead along the ridge north of town, self-evident or invariably guided by school children eager to practice their English.

A leisurely all-day hike can be undertaken to visit **Namo Buddha** (meaning "Hail to the Buddha"), a sacred site which for untold centuries has drawn reverent pilgrims. Legend tells that the Buddha sacrificed his body here to feed a starving tigress and her cubs. A carved stone slab on the top of the hill depicts the moving story, a lesson in compassion and selfless giving.

Clustered around the main stupa are tea shops selling *chiya, alu daam* and *chiura* (tea, potato curry and beaten rice) and a huge prayerwheel; on the hilltop above are a Buddhist retreat ringed with prayer flags and a line of nine white stupas. A dirt road (sometimes suitable for vehicles) reaches Namo Buddha from Dhulikhel via Kavre and is a pleasant roundtrip walk of eight hours. From the stupa still another road drops west downhill through a sacred forest and across a wide valley for a two hours' walk or a half-hour

drive to **Panauti** (see page 236). Check the prevailing road condition before you attempt to drive.

An all day hike reaches Nagarkot via Banepa and Nala (see page 239) where lodges are available. White-water rafting on the Sunkosi River (see page 129) combined with a drive to the Tibet border at Kodari are alternative day excursions. A China visa must be arranged in advance in order to cross the border into Tibet.

Views from the Valley Rim: The tiny settlement of **Nagarkot** clings to a hilltop east of Kathmandu (2,099 meters, 6,886 feet), far from city noise and traffic. A one-hour drive up the winding road from Bhaktapur greets the fresh hill breezes and Valley views east and west, eclipsed by the best close range Himalayan vantage-point from anywhere on the Kathmandu Valley rim. From the Annapurnas to Everest, the peaks seem no more than a day's walk away.

Clustered at the base of a small Shiva temple, lodges outnumber farmhouses, most offering basic accommodations

for no more than a few dollars with simple meals. Two have more up-market facilities: the government-managed **Taragaon Resort** and **Hotel Flora Hill**, both accessible from the main road five minutes below. Travel agents in Kathmandu can arrange overnight private taxi services or guided tours for viewing the sunset or sunrise. The local bus from Bhaktapur takes two to three hours with many stops.

The more active-spirited traveller might hitch a ride up to Nagarkot and walk down via any of several routes. Mountain bikers find little traffic going up the paved road and a fun, zigzag descent to Sankhu on a dirt road (see page 239). When military exercises are not in progress, visitors can enter the army camp and mount the tower for an even better 360-degree perspective.

Crowning a knoll on the opposite side of the Kathmandu Valley is **Kakani**, its hilltop **Taragaon Resort** shared by the British Ambassador's private residence and a police training academy. The main road to Trisuli Bazaar climbs from **Baleju** through steeply terraced paddies to the Kakani turn-off. From the hotel terrace at 2,073 meters (6,801 feet), Ganesh Himal and Langtang Lirung dominate the centre-stage with Annapurna II and Himalchuli, Lenpogang (Great White Peak) and Gauri Shankar in the left and right wings. Several day hikes and Valley rim treks begin or end at Kakani (see page 240).

New and Old Look-out Sites: The commanding fortress site of **Nuwakot** is an interesting side trip from **Trisuli Bazaar**, reachable in an hour's climb from the road. Prithvi Narayan Shah captured Nuwakot in 1744, thereby cutting off one of the Valley's primary supply routes, then launched his heroic siege whilst based here. The seven-story palace fortress stands little marred by time despite a history of attacks by Malla and later Chinese forces. Basic lodging is available in Trisuli, or a day trip can be made from Kathmandu or Kakani.

Gorkha, the original home of the Shah kings, remains an historical and commercial centre reached by a well-maintained paved road from Khaireni

Left, Hills and houses near Nagarkot, Kathmandu's favourite viewpoint.

on the Kathmandu to Pokhara highway. Basic to medium-standard accommodation is available. A number of treks begin from here, which day-hikers can explore as well (see page 257).

A 300-meter (1,000-feet) climb up a well-tended stairway to the northern hilltop is worthwhile not only for a lovely view of Baudha, Himalchuli and the shoulder of Manaslu but for a visit to Prithvi Narayan Shah's palace, although periodically it is closed to foreigners. The outer courtyard's stone-carving and woodwork is beautifully crafted and the structure's massive stone-block construction impressive. The inner sanctum is heavily guarded and contains a Kali image which demands a prodigious number of animal sacrifices, particularly during Dasain when the palace compound runs red with the blood of hundreds of buffalos, goats and chickens.

On the drive to Gorkha or Pokhara from Kathmandu, a side trip to the temple of **Manakamana** (1,713 meters, 5,620 feet) follows a steep footpath travelled at least once in a lifetime by nearly every Nepali. The devout and the superstitious pray at this temple site for the mandatory male offspring or before setting out on any major venture – physical, spiritual or commercial. Another site only recently brought to public attention is the **Bandipur Caves**, accessible by foot from near Dumre.

Though most of Pokhara's attractions are in the valley (see page 269), the **Tiger Mountain Lodge** located on a ridge-top northeast of the town is a resort destination all of its own. Opening in September 1993 this newest of Tiger Tops' popular venues will command superb views of Annapurnas and accross the Pokhara valley. A central lodge and deluxe bungalow units are designed in the traditional architectural style using local materials yet with all modern comforts and facilities – including a swimming pool.

A half day's drive from Pokhara along the Siddartha Raj Marg towards Butwal reaches the enchanting trading town of **Tansen** (1,400 meters, 4,600

The plaque at Namo Buddha depicts the legend of Buddha sacrificing himself to the starving tigress.

feet). Few tourists discover Tansen's off-the-beaten-track serenity nor its bazaars famed for their colourful *dhaka*-cloth *topis* (Nepali hats) and hand-tooled metal-ware. This town of 16,000 was the capital of the powerful Palpa kingdom until a final subjection by the Shah kings which dragged on into the early 19th century. The remains of several fortresses can be visited by a short drive and walk. Day hikes through oak, chestnut, pine and rhododendron forests and Magar villages lead to quiet lakes, caves and the decayed **Ranighat Palace** on the banks of the Kali Gandaki river. From a pleasant hilltop lodge, the Himalaya are visible from Dhaulagiri to Gauri Shankar; to the south the Tinau River cuts through the Mahabharat range and beyond, the Siwalik hills rise from the shimmering Terai. Flights from Kathmandu to Bhairawa shorten the trip from a long day's drive to less than two hours.

Except for hard-core bikers who have snaked up the 2,100-meter (6,900-foot) hill from Hetauda, **Daman** remains an underrated and unknown hill station with the broadest Himalayan views of all. From its 2,400-meter (7,874-foot) vantage-point, enhanced by a circular view tower with two high-power mounted telescopes, a full 400 kilometers (250 miles) of ice-cast peaks are visible – from Dhaulagiri to Everest and beyond – even from the dormitory beds inside the glassed-in observation tower. A few shops and simple lodges define the primarily Sherpa community and provide an overnight halt for truck drivers who ply the Tribhuvan Raj Path between Kathmandu and Birgunj. One can hitch a ride on a truck or hire a private car and driver in Kathmandu for the winding three-hour drive. Travellers en route to or from Chitwan can request the driver to take this longer route as an alternative to the familiar road via Mugling.

From Daman's often windy, pine-forested hill the lovely **Palung Valley**, with its jig-saw patterned terraces, stretches to the north and west. A small Buddhist *gompa* tended by monks and

Winter sunshine bathes the peaks of Ganesh Himal.

nuns from Bhutan can be reached in an hour's walk from the tower, down a marked trail through the forest.

Views from on High: Undoubtedly the best mountain views are from still higher, close to the bases of the world's highest peaks. But not everyone is able to walk there. Nepal's network of STOL (Short Take Off and Landing) airstrips allow the less hardy traveller to be in the heart of the Himalaya with minimal effort, although it must be stressed that weather and delays can disrupt the best-laid airline plans.

The **Hotel Everest View** at 3,962 meters (13,000 feet) at **Syangboche** in the Khumbu distinguishes itself as the highest hotel in the world. From expansive windows in the 12-room, Japanese-built hotel, guests look out onto Mount Everest, Nupste, Lhotse, Ama Dablam and surrounding peaks. Every room has a view and many of the conveniences of a city hotel. Charter flights from Kathmandu land 100 meters (300 feet) below the hotel. Oxygen and medical assistance are available in case guests experience difficulty in acclimatising to the high altitude. Day hikes or treks to some of the Khumbu's famous spots can be arranged.

Down-valley at **Lukla** (2,866 meters, 9,403 feet), the gateway for scheduled daily flights into Khumbu, numerous lodges accommodate all travellers' tastes. The **Hotel Sagarmatha** is one of the nicest of many Sherpa-run hotels. Although Mount Everest is not visible from Lukla, others are, and a day and a half walk to Namche Bazaar brings Everest and many of the Khumbu's primary peaks into view.

If these high elevation gains are intimidating, the more moderate-level Sherpa town of **Phaplu** (2,370 meters, 7,775 feet) in the Solu Khumbu is a good substitute. Although views of the Himalaya are more distant and flights even less reliable, the forests and vales of Solu exude a special charm of their own . The *Hostelrie des Sherpas* mimics some of Solu's mansion-like homes with its colourful window shutters and congenial atmosphere.

Comfortable resorts near Dhulikhel offer spectacular views.

Nearly everyone comes to Nepal to see Mount Everest, at 8,848 meters (29,028 feet) the highest point, and truly one of the greatest spectacles on earth. Some are lucky enough to glimpse it on their flight into Kathmandu, or from one of the Valley rim viewpoints if the weather is clear. Thousands hike to its base every year, but only the fit should attempt such heights (5,357 meters or 17,575 feet).

Fortunately, for the rest of mountain lovers, Royal Nepal Airlines, the domestic flag-carrier, arranges a one-hour mountain flight east from Kathmandu every day to see Mount Everest and the entire central and eastern Himalayan range.

The Mountain Flight is an experience none should miss. Flying at approximately 7,500 to 8,500 meters (25,000 to 28,000 feet) – eye level with the peaks at some 22 kilometers (14 miles) distance – passengers get a magnificent close up perspective. The flight route parallels the mountains for 160 kilometers (100 miles) east of Kathmandu, and then turns around to give both sides the same view. This "fly past" of the world's greatest peaks is usually in the morning when the weather is most likely to be clear – your money is refunded if it is not – and is operated in either an Avro or Boeing aircraft. Smaller aeroplanes can be chartered, usually with great difficulty and considerable cost.

Just as interesting as the awesome white mountains are the middle hills of Nepal, with their intricate cobwebs of green and yellow terraces and fairytale villages clinging to ridgetops, dissected with great grey-green rivers snaking through their narrow valleys. Lofty views extend north onto the Tibetan plateau and south over the vast Ganges plains. Often visitors are invited into the cockpit to photograph or just to enjoy being captivated by the country spread below.

Nepal has eight of the earth's fourteen 8,000-meter (26,250-feet) mountains either within or on its borders, and eight of the ten

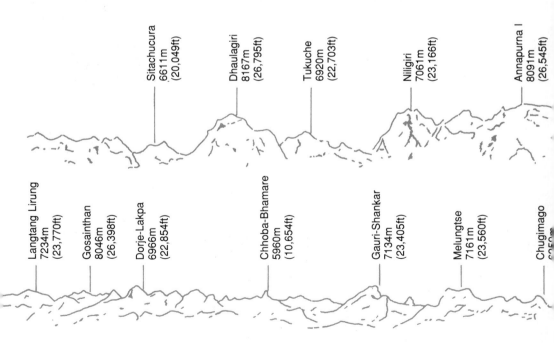

highest mountains in the world. In addition to these giants, there are a large number of "smaller" peaks – most of them thousands of feet higher than any of the summits of Europe or the Americas – which march range after range across the northern reaches of this small nation. Indeed, Nepal's base camps at the foot of a mountain generally lie at about 5,500 meters (18,000 feet) elevation, higher than any mountain in Europe. The time and effort expended trekking just to reach them is for most people a complete lifetime adventure in itself. The sheer magnitude of the Himalaya is intimidating.

Mount Everest, which bestrides the Nepal Tibet border in the east of the country, is known to Nepalis as Sagarmatha (Mother of the Universe) and in Tibet as Chomolungma (Mother Goddess). Everest was named after George Everest, a British surveyor-general

Outline sketch of the mountain range from west to east.

in late 19th-century India. The highest mountain in the world was eventually climbed on 29th May, 1953, by Sir Edmund Hillary of New Zealand and Tenzing Norgay Sherpa of India (see page 178).

There had been a number of earlier attempts, mostly from the north side, the first one being in 1922 by the British. Nepal was not open for foreign mountaineers until 1949, and Nepalis were not interested in scaling the peaks. So it has only been in the most recent decades that the many peaks of Nepal's Himalaya have been explored and climbed (see page 147).

Annapurna I (8,091 meters, 26,545 feet) was the first 8,000-meter peak to be successfully climbed in the world, when in June 1950 a French expedition reached the top. The summiteers on this historic ascent were the team's leader, Maurice Herzog, and his climbing partner, Louis Lachenal. By 1960 all the remaining 8,000 meter mountains in Nepal had been scaled (see page 162).

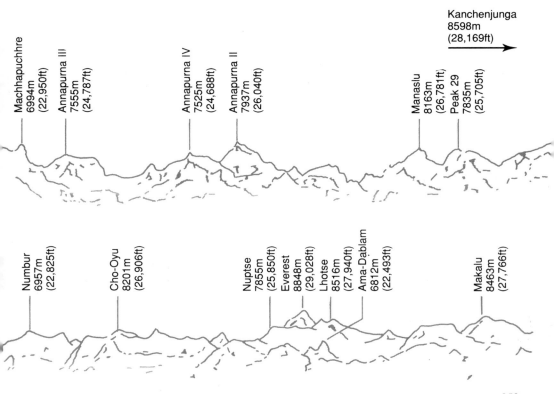

Kanchenjunga
8598m
(28,169ft)

Machhapuchhre 6994m (22,950ft)
Annapurna III 7555m (24,787ft)
Annapurna IV 7525m (24,688ft)
Annapurna II 7937m (26,040ft)
Manaslu 8163m (26,781ft)
Peak 29 7835m (25,705ft)

Numbur 6957m (22,825ft)
Cho-Oyu 8201m (26,906ft)
Nuptse 7855m (25,850ft)
Everest 8848m (29,028ft)
Lhotse 8516m (27,940ft)
Ama-Dablam 6812m (22,493ft)
Makalu 8463m (27,766ft)

Langtang Himal and East Nepal

12 km/ 7,5 miles

Langtang Ri
7205

Chusudo Ri
6248

Phentang Ri
6342

LANGTANG
HIMAL

Langtang Lirung
7245

Langshisa
(4080)

Langshisa Ri
6427

Lengpo Gang
7083

Langtang
(3300)

Kyangjin
(3749)

Yala

Dorje Lakpa
6966

Phurbi Chyachu
6637

Ghora Tabela

Naya Kanga
5846

Ganja La
(5120)

Tilman's Col

Dasi

Pò Chlau

Ch
Ba

Gatlang

Syabrubensi

LANGTANG NATIONAL
PARK

JUGAL

Pangsing
Bhanjyang

Syabru

Phalang Gyang

Tin Pokhari

HIMAL

Dhunche
(1966)

Thare

Trisuli River

GOSAINKUND
LEKH

Gosainkund
Lakes (4328)

Melamchi K.

Panch
Pokhari
(3692)

Thempatang

Bhairav Kund

Dram

Betrawati

Melamchigaun
(2590)

Tarkyegyang

Monastery

BHAIRAV KUND

LEKH

Kodari

Kutumsang

Sermathang

Balephi Khola

Nuwakot
(Old Fortification)

Tadi Khola

Gul Bhanjyang

Indrawati Khola

Lartza

Tinsahg La
(3313)

Dilli Bazar

Talamarang

Vantage point

Pati Bhanjyang

Burlang
Bhanjyang

Sindhu Khola

Melamchi
Phul

Barabise
(823)

Kalinchok
3759

Kakani

Trisuli
Bazar

Chautara

Lamosangu

Gur

Kathmandu

Bodhnath

Sundarijal

Balephi

Muldi

Nigale

Charikot

Swayambhunath

Thimi

Nagarkot
(2099)

Indrawati K.

Kirtipur

Lalitpur

Bhaktapur

Sanga

Panchkaal

Dolalghat

Phunri

Tribeni

Bungmati

Harisiddhi

Banepa

Pharping

Godavari

Dhulikhel

Panauti

Vantage point
Bhagvati Temple

Lele

Brahmayani Temple
Indreshwar Mahadev
Temple

Rosi Khola

Sunkosi

Phulasi

Phaklang

Bagmati

Kethi Chauk

Nepalthok

Chisapani

Ch

Makwanpur Garhi

Bagmati

Thumki

Chainpur

Phulbari

Chinpurtar

Suna

Kokhajor K.

Kapilkot

Rame

Jhayandi

Sindhulimadi

Sunkosi

••••••••• Rolwaling Valley Trek
••••••••• Solu Trek: Jiri to Namche Bazar
••••••••• Salpa Pass Trek
••••••••• Everest Base Camp with Chhukung Trek
••••••••• Gokyo Trek with Cho La
••••••••• Thame Trek
••••••••• Langtang Trek
••••••••• Panch Pokhari-Jugal Himal Trek
••••••••• Gosainkund and Helambu Trek

Dhungaybas

Chhiame Khola

Trisuli River

Lende Khola

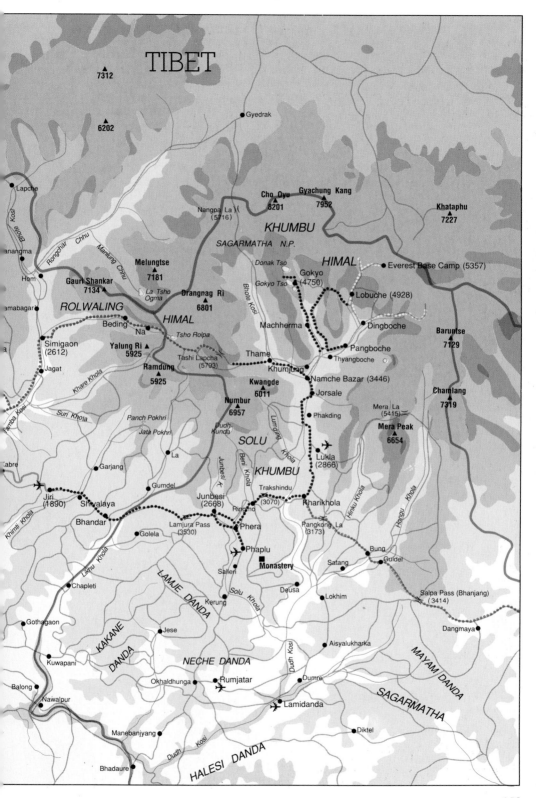

TIBET

▲ 7312

▲ 6202

Gyedrak

Lapche

Bhote Kosi

Cho Oyu
8201

Gyachung Kang
7952

Nangpa La
(5716)

KHUMBU

Khataphu
7227

SAGARMATHA N.P.

Rongchar Chhu

Mamlung Chhu

Melungtse
7181

Donak Tso

HIMAL

Everest Base Camp (5357)

anangma

Hom

Gauri Shankar
7134

La Tsho
Ogma

Drangnag Ri
6801

Gokyo
(4750)

Gokyo Tso

Bhote Kosi

Lobuche (4928)

amabagar

ROLWALING

Beding

Na

HIMAL

Tsho Rolpa

Machherma

Dingboche

Baruntse
7129

Simigaon
(2612)

Yalung Ri ▲
5925

Tashi Lapcha
(5793)

Thame

Pangboche

Thyangboche

Jagat

Khare Khola

Ramdung
5925

Khumjung

Namche Bazar (3446)

Chamlang
7319

Suri Khola

Panch Pokhri

Jata Pokhri

Kwangde
6011

Jorsale

Mera La
(5415)

abre

Tamba Kosi

Dudh
Kunda

Numbur
6957

Phakding

Mera Peak
6654

La

Lumding Khola

SOLU

Garjang

Gumdel

Beni Khola

Junbesi K.

KHUMBU

Lukla
(2866)

Hinku Khola

Jiri
(1890)

Shivalaya

Junbesi
(2668)

Trakshindu
(3070)

Kharikhola

Hongu Khola

Khimti Khola

Bhandar

Ringmo

Phera

Rangkong La
(3173)

Bung

Guidel

Golela

Lamjura Pass
(3530)

Phaplu

Salleri

Monastery

Satang

Salpa Pass (Bhanjang)
(3414)

Chapleti

LAMJE DANDA

Likhu Khola

Kerung

Solu Khola

Deusa

Lokhim

Dangmaya

Gothagaon

KAKANE

Jese

Dudh Kosi

Aisyalukharka

MAYAM DANDA

Kuwapani

DANDA

NECHE DANDA

Okhaldhunga

Rumjatar

Dumre

SAGARMATHA

Balong

Nawalpur

Lamidanda

Manebanjyang

Dudh

Kosi

Diktel

Bhadaure

HALESI DANDA

CENTRAL NEPAL TREKS

Other than the Langtang-Gosainkund-Helambu area, central Nepal is vastly underutilized by trekkers, despite its easy access and extensive network of trails. Few trekking agents promote the Manaslu, Ganesh or Jugal Himal, which flank the Langtang range west and east. The custom-outfitted group, and the independent trekker willing to sleep in smokey homes and carry a few days' food supplies, will discover an environment little changed in centuries.

In the mid-1700s, the area now known as Nepal, extending slightly north and west, was politically divided into some 80 principalities. They were in constant flux, borders changing, contracts dissolving, and the *rajas* – heads of state, mostly emigrant Rajputs – spent precious resources defending their territories against neighbouring states.

The state of Gorkha, centering on the present-day town of Gorkha (see page 248) half way between Kathmandu and Pokhara, was neither the largest nor the strongest force. Its manpower was no more than 15,000 to 20,000, a figure later extrapolated from a recorded "12,000 roofs." But its leader, Prithvi Narayan Shah, was the most able and determined and he led a campaign to conquer the Kathmandu Valley and form a unified kingdom. His palace still stands on the hilltop above Gorkha, overlooking the fertile hills which once supported his ambitions.

Gorkha Treks: A number of short and long treks begin in the town of Gorkha, making concentric loops into the Himalaya which end at Dumre or the Gorkha access road. From nearly any point, the stalwart ramparts of **Manaslu**, **Himalchuli** (7,893 meters, 25,895 feet), **Baudha** (6,672 meters, 21,890 feet) or **Ganesh Himal** (7,111 meters, 23,330 feet) all give bearing to the wayfarer.

On arrival from a half-day drive from Kathmandu, most trekkers stay in Gorkha or camp nearby after a visit to Prithvi Narayan Shah's palace. The low path to Pokhara descends west to the **Darondi Khola** down a slippery hillside screeching with monkeys. The high trail sets off to the northwest, riding a corrugated ridgeline between the Darondi and **Buri Gandaki** rivers. By day three, the lush millet terraces are left behind and camp is made in the forest on top of bulky **Darchya** (3,048 meters, 10,000 feet), from where the Himalaya appear in their snowy finery.

Beyond Darchya, the route splits in three directions. The eastward trail descends to the village of **Laprag,** facing a silent waterfall as it plummets to a tributary stream of the Buri Gandaki. The westward route winds down through rhododendron forest to the pleasant Gurung town of **Barpak**, with its flagstone walkways and smells of freshly distilled millet *rakshi*. Continuing westward, a steep descent into the valley meets a pedestrian highway that parallels the gentle Darondi down to **Khoplang** and back to Gorkha completing a week-long trek.

The northern path leads to **Rupina**

Left, Lama dancing at a monastery festival in Helambu. Right, rice terraces below the peaks of Ganesh Himal.

La (approximately 4,600 meters, 15,100 feet) which connects the headwaters of the Darondi and Buri Gandaki rivers. Beyond the cairn-marked summit, a sketchy trail skirts the **Chhuling Glacier** and eventually joins the Buri Gandaki at **Nyak**.

Sacred Lakes: The Nepalese invest sacred meaning in nature, particularly water and high points, expressed by strings of prayer flags and *mani* stone piles. Many high lakes like Dudh Pokhari and Bara Pokhari are important places of pilgrimage.

Dudh Pokhari ("Milk Lake") lies at approximately 4,270 meters (14,000 feet) on the ridge west of the Darondi. Days above permanent settlements, only wood-cutters, shepherds or devotees are encountered on the trail. A two-week trek from Gorkha via Darchya and Barpak, crossing the Darondi, reaches the hidden waters only with the help of a guide and staff to carry supplies. The return route stays high along **Sirandanda** ridge and exits east to the Gorkha road or west via the **Chepe Khola** to Dumre.

A five-day round trip to **Bara Pokhari** (3,110 meters, 10,200 feet) follows braided trails east from **Phalesangu** and **Ngadi** on the lower Marsyangdi River. Paths also connect it west to Sirandanda, three to four days away. The lake often has snow till late spring.

Around Manaslu: A much more challenging trek reaches north of the Himalaya circling the Manaslu-Himalchuli-Baudha massif via **Larkya La** (5,213 meters, 17,103 feet). The 18-21 day trip can begin from either Besisahar on the Marsyangdi, or Gorkha. From **Thonje,** above the Marsyangdi, to Nyak in the upper the Buri Gandaki, travel is permitted only to holders of a special trekking or expedition permits. Tents and food for at least a week and a guide are essential.

Guarded by the northern flanks of Manaslu and Larkya Himal, Larkya La is within ten kilometers (six miles) of the Tibet border. On the east side, descendants of Tibetan immigrants have settled in hamlets such as **Sama** and

A porter pauses by Gosainkund Lake.

Lho. Carved stone images of Milrepa, an 11th-century Tibetan poet and teacher of Buddhism, record his visits to the region for meditational retreat. At Nyak, the Buri Gandaki heads south through a steamy gorge to **Arughat** (488 meters, 1,601 feet) in three to four days. The route then climbs westward onto the ridge via **Khanchok** to Gorkha.

A 16-18 day Gorkha-to-Trisuli trek traverses undulating ridges at the base of Ganesh Himal. From the upper Buri Gandaki the route heads northeast to **Tirudanda**, ending either at **Betrawati** on the **Trisuli River** or at Syabrubensi, where the Langtang river enters the **Bhote Kosi** valley giving birth to the mighty Trisuli River. Tamangs, the predominant hill-people across Nepal, populate these slopes and ridges. Their Tibetan heritage is evident by Mongoloid features and an adherence to Buddhism. They marry young, usually an arranged union, entitling the young man's family to his wife's labours.

Kathmandu to Pokhara: Less than 20 years ago, anyone wishing to get to Pokhara from Kathmandu had two choices; to fly or to walk. Most Nepalis walked, covering the distance in four or five days.

In 1974, the 200-kilometer (124-mile) Prithvi Raj Marg connecting Kathmandu with Pokhara was completed with Chinese aid, speeding travel time to six or seven hours, depending on road re-construction delays. But the old pedestrian "highway" remains a worthwhile journey, heavily plied by locals who delight in seeing and sharing a meal with a stranger from another land.

For *bideshis* (foreigners), the eight to nine day walk is an excellent introduction to trekking in Nepal, with relatively low passes – maximum 1,300 meters (4,250 feet) – frequent tea houses and several premature exit spots should the experience prove tiring. It is best to do this trek in winter as the lowland heat is draining.

A few highlights along the way include **Nuwakot**, one of Prithvi Narayan Shah's fortress sites, above Trisuli, nu-

Langtang Lirung just shows behind Yala peak.

merous stream crossings availing a dunk in the rushing waters, views of Ganesh Himal (named for the elephant-headed god), Himalchuli, Ngadi Himal, Manaslu and the Annapurnas, and optional side-trips to Gorkha or to **Ampipal's** project hospital and primary school. Newars, Brahmans, Chhetris, Tamangs, Gurungs and Magars populate this corridor. Old men sit cross-legged sucking tobacco smoke through a *hookah* (water pipe); school rooms full of boys and girls pronounce their lessons aloud; women weave on back-looms stretched taut across their backs – countless memorable scenes out of a slice-of-life scenerio.

The Langtang Valley: From downtown Kathmandu the black-rock roof of **Langtang Himal** crowned by a snow-capped **Langtang Lirung** (7,234 meters, 23,734 feet) can be seen on a clear day jutting above the city's own Shivapuri summit. Some 30 kilometers away, the long glaciated valley known as Langtang divides the northern range from **Gosainkund Lekh** (4,590 meters, 15,060 feet) and the Jugal Himal.

Legend tells that the upper Langtang Valley was discovered by a man in search of his yak, thus the name which means "in pursuit of a yak." The inhabitants are thought to be descendants of Tibetans who intermingled with Tamangs from Helambu. They are mainly sheep and yak herders, but grow some buckwheat, potatoes and barley as well.

Trekking in Langtang suits those with limited time who want to explore relatively high ground, and to see yaks. A tarmac road connects Kathmandu to Trisuli and continues unpaved to **Dhunche**, entance to **Langtang National Park**, and take-off point for treks into Langtang and to the Gosainkund Lakes.

In 1976, Langtang became Nepal's second largest national park. Healthy forests of rhododendron, fir, blue and chir pine, and birch stand out amidst central Nepal's predominantly cultivated hillsides. Wildlife of the park includes leopard, musk deer, Himalayan black bear, rhesus and langur monkeys

Sherpanis dancing at Tarkeghyang in Helambu.

and the endangered red panda. But most are kept at bay by the herders' Tibetan mastiff guard dogs. The Bhote Kosi-Trisuli river is an important migratory route for birds travelling between India and Tibet. A national park intrepretive centre at Dhunche introduces the park's ecology.

Two main tracks enter the valley of Langtang, each with lodging for every night as far as Kyangjin Gompa. The longer route goes through **Syabrubensi**, clinging to the steep, dry south-facing hillside in contrast to thick forests on the opposite side. At **Ghora Tabela** ("Horse Stable"), high cliffs rim the meadows.

Langtang village (3,300 meters, 10,850 feet) is the largest and last permanent settlement. Beyond is **Kyangjin**, a cluster of stone huts surrounded by potato and turnip fields, with a small Buddhist *gompa*. A Swiss-initiated government cheese factory makes remarkably Swiss-like yak cheese (but without the holes) and creamy yoghurt. Kyangjin can be reached in three fast days from Dhunche, but at 3,750 meters (12,300 feet) a slower pace is advised. A nearby airstrip is serviced by charter flights.

Kyangjin is as far as most trekkers go. But beyond, several day hikes are possible and for the self-sufficient hiker, days of exploring the upper valley to **Langshisa** (4,080 meters, 13,400 feet). **Tilman's Col**, a difficult crossing named for H.W. Tilman, the first Westerner to visit Langtang in 1949, leads east toward Panch Pokhari ("Five Lakes"). **Ganja La**, a 5,120 meter (16,800 foot) snowy and often cloud-bound pass, leads south to Helambu. Hikers with techinical experience, food, tents and a guide can reach Tarkeghyang on the other side in three to four days.

The easiest return route from upper Langtang is back down the valley. Below Ghora Tabela, the path scrambles south up a landslide to **Syabru**, its single row of timber houses stretched far down the ridgeline. Beautifully carved wooden windows compete with multi-

Village dwarfed by its surroundings in Langtang Valley.

coloured lodge signs for attention. A day's walk to Dhunche completes the eight or nine-day trek.

A Shiva Pilgrimage: Langtang National Park also includes the sacred **Gosainkund Lakes**, a pilgrimage site for thousands of Shiva devotees during the July-August full-moon festival of Janai Purnima. Hindus throng to bathe in the lakes' holy waters; males change a string worn around one shoulder renewing their devotion to Shiva, god of reproduction and destruction. *Jhankris* (shaman) dance in an induced trance to all night singing and drum beating. According to legend, Shiva formed the lakes by thrusting his *trisul* (trident) into the mountainside, creating three gushing springs and giving title to the Trisuli River.

The trail to Gosainkund (4,328 meters, 14,200 feet) climbs from either Dhunche or Syabru through lush rhododendron hillsides to **Sing Gompa**, where there is another cheese factory. The 2,400 meter (7,800 foot) elevation gain from Dhunche requires three days for proper acclimatisation. Food and lodging are available at the lakes during trekking season.

East of the lakes **Laurebina La** (4,600 meters, 15,100 feet) leads to Helambu. Scores of rock piles left by pilgrims seeking good fortune dot the treeless landscape. The path descends to a cluster of shepherds' huts at **Tharepati**, where it divides into two return routes to Kathmandu. The shorter way rides the ridge south through cool rhododendron forests (crawling with leeches during monsoon season) passing several Tamang villages, and crests the Kathmandu Valley rim at **Burlang Bhanjyang,** some 1,100 meters (3,600 feet) above Sundarijal. This ridge forms the divide between two of Nepal's major river systems; the Gandaki, which extends west to Dhaulagiri, and the Sapt Kosi whose tributaries extend east to Kangchenjunga on the border with Sikkim.

The other trail from Tharepati plunges 1,000 meters (3,300 feet) to a

Langtang village girl with her *doko* basket and goat.

tributary of the **Melamchi Khola** and above it the aging village of **Melamchigaun**. Stone houses scatter across the terraced fields above an old *gompa* dressed with tall prayer flags. The people of Helambu call themselves Sherpas but their link with the Sherpas of Solu Khumbu is distant, underlined by different dialects, clothes and family lines. Inside the heavy timber homes of **Tarkeghyang** and **Sermathang,** rows of polished copper cauldrons and brass plates line the sitting room. A *gompa* set on the ridge above Tarkeghyang commands excellent views of the Himalaya, looking north toward Ganja La and **Dorje Lakpa** (6,966 meters, 22,854 feet) and a harem of peaks over 6,000 meters (20,000 feet). Late-summer apples are a treat in this area as is spring's flower show of *laligurans* and purple irises.

The next few days' walk into the Melamchi Khola valley and out through **Talamarang** and the rice paddies of Melamchi Phul are sweaty, and once on the dirt road to **Panchkaal,** monotonous. To escape the heat, an alternative

trail climbs back up to 1,890 meters (6,200 feet) and joins **Pati Bhanjyang** on the way to Sundarijal. An eight or nine-day loop trip up to Tharepati and Melamchigaun is a short, enjoyable trek suitable during any season, with the chance of winter snow on high grounds.

Another set of sacred lakes east of Helambu called **Panch Pokhari** (Five Lakes) introduces trekkers to the saw-toothed Jugal Himal. The trek from Tarkeghyang crosses the **Indrawati Khola**, brown with the hills' red clay which it carries to the **Sunkosi**, and mounts a 3,600-meter (12,000-foot) ridge to the lakes. The shortest exit route heads straight down the ridge to **Chautara**, a large bazaar connected to the Kathmandu-Kodari road by jeep or bus. Another route continues eastward visiting the hauntingly beautiful **Lake Bhairav Kund** and Sherpa and Tamang villages that once straddled the Tibet trade route through the Khasa gorge. From Tarkeghyang or Chautara, a leisurly two-week trek ends at **Balephi** on the road to Kathmandu.

Sherpa teahouse in Helambu.

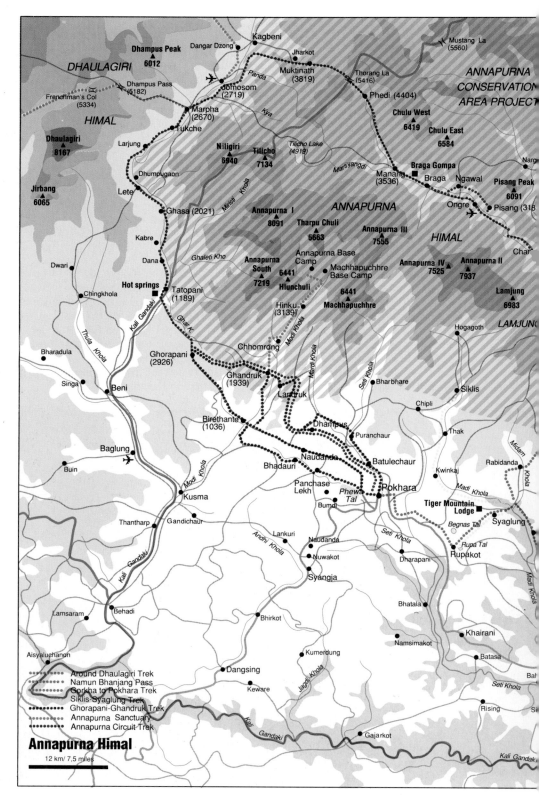

DHAULAGIRI

Kagbeni
Dangar Dzong
Jharkot
Muktinath
(3819)
Mustang La
(5560)

ANNAPURNA
CONSERVATION
AREA PROJECT

Dhampus Peak
6012

Dhampus Pass
(5182)
Frenchman's Col
(5334)
Jomosom
(2719)
Panda
Thorang La
(5416)
Phedi (4404)

Chulu West
6419
Chulu East
6584

HIMAL

Marpha
(2670)
Tukche
Kya

Dhaulagiri
8167

Larjung

Niligiri
6940
Tilicho
7134
Tilicho Lake
(4919)
Marsyangdi
Manang
(3536)
Braga Gompa
Braga
Ngawal
Pisang Peak
6091
Narg

Dhumpugaon

Jirbang
6065

Lete

Ghasa (2021)

Annapurna I
8091
ANNAPURNA
Ongre
Pisang (318

Char

Kabre

Dana

Ghaleti Kho

Annapurna South
7219
Tharpu Chuli
5663
Annapurna III
7555
HIMAL

Annapurna Base
Camp

Annapurna IV
7525
Annapurna II
7937

Dwari

Chingkhola

Hot springs
Tatopani
(1189)

Annapurna
South
6441
Hiunchuli
Machhapuchhre
Base Camp

6441
Machhapuchhre

Lamjung
6983

Hinku
(3139)

Ghar K.

Modi Khola

Hogagoth
LAMJUN

Bharadula

Thula Khola

Ghorapani
(2926)

Chhomrong

Mardi Khola

Seti Khola

Bharbhare

Siklis

Singa

Beni

Kali Gandaki

Ghandruk
(1939)

Landruk

Chipli

Thak

Baglung

Buin

Modi Khola

Birethante
(1036)

Dhampus
Puranchaur

Naudanda

Bhadauri

Batulechaur

Kwinkaj

Rabidanda

Midam
Khola

Kusma

Thantharp
Gandichaur

Andhi Khola

Lankuri

Panchase
Lekh
Bumdi
Phewa
Tal
Pokhara

Madi Khola

Tiger Mountain
Lodge

Begnas Tal
Syaglung

Naudanda

Seti Khola

Rupa Tal

Rupakot

Lamsaram

Behadi

Bhirkot

Nuwakot

Syangja

Dharapani

Bhatala

Khairani

Aisyaluchanon

Kumerdung

Dangsing

Keware

Jagdi Khola

Namsimakot

Batasa

Bah

Kali Gandaki

Seti Khola

Rising

Si

•••••••• Around Dhaulagiri Trek
•••••••• Namun Bhanjang Pass
—— Gorkha to Pokhara Trek
•••••••• Siklis-Syaglung Trek
•••••••• Ghorapani-Ghandruk Trek
•••••••• Annapurna Sanctuary
•••••••• Annapurna Circuit Trek

Gajarkot

Kali Gandak

Annapurna Himal

12 km/ 7,5 miles

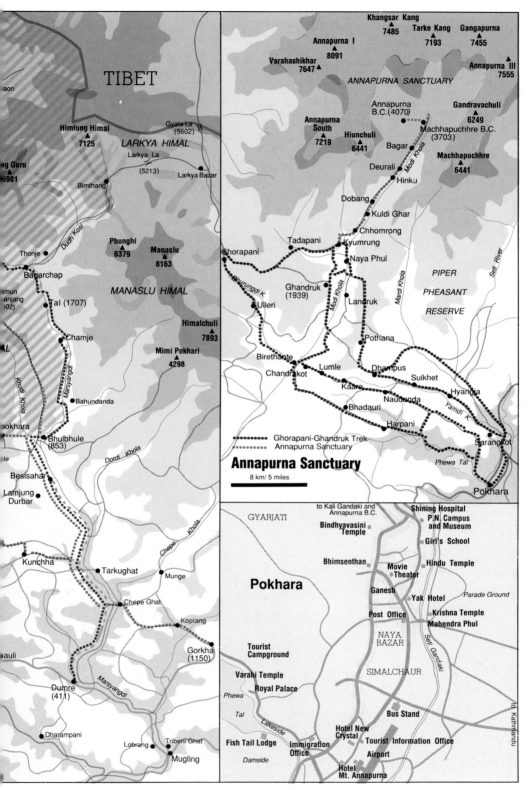

TIBET

LARKYA HIMAL

Himlung Himal
7125

Gyala La
(5602)

Larkya La
(5213)

Larkya Bazar

Bimthang

ng Guru
6981

Thonje

Bagarchap

Phunghi
6379

Manaslu
8163

MANASLU HIMAL

mun
anjang
502)

Tal (1707)

Chamje

Himalchuli
7893

Bahundanda

Mimi Pokhari
4298

okhara

Bhulbhule
(853)

Besisahar

Lamjung
Durbar

Dordi Khola

Chepe Khola

Kunchha

Tarkughat

Munge

Chepe Ghat

Koplang

auli

Gorkha
(1150)

Dumre
(411)

Marsyangdi

Dharampani

Lobrang

Tribeni Ghat

Mugling

Khangsar Kang
7485

Tarke Kang
7193

Gangapurna
7455

Annapurna I
8091

Varahashikhar
7647

ANNAPURNA SANCTUARY

Annapurna III
7555

Annapurna
B.C.(4070)

Gandravachuli
6249

Annapurna
South
7219

Hiunchuli
6441

Bagar

Machhapuchhre B.C.
(3703)

Deurali

Machhapuchhre
6441

Hinku

Dobang

Kuldi Ghar

Chhomrong

Tadapani

Kyumrung

Ghorapani

Naya Phul

PIPER

PHEASANT

RESERVE

Ghandruk
(1939)

Landruk

Ulleri

Pothana

Birethante

Lumle

Dhampus

Suikhet

Chandrakot

Kaare

Naudanda

Hyangja

Bhadauri

Harpani

Sarangkot

●●●●● Ghorapani-Ghandruk Trek
○○○○○ Annapurna Sanctuary

Phewa Tal

Pokhara

Annapurna Sanctuary

8 km/ 5 miles

GYARJATI

to Kali Gandaki and
Annapurna B.C.

Shining Hospital

P.N. Campus
and Museum

Bindhyavasini
Temple

Girl's School

Bhimsenthan

Hindu Temple

Movie
Theater

Pokhara

Ganesh

Yak Hotel

Parade Ground

Post Office

Krishna Temple

Mahendra Phul

NAYA
BAZAR

Tourist
Campground

SIMALCHAUR

Varahi Temple

Royal Palace

Phewa

Bus Stand

Tal

Lakeside

Hotel New
Crystal

Tourist Information Office

Fish Tail Lodge

Immigration
Office

Airport

Damside

Hotel
Mt. Annapurna

POKHARA VALLEY

Nestled beneath the snow-crested Annapurna Massif 200 kilometers (124 miles) west of Kathmandu, the lush **Pokhara Valley** has quietly won the hearts of travellers from around the world. Many visitors find that their most lasting impression of Nepal is **Machhapuchhre's** razor-edged "fish tail" peak piercing the skyline or reflected in the still waters of **Phewa Lake**. The antithesis of Kathmandu's flurry of cars, concrete and temples, Pokhara is a laid-back and spread-out bazaar town where farm houses nudge against tourist lodges and a new-age T-shirt is *haute couture* for even the best hotels.

Pokhara is Nepal's second most popular tourist destination; a quarter of all visitors travel here, many on their way to trekking in the Annapurnas, or to enjoy a relaxing holiday with incomparable mountain views.

Annapurna I, crowning a 140 kilometer (87 mile) horizon stretching from Dhaulagiri to Himalchuli, lies just 48 kilometers (30 miles) from the lake's edge as the crow flies. Machhapuchhre, just 30 kilometers' (19 miles) away, seemingly erupts from the valley. The elevational differences are equally impressive; 7,000 meters (23,500 feet) from the valley floor to the tip of Annapurna I, tenth highest mountain in the world at 8,091 meters (26,545 feet) above sea level.

Pokhara sits at about 900 meters (3,000 feet) elevation, significantly lower than Kathmandu and generally several degrees warmer. The fertile valley and an annual rainfall of 4,000 millimeters (157 inches) produce a gardenscape of subtropical flora.

Flowering cacti, poinsettias, citrus and banana trees line the rice and mustard fields; garden walls are hedged with thorny spurge spiked with red blossoms, and the knarled roots of *pipal* and banyan trees burst from stone *chautaras*. A lakeside forest of mixed oak and evergreen conifers borders the extensively cultivated Mahabharat hills to the south.

The 20th Century Arrives by Plane: Until a quarter of a century ago, Pokhara was a quiet Newar and Gurung farming community which came alive only during winter when caravans from Mustang – announced by the jingle of mule bells – and heavily laden porters from Butwal congregated to exchange goods. The wheel was not yet in use when the first airplane landed at Pokhara in 1952. Six years later, a novel jeep flew in by plane even before the primitive wooden bullock cart arrived by the same means in 1961.

The eradication of malaria in the late 1950s, the commissioning of hydroelectric power in 1968, and the completion of the Kathmandu-Pokhara and Pokhara-Sonauli highways in the early 1970s rocketed Pokhara into the 20th century – but without much planning.

Nevertheless, it has become a regional centre for administration, commerce and cottage industry. The **Shining Hospital** and **Prithvi Narayan**

Campus are located in the northern part of town as is the **Bindhyavasini Temple** overlooking a modest amusement park. Shining Hospital is the trailhead for most Annapurna treks and is a good place to hire porters who gather there for work. The campus **Natural History Museum** features displays on the peoples and wildlife of the Annapurna Conservation Area, whose project headquarters is three days' walk away in Ghandruk.

The bus station sprawls at the eastern entrance to town, not far from Pokhara's gravel-runway **airport**, the **Tourist Information Centre**, several medium-priced hotels and trekking agencies. Five minutes' taxi ride past the **Immigration Office** are **Lakeside** and **Damside**, the most congenial spots for visitors. Scores of inexpensive lodges, restaurants and shops selling Tibetan jewellery and artifacts, carpets, clothes, books and trekking equipment line the lanes. Many former denizens of Kathmandu's "Freak Street" have migrated here. A visit to the Tibetan carpet factory and handicraft centre at **Hyangja**, located several hours' walk or a taxi drive up valley, makes an interesting day outing.

Fish Tail Lodge, Pokhara's nicest hotel, is set on an island peninsula reachable by flotation raft. The lake edge just beyond the hotel grounds is the best vantage point for photographing Machhapuchhre's reflection in the clear morning light. The hotel with the best close-up mountain views however is the new deluxe **Tiger Mountain Lodge**, located on a ridge northeast of Pokhara.

Lakes and Caves: A **Tourist Campground** edges the water near the demarcated swimmers' beach. Row boats and a few sailboats can be rented along the shore for exploring the two and a half kilometer long lake, criss-crossed by local fishermen and village farmers paddling dugout canoes. The **Golden Temple of Varahi** on a tiny shaded island draws pilgrims and romantics, just opposite the modest winter palace of King Birendra.

Brahman and Chhetri villages thrive on the gentle hills around Pokhara.

270

Lake Phewa is one of eight lakes in the Pokhara valley. Few others are known to tourists except **Rupa** and **Begnas**, pleasant lakes for day hikes or picnics located about 15 kilometers (nine miles) east of Pokhara by road.

Ancient subsurface lakes have left limestone caverns large enough to walk upright through at **Mahendra Caves** in **Batulechaur**, north of the bazaar. For a few rupees young boys with flashlights lead the way pointing out stalactite and stalagmite features which locals interpret as images of deities. The **Seti Khola** has carved a narrow chasm on its course through the valley, visible from the **Mahendra Phul** (bridge) near the airport where the river rushes 30 meters (100 feet) below in a nine-meter (30-foot) wide gap in the earth.

There are numerous trails leading into the hills surrounding Pokhara. **Sarankot**, **Naudanda**, and **Bumdi** are all accessible on day hikes (Naudanda is now reachable by the newly built "Chinese" road); lodges at Sarankot and Naudanda offer simple other accommodations (see page 274). Agents in Pokhara can arrange pony treks. Some of the other more scenic excursions include a drive west on the Siddhartha Raj Marg to **Kubhinde Pass** for a spectacular sunrise over the Annapurna massif. Like the fortress ruins site at Sarankot, **Nuwakot**, located 15 kilometers (nine miles) south of Pokhara, served as a lookout for Kaski kings prior to conquest by Prithvi Narayan Shah.

Located in the geographical centre of Nepal on a main highway from Kathmandu, Pokhara is accessible by tourist bus or private taxi in a six hour drive through a scenic cross-section of Nepal's middle hills. Due to ongoing road construction, the ride can be slow or delayed.

Royal Nepal Airlines ferries passengers two to three times daily from Kathmandu, featuring panoramic views of the Annapurnas and central Himalaya. Royal Chitwan National Park, Lumbini, Tansen, white-water rafting and tourist attractions in western Nepal are all accessible by road from Pokhara.

An old man with children enjoys watching the world go by.

ANNAPURNA HIMAL

Dawn's rays gild **Annapurna I** before any of her sister peaks in the majestic **Annapurna Himal**. At 8,091 meters (26,545 feet), she crowns a range which scarcely dips below 6,000 meters (20,000 feet). This is a land of astonishing altitudinal variation and ecological diversity, encompassing the tropical Pokhara Valley to the frozen tips of the some of the world's highest peaks – a region brimming with natural beauty and preeminently the most popular trekking area in Nepal.

Marking a convergence of biogeographical zones east and west, the Annapurnas host a wide assortment of flora and fauna. The massif's southern flanks are blanketed in lush deciduous forests, fed by some of the country's greatest rainfall. Fir, pine and juniper tend the upper slopes while the mountains' rainshadow effect keeps the high valleys brown and barren.

Wildlife once abounded in every habitat but has been driven to remote corners by widespread land clearing and hunting. Still the low-swinging rhesus and langur monkeys, jungle cats and wild boar give way to mid-elevation black bear, musk deer and yellow throated marten. The long-haired *tahr* (mountain goat), *bharal* (blue sheep) and snow leopard prowl the loftiest reaches. Among the 440 recorded bird species are the monal and Impeyan pheasants, and some 40 migratory varieties which take refuge en route to and from Tibet.

The human community of 40,000 is a melting pot as well. Seven ethnic groups live side by side wearing distinctive dress, revering different deities and speaking their own languages. High caste Brahmans and Chhetris, Newars and the occupational Kamis (blacksmiths), Damais (tailors) and Sarkis (shoemakers), primarily Hindus, occupy lowland valleys. Hill-peoples, some distant descendants of Tibetans, include the Gurungs, Magars and Thakalis. Most follow the Buddhist doctrine or a syncretism of the two religions. Living close to the border are peoples more recently migrated from Tibet, such as the Lopa of Kagbeni, who cling to the Bon religion (see page 101), or the Manangis, who as skilled traders have benefitted from centuries of preferential commerce laws.

A Magnet for Trekkers: More than 38,000 trekkers visit the Annapurna area each year, three times the number who hike in Everest, the next most trekked region. Combined with increasing numbers of tourists, growth in the native population has contributed to deforestation, intensive cultivation and livestock grazing, poor sanitation, littering and water pollution. In the last few years, the non-governmental Annapurna Conservation Area Project (ACAP) has been organising villagers to take up measures of resource management, low-tech conservation, alternative energy schemes and community development programmes. The results are inspiring (see page 56).

The nearly month-long walk around

Preceding pages: the stupendous bulk of the Annapurna massif dominates the region. **Left,** inside the monastery at Braga in the Manang valley. **Right,** Brahman farmer ploughing his fields in the Annapurna foothills.

the Annapurna massif is considered by many as the classic Nepal trek. The route circles the Annapurna and **Lamjung Himals** (6,983 meters, 22,910 feet), including Annapurna I, tenth highest peak in the world, **Annapurna II** (7,937 meters, 26,040 feet), **Annapurna IV** (7,525 meters, 24,688 feet), **Annapurna III** (7,555 meters, 24,787 feet) and **Gangapurna** (7,455 meters, 24,458 feet). On the eastern front, it traces the **Marsyangdi River** up and over **Thorong La** pass (5,416 meters, 17,769 feet) then descends the **Kali Gandaki** to the west. The trek can be done in reverse but requires a greater one day elevation gain to get over the pass. Lodges are spaced for every night and snack stops are available throughout the day.

The trek commonly begins in **Dumre**, a road stop two to three hours' drive east from Pokhara. Trucks and jeeps go as far as **Besisahar** on an unpaved seasonal road. Alternatively, the trail enters the Marsyangdi valley at **Tarkughat**, two days west of the town of **Gorkha**, or at **Khudi** a slightly longer walk from Pokhara. These less-travelled sections give a taste of hill life which is unadulterated by tourist-catering entrepreneurs.

The first days' walk up the Marsyangdi River affords excellent and ever-changing views of the high Himalaya. To the north and west loom **Machhapuchhre** (6,994 meters, 22,950 feet) and Annapurnas II to IV. Dominating the eastern skyline are **Manaslu** (8,163 meters, 26,781 feet), the world's eighth highest peak, **Himalchuli** (7,893 meter, 25,896 feet), **Peak 29** (7,835 meters, 25,705 feet) – locally known as **Ngadi Himal** – and **Baudha Himal** (6,672 meters, 21,889 feet).

The trail climbs gently through banana palms and rice fields, shaded by welcome *chautaras* beneath the sprawling limbs of aged *pipal* and *bahar* or *banyan* trees; or sometimes both, symbolizing a male-female union. At **Bahundanda** (1,310 meters, 4,300 feet), lowland Hindu communities give way to Gurung and Magar villages.

Street in the Thakali village of Marpha in the Kali Gandaki valley.

276

Typical two-toned ochre and white-washed houses mirror the amalgamation of two cultures and ecological zones. Here, the wide valley squeezes into a rock-bound cleft, millet replaces rice cultivation, and oak-rhododendron-spruce covered slopes take over.

At the bazaar town of **Bagarchap**, the valley swerves due west to enter the 24-kilometer (15-mile) long **Manang Valley**. A new trail blasted out of solid rock avoids a section once considered too dangerous even for pack animals. In earlier times, the only southern entry into the Marsyangdi gorge was a high trail over the treacherous **Namun Bhanjang** pass (5,502 meters, 18,050 feet) to Ghanpokhara, Khudi or west to the Modi Khola.

As the climate cools, forests turn to pine. At **Tal** ("lake"), tourist inns outshine the dark, cramped quarters previously shared with herdsmen and traders. **Chame** (2,655 meters, 8,710 feet) is the district headquarters and checkpost for Manang, with electricity and natural hot springs (as at Bahundanda).

The **Nar Valley**, off limits to foreigners, enters from the north. The people of Nar and **Phu** villages were originally from Tibet and, like those of Dolpo, remain largely out of touch with the rest of the world. In such a high, cold environment only barley, buckwheat and potatoes grows, supplemented with summer greens, yak meat and dairy products.

A kilometer beyond **Brathang** a sweeping rock face of dark limestone spans two promontory points some 1,650 meters above the river. Known as "ghost rock," it represents the arduous route to heaven among local Gurungs. The main trail continues up through thinning pine forest and enters the broad **Nyeshang** (or upper Manang) valley.

With their tight clusters of flat-roofed stone buildings huddled against eroding sandstone cliffs, the villages of **Pisang** and **Braga** are reminiscent of native American Hopi Indian communities. Buddhist prayer flags flying from the houses' corners, however, and the massive northern flanks of An-

Muktinath temple with its 108 sacred waterspouts is an important pilgrimage place for Hindus and Buddhists alike.

napurna II, IV, and further up Annapurna III, Gangapurna, **Glacier Dome** or **Tarkekang** (7,193 meters, 23,599 feet) and **Tilicho Peak** (7,134 meters, 23,405 feet), dissolve any question of whereabouts.

An alternative high trail connects Pisang to Braga through the traditional villages of **Ghyaru** and **Ngawal**. **Pisang Peak** (6,091 meters, 19,983 feet) towers to the east. Like nearby **Chulu East** and **West** (both approximately 6,500 meters or 21,000 feet), it is a Trekking Peak open for non-expeditionary ascents (see page 155).

There is much to see and do in the upper valley warranting a rest-day at either Braga or Manang, which can doubly serve for acclimatisation. Doctors advise that once above 3,400 meters (11,000 feet), trekkers should not sleep more than 300 meters (1,000 feet) above the previous night's stay.

Braga's 400 to 500 year old *gompa* is one of the cultural highlights of the valley. A series of *terra cotta* statues of the Kargyupa *lama* lineage lines its outer walls. Manang village (3,535 meters, 11,600 feet), the largest and last significant settlement in the valley, also has a monastery. It is customary to remove shoes before entering a *gompa* and to make an offering such as a small donation to help with its upkeep.

Day hikes to higher elevations help with acclimatisation. One trip reaches a forested plateau overlooking the Gangapurna ice waterfall which feeds a stunning glacial lake. Another ascends to **Khangsar** along the difficult 18-kilometer (11-mile) track to **Tilicho Lake** (4,919 meters, 16,138 feet). Entry is restricted, however.

Trekkers number upward of 300 per day through Manang during peak season. Scheduled flights from Pokhara will bring others not so well acclimatised. The Himalayan Rescue Association (H.R.A.) Trekkers' Aid Post, which is seasonally staffed by volunteer Western physicians, treats trekkers and villagers. The **Manang Mountaineering School**, built in 1979 by Yugoslavians to honour a Sherpa killed on Everest, offers summer classes in climbing techniques and safety.

Proceeding slowly up from Manang, a night at **Leder** and then at **Phedi** (4,404 meters, 14,449 feet) bodes well for crossing the Thorong La. The first part of the pass is the steepest, leveling off in a series of false summits before the top, which is unmistakably marked with stone cairns and wind-whipped prayer flags. Magnificent views unfold all around. The icy trail descends to Muktinath (3,810 meters, 12,500 feet), completing an eight to ten hour hike from Phedi.

"Place of a Hundred Springs": Besides Pashupatinath temple in the Kathmandu Valley, **Muktinath** is the most sacred Hindu site in Nepal. Pilgrims come to bathe in the pure spring waters that gush from 108 water spouts shaped as cows' heads. Buddhists come to pay homage at a shrine enclosing a blue flame of natural gas which burns eternally above a trickle of water, a wondrous union of fire, air and water.

Ammonite fossils called *shaligrams* – evidence of the Himalaya's former

Left, Brahman farmer ploughing his fields in the Annapurna foothills. Right, Annapurna is one of the most pleasant trekking areas. A young porter rests with his load.

position beneath the Tethys Sea (see page 31) – are revered as embodiments of Vishnu.

Full moon is a propitious time to visit Muktinath, and, especially during August-September, to witness a rowdy festival called Yartung wherein local Tibetans hold horse races amidst much wild drinking, gambling and dancing.

Near **Kagbeni**, a fascinating old citadel, the trail divides in four directions; north into distant **Mustang,** one of the few remaining Tibetan dominions ruled by ancestral nobility; south down the Kali Gandaki, dividing the Dhaulagiri Himal from the Annapurnas; west to **Dangar Dzong** and Dolpo; and east from Muktinath. A myriad of paths explore the region; to **Jharkot** fortress perched above Kagbeni, or along a ridge north of Muktinath looking down into Mustang.

The upper Kali Gandaki is known as the **Thak Khola**, home of the Thakali people whose *bhattis* (lodges) are legendary among trekkers for their cleanliness and among traders for their unbeatable *dal bhaat*. The Thakalis have also prospered in the salt trade, and can be seen (and heard) accompanying colourful caravans of mules adorned in plumes, bells and streamers of discarded casette ribbon along the old trade route to Pokhara.

Royal Nepal's Twin Otter flies the same course in and out of **Jomosom** (2,710 meters, 8,900 feet) through a narrow slice between and well below the tips of **Dhaulagiri I** (8,167 meters, 26,795 feet) and Annapurna I. These two giants tower nearly seven kilometers (four miles) above the Kali Gandaki at the village of Tatopani, making this the deepest gorge on earth. Those who fly into Jomosom should be aware of altitude symptoms. The Jomosom to Pokhara trek takes eight to ten days, twelve in reverse; extra days may be needed in case of flight delay.

A trip strictly for leather-skinned trekkers encircles the **Dhaulagiri Himal**, comprising Dhaulagiri I-VI all over 7,260 meters (23,800 feet), through partially restricted, semi-wild

Braga village in the Manang valley.

territory. A month-long trek heads west from Dangar Dzong crossing two high passes and on to Tarakot in Dolpo, returning to Pokhara via Dhorpatan (see page 312). A short cut itinerary climbs out of the Kali Gandaki and over **Dhampus** and **French Passes** via **Hidden Valley**, then turns southeast to follow the **Mayangdi Khola** to Beni, west of Pokhara.

Apricot Brandy and Hot Springs: Marpha is a gastronomic delight with garden vegetables and juicy apples, apricots and peaches sold fresh, dry and as robust *rakshi* (distilled liquor). Both Marpha and **Tukuche** (2,590 meters, 8,480 feet) have retained their indigenous charm despite electrification.

Traces of forest appear on the hillsides, leaving behind the dry moonscape, and a strong wind tears with midday regularity through the valley. Exploratory trips such as up the **Dhaulagiri Icefall** reward those with a flexible schedule. A seven-day hike up to **Annapurna Base Camp** and back follows the spectacular route discov-

ered by French climbers with Maurice Herzog in 1950 on the first ever ascent of an 8,000-meter peak (Annapurna I).

Below **Ghasa** the Kali Gandaki plunges through a narrow chasm, and the transition from pines to broadleaf, deciduous trees marks the lower reaches of Thakali *bhattis* and Tibetan Lamaistic influence. At **Tatopani** (1,189 meters, 3,900 feet), whose name means "hot springs," lodgekeepers capitalize on natural hot springs and a balmy, floral setting, tempting the trekkers with hydro-generated videos and oven-baked pizza. The long climb up through rhododendron and oak forests to **Ghorapani Pass** regains 1,660 meters (5,450 feet), with primo views back to number seven in the world: Dhaulagiri I.

Sunrise from Pun Hill: Ghorapani ("horse water"), a jumble of trekker lodges literally carved out of a denuded landscape, was once a movie-set tradepost. Now it is an easy destination for trekkers – where Tibetan refugees hawk "yak bone artifacts" – boasting glorious

The Himalayan foothills can be clement and fertile.

views of **Annapurna South** (7,219 meters, 23,684 feet), **Hiunchuli** (6,441 meters, 21,130 feet) and from the top of **Pun Hill** (approximately 3,200 meters, 10,500 feet) an unforgettable sunrise over Machhapuchhre. Inspired by an Australian conservation project, lodge-keepers have installed fuel-efficient stoves and composting toilets, and on their own have removed lodges from Pun Hill (named for a prevalent Magar clan), establishing it as a protected area.

From Ghorapani there are two main return routes to Pokhara, each taking four to five days. One follows the donkey trains down some 3,700 steps from **Ulleri** to **Tirkhedhunga** (1,577 meters, 5,175 feet) and on to **Birethante's** riverside lodges in a long day. From the confluence of the Modi and **Bhurungdi Kholas**, the old trail continues up to **Chandrakot** and contours through **Lumle** where it meets the new Chinese-built road which obliterates the trail onward through **Khare** and **Naudanda**. An alternative skirts to the next ridge south via **Jhobang** and **Bhadauri**

before descending to the Harpan **Khola** and across **Phewa Tal** (lake) by paddle boat to Pokhara.

Many trekkers make an eight to ten day Pokhara-Ghorapani-Ghandruk loop, or vice versa. The walk from Ghorapani (2,853 meters, 9,360 feet) to **Ghandruk** – also known as Ghandrung – can be done in one day but might be split at either **Tadapani** or **Banthante** if going the other way. The trail tunnels through an incredible rhododendron forest whose bronze twisted limbs inspired Tolkien's *Hobbit* forest. During March and April, the Annapurna forests, as throughout much of Nepal's mid-region, are smothered with *laligurans* (rhododendron) trees ablaze with ivory, rose, apricot and crimson bouquets. The sweet frangrance of *daphne* blossoms fills the air.

The Annapurna Sanctuary: Ghandruk's sprawling split-level town is one of the biggest Gurung settlements in Nepal. A layover day is well spent roaming its maze of stone-paved paths among handsome slate-roofed houses.

A woman at Chame weaves on a traditional loom.

The community prospers, as do others in the region, from its young men serving in the Gurkha regiments.

The **Annapurna Conservation Area** headquarters, with a museum and informative staff, sets on a promontory behind the health post. The site provides an unbeatable photo-op taking in Annapurna South, Hiunchuli, Machhapuchhre and the steep sided **Modi Khola** valley leading into the **Annapurna Sanctuary**.

Long before trekkers came flocking to the Himalaya, *Deothal* as the Gurungs know it, was a place of refuge and spiritual renewal, where nothing should be slaughtered nor meat eaten. Lt. Col. Jimmy Roberts christened it the "Annapurna Sanctuary" during his 1956 unsuccessful attempt to climb Machhapuchhre, itself a sacred summit subsequently closed to expeditions.

A natural amphitheatre surrounded by eleven peaks over 6,400 meters (21,000 feet), the Sanctuary affords trekkers a spot amidst a panoply of enormous peaks, a high usually reserved for mountaineers. **Annapurna Base Camp** (4,070 meters, 13,550 feet), a large snow-covered meadow with several small lodges, is only a week's walk from Pokhara, through **Dhampus** and **Landruk** (also called Landrung) in one direction and Ghandruk and Birethante in the other.

Tea houses, many trimmed with flower beds , provide some of the highest standard trek lodging in Nepal. The ACAP "demonstration" lodge at **Kuldi Ghar** features fresh garden vegetables and a hot shower heated by the efficient back-boiler system. In order to save trees, ACAP regulations prohibit fires in the Sanctuary (kerosene can be purchased and stoves rented in **Chhomrong**). Weather is fickle and the Modi valley gorge is susceptible to avalanches and early snow. Non-expedition climbers can try out **Tharpu Chuli** (Tent Peak, 5,663 meters, 18,550 feet) with a Trekking Peak permit.

Historic Hill Treks: Siklis, one of the early southern Gurung settlements, retains an aura of olden times where tradi-

Tea shops provide alternative accommodation for trekkers.

tions run strong. The *jhankri* (shaman) and *lama* (priest) each have a place in the Buddhist community, in marriage, death and dealing with ill-fate. Village elders oversee an effective forest management system whereby the entire year's wood supply is cut during three frenzied days, culminating in a frolicsome celebration.

Dasain, Nepal's great fall festival, is a time of home-coming, feasting, dancing for Siklis as for much of the hill country. Hindus sacrifice goats, chickens and buffalo in the name of goddess Durga, and are blessed with a *tika*.

On an east-facing slope above the **Madi Khola** at 1,981 meters (6,500 feet), Siklis looks north on Annapurna IV, and east to Annapurna II and Lamjung Himal. From Pokhara, a two day trek to Siklis continues west to the **Piper Pheasant Reserve** where hunting is permitted. A seven to ten day trek returns along the Modi Khola southeast from Siklis, climbs to **Kalikathan** and **Syaglung** on a ridge paralleling the east-west Annapurna Himal, and de-

scends to **Rupa** and **Begnas Tals** (lakes) in the eastern Pokhara valley. Britain's Prince Charles tramped in this area in 1980, calling on the Gurkha recruits' home hamlets. A four-day "Royal Trek" mimicking his route encompasses village life and striking mountain panoramas.

The Annapurna hills are alive with battle tales between rival kings from the days of fierce trade feuds and territorial skirmishes. The faded glory of **Ghanpokhara's** rich woodwork and oversized houses tells its story as controller of the Marsyangdi salt trade. A prominent hilltop position (2,165 meters, 7,100 feet) grants it sweeping views of Lamjung, Manaslu and Gorkha Himals.

Stone ramparts of the old **Lamjung Durba** royal fort, residence of Ghale and later Thakuri kings, remain from this ancestral home of the lineage which in 1559 conquered Gorkha and later gave birth to the kingdom of Nepal.

Today, Gurungs of northern Lamjung raise sheep and goats for wool which the women weave into attractive striped blankets called *baakhu*, as well as kitten soft *pachuri* shawls and jackets sold in Pokhara's and Kathmandu's markets. The Gurungs' dress is distinctive; the women often wear a burgundy velvet blouse *(chol)* over a colourful *ghuniyo* (loongi) and hefty golden nose and ear ornaments. The men sport a *bhot* (vest) and the traditional *kachada*, a short skirt-like wrap. A handwoven white cotton square *(bhanggra)* is loosely tied across the men's chests, creating a back-sack in which light goods can be carried.

Climbing to the west of Pokhara gains excellent views of the Annapurnas and Machhapuchhre. An overnight trek to **Sarangkot**, another fortress site, and along the crest toward Naudanda circles south and returns via the Harpan valley. Above Lake Phewa's southern rim set picturesque **Pumdi** and **Bumdi**, with their old style oval-shaped, red clay houses; in early times, evil spirits were thought to dwell in corners, thus the rounded walls. Just minutes from modern Pokhara, traditions hold firm.

Left, highland man of Tibetan origin.

A DAY IN THE LIFE OF A GURUNG HILLWOMAN

"Kaanchi! Oh Kaanchi!" Sun Kumari calls her youngest daughter into the dim light of the coming day. She and her husband have been up since dawn, he reciting the morning prayers to a medley of Hindu and Buddhist gods, she stoking the coals of last night's fire to brew a fresh pot of milk tea.

Kaanchi arises from a shapeless pile of children and goat-hair blankets and sleepily adjusts the *naamlo* (rope headstrap) and jug that are her tools for fetching water, the first chore of the day. Barefoot, she enters the mist, her small calloused feet padding silently down the slate steps that overlook the precipitous canyon walls of the Modi Khola.

Sunlight filters through the glassless windows of the tidy stone house, piercing the smoky interior and spotlighting an assortment of copper pots and utensils. The other children rise and drink tea as their grandmother, the *Bajai*, sits up and with a toothless grin, lights a Yak brand cigarette. Sun Kumari squats by the doorway and spreads a layer of fresh ochre-coloured mud on the inside floor, a daily ritual performed by Gurung women to cleanse their homes of malevolent spirits. The day comes to life punctuated by laughter, good natured teasing and the scratchy sounds of Radio Nepal.

After the morning meal of *dhero*, a gruel of ground, boiled millet, with venison curry, the older children go to school, the younger ones wander into the forest to collect firewood and fodder, and the adults migrate to the sunny stone courtyard. Sun Kumari beats and winnows rice to be distilled into *rakshi* or cooked as *dhal bhaat*. Her husband weaves a bamboo basket and *Bajai* soaks up the sun, her pendulous golden earrings glistening like ice crystals.

The hard work of the harvest is over; the corn and chilies hang in colourful clumps on the drying racks, the sheep and goats graze in the Pokhara lowlands, and Sun Kumari spends her afternoons spinning wool and weaving carpets. Today some neighbour women drop by for an impromptu weaving and gossip session that lasts well into the night. Their usual light-hearted exchange grows uneasy as one recounts a story about several young village men who were caught fighting with a gang from over the hill. Once before they were reportedly drunk and watching lurid videos in Pokhara.

Times are changing; young people's behaviour is unprecedented and bewildering, causing disruption in the peaceful village. The youth are losing respect for Gurung ways; they seem angry and dissatisfied. If they go, who will run the village after the old folks die? Who will look after the fields and animals, and weave the baskets and blankets? Sun Kumari pauses for a moment to ponder the situation and says a quiet prayer of thanks that this destructive spirit has not afflicted her family. She weaves a band of soft brown wool into a new *baakhu*, a blanket for her son, and turns her thoughts to tomorrow's morning meal.

Spreading *pipal* tree is the centre of a Gurung village near Gorkha.

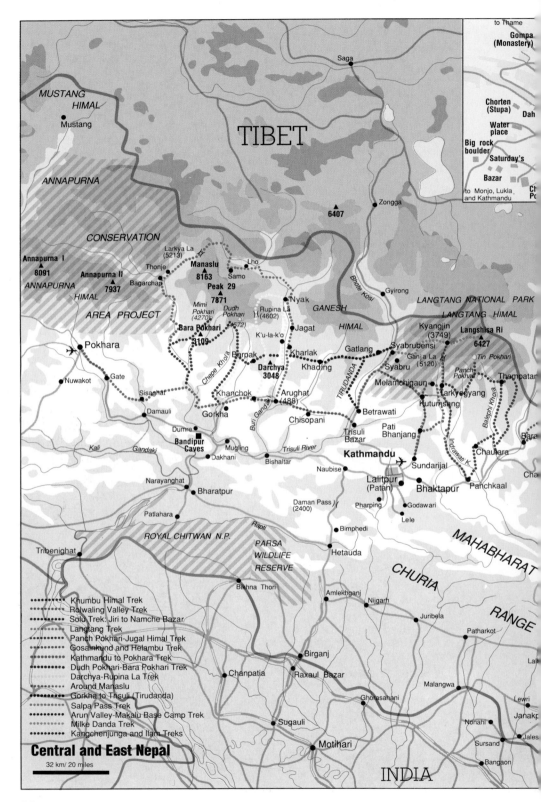

MUSTANG
HIMAL

• Mustang

TIBET

ANNAPURNA

CONSERVATION

• Zongga

▲ 6407

Larkya La
(5213)

Thonje

Manaslu
▲ 8163

Lho
Samo

Annapurna I
▲ 8091

Annapurna II
▲ 7937

ANNAPURNA
HIMAL

Bagarchap

Peak 29
▲ 7871

AREA PROJECT

Mimi
Pokhari
(4270)

Dudh
Pokhari

Rupina La
(4602)

Nyak

GANESH

Gyirong

LANGTANG NATIONAL PARK

LANGTANG HIMAL

Bhote Kosi

Bara Pokhari
▲ 3109

(572)

K'u-la-k'o

Jagat

HIMAL

Kyangjin
(3749)

Langshisa Ri
▲ 6427

Pokhara

Barpak

Chepe Khola

Darchya
▲ 3048

Kharlak

Khading

Gatlang

Syabrubensi

Ganja La
(5120)

Tin Pokhari

Nuwakot

Gate

Sisaghat

Khanchok

Buri Gandaki

Arughat
(488)

TIRUDANDA

Syabru

Melamchigaun

Panch
Pokhari

Thampatar

Damauli

Gorkha

Chisopani

Betrawati

Kutumsang

Tarkyegyang

Balephi Khola

Chautara

Dumre

Bandipur
Caves

Mugling

Dakhani

Trisuli River

Bishaltar

Trisuli
Bazar

Pati
Bhanjang

Indrawati K.

Bara

Kali

Gandaki

Narayanghat

Bharatpur

Naubise

Kathmandu

Lalitpur
(Patan)

Sundarijal

Bhaktapur

Panchkaal

Cha

Patlahara

Daman Pass
(2400)

Pharping

Lele

Godawari

Rapti

ROYAL CHITWAN N.P.

PARSA
WILDLIFE
RESERVE

Bimphedi

Hetauda

CHURIA

MAHABHARAT

Tribenighat

Bikhna Thori

Amlekhganj

Nijgarh

Juribela

RANGE

Patharkot

Lal

•••••••• Khumbu Himal Trek
•••••••• Rolwaling Valley Trek
•••••••• Solu Trek: Jiri to Namche Bazar
•••••••• Langtang Trek
•••••••• Panch Pokhari-Jugal Himal Trek
•••••••• Gosainkund and Helambu Trek
•••••••• Kathmandu to Pokhara Trek
•••••••• Dudh Pokhari-Bara Pokhari Trek
•••••••• Darchya-Rupina La Trek
•••••••• Around Manaslu
•••••••• Gorkha to Trisuli (Tirudanda)
•••••••• Salpa Pass Trek
•••••••• Arun Valley-Makalu Base Camp Trek
•••••••• Milke Danda Trek
•••••••• Kangchenjunga and Ilam Treks

Birganj

Chanpatia

Raxaul Bazar

Malangwa

Lewri

Janakp

Central and East Nepal

32 km/ 20 miles

Sugauli

Motihari

Nonahi

Sursand

Bangaon

Jales

INDIA

to Thame

Gompa
(Monastery)

Chorten
(Stupa)   Dah

Water
place

Big rock
boulder

Saturday's

Bazar

to Monjo, Lukla
and Kathmandu

Ch
Po

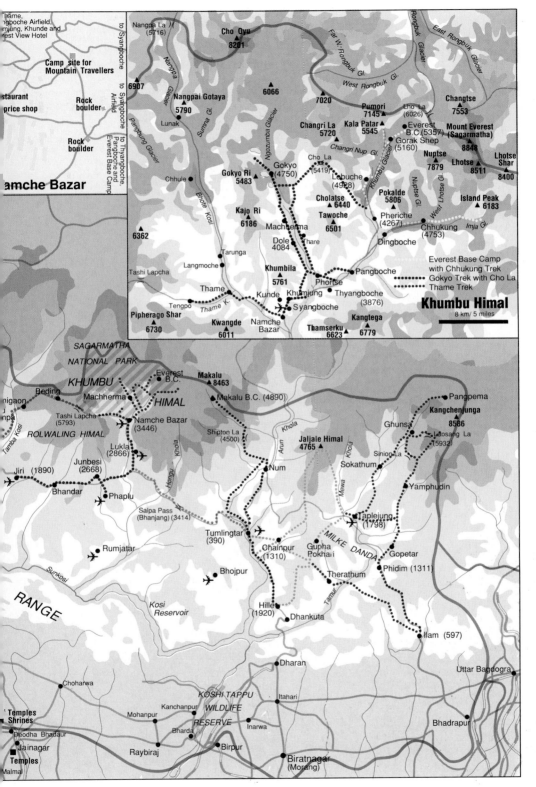

to Thame,
Syangboche Airfield,
Khumjung, Khunde and
Everest View Hotel

Camp site for
Mountain Travellers

restaurant
price shop

Rock
boulder

Rock
boulder

to Syangboche

to Syangboche
Airfield

to Thyangboche,
Pangboche and
Everest Base Camp

amche Bazar

Nangpa La
(5716)

Cho Oyu
8201

6907

Nangpai Gotaya
5790

Lunak

Chhule

6362

Far W. Rongbuk Gl.

West Rongbuk Gl.

Rongbuk Glacier

East Rongbuk Glacier

6066

7020

Pumori
7145

Lho La
(6026)

Changtse
7553

Changri La
5720

Kala Patar
5545

Everest
B.C.(5357)

Mount Everest
(Sagarmatha)

8848

Changri Nup Gl.

Gorak Shep
(5160)

Nuptse
7879

Lhotse
8511

Lhotse
Shar
8400

Cho La
(5419)

Gokyo Ri
5483

Gokyo
(4750)

Lobuche
(4928)

Pokalde
5806

Island Peak
6183

Kajo Ri
6186

Cholatse
6440

Tawoche
6501

Pheriche
(4267)

Chhukung
(4753)

Machherma

Dingboche

Imja Gl.

Dole
4084

Thare

Tarunga

Langmoche

Khumbila
5761

Phortse

Pangboche

Everest Base Camp
with Chhukung Trek
•••••• Gokyo Trek with Cho La
•••••• Thame Trek

Tashi Lapcha

Thame

Kunde

Khumjung

Thyangboche
(3876)

Khumbu Himal

8 km/ 5 miles

Tengpo

Thame K.

Syangboche

Pipherago Shar
6730

Kwangde
6011

Namche
Bazar

Thamserku
6623

Kangtega
6779

SAGARMATHA

NATIONAL PARK

KHUMBU

Everest
B.C.

Makalu
8463

Makalu B.C. (4890)

Pangpema

Kangchenjunga
8586

nigaon

Beding

Machherma

HIMAL

Tashi Lapcha
(5793)

Namche Bazar
(3446)

Shipton La
(4500)

Ghunsa

Laosang La
(5932)

npa

ROLWALING HIMAL

Lukla
(2866)

Arun Khola

Jaljale Himal
4765

Sinion La

Jiri (1890)

Junbesi
(2668)

Bhandar

Phaplu

Hongu Khola

Num

Sokathum

Yamphudin

Salpa Pass
(Bhanjang) (3414)

Tumlingtar
(390)

MILKE DANDA

Taplejung
(1798)

Rumjatar

Chainpur
(1310)

Gupha
Pokhari

Mewa Khola

Gopetar

Bhojpur

Therathum

Phidim (1311)

Sunkosi

Kosi
Reservoir

Hille
(1920)

Dhankuta

Tamur

Ilam (597)

RANGE

Dharan

Uttar Bagdogra

Choharwa

KOSHI TAPPU

Kanchanpur

WILDLIFE

Itahari

Temples
Shrines

Mohanpur

RESERVE

Inarwa

Bhadrapur

Deodha Bhadaur

Bharda

Jainagar

Raybiraj

Birpur

Biratnagar
(Morang)

Temples

Malma

EVEREST
AND THE EAST

East Nepal epitomizes the name *Himalaya, The Abode of the Gods.* Five of the world's ten highest peaks including **Mount Everest** at 8,848 meters (29,028 feet) – known as Sagarmatha to the Nepalese and Chomolungma to the Tibetans – preside over a land of great spiritual sanctuary, a region of geographical and cultural contrasts. In ancient Tibetan literature, valleys such as Khumbu and Rolwaling were sanctified as *beyuls*, hidden places of refuge for troubled times (see page 157). A wide variety of Himalayan wildlife find the eastern hills a hospitable environment nourished by an adolescent monsoon.

The first people known to inhabit east Nepal are the Kiratis, a Mongolian tribal people. In the 7th or 8th century B.C., they invaded the Kathmandu Valley and established a thriving kingdom which ruled until about 300 A.D. Their descendants, the Rais and Limbus, are still prevalent in the east and have carried on militarily as valued recruits in the British and Indian Gurkha regiments.

The east is home to at least a dozen ethnic hill-peoples including the celebrated Sherpas of mountaineering fame. The Sherpas, whose name "easterner" denotes their original home in eastern Tibet, settled in Khumbu, the Everest region, around 1533. They continued to trade over the Nangpa La pass, carrying salt, wool, carpets, Tibetan artifacts and mastiff dogs south from Tibet and grains, raw iron, paper, cotton cloth and *dzo* (a cross-breed of hill cattle and female yak) north from the lowlands. When trans-Himalayan trade subsided in the early 1960s, the Sherpas had already proven adept as mountain guides and high altitude porters. Since the 1970s, they have prospered from tourism more than any other ethnic group as lodgekeepers in Khumbu and in the Kathmandu-based trekking industry.

Trekking in the east avails a wide range of wilderness and cultural encounters. Most first-timers choose to live out their dreams of standing at the foot of Mount Everest. Others prefer the less trekked areas – everywhere east of Khumbu, including the newly de-restricted Kangchenjunga region – or a middle ground, such as Solu.

The Land of Milk and Honey: Solu, or Sho Rung as the Sherpas know it, lies between 2,600 and 3,200 meters (8,500 and 10,500 feet) elevation, extending from **Jiri** east to the **Dudh Kosi** ("Milk River"). It is a land blessed with temperate climate, well-watered forests and pasturelands, and rolling farmlands cultivated in maize, wheat, barley and apples. Buddhist *lamas*, monks and nuns led by *Rinpoches* (reincarnate *lamas*) serve the predominantly Sherpa communities from *gompas* patterned after those built by their ancestors in Tibet (see page 304).

This land of milk and honey is ideal for trekkers without a destination. Much more than a path to Khumbu's high country, Solu invites a leisurely pace – time for a retreat at **Junbesi's**

Preceding pages: the highest mountain in the world, Mount Everest, is flanked by Nuptse and Lhotse. Left, Sherpa mother and child of Pangboche village with Ama Dablan framed in the window. Right, this arrangement for a child near Kangchenjunga is a practical way to avoid the cold.

Thupten Choling or **Salleri** and **Phaplu's Chiwong** monasteries, or to photograph spring rhodododendron and magnolia blooms more profuse here than almost anywhere in Nepal. The mountains are present as well: a wilderness trek to **Dudh Kunda** reaches the base of **Numbur** (6,957 meters, 22,825 feet), Solu's sacred peak. Everest and the Khumbu range rise to the east while **Gauri Shanker** (7,145 meters, 23,442 feet) and **Menlungtse** (7,181 meters, 23,560 feet) tower to the north.

Most treks through Solu follow the route used by early Everest expeditions, but nowadays beginning in Jiri (1,905 meters, 6,250 feet) cutting several days off the old trail from **Lamosangu**. The region's mid-elevation does not signal an easy trek however. On a nine to ten-day hike to **Namche Bazaar**, gateway to Khumbu, the track crosses seven ridges, three at 3,000 meters (9,850 feet) or higher. Frequent lodges, some with private rooms and delicacies such as fresh apple pie, allow the independ-

ent trekker to travel light. Campers have more flexibility to get off the beaten track. Air service to mid-elevation airstrips at Jiri, Phaplu and Lukla, or to lowland **Ramechap, Okhaldhunga/ Rumjatar**, and **Lamidanda** reduce travel time from Kathmandu.

Trekking in Khumbu: Khumbu is too beautiful and too friendly a place to hurry. Besides, at such elevations, it can be dangerous to trek too high too fast (see page 173). Fortunately for trekkers, there are two medical stations in Khumbu staffed by Western doctors during the trekking seasons: a small hospital at Kunde developed with assistance from Sir Edmund Hillary's Himalayan Trust, and the Trekkers' Aid Post at Pheriche, under the auspices of the Himalayan Rescue Association. The Trust has assisted in building numerous schools, health posts, bridges and water pipelines throughout Solu Khumbu.

For visitors with limited time, the best way to approach Khumbu is to fly to **Lukla** (2,866 meters, 9,403 feet). Royal Nepal Airlines flies three or four times daily during peak season, weather permitting. The 40-minute flight gives a thrill of a lifetime as the little plane descends below the peaks into the Dudh Kosi gorge and bounces up the gravel runway which ends in a mountain face. Erratic scheduling and wind patterns often result in delayed or cancelled flights.

From Lukla, the trail climbs gradually up the steep-sided Dudh Kosi valley, crossing from side to side and passing through forests of blue pine, fir, juniper, rhododendron, birch and oak. Many villages, particularly **Phakding**, the standard first night's stop, cater to trekkers with Western style food and dormitory lodging.

Narrow bench-lands are cultivated in wheat, potatoes, spinach, onions and radishes. Piled stone walls and huge boulders are carved with the Buddhist *mantra "Om mani padme hum."* On Fridays, hundreds of barefoot porters line the trail like a string of ants toting food and wares up the mountainside to Namche's Saturday market.

All of Khumbu falls within **Sagar-**

Statue of the Buddha in the Junbesi monastery, Solu Khumbu.

matha National Park, established in 1976 with help from the government of New Zealand, Sir Edmund Hillary's native country. The Sherpa culture is an important part of the environment worthy of protection, recognized in the 1979 declaration of Khumbu as a World Heritage Site. There is a visitor centre above Namche Bazaar, and an entry post at **Jorsale** where trekkers register and pay a fee.

Crampons and Canned *Pate*: At the confluence of the Dudh Kosi and **Bhote Kosi** (another river named for its Tibetan origins), the trail crosses a high, sturdy bridge built with Swiss assistance and begins a grueling ascent to Namche (3,446 meters, 11,300 feet). On the way, the first glimpses of Everest and **Lhotse** (8,511 meters, 27,923 feet) are revealed. The Bhote Kosi leads northwest to **Thame** village and over the **Nangpa La** (5,716 meters, 18,753 feet) to Tibet.

The prosperous town of Namche, with its two and three-story glass-windowed houses cum lodges, a bank and post office sets in a U-shaped west-facing valley. Stone-paved lanes are lined with shops selling (and renting) an amazing selection of mountaineering ware and gourmet expedition food featuring Swiss chocolate and French *pate*. The sacred mountain **Khumbila** (5,761 meters, 18,900 feet) guards the north while **Thamserku** (6,608 meters, 21,680 feet) stands to the east and **Kwangde Ri** (6,187 meters, 20,298 feet) to the west.

An hour north of Namche, beyond the ridge hamlet of **Syangboche** airstrip serving the recently re-opened **Hotel Everest View**, are the two traditional villages of **Khumjung** and **Kunde**. Rock walls separate families' potato fields, curiously delineated as a honeycomb pattern on the superb Schneider map of Khumbu and the beautiful National Geographic map of Everest.

Sherpa painters have created a market for their whimsical artwork which portrays yetis and trekkers amidst the Khumbu village-scape in primitive Tibetan mural style.

Tulshey Rinpoche and monks of Thupten Choling monastery in Solu Khumbu.

The Trail to Everest Base Camp: By far the most travelled trail in Khumbu leads to Everest Base Camp. Most trekkers take at least six days from Namche, including time for acclimatisation. But with side trips and days to just soak in the mountains' wonders, two, preferably three weeks are needed to see Khumbu without rushing.

Until a fire destroyed it in January 1989, **Thyangboche** monastery was one of Khumbu's most important and beautiful cultural centres. With donations from the Sherpa and international communities, the monastery is being rebuilt in a nearly identical style, requiring years of detailed craftsmanship and painters specialized in replicating the interior's Tibetan Buddhist frescoes. The monastery site is perched on a high forested promontory at 3,876 meters (12,716 feet) on the main Base Camp trail. From here **Ama Dablam** (6,856 meters, 22,493 feet), Everest, **Nuptse** (7,879 meters, 25,850 feet) and Lhotse (8,516 meters, 27,940 feet) make a perfect picture to the north. A **Sherpa**

Cultural Centre with informative displays explaining the religious and home lives of Sherpas, and several lodges share the meadow site.

Many trekkers know Thyangboche as the site of the yearly **Mani Rimdu** festival, a dance-drama in which monks dressed in brilliant masks and silk robes perform ritual dances depicting Buddhism's subjugation of the ancient Bon religion – basically the victory of good over evil. It is held at Thyangboche every October or November, also at Thame's monastery in May and at Solu's Chiwong monastery in autumn.

The forest surrounding Thyangboche is considered sacred and wild animals roam fearlessly, such as the "fanged" musk deer and iridescent *danphe*. The trail wanders down through a magical forest which is heavy with moss and crosses the **Imja Khola's** seething waters on a plank bridge. The climb to **Pangboche,** site of Khumbu's oldest *gompa* where a yeti scalp and hand relic are displayed, passes by skillfully etched *mani* stones and the last scat-

The monastery of Thupten Choling bathed in afternoon light.

tered trees below timberline.

Soon the canyon widens into alpine meadows, and the river and trail divide. The Imja Khola leads east toward the high, uncommercialized settlements of **Dingboche** and **Chhukung**. At Chhukung (4,753 meters, 15,594 feet), five glaciers descend; a path edging Imja and Lhotse Glaciers passes a lake on the way to **Island Peak (Imja Tse) Base Camp**, take-off point for the two-day ascent of this 6,160 meter (20,210 foot) Trekking Peak. To the south, **Amphu Labtsa** pass (5,780 meters, 18,963 feet) leads to the wild and rugged **Hongu Basin**. This huge glacial cirque nestles five small lakes (**Panch Pokhari**) amidst a number of peaks over 6,000 meters (19,685 feet). The Hongu can also be reached via **Mingbo La** (5,817 meters, 19,084 feet) on the southeast ridge of Ama Dablam, as from over the high but gentle **Mera La** (5,415 meters, 17,766 feet) from Lukla, or from the Salpa Pass trail (see below).

Tourism's Two Sides: From the confluence of the Imja and **Lobuche Kholas,** the left-hand trail climbs gradually to **Pheriche**, an unimpressive settlement with tea shops and the trekkers' medical post midway up a hillocky windswept valley. Yak trains carrying goods whose prices increase incrementally with elevation plod up the eroded slope to **Dugla** and over the crest where a line of stone *chortens* memorialises climbers killed on Everest (see page 169). Many Sherpas have lost their lives in the course of a day's work. Ang Rita Sherpa is the only person to have summitted Everest six times and stands as a Nepalese hero.

Lobuche's cluster of lodges set at the edge of the **Khumbu Glacier** (4,928 meters, 16,168 feet) is the staging ground for forays to **Kala Pattar** ("Black Rock"), Everest Base Camp and climbs on the Trekking Peak **Lobuche Peak**. A two-hour hike through a morass of morainal boulders reaches **Gorak Shep** ("dead crow"), where one or two small lodges offer drafty quarters. The climb to Kala Pattar (5,545 meters, 18,192 feet) takes one to

Namche Bazaar in its dramatic amphitheatre beneath swirling October mists.

two hours and is worth every step for the views of Sagarmatha's distinctive black triangle amidst a gallery of giants. During winter, a jet-stream from the west blasts all snow off Everest's towering face, and produces the characteristic plume from its summit. Gentler summer winds from the east leave its white mantle intact.

Pumori (7,145 meters, 23,442 feet) looms immediately to the rear of Kala Pattar while Nuptse shows its vast marbled face directly in front. Base Camp and the unforgiving **Khumbu Icefall** stretch across the foreground, and less than six kilometers (3.7 miles) away across **Lho La** (6,026 meters, 19,770 feet) lies the Rongbuk Glacier and Tibet. If only we had wings!

The trail to Base Camp (5,357 meters, 17,575 feet) crosses the jumbled glacier amidst transluscent blue ice seracs, some topped with boulders. Hikers are often disappointed upon reaching Base Camp, from where Everest is not even visible. Piles of garbage further spoil the illusion, emblematic of the nation's growing environmental woes compounded by tourism. Monumental efforts are periodically mounted to clear away expedition litter but the ultimate solution lies in mountaineers cleaning up after themselves.

The effects of mountain tourism on the local environment, both social and natural, are not hard to overlook in Khumbu. Before national park regulations stopped tree cutting for fuel and construction uses, much of Khumbu's forests had already disappeared; and it takes 60 years at such elevations for trees to grow back. Now trekking groups are required to be self-sufficient in kerosene for clients' cooking needs, but porters and lodges still rely on local wood.

Individual trekkers stay in Sherpa lodges where the cooking hearth has traditionally been a congenial gathering spot, these days kept warmer by the large amounts of firewood burned to feed hungry foreigners. Recent innovations to save firewood include a "back boiler" system that heats water via a

Exquisitely carved *mani* stones are a feature of the Everest region.

pipe through the hearth and several mini-hydroelectric projects which primarily provide lighting not cooking power. Lodge operators can pass the inflationary costs of cooking and heating on to the trekker but this does not solve the problem.

Whereas the Khumbu Sherpas have certainly benefitted economically from tourism, changes in dress, values and even some monks' waning devotion to their studies are evidence of the two-sided sword.

The Gokyo Valley: The return trip to Namche can be accomplished much more quickly, either following the same route down or exploring side valleys such as **Gokyo**. Churning with glaciers that melt into turquoise lakes, and rimmed with savage mountain scenery, the Gokyo Valley is veteran trekkers' favourite side of Khumbu. Trails cling to both sides of the steep Dudh Kosi gorge, joining at the toe of the **Ngozumpa Glacier** and continuing up its lateral moraine past half-frozen lakes to a cluster of lodges at Gokyo. The west

side's trail passes lodges at **Dole**, **Lhabarma**, **Luza** and **Machherma** suggesting four half days (or three full days with a layover) from Namche or Khumjung for proper acclimatisation. The opposite trail is visibly unpopulated except for one tea shop in **Thare**.

Himalayan *tahr* are often seen grazing on narrow ledges in the lower reaches, their long golden-brown hair barely visible against the same coloured grasses. Below Dole, the trail winds up through rhododendron, poplar and birch, its thin smooth bark, like brown mylar, peeling off layers at a time.

The entire Gokyo Valley is sparsely populated, with sheltering found only for summer yak herder settlements, which are also shared by trekker lodges. Above Machherma, there is no food or lodging to Gokyo. Well above treeline only scrub rhododendron, azelea and hardy grasses can survive. Around the lakes, the ground is snow-covered much of the year except during monsoon when buttercups, asters, edelweiss and gentians bloom.

Yaks cross a precarious suspension bridge above the Dudh Kosi.

GOMPAS: SHERPA MONASTERIES OF SOLU KHUMBU

Gompas are the physical and spiritual centers of Sherpa communities of Solu Khumbu.

Sherpas follow the Mahayana Buddhist practice known as *Nyingma*. The first *gompas* at Pangboche and Thame, established by Lama Sanga Dorje between three and four hundred years ago, served as the focus of the Sherpas' religious and cultural activities. It was not until 1916 that the first celibate monastery was established for religious study.

Sherpa *gompas* follow a traditional pattern of construction. At the front are three statues. The central is the historical Buddha who lived 2,500 years ago and taught a means for developing one's spiritual potential. On the right is Guru Rinpoche, an Indian mystic who established Buddhism in Tibet about 730 A.D. and on the left is the god

embodying compassion. Books of Sherpa history and religious teachings are kept in the *gompa*.

Villagers take turns as the *gompa* custodian while *lamas* and celibate monks fill the religous roles. The title *lama* is reserved for religious teachers, whether or not they have taken vows of celibacy. They have studied the Sherpa beliefs, can read the scriptures, perform rituals and teach Buddhist principles.

A *lama* who has attained the highest level of spiritual achievement is called *Rinpoche*, "precious one." He may earn this respected title through study and wisdom attained in this lifetime or by being recognised as the incarnation of a previous *lama*. The reincarnate's identity is determined when as a child he exhibits the characteristics of the late *Rinpoche* and can identify the deceased's belongings. The young *lama* is then raised in the monastery and given a religious and secular education.

Just as not all *lamas* are monks, not all monks are *lamas*. Monks devote their lives to religious practice, studying, teaching and performing religious rites for the Sherpa community. As well as helping with monastery work, they may be stewards, custodians, artists or prayer leaders.

Women may take vows to become nuns and live in religious communities. Monks and nuns are usually supported by their relatives, who consider it an honour to the family. A man or a woman is free to leave the monastery and return to lay life without discredit.

Students enter the monastery school at age seven. They learn to read and write Tibetan and study religion, history, grammer, psychology and medicine. During their studies, students may take vows of commitment to monastic life. To take the final *Gelung* vows, a man must be celibate and at least 20 years old.

Previously, students of higher level Buddhist teachings went to Tibet to study with the most respected *Rinpoche*s. Nowadays a complete spiritual education is much more accessible, in Nepal and India as well as the West – as interest in Tibetan Buddhism is growing.

The beautifully painted monastery of Chiwong in Solu Khumbu.

Gokyo sits on the third lake **Dudh Pokhari** at 4,750 meters (15,580 feet), and rising above it is the easily climbable **Gokyo Ri** (5,483 meters, 17,984 feet). From the top, a panoply of peaks loom on every horizon. To the north, **Cho Oyu**, at 8,201 meters (26,906 feet), the sixth highest in the world, and **Gyachung Kang** (7,952 meters, 25,991 feet) grow out of corrugated ice folds which tumble to the glacier. Pumori, **Changtse**, Everest, Nuptse, **Makalu** (at 8,463 meters, 27,766 feet, the world's fifth highest), Ama Dablam and Thamserku stretch to the east and south. Beyond a 5,900 meter (19,360 foot) ridge to the west lies the Bhote Kosi leading to Nangpa La.

Besides day hikes from Gokyo along the lateral moraine, a short-cut route crossing **Cho La** (5,420 meters, 17,782 feet), called **Chuguma** by the locals, saves two days' walking to Lobuche. The pass requires some basic rope work, and food and tent for one night. The eastern side skirts **Tshola Tsho** lake and crosses the moraines between Cholatse and **Tawoche** (6,501 meters, 21,330 feet), emerging above the village of Pheriche.

Locals walk from Gokyo down to Namche on the Machherma-Dole trail in one day, but a more moderate pace requires two to three days. If heading to Pangboche, the Dudh Kosi's east side trail via Phortse offers an unparalleled perspective on Khumbila, Thamserku, **Kang Taiga** (6,685 meters, 21,932 feet) and Ama Dablam. Set above a steep ravine facing Thyangboche to the west, Phortse is a peaceful farming community off the main trekker route. Potato fields stretch to the cliff's edge, marked by three centuries-old stone *chortens* and a fringe of birch forest from where the bold *danphe* raid newly planted fields. The two to three hour walk to Pangboche along precipitous slopes is memorable for its high vantage over the Imja Khola.

Quiet Thame and Rolwaling: A three to four hour walk up the Bhote Kosi from Namche Bazaar reaches the peaceful settlement of **Thame**. Its mud walled, Sherpa-style houses surrounded by po-

tato fields reveal little of the 20th century. Here is the perfect remedy to noisy trekker lodges. Thame's monastery clings to the ridge above, which looks upvalley toward Nangpa La whose territory is closed to trekkers. Guests at the monastery may be offered a cup of Tibetan butter tea – a mild black tea churned in a wooden cylinder with yak butter and salt, often unappealing to the naive tongue.

Crowning the tributary valley west of Thame is the infamous **Tashi Lapcha** pass (5,753 meters, 18,875 feet) to the Rolwaling Valley. Trekkers have died from rock fall on this extremely rugged route, now restricted to foreigners. Ice ax, crampons, rope and a blessing from the Thame *lama* are advised. Most mountaineering expeditions in Khumbu follow the Sherpa practice of making a *puja*, an offering, to the mountain dieties before beginning a climb.

The **Rolwaling Valley** is more easily accessible from **Charikot** on the Lamosangu-Jiri road. **Gauri Shankar** (7,134 meters, 23,405 feet), long

Churning the famous salt butter tea of Tibet, much savoured by Sherpas.

thought to be highest in the world, resisted all mountaineering attempts until a joint Nepalese-American team scaled it in 1979. Three peaks, including **Ramdung** (5,925 meters, 19,439 feet), are open as Trekking Peaks.

Several days' walk up the **Bhote Kosi** is **Simigaon**, where the Rolwaling Khola enters from the east. **Beding**, the only settlement in the upper Rolwaling, is gray and barren save for the stone houses' window shutters painted red, blue and yellow. Beyond is the summer yak herders' settlement of **Na**, and still further, the stark beauty of craggy glaciers and glazed ice slopes. To trek this far and return down valley is worthwhile for the high altitude experience and the serenity of a silent white world.

From the lower Bhote Kosi, an alternative trail heads west up the **Sangawa Khola** and climbs to **Bigu Gompa** (2,512 meters, 8,240 feet) with its forest sheltered nuns' convent. The path continues upward, beyond habitation to cross **Tinsang La** (3,319 meters, 10,890 feet) and descends to **Barabise**;

another follows the ridge north past **Deodunga** ("god's rock") to within a kilometer of the Tibet border where the trail turns west to meet the Kodari-Kathmandu road.

The Arun Valley: Like Nepal's far west, east of Everest is seldom visited by foreigners, but the similarities stop there. The east is far more populated than the west, in part due to a wetter climate; it is narrower north to south and much more accessible; and its people are generally better off, having benefitted from the geography as well as participation in the Gurkha regiments. The east is a fascinating area in which to trek, enlivened by weekly open-air markets attracting a carnival of variously costumed peoples. Naturalists rate the eastern Himalaya high, especially bird-watchers who can rack up scores of new sightings with the help of the Flemings' authoritative book *Birds of Nepal.*

A little known trail which leaves the crowds of Khumbu behind follows an up and down trade route east over **Salpa**

Sherpani sisters tend the family hearth.

Pass (3,414 meters, 11,200 feet). This seven to eight day walk from **Kharte** on the Dudh Kosi to **Tumlingtar** on the Arun crosses three ridges and two main rivers, the **Inukhu** (or **Hinku**) and **Hongu Kholas**. From Tumlingtar, planes fly several times a week to Kathmandu; trails connect to the bazaar towns of **Hille** and **Dhankuta** north of **Biratnagar**, with daily flight service to Kathmandu. Whereas food and shelter are sporadically available at Sherpa and Rai villages along the main Salpa trail, trekkers are advised to take food for a few days' and a guide who knows the way. This trail also provides southern access into the upper Hongu Basin where well-equipped trekkers might venture (see above).

Standing in the broiling sun on Tumlingtar's red clay airfield at 390 meters (1,280 feet) above sea level, the idea of climbing nearly 4,500 meters (14,800 feet) to the base of Makalu is indeed daunting. Trekking into the upper **Arun Valley** is a near-expedition undertaking, requiring four weeks to

Jewellery is family wealth and only worn on special occasions.

and from **Makalu Base Camp** if the weather cooperates. A vast range in temperatures is confronted, from steamy in the lowlands to serious snow storms on high which can block the route if ill-timed. Weather alone deters most trekkers from the Arun, and dictates others' schedule to a narrow window in March or October-November.

The mighty Arun, one of Nepal's two largest rivers besides the Karnali, flows from Tibet through a narrow gorge which is thought to pre-date the rise of the Himalayan massif. At its uppermost reaches within Nepal, it receives meltwaters from the **Barun Glacier** off the slopes of **Baruntse** (7,129 meters, 23,389 feet), Makalu and **Lhotse Shar** (8,386 meters, 27,513 feet), and then heads due south to join the Sapt Kosi (Seven Rivers) of east Nepal.

The Tumlingtar airstrip, or Hille, are the most convenient entry points to the Arun Valley. The people of Tumlingtar are mostly Kumals (potters) who live in elevated bamboo houses and cultivate dry crops such as black lentil (*dal*) and sesame. Bulbous clay pots like those sold nearby at **Khandbari** are used for carrying water or storing millet as it ferments into *tongba*. Virtually all of east Nepal (and Sikkim) drinks *tongba*, a tasty brew made by pouring boiling water into a bamboo or wooden cylinder filled with fermented millet. The liquid is drunk through a straw seived to keep out the millet kernels. The Sherpas and Bhotias of colder climes appreciate *tongba's* warming effects. *Suntala,* similar to Mandarin oranges, are another speciality of the east savoured on warm days from October through March.

If starting from Hille, the ridge-top bazaar town of **Chainpur** is well worth a visit, especially for the Friday market. People of the surrounding hills come to sell a variety of goods; tobacco, grains, vegetables, cloth and well reputed brassware. Tamang porters stop on the trail to rest their loads on handsomely smoothed wooden T-sticks. Women dressed in brightly flowered skirts, burgundy velveteen blouses and hefty coin necklaces gather in the tea shops and share the week's news. And Newar businessmen display their Dhaka-patterned *topis* (hats) made of handwoven cotton of colourful geometric designs. Chainpur is a pleasant stop anytime with its flagstone walkways and shops spilling over with shiny brass pots sold at great mark-up in Kathmandu outlets.

Another approach to the Arun is via a flight to **Bhojpur**, famed for its hardened steel *khukri* knives wielded by the Gurkhas from the Falklands to Cypress and the Suez (see page 91).

From Tumlingtar, the trail parallels the river along a ridge to the east, passing first through Brahman and Chhetri, then Rai, Limbu, Gurung and Newar villages. Oak, chestnut and rhododendron forests are aflutter with bird and animal life. Precursory views of Makalu, Baruntse, **Chamlang**, and the Khumbu peaks open to the west, and Milke Danda, one of the longest ridges in Nepal, rises to the east.

At **Num**, the trail crosses the Arun and starts up the **Kasuwa Khola** toward Makalu Base Camp in the upper **Barun Valley**. This is wild country, and should only be attempted with an experienced guide, food for 12 to 14 days, and snow gear. There are no settlements beyond the Sherpa village of **Tashigaon**, and for six to seven days the path crosses rugged terrain rising to three passes, including **Shipton La** (approximately 4,500 meters, 14,760 feet) and **Barun La** (4,400 meters, 14,440 feet).

From the high points, panoramic views of the eastern Himalaya from Everest to Kangchenjunga and north into Tibet reward the steadfast trekker. Campsites are memorable, among alpine meadows and at the base of Makalu's pink face as it reflects dusk's light off the surrounding peaks. Day hikes up the glacier or to Camp I offer even more spectacular views. On the way down, the moss-laden forests of birch, rhododendron and oak are a blaring contrast to the upper horizons of ice and rock.

The return to Tumlingtar can be routed along the west side of the Arun, sharing a jungly trail with chattering rhesus monkeys and swimming holes with equally boisterous children. Or trekkers with a special permit in hand can continue up the Arun from Num into remote reaches populated with Lhomis, most of whom practice Bon religion.

Within the next ten years, much of the Arun valley will be altered by the installation of a hydroelectric facility. To compensate, parts of the the Barun and Arun watersheds will be protected as the Makalu-Barun National Park and Conservation Area while recognising the needs of the local peoples.

Newly Opened Kangchenjunga: In 1988 His Majesty's Government opened two previously restricted northern border zones to foreign trekkers, Dolpo in west Nepal and **Kangchenjunga**. Wary of the potential effects of tourism in such virgin territories, regulations aimed at protecting the environment and local economies were imposed, for the first time outside of a national park or natural reserve. Trekkers must go through a registered trekking agency, guarantee self-sufficiency in food and fuel so as not to deplete the native supplies, and

Dancing skeletons represent protector deitiies.

neither litter nor pollute the area.

The Kangchenjunga trekking region, roughly defined as the **Tamur Kosi** watershed which drains the west side of Kangchenjunga (8,586 meters, 28,169 feet), third highest peak on earth, has received more attention than Dolpo, being relatively easier to get to and topographically more hospitable. Still, a Kangchenjunga trek requires minimum three to four weeks' hiking on unrefined trails crossing ridge and gully to visit the mountain's base either south or north. **Pangpema**, at close to 5,000 meters (16,000 feet), base camp for Kangchenjunga's northern face, sits on a glacier within ten kilometers of the Tibet border surrounded by peaks upward of 6,500 meters (21,300 feet). It is a long way from emergency treatment should problems arise. Numerous trekking groups have had to turn back just days short of base camp for lack of adequate acclimatisation time.

Flying in and out of **Taplejung** saves considerable driving time from Kathmandu (16-20 hours) but as with all mountain airstrips flights are often unreliable. A compromise solution is to fly to and from Biratnagar (daily flights from Kathmandu) and drive four to six hours to trailheads at Hille (1,920 meters, 6,300 feet) via the **Dharan/Dhankuta** road, or **Phidim** (1,311 meters, 4,300 feet) north of **Ilam**. Hille sports a lively weekly market on Thursdays, and being so close to Dhankuta's Gurkha camps is well stocked with food and drink, a good place to start out. Phidim is at the end of a newly completed dry season dirt road which traverses Ilam's young tea estates.

Heading northeast out of Hille, the trail climbs gradually through settlements of recent migrants from the northern Walungchung region, trans-Himalayan yak drivers who live for months on *tsampa* (roasted barley flour), dried yak meat and cheese, and *chhang* (fermented rice beer) or *tongba*. **Gupha Pokhari** (3,150 meters, 10,300 feet), the second night's rest, is a serene meditational lake set on a ridge looking east at the Kangchenjunga massif and

Kangchenjunga (8,586 meters, 28,169 feet) guards Nepal's eastern border.

west at Makalu and the Khumbu Himal. From here, a shorter trek follows the **Milke Danda** ridge due north, climbing to 4,700 meters (15,400 feet) into the **Jaljale Himal**, a remote area spotted with lakes and inhabited by mountain peoples from Tibet. The trail up Milke Danda ridge finds little water and a sketchy, rocky way often emersed in clouds. With a guide who knows the area, the return route can descend east to the **Mewa Khola** (Papaya River) and on to Taplejung's airfield (approximately two weeks' walking time from Hille), or head back down the ridge and turn west via **Nundhaki** to Chainpur and Tumlingtar (10-12 days).

The main Kangchenjunga trail crosses the Mewa Khola at **Dobhan,** and follows the Tamur Kosi, jousting from side to side to skirt steep valley walls. The hills are densely forested in rhododendron, oak, and pine; wooden houses and frequent waterfalls confirm a copious monsoon. The indomitable bamboo appears in many varieties, often the last lanky vegetation to give way

to alpine grasses and scrub rhododendron. At **Ghunsa**, a Sherpa village marked with prayer flags and a *gompa*, two trails from Kangchenjunga's southern flanks join the northbound route.

Now close to 3,500 meters (11,500 feet), full days of trekking may gain elevation too fast. The last three days to Pangpema are increasingly cold and spectacular as mountains close in from both sides of the valley. A small stone hut defines **Lhonak** and a level snowy pad is Pangpema, where expedition support teams spend months as lead climbers make camps far above. Day hikes onto the glacier and to higher ground for even better vantages of Kangchenjunga delay departure from this mind-bending spot.

For another perspective on Kangchenjunga and the sometimes favoured face of **Jannu** (7,710 meters, 25,300 feet), and to avoid backtracking, a 30-day trek visits the southern **Yalung Glacier** on the return to Pangpema. Two trails head south from Ghunsa. The easterly route scrambles over loose, snow-covered rock to cross higher **Lapsang La** (5,932 meters, 19,460 feet) while the lower alternative traverses three passes, the highest being **Sinion La** which stands at nearly 4,800 meters (15,750 feet). Both routes require at least a one night stay at high altitudes. Above the crystalline lake of **Ramser**, a trail skirts the massive Yalung Glacier up to **Oktang** for prime views of Jannu, the southern face of Kangchenjunga and a line of peaks which divide Nepal from Sikkim.

No time to relax, for a roller-coaster retreat still lies ahead. Starting down the **Simbua Khola**, the preferred trail diverts south through **Yamphudin** then either west to Taplejung (sending someone ahead to try to confirm a flight) or south to enter the subtropical **Kabeli Khola** valley, and on the Phidim or Ilam. Like treks into the Arun and other far-reaching areas, the Kangchenjunga trek encounters a vast range of elevations and temperatures, best planned for October-November or March-April, with the possibility of snowfall at any time of year.

Left, Thyangboche Rinpoche with Tamserku behind. Right, trekking near Gokyo in the Khumbu.

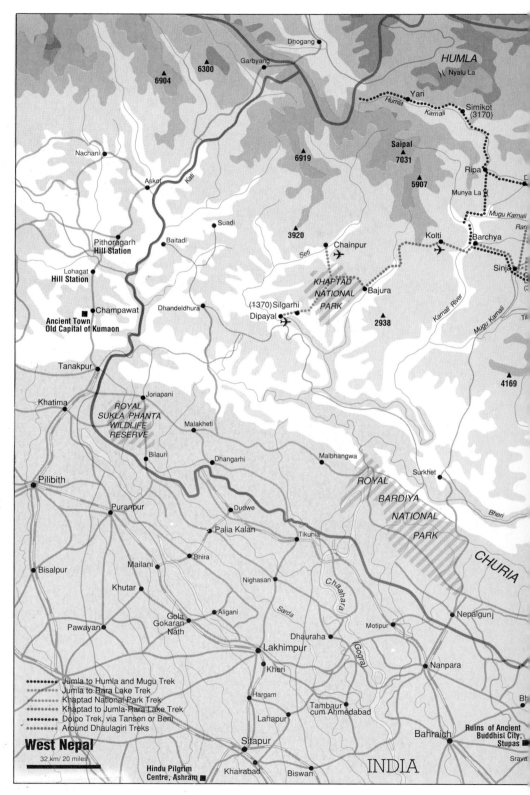

West Nepal

32 km/ 20 miles

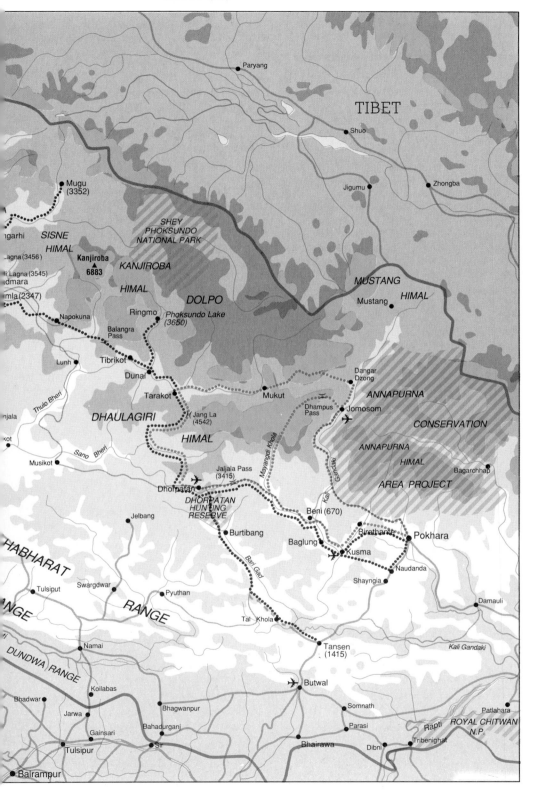

TREKS IN WEST NEPAL

More than a third of Nepal, everything west of the **Kali Gandaki River**, is loosely referred to as west Nepal, and further west, in the basin of the **Karnali River**, as the far west. Together this largely untamed, seldom travelled region is so remote that even some visiting Nepalese are often mistaken for foreigners.

Here, the Nepal Himalaya are at their widest, unfolding as broad ridges (generally over 3,600 meters, 11,800 feet) known as *lekhs*. The great Karnali river system bevels these high pasturelands into oak-pine forested valleys. Jumla, an administrative and commercial centre, shivers at 2,347 meters (7,677 feet) under a meter of snow throughout winter, while **Dipayal**, at 600 meters (1,970 feet) records some of the country's highest temperatures. A petered-out monsoon squeezes its last drops onto the west's summer-parched farmlands

in the far reaching rainshadow of the Dhaulagiri massif.

The Khasa Malla kings governed west Nepal and Tibet through the 14th century, when Indian Rajput chieftains fleeing Muslim invaders settled and carved out petty principalities. Occupational castes followed, settling in the valleys and low hills while peoples from Tibet extended their niche into the inner Himalaya, establishing an unassimilated settlement pattern that persists today. The crusade of Prithvi Narayan Shah reached Jumla in 1788 and thereafter the west answered to Kathmandu, or for a period to local authorities of neighbouring Mustang.

Today, hilltop *chortens,* crude human effigies and folk song traditions recall the west's mixed ethnic heritage. Like the villagers who practice them, religions show altitudinal preferences: Buddhism in the highlands, Hinduism in the lowlands, with a form of kinship deity worship intertwined.

Trekking in the West: Trekkers bound for west Nepal enter a world far re-

Trekking with a reliable agency ensures a healthy and varied diet.

moved from the apple pie-tea houses of Solu Khumbu. Except for the Terai and silt-fed valleys, the region is agriculturally impoverished; trekkers must carry all food from Kathmandu. Customarily ill-prepared to accommodate outsiders – peoples such as the Thakuris consider it polluting to house a stranger – tents and camping equipment are also required. A trekking guide can prove invaluable in finding elusive paths and dealing with non-English speaking porters.

Jumla is where most treks begin. Royal Nepal Airlines flies weekly from Kathmandu to Jumla via Nepalgunj; flights are erratic due to weather conditions. Planes also fly direct, covering the 360 kilometer (224 mile) journey in just 45 minutes.

Rara National Park is the far west's most popular trekking destination, though it receives no more than a few dozen tourists each year. Set at 2,980 meters (9,777 feet), **Rara Daha**'s (Lake) royal blue waters reflect a snow-clad **Ghurchi Lekh** framed in ever-greens. During November and April, shoreline reeds are aflutter with migrating wild fowl. The 106 square kilometer (41 square mile) protected area harbours the Himalayan black bear, *tahr*, musk deer, leopard and other wildlife.

Two main trails connect Jumla to Rara, each requiring three to four days. The more westerly route heads north from Jumla, up the valley and across grassy slopes calicoed with coniferous forests, reaching the ancient Khasa capital of **Sinja** in two days. Leaving lowland Brahman, Chhetri and Thakuri villages behind, the trail crosses a second pass, **Chuchemara Danda**, and traverses a 3,800-meter (12,500-foot) ridge overlooking Rara Lake and the distant Humla and **Mugu Valleys**. Typical of this area, a handsome bridge with railing posts carved into human likenesses spans the final approach to Rara Lake.

Villages dotting the area were relocated when it became a national park. Subsequently, as in Langtang and Sagarmatha National Parks, human

Lake Rara is one of the most beautiful spots in Nepal.

dwellers have been seen as integral to the park purposes, and villages have remained.

It takes one full day to walk around the lake on a trail that was cleared for King Mahendra when he visited here in 1964. Unlike many Himalayan lakes, Rara is not a pilgrimage site. A warden's house and guest lodge providing sleeping quarters (food is not available) are built along the northern shoreline. Alpine meadows amidst a spruce forest attract campers to the southern side.

The return to Jumla leaves from the lake's southern rim and descends to **Pina** (2,430 meters, 7,970 feet). Once over **Ghurchi Lagna** (3,456 meters, 11,340 feet) – "*lagna*" or "*la*" mean "pass"– trail-side milestones indicate the distance to Kathmandu's Hanuman Dhoka (royal palace), 176 *kos,* or 520 kilometers (323 miles), – marking the old track by which Jumla's famous red rice was carried to the Rana Prime Ministers' kitchens.

Beyond **Bumra** and the **Lah Gad River**, the trail climbs to a meadow where it forks. The westerly branch crosses **Danphya Lagna** (3,658 meters, 12,000 feet), named for Nepal's national bird the *danphe*, the iridescent Impeyan pheasant. The easterly route scales a slightly lower **Khali Lagna** and descends along the **Chaudabise Khola** (river) to where it enters the **Tila River** at Jumla.

Jumla to Humla and Mugu: The distance from Jumla to **Humla** is far greater than the jingle in their names implies. Located ten days' walk northwest of Jumla in Nepal's furthermost corner, Humal knows but a handful of Westerners and few of the modern world's accoutrements. Ironically, a STOL airstrip at **Simikot** (3,170 meters, 10,400 feet) enables speedy travel in and out of the 20th century. The majority of those who pass through on foot are families of the upper reaches who are taking their sheep and goats down to the lowlands for winter. Hindu and Buddhist pilgrims bisect Humla en route to the holy **Lake Mansarovar** and **Mount Kailas**, in nearby Tibet.

The villages of Dolpo are stone built and can have flat roofs due to the relatively low rainfall.

Trekkers who aim to venture far afield will find their pioneering interests fulfilled here – but not food and shelter.

From the lovely valley of **Surkhet**, a historic trade highway follows the Karnali river up toward Humla. Trekkers who ply this route are ensured of lively encounters with Thakuri and highland travellers. The trans-Himalayan salt trade was the mainstay economy of Nepal's mountain peoples until 1959. Every summer, yak caravans crossed snowbound passes, such as **Ninyan La** at 4,900 meters (16,080 feet) north of Simikot, sometimes enduring days without food and nights at temperatures down to 20 degrees Celsius (four degrees Fahrenheit) below zero. Terai-grown grains brought up during winter were exchanged for the essential salt as well as wool, butter and Tibetan brick tea in a thriving but perilous barter business.

The trail from Jumla to Humla shortcuts travel up the Karnali, joining the great river below **Barchya** (via Sinja, as described above). Threading along dry river banks, the route crosses 3,800 meter (12,500 foot) **Munya La** and drops to **Ripa** where it enters Humla proper. Trekkers are allowed no further upvalley than the checkpost at **Munchu**.

For years, Nepalese officials have discussed opening the **Yari** to Mansarovar-Kailas route through Humla to foreigners; but for now, visitors must be satisfied with a glimpse of Mount Kailas from the top of **Nyalu La**, a pass leading to the northern Limi valley.

The **Mugu Valley**, a restricted area for which special permission is needed, is accessible from **Pina**, or via **Chankheli La** (3,570 meters, 11,700 feet) on return from Humla. The people of Mugu appear much like their Tibetan ancestors. They wear home-spun *chubas*; the men's are low-belted, rough woolen robes, the women's long wrapped dresses tied with an earth-tone striped apron. Once industrious traders whose profession dried up with the border closing, they abandoned their original settlement **Purano Mugu** (Old Mugu) in favour of the present more agriculturally productive site.

Khaptad: Unusual among natural preserves, **Khaptad National Park** guards a place of religious importance as well as a prime sample of the far west's forested *lekhs* and high plateau pastures. Five of the park's 225 square kilometers (89 square miles) are in sacred reserve, sheltering shrines and streams that feed the Ganges river. Khaptad Baba, a Hindu guru, is the self-appointed caretaker of this spiritual haven. For the last 40 years he has proffered spiritual counseling, and suprises visitors with his fluent English.

Getting to Khaptad is not difficult; flights to any of four western airports (**Kolti, Sanphebagar**, **Chainpur** or **Dipayal**) can be reached within two to three days' walk of the park. Procuring a flight is what may take time. From Chainpur in the upper Seti Valley, the trail mounts 3,050 meter (10,000 foot) Khaptad Lekh to the Park Headquarters. An alternative return route heads south along a forested ridge down to **Silgarhi**, a prosperous Newari hill ba-

The people of Jumla lead a hard life in this food deficit area.

zaar with stone-paved streets a short walk from Dipayal. Seven to ten days are needed for the entire trip.

Mysterious Dolpo: Sequestered from the outside world by torturously high mountain passes and restricted entry, **Dolpo** has long fascinated and frustrated travellers. David Snellgrove first revealed the mysteries of Dolpo in his book *Himalayan Pilgrimage (1961)*. Peter Matthiessen's description of **Shey Gompa ("Crystal Monastery")** in *The Snow Leopard* (1979) further piqued readers' interest.

In 1988, the valleys leading to Dolpo's **Shey-Phoksundo National Park** were de-restricted to organised trekking groups who are self-sufficient in food and fuel. Shey Gompa and the rest of the huge 1,373 square kilometer (3,555 square mile) park above Phoksundo Lake remain off limits.

A three to four week trek into Dolpo requires the mindset to endure hardships of travelling in a remote, impoverished landscape. There are several approach routes; from Pokhara, Jumla,

or following Snellgrove's 1956 path up the **Bheri River**. Flights are available to **Dunai** (also known as **Dunyer**) and potentially on charter basis to Dhorpatan.

The walk from Pokhara begins in **Naudanda** on the Pokhara-Tansen road, or from the main Ghorapani trail via Beni (670 meters, 2,200 feet). A Chinese-built road under construction from Pokhara will eventually reach Beni.

Village tea houses are readily available along this corridor as far as **Lumsum**, from where the trail climbs steeply through pine and rhododendron forest to **Jaljala Pass** (3,415 meters, 11,200 feet). A *chautara* (tree shaded rest stop) marks the top, where a fine camp spot looks on the Dhaulagiri and Annapurna Himals. **Dhorpatan** (2,760 meters, 9,055 feet) is reachable in seven days from Pokhara.

An alternative trail leaves from **Tansen** (1,415 meters, 4,650 feet), a historic fortress-town connected by road to Pokhara and **Butwal**. Following a northwesterly route through Brahman and Chhetri bazaars skirted by sal and chir pine forests, Dhorpatan lies over a 2,930 meter (9,600 foot) pass five to six days from the trailhead. At the **Dhorpatan Hunting Reserve**, blue sheep and other prize animals can be hunted with a permit.

The next leg of the journey, Dhorpatan to Dunai, takes a roller-coaster track over three passes through a desolate landscape. For five or six days food and supplies are not available, until **Tarakot**, known locally as **Dzong** for its hilltop fortress. The people of Tarakot call themselves Magars but dress and live like Tibetans.

At Dunai, the district headquarters and checkpost stop, the **Suli Gad** river enters the Bheri carrying waters of Lake Phoksundo for their long passage via the Ganges into the Bay of Bengal. The trail follows a narrow gorge – by early May rimmed with primulas, violets and gentians and shaded by tall spruce – passing a magnificent waterfall which **Lake** tumbles 1,670 meters (5,480 feet) down **Phoksundo in** a series of rock shelves. The park en- **distant Dolpo.**

312

trance is at **Raha**, still two days from the lake. Blue sheep, musk deer, goral, snow leopard, *tahr* and bear inhabit the park, set aside to protect an ecosystem typical of the high arid Tibetan plateau.

Hikers' first glimpse of **Lake Phoksundo** reveals a scene of unearthly beauty; a white glimmer of silver birch edges the lake's radiant turquoise-blue waters, set in a cleft between rocks that rise 2,000 meters (6,500 feet) into the clear mountain skies. **Kanjiroba**, at 6,883 meters (22,582 feet) one of the highest in the region, can be seen from the tops of these surrounding peaks.

At the southern end of the lake sets the hamlet of **Ringmo** (3,630 meters, 11,900 feet) whose inhabitants subsist on buckwheat, wheat and potatoes, a prosperous existence compared to the peoples of upper Dolpo who depend on barley as a sole crop. The stalwart yak is a vital source of food, transport and dung fuel.

Some peoples of Dolpo still practice the pre-Buddhist Bon religion, which except for scattered pockets in places such as Mustang and the Annapurnas' Nar and Phu valleys, disappeared from Tibet in the 9th century. Bon and Buddhism are outwardly indistinguishable to all but an expert. One tell-tale sign is the swastika, an ancient Sanskrit symbol for good fortune; it points counterclockwise on a Bon *gompa* and clockwise on a Buddhist one.

Turning down the Suli Gad and continuing west to **Tibrikot**, another fort town doubly guarded with rooftop human effigies, the trail diverges, southward along the Bheri to **Jajarkot** and Surkhet, accessible by road from Nepalganj, or westward to Jumla. Most trekkers prefer the five to six-day journey to Jumla, across the 3,840 meter (12,590 foot) **Balangra Pass** and on through **Rimi** to **Napokuna** in the upper Tila Valley. The entire Pokhara or Tansen-Dolpo-Jumla trek can also be done in reverse. In either direction, weather will be a major factor as high passes can be snowbound between late October and early May.

Planting rice in the Tila valley of Jumla.

THE TERAI: GRANARY OF NEPAL

The name Terai, meaning "land of fever," has long evoked the dangers of this lowland belt of unhealthy jungle and swamps which runs the length of the country and has historically provided a natural barrier between Nepal and India.

The lowest Himalayan range, the **Siwalik hills** (also known as the **Churia**), forms the Terai's northern boundary. Where the hills divide, smaller Inner Terai valleys such as Chitwan, Dang, Deokhuri and Surkhet abut foothills covered with giant sal trees *(Shorea robusta)*. Tumbling streams carry stones, gravel and sand from the high mountains and deposit them in rivers which, laden with rich alluvial debris, slow and widen. Swamp and forest merge to create the Terai's beautiful, serene landscape. Giant grasses and trees, such as the khair *(Acacia catechu)*, sissu *(Dalbergia sisso)*, simal *(Bombax ceiba)* and sal, provide refuge for a rich fauna of tiger, elephant and rhinoceros.

During winter, streams dry up leaving wide rocky beds and large rivers recede to reveal great stretches of white sandy beaches. The climate is pleasant though cold at night. In December morning mist shrouds the landscape, sometimes lasting until midday. From April to June mosquitoes invade the towns and a violent, dusty wind parches everything.

The summer monsoon follows, sending water racing into old and new river beds. Greenness, dampness and fevers succeed the dust and heat. Despite the floods, which can isolate villages from muddy lanes, the rains give the land its most wild and verdant appearance. Silvery, downy grasses wave on the river banks and young crops flourish in the fields.

The best season to visit the Terai is after the monsoon rains in October and November, when emerald rice covers the fields and bright yellow mustard contrasts with the deep blue sky; or during February and March when spring flowers emblazon the landscape with splashes of scarlet bougainvillaea, red bombax and the orange flame of the forest.

Early Settlers: Throughout history Terai dangers repelled invaders, while its fertility attracted migrants. Palaeolithic and Neolithic remains have been found at the foot of the Siwaliks in the Dang valley. In the 6th century B.C., during a period of great prosperity, the Lord Buddha was born in Lumbini (see page 323). Waves of settlers were forced to retreat due to local border conflicts or feudal oppression and the jungle soon reestablished itself. Only a few scattered groups stubbornly remained to tend the rich land in such unhealthy conditions; the most numerous are the Tharu (see page 143) and small groups of the Bote, Majhi and Raji, all fishermen and ferrymen, and the Kumhal potters.

In this century the Terai has yielded its virgin forests to settlements of impoverished farmers fleeing the over-

Left, the Janak temple of Janakpur, celebrated as the birthplace of Sita, is the object of pilgrimage for many devotees. **Right**, the cultivated fertile plains of the Terai are the granary of Nepal.

populated middle hills. Cultivation accelerated following the political change of the 1950s and the eradication of malaria in the 1960s. The "land of fever" became the granary of Nepal. Its fertile soils favour rice and grain as well as oil seeds and more recently cash crops such as sugar cane, cotton, jute and vegetables.

Today nearly half of Nepal's people live in the Terai. The population is multiplying faster than that of the country as a whole: 50 percent growth over the last decade compared to 30 percent throughout Nepal.

The eastern Terai is the most densely populated, particularly Jhapa District where native Tharu, Rajbamsi, Dhimal and people of Indian origin have settled with the more recently-arrived Rai and Limbu. In central Terai, Tharu, Kumal and Bote tribes are neighbours with hill peoples such as Brahman, Chhetri and Gurung. Until the 1970s far western Terai was heavily forested but legal and illegal settlers from the western hills, mostly Brahman and Chhetri, have joined the original Tharu tribes of Danguara, Rana and Katharya. Still, the western Terai is sparsely populated (70 persons per 98 square kilometers) and far less developed than the east which has benefitted from foreign aid.

Nepal's Future: Roads are now being built across the Terai paving the way for industrial development. Where decades ago were forests, now are bustling bazaars; long-distance transport trucks are washed on sandy beaches where ferry boats used to wait all day for a passenger. The jungle has diminished forever, now confined to scattered patches and tracts protected as national parks and wildlife reserves at Koshi Tappu, Royal Chitwan, Royal Bardiya and Sukla Phanta (see page 135).

Though early on an untamed border region, the Terai has also been an unavoidable zone of commercial contact, linking the mountains with the Gangetic plains. Trans-Himalayan trading gave birth to seasonal markets where merchants and villagers swapped news and goods. Bazaars grew into border towns when the British Raj imposed its commercial hegemony and the Indian railways reached southern Nepal.

Terai markets have continued to prosper by their proximity to India, inevitably Nepal's number one trade partner. Most of Nepal's agriculturally-based industries are situated in eastern and central Terai, besides the Kathmandu Valley. Successful sugar mills were opened in Biratnagar in 1946, in Birgunj in 1964 and recently in Bhairawa.

Manufacturing plants produce Nepalese brand cigarettes, *beedees* (the indigenous smokes), matches and soap. Nepal's first Industrial Estate with a brewery, tobacco factory, cotton textile and cereal mills was established in Hetauda. Although still small, Nepal's industrial sector is growing quickly, introducing not only new products and an increasing number of jobs but an entirely new way of thinking.

East-West Highway: Until the mid-1950s Nepal had very few motorable roads. Early visitors reached Kathmandu by foot or on horseback from

A suspension bridge stretches across the Arun river in east Nepal.

Hetauda. The first road, the Tribhuvan Raj Marg, was completed in 1956 and linked Birgunj to Kathmandu. It remained the only gateway to the capital city until the Siddhartha Raj Marg linking Bhairawa to Pokhara and Kathmandu was completed in 1968. Today few travellers brave the hairpin bends on the road from Hetauda over **Daman Pass** to **Naubise**. The main border entry points from India are Birgunj, close to the Raxaul train-line and Bhairawa, connected to Nautanwa station. Foreigners are only allowed to enter Nepal from India at Kakarbhitta, Birgunj and Sonauli, near Bhairawa, but it is advisable to check as regulations change.

Transport and communication across the Terai east to west was greatly facilitated with the completion of the 1,030-kilometer (640-mile) Mahendra Raj Marg in the late 1960s. Part of the Pan-Asian Highway, but popularly known as the East-West Highway, it was constructed in phases with assistance from U.S.S.R., U.S.A., U.K. and India. The road link is still incomplete in the far

The only railway in Nepal runs from the Indian border to Janakpur.

west, awaiting the construction of a bridge over the Karnali river at Chisopani.

Bazaars have sprung up along the East-West Highway at truck stops and crossroads, spreading untidy rows of thatched tea shops and fruit stalls. Shiny apples, heaps of oranges and bananas displayed against the jungle backdrop of statuesque sal trees and scrubby undergrowth are an enduring image of a Terai journey.

Narayanghat and adjoining **Bharatpur**, located five hours by car southwest of Kathmandu – gateways to **Royal Chitwan National Park** – mark the hub of the Terai road network. All vehicles, whatever their final destination, must pass through this mushrooming town, situated on the banks of the Narayani river.

Narayanghat is the prototype of a Terai town, with its straight grid roads, pastel-coloured concrete buildings and North-Indian style hotels and restaurants. Shops and stalls sell imported electronic products, fashions, fruit, bis-

cuits and chocolate. Nepalese beer, Fanta and Coke are cooled in huge refrigerators or red portable freezer boxes. Windowless restaurants cooled with ceiling fans provide welcome shelter from hot and dusty streets which throng with gaily painted rickshaws and hooting trucks.

Devghat, a sacred confluence where devotees congregate in January for the great purificatory festival of Magh Sankranti, lies ten kilometers (six miles) north of Narayanghat. Dugout canoes wait to ferry visitors to the shrine, tended by a *baba*, a famous holy man whose counsel is much sought by visiting pilgrims. This is also the take-out point for many Chitwan-bound rafting trips.

Janakpur, Birthplace of Sita: From Narayanghat the road passes east through the thriving industrial town of **Hetauda** (70 kilometers, 44 miles away) and continues another 110 kilometers (68 miles) to **Dhalkelwar** (Lalbiti) bazaar. Here a road leads south to the sacred town of **Janakpur** (20 kilometers, 12 miles), an interesting detour into history.

The Hindu epic Ramayana tells the story of "the city of King Janak," Janakpur, legendarily the birthplace of the king's adopted daughter Sita, whom he found while tilling the soil with a golden plough. Ram, hero of the epic and an incarnation of Vishnu, won Sita in marriage by bending the great bow of Shiva, as no other man could do. The loving couple were gloriously married in Janakpur.

Janakpur has been an important pilgrimage site since the 16th century when artifacts – holy images of Sita and Ram and a piece of Shiva's sacred bow – were reportedly discovered in the jungle by ascetics. In 1882, a Nepalese style temple to Ram was built and in 1911 the main temple was constructed over the spot where Sita's image was found. It is one of the few buildings in Nepal of Moghul architecture.

Two annual festivals in Janakpur attract hundreds of thousands of devotees to bathe in the city's 24 water tanks. The

Below, bathing at the festival of Biha Panchami. All Nepal rivers drain eventually into the holy Ganges. Right, Marigolds are sold as offerings for devout Hindus at Janakpur.

most important celebration is Ram Nawami, Ram's birthday, in April. December marks the festival of Biha Panchami reenacting Ram and Sita's marriage in a procession of elephants, horses, and chariots accompanied by musicians beating drums.

Janakpur is also of historical importance as the capital city of Videha, an ancient state that once covered much of India's northern Bihar and the Terai from the Sapt Kosi to the Gandaki. The Mithila culture of Videha, with its very own language and literary traditions, prevails today as vividly illustrated in the colourful wall paintings done by the Mithila women now just as they did over 3,000 years ago. Recently some of these women have begun painting commercially.

Janakpur is linked to the sleepy Indian border village of Madhubani by the only railway in Nepal. In addition to its religious and historic significance, Janakpur is a modern developing town with a thriving cigarette manufacturing industry.

Returning to Dhalkelwar, the highway continues east through scrub jungle to the **Koshi Tappu Wildlife Reserve**, famous for its birdlife and wild buffalos (see page 142). Beyond the Kosi River bridge is **Itahari**, an unremarkable crossroads town midway between Dharan at the foot of the Siwalik hills and Biratnagar, just six kilometers from the Indian border.

The pleasant hill-style bazaar of **Dharan** was badly damaged in the August 1988 earthquake. Until 1989, it was the headquarters of the British Gurkhas in Nepal, before they moved to Kathmandu. A British-built road winds from Dharan up into the hills to **Dhankuta** and **Hille**, the starting point for Kangchenjunga and many of the other east Nepal treks (see page 301).

Nepal's Second City: With a population of 100,000, **Biratnagar** is the second largest city in Nepal. Its geographical position has kept it at the forefront of the country's industrial development. Nepal's very first industry, Biratnagar Jute Mills, was established here in 1936. The Nepal-Indian enterprise prospered with the rise of jute prices following the Second World War; more mills were opened and jute remains a significant export. Biratnagar's other industries include sugar mills, textile factories and manufacturing of stainless steel kitchen-ware. Daily flights link Biratnagar with Kathmandu.

The eastern **Jhapa District** has a rich mixture of ethnic groups and an equally varied physical look: wooden houses elevated on high poles stand juxtaposed to charmless concrete structures. At the weekly market of **Damak**, a diversity of ethnic dress is apparent, such as the Dhimal women who wear hand-woven black sarongs tied with red belts, their shoulders naked.

Further east, the recently established tea gardens and processing industry centre around the hill town of **Ilam**. The Mahendra Raj Marg leaves Nepal at the eastern border crossing of **Kakarbhitta**, gateway to the Indian hillstation of Darjeeling and Sikkim.

Chitwan and Deokhuri: The British and Indian-built western sections of the

Elaborate traps to catch fish are constructed by some Terai tribes.

East-West Highway opened to traffic only in the last decade. The bridge at Narayanghat was completed in the early 1980s. The excellent stretch of road west of Narayanghat follows the Narayani river through the **Chitwan valley**, past a paper factory and the Tuborg brewery. A well-marked village road leads south to the **Tiger Tops Tharu Safari Resort** on the western edge of Royal Chitwan National Park. The road winds out of the Inner Terai Chitwan valley and through the forested Siwaliks.

The highway runs between stands of leafy sal trees, complimenting the red soil and scattered golden and cream-coloured houses. From the far-reaching flatlands which stretch along the roadside, people seemingly appear from nowhere. Young children tend water buffalos and goats grazing nearby the deserted road.

Located 120 kilometers (75 miles) west of Narayanghat at the base of the foothills, is the pleasant cross-roads town of **Butwal**. Gurungs and Thakali people

originally from the uplands make up the majority of its population. From here, a scenic road runs north through the hills to Pokhara via the viewpoint of Tansen. Another route heads south for 20 kilometers (13 miles) to the large industrial town of **Bhairawa**, the border crossing at **Sonauli**.

This area is full of places of historical and cultural interest. Twenty kilometers (12 miles) west of Bhairawa on a well marked road is **Lumbini**, the birthplace of the Lord Buddha and an important pilgrimage place for all Asia (see page 323). Another ancient civilization site, **Kapilavastu**, lies further west (27 kilometers, 17 miles) at **Tilaurakot**, the former capital of Prince Siddhartha father's kingdom. Near the dam at **Tribenighat**, a historic temple marks the site of Sita's banishment, as told in the great Ramayana epic.

The East-West Highway climbs through the Siwalik range into the beautiful **Deokhuri** valley, an Inner Terai *dun* watered by the Rapti river. This is home to the Dangaura Tharu people

Brahmany ducks, or Ruddy Sheldrake, fly low over the Terai rivers where they like to winter before returning through the Himalayan range to Tibet.

whose long mud houses surrounded by fertile fields can be seen from the road. Young women wear stri-king black and red skirts and a distinctive headdress adorned with tassels and beads upon which they balance loads. The less-visited **Dang** valley lies north.

The Remote Far West: Until a few years ago, the easiest way to reach far west Nepal was via India, especially during monsoon when floods swell the rivers. Beyond the Deokhuri valley, the highway penetrates the most remote part of the Terai. Here is the feeling of the "wild west." The four districts of **Banke**, **Bardiya**, **Kailali** and **Kanchanpur** are still known as the *naya muluk*, or new territories, as they were returned to Nepal by British India as late as 1860. Before the Land Reform Act of 1964, these districts were inhabited by only Dangaura, Katharya and Rana Tharu. Migrants subsequently settled from the hills, clearing and claiming these virgin lands.

Nepalgunj is the far west's largest city and is considered to be one of the

hottest places in Nepal. For centuries it has been an important market, attracting Indians, Tharu and highlanders from Jumla and Tibet to its bustling bazaars. Today the population, including many Indians, is less than 40,000; it has yet to benefit from industrialisation, although small scale handicraft production such as silver jewellery is evident along the main street.

An important regional communications and transportation centre, Nepalgunj is the far west's link with Kathmandu. Flights connect to the hill town of **Jumla** (see page 309) and roads service the Tiger Tops Karnali Lodge and Tented Camp in **Royal Bardiya National Park** and **Sukla Phanta Wildlife Reserve**, near the western border. A fine road leads north to the pleasant and fertile valley of **Surkhet**, now renamed **Birendranagar**, once so malarious that travellers feared to stay even one night.

West of Nepalgunj the East-West Highway is still under construction through the untouched forests of Royal Bardiya National Park to **Chisopani**, a village on the banks of the Karnali River (350 kilometers, 218 miles west of Narayanghat). Passengers, along with buses and trucks, must cross the swift-flowing river on a flat ferry boat. Eventually a huge single-tower suspension bridge will link the far west to the rest of Nepal. Very few tourists venture into these parts. The border town of **Dhanghari** draws Indian shoppers with its imported goods. The challenges of a new cultural identity evident in such remote areas is apparent in booming **Mahendranagar**, which has doubled its population in the last ten years and is now bigger than Nepalgunj. In contrast, villages inhabited by the native Rana Tharu are distinguished by women in colourfully embroidered skirts topped with black shawls.

Though not one of Nepal's primary tourist attractions, the Terai offers a certain fascination as a melding point of Indian and Nepalese hill traditions and a centre of burgeoning commercialism speeding whole-heartedly into the 20th century.

The sacred thread of a Brahman is renewed every year.

322

BIRTHPLACE OF LORD BUDDHA

Lumbini in southern Nepal is the birthplace of the Buddha, born in 543 B.C. as the Sakya Prince, Siddhartha Gautama. It is situated 21 kilometers (13 miles) west of the modern town of Bhairawa, formerly known as Siddhar-thanagar, and is set in five square miles of landscaped gardens.

An important place of pilgrimage for Buddhists as well as Hindus, Lumbini was "lost" for centuries. In the 4th century A.D. the Chinese monk, Fa-Hien, travelled to India in search of Buddhist manuscripts and returned with vivid descriptions of the remains he found at Lumbini. Already it was in ruins and had been overgrown by the jungle. Fa-Hien wrote: "On the road people have to guard against elephants and lions."

Only in 1895 did archaeologists unearth the inscribed pillar, erected to commemorate the visit of the Maurayan Emperor Ashoka in 249 B.C. Since 1970 the sacred site has been protected by the Lumbini Development Trust. Excavations have been made and pottery, figurines and coins found amongst the ancient brick foundations of monasteries and stupas. A new Tibetan monastery has been built, trees planted and a museum, library, hotel and garden are under construction.

The massive Ashoka pillar marks the place of Buddha's birth and the Mayadevi Temple contains a panel depicting the miraculous event. The myth tells how Buddha was conceived by entering his mother's womb in the form of a white elephant. When the time came his mother, Mayadevi, leaning on a fig tree, gave birth to Prince Siddhartha from her right side. She placed the new born child in a lotus flower, but he stood and walked seven steps in each of the four directions, announcing his great destiny. After seven days Mayadevi died.

The original temple was built by Emperor Ashoka and reconstructed in the 5th century A.D. in the *shikara* style. The present building dates from the 19th century and is sheltered by an an-

cient *pipal* tree. Adjacent is the sacred pond in which Prince Siddhartha was bathed after his birth. Mayadevi is also greatly revered by Hindus.

The story of the Buddha is known to all Buddhists. He lived a life of luxury, marrying a princess, fathering a child and enjoying his youth. Only as an adult did he venture beyond the walls of the palace where he encountered a poor man, a sick man and a dead man. He was so disturbed by this suffering that he abandoned his comfortable life to become an ascetic.

Tilaurakot, the ancient capital of Kapilavastu, is 27 kilometers (17 miles) west of Lumbini. In a lovely mango grove, excavations have revealed the brick remains of the eastern and western gates of the palace complex in which Prince Siddharta lived with his father, King Suddhodhana. The museum in the village contains pieces found dating between the 4th century B.C. and the 4th century A.D. Near Tilaurakot are the damaged Ashoka pillars of Niglihawa and Kotihawa.

Right, a Licchavi statue of the Lord Buddha, the Compassionate One, born at Lumbini. **Following page**: a misty morning on Nuptse.

TRAVEL TIPS

GETTING THERE

BY AIR

More than 90 percent of all non-Indian visitors to Nepal arrive by air at Tribhuvan International Airport, about 8 km (5 miles) from Kathmandu.

Many air carriers serve the Kingdom including the national flag carrier, Royal Nepal Airlines Corporation (RNAC), Aeroflot, Bangladesh Biman, Burma Airways, China Airlines (CAAC), Dragon Air, Indian Airlines, Lufthansa, Pakistan International Airlines, Royal Bhutan Airlines (Druz Air), Singapore Airlines and Thai International.

Kathmandu can be accessed by flights directly from Europe (Frankfurt, London and Moscow), Dubai and Karachi as well as the traditional route from the west via Delhi. From the east there are flights from Hong Kong, Singapore and Bangkok. Additional regional destinations served are Bombay, Calcutta, Dhaka, Lhasa, Paro, Patna, Rangoon and Varanasi. RNAC provides charter service to Brunei, Hong Kong, Japan and the Middle East.

FARES

All air fares must be paid in foreign exchange by foreigners in Nepal and there are a number of special fares available in Kathmandu. As some airfares fluctuate with the exchange rate, check with a travel agent. Only Nepalese and Indian nationals may pay in rupees for any air passage between Nepal and India.

When coming from the west to Kathmandu on a clear day you will see close in succession the western Himalaya: Gurja Himal (7,193 meters), Dhaulagiri (8,167 meters), the dark, deep valley of the Kali Gandaki River leading north to Mustang, the six peaks of the Annapurna Range including Annapurna I (8,091 meters), the pointed Manaslu (8,163 meters) and the three lumps of Ganesh Himal (7,429 meters) which dominate the Kathmandu Valley.

Coming from the east you can view successively the flat-topped Kangchenjunga (8,586 meters), the rocky Makalu (8,463 meters), the giant of them all, Mount Everest (8,848 meters), Cho Oyu (8,201 meters), Dorje Lhakpa (6,966 meters) and Langtang Lirung (7,234 meters) standing above the Kathmandu Valley.

The twice weekly service to Lhasa flies directly over the Himalaya and must be one of the most spectacular flights in the world. Check with local travel agents as these flights are seasonal and sometimes do not operate for political reasons.

Be sure to reconfirm your international departure flight tickets not less than three days before departure or they will be subject to cancellation. The baggage allowance on international is 20 kilos in economy class. Overweight charges will be levied in foreign exchange.

Do take note there is a Rs. 450 departure tax payable upon check-in on all departing international flights.

BY RAIL

Within India, trains are a convenient means of transportation but there is no railway to speak of in Nepal. A 47-km line was built in 1925 between Raxaul, India and Amlekhganj, south of Kathmandu. Further east, a second line was built in 1940 between the Indian border and Janakpur, some 50 kms. north. But that's all.

Combining Indian rail with Indian and Nepalese roads, it takes about three days of travel from Delhi to Kathmandu by way of Agra, Varanasi and Patna, crossing the border at Birgunj.

If you are coming from the Indian hill station of Darjeeling, you can take to train to Siligiri. From there it is a one-hour taxi journey to Kakarbhitta, a Nepalese border post from where you catch a bus or taxi to Biratnagar. Tourists wishing to enter the Indian state of Sikkim can now get a 15-day tourist visa at Siliguri.

BY ROAD

In addition to Tribhuvan International Airport there are only five official entry points. Check local political conditions as even these are sometimes closed temporarily. These points are:

Rani Sikiyahi (Kosi Zone) just south of Biratnagar.

Birgunj (Narayani Zone) near Raxaul, India, the most common entry point for overland travelers.

Kodari (Bagmati Zone) on the Chinese Tibetan border, open to tourists with Chinese visas, providing road access to Lhasa.

Sonauli (Lumbini Zone) near Bhairawa on the road to Pokhara.

Kakarbhitta (Mechi Zone) with connections to Darjeeling, Sikkim and Siliguri, India (see above).

An Indian visa is required for all foreign passport holders in order to enter India. If you are planning to commute more than once between Nepal and India be sure to get a double or multiple entry visa. Visas are most conveniently secured from the Indian Embassy in your country of residence, although it is possible to get them from the Indian embassy in Kathmandu.

If you are entering Nepal by private car, be prepared to wait for several hours to get through any of the Indian border posts. Private vehicles are not

THE PROBLEMS OF A

HEAVY TRAFFIC.

You'll come across massive Thai jumbos at work and play in their natural habitat. In Thailand, elephants are part of everyday rural life.

FALLING MASONRY.

A visit to the ruined cities of Sukhothai or Ayutthaya will remind you of the country's long and event-filled history.

EYESTRAIN.

A problem everyone seems to enjoy. The beauty of our exotic land is only matched by the beauty and gentle nature of the Thai people.

GETTING LOST.

From the palm-fringed beaches of Phuket to the highlands of Chiang Mai there are numerous places to get away from it all.

OLIDAY IN THAILAND.

GETTING TRAPPED.

In bunkers mostly. The fairways, superb club houses and helpful caddies make a golf trap for players of all standards.

HIGH DRAMA.

A performance of the 'Khon' drama, with gods and demons acting out a never-ending battle between good and evil, should not be missed.

EXCESS BAGGAGE.

Thai food is so delicious you'll want to eat more and more of it. Of course, on Thai there's no charge for extra kilos in this area.

MISSING YOUR FLIGHT.

In Thailand, this isn't a problem. Talk to us or your local travel agent about Royal Orchid Holidays in Thailand.

Thai
We reach for the sky.

HOLIDAY MAKERS'
N·E·P·A·L

Nepal is a dream travel destination. Towering Himalayas. Enchanting countryside. Hidden Valleys. Ancient culture and tradition – so colourful to match your holiday spirit. Mountaineering. Whitewater rafting. Leisurely treks. Exploration tours. Wildlife explorations and above all, the discovery of medieval culture.

Come to Nepal where a Shangri-La experience awaits you.
There is no better way to reach Nepal than by Royal Nepal Airlines. The holiday starts the moment you board Royal Nepal flight.

Royal Nepal Airlines

HONG KONG	SINGAPORE	DELHI	CALCUTTA	NEWYORK	LONDON	PARIS	FRANKFURT	KATHMANDU	BANGKOK
3699151/2	2257575	3321572	298534	(212) 6614435	071-3871541	(01) 40459521	(069) 250106/07	220757	233-3921-4

permitted to enter China from Nepal. A *carnet de passage en douanes* is required for cars and motorbikes. These exempt the owner of the vehicle from customs duty for three months. A driver's license is also required. Motor vehicles in Nepal are driven on the left side of the road.

TRAVEL ESSENTIALS

VISAS AND PASSPORTS

Except for Indian and Bhutanese citizens, all passport holders require a visa for entry into Nepal.

A tourist visa can be isssued by a Nepalese Embassy. This visa is valid for 30 days in the Kathmandu Valley, Pokhara, the Terai and other parts of Nepal linked by highways. A single entry visa to Nepal costs US$10 for 30 days for all foreign nationals except British passport holders for whom it costs UK£20. Visas can be extended for up to three months at a rate of Rs. 75 per week for the second month and Rs. 150 a week for the third month. Tourist visas will not be granted for more than three months in any 12 month period.

A 15-day visa can also be issued on arrival at Kathmandu's Tribhuvan Airport for the same cost as a 30 day single entry visa. This can be extended to the full 30-day period at no extra cost.

Extensions are granted at the Department of Immigration, Keshar Mahal, Thamel, Kathmandu; tel: 412337 (open from 10 a.m. to 4 p.m. except Saturdays and government holidays). A normal visa extension or trekking permit (within the first three months) usually takes one or two days.

It is required to show that you have changed money (at least US$20 per day) to obtain a visa extension so bring your currency card or Foreign Exchange Encashment Receipts with your passport and two passport-size photos.

Persons intending to trek off the main highway into the hills must obtain a trekking permit for the specific area they are planning to visit. These are colour coded and require three passport-size photographs. Trekking permits are available at the Department of Immigration in Kathmandu and, for limited periods, in Pokhara.

Get a multiple entry visa if you are planning a short visit to Tibet or India within your three month period.

MONEY MATTERS

Most hotel, airline and travel agency payments are required to be made in foreign exchange. Credit cards such as American Express and Visa are widely accepted. Others are not.

Every time you make a foreign exchange payment or exchange currency for Nepalese rupees, make sure the transaction is recorded with a Foreign Exchange Encashment Receipt.

At the end of your stay, excess Nepalese rupees can be converted back into hard currency, but no more than 10 per cent of the total amount changed.

Non-Indian visitors are not allowed to import or export Nepalese nor Indian rupees.

For currency exchange, there is an exchange counter at Tribhuvan Airport, in banks and at most hotels.

You may purchase US dollar Travellers Cheques with American Express credit card at their office in Durbar Marg or with Visa card at their representatives, Nepal Grindlays Bank at Kantipath. It is possible to have money sent to you at foreign banks which can be collected in US dollar Traveller Cheques but this proceedure is not recommended unless in emergency as it is time consuming and unreliable.

The official rate of exchange fluctuates against all currencies. In early 1992 the rate was 42.60 to US$1. It is published daily on the back page of the *Rising Nepal* newspaper and broadcast every day on Radio Nepal in the Nepali language.

Hard currency is in high demand and there is a black market in Kathmandu. Buyers should be cautious and remember currency receipt requirements.

There are banknotes in denominations of Nepalese Rupees, 1,000, 500, 100, 50, 20, 10, 5, 2 and 1, and coins of one rupee and of 50, 25, 10 and 5 *paisa*. There are 100 *paisa* to one rupee.

HEALTH

Visitors should possess a valid health certificate of inoculation against yellow fever if coming from an infected area. Checking of health certificates is haphazard.

Although there is not more danger to health in Nepal that in many other countries, elementary sanitary precautions are in order. Health requirements are lax for entry, but travellers are advised to get injections against typhoid and meningitis and to have gamma globulin against hepatitis. Make sure your routine tetanus and polio inoculations are up to date. Cholera inoculation is not required nor recommended.

Never drink unboiled and untreated water and do not trust ice cubes anywhere except in the best hotels. Avoid eating raw vegetables and peel fruit before consuming. Never walk barefoot and wash your hands often. If you follow these basic guidelines you should avoid many of the intestinal infections which lead to diarrhoea.

Nevertheless, it is not uncommon for minor problems to occur soon after arrival in the country especially after those long inter-continental flights. "Traveller's tummy" should clear up after a couple of days but if it is particularly severe and persistest or interferes with your travel plans, get a stool text and medical assistance.

The foreign-staffed CIWEC Clinic at Baluwater opposite the Russian Embassy tel: 410983 is particularly convenient and experienced with travellers.

WHAT TO WEAR

Your wardrobe will depend upon when you are going to Nepal and what you intend to do there. Unless you are planning to meet government or embassy officials, there is no need to bring anything but the most casual clothing.

From mid-September to March light clothing is fine in the Kathmandu Valley. For evenings and early mornings, a heavy woollen sweater or a padded anorak or jacket will be needed. Blue jeans, corduroy trousers or below-the-knee skirts are in order and comfortable shoes are a must, even if you do not intend to go trekking. High heels are out and sneakers are ideal. Do not bother to bring a rain coat; a locally bought umbrella will suffice against the sun as well as the rain.

Special gear required for trekking can be hired or bought in Kathmandu or Pokhara, in standard Western sizes. The same applies for sweaters, caps and other woollen or down clothing, though it is best to arrive self-sufficient.

From April to September only light clothes, preferably cotton, are needed in Kathmandu. Avoid synthetic fibres which irritate the skin.

The Terai, being lower in altitude, is generally warmer than Kathmandu throughout the year. Safari-type clothing is most appropriate for visits to the lowland National Parks. But the cold winter nights in December and January make a sweater and jacket essential.

CUSTOMS

The traveller may bring in 200 cigarettes, 20 cigars, one bottle of spirits and one bottle of wine. Also duty-free are the following personal effects: one pair of binoculars, a camera with a reasonable amount of film, a tape recorder with 15 tapes, a musical instrument, a transistor radio, one video camera (without deck) and a fishing rod.

Controls are quite strict at Tribhuvan Airport and customs officials must chalk all your luggage before you leave. Prohibited are fire-arms and ammunition (unless an import licence has been obtained in advance), radio transmitters, walkie-talkies and drugs. Special film permits are required for 16mm cameras.

Customs are also quite sensitive about video cameras and radios and these may be recorded in your passport, thus ensuring they are exported when you depart.

You must also clear customs when you leave the country. To avoid hassles, be aware of the following:

1. **Souvenirs** can be exported freely but **antiques and art objects** require a special certificate from the Department of Archaeology, National Archives Building, Ram Shah Path, Kathmandu. It takes at least two days to secure. It is forbidden to export any object more that 100 years old.

2. **Precious and rare commodities** are strictly forbidden to be exported from Nepal. These include precious stones, gold, silver, weapons and drugs. Animal hides, fangs or wild animals may not be exported with special licenses. Live pet animals such as Tibetan dogs may be taken out.

3. **Currency** – Keep receipts for any handicrafts and purchases you have made and remember to have your Foreign Exchange Encashment Receipts ready for inspection if necessary.

GETTING ACQUAINTED

GOVERNMENT & ECONOMY

Nepal is a constitutional monarchy headed by His Majesty King Birendra Bir Bikram Shah Dev who holds powers similar to those of the Queen of England. Today's multi-party parliamentary system was achieved by the "revolution" of April 1990 and formalised in the November 1990 constitution which guaranteed sovereignty in the people and universal franchise for citizens 18 years and older. In the May 1991 general election, the Nepali Congress Party, which is social democratic in outlook, gained a small majority and its leader is Prime Minister Girija Prasad Koirala. The main opposition is the Communist Party of Nepal (United Marxist-Leninist) which also supports parliamentary democracy.

The King (born 28th December, 1945) and Queen Aishwarya Rajya Lakshmi Devi Shah (born 7th November, 1949) have three children; the older, His Royal Highness Crown Prince Dipendra (born 27th June, 1971) is heir to the throne.

Nepal's population is about 19 million, 50 percent of it under the age of 15. The annual rate of population growth is 2.7 percent. Nepal is classified by the United Nations as one of the world's least developed nations with one of the world's half dozen lowest per capita incomes at about US$180 per annum.

The majority of the population is dependent on agriculture for their livelihood and much of this is subsistence farming on small plots on terraced hillsides. Only 10 percent of the labourforce is employed in other areas.

The majority of imported goods come from or via India, Calcutta being Nepal's official port of entry. This makes Nepal particularly vulnerable as was demonstrated by the problems that arose with India when the trade and transit treaties expired in 1989.

The revenue of hand-made wool carpets reached over US$ 70 million in 1990 and overtook tourism (some US$ 60 million in 1990) as the largest source of foreign exchange. Carpets accounted for over 50 percent of Nepal's total exports.

Nepal is heavily dependent on foreign aid for its economic development as it tries to provide basic necessities for all its citizens by the year 2000.

Two-thirds of its development budget comes from foreign aid, both bilateral and multilateral. The foreign aid commitment for 1990/91 was about US$500 million.

Literacy is very low with less than a quarter of the population being able to write their names. Health care is minimal with one doctor for every 25,000 population and with only 3,000 hospital beds in Kathmandu. Infant mortality is "very high" and one child in every six dies before their fifth birthday. Life expectancy for adults is little more than 50 years, with women unusually having a lower life expectancy than men.

TIME ZONES

Nepal is five hours, 45 minutes ahead of Greenwich Mean Time and 15 minutes ahead of Indian Standard Time. Thus international time differences are rather staggered as follows:

Kathmandu	12 noon
New Delhi	11.45 a.m. today
Paris	7.15 a.m. today
London	6.15 a.m. today
San Francisco	10.15 p.m. yesterday
Hawaii	8.15 p.m. yesterday
Sydney	4.15 p.m. today
Tokyo	3.15 p.m. today
Hong Kong	2.15 p.m. today
Bangkok	1.15 p.m. today
Rangoon	12.45 p.m. today

CALENDARS

Five different calendars are used simultaneously in Nepal. These include the Gregorian calendar familiar to the West and the Tibetan calendar.

The traditional ones are the Sakya Era calendar which began counting years in 108 A.D., and the Newari calendar, starting in 879-880 A.D.

The official calendar is the Vikram Sambat calendar, named after the legendary North Indian King Vikramaditya. Day One of Vikram Sambat was 23rd February, 57 B.C. Hence the year 1991 of the Christian era is 2048 of the Vikram era.

This system is the only one you will find in newspapers, public services and the world of government bureaucracy.

The Nepalese celebrate their New Year in mid-April, according to the Western calendar. The fiscal and budgetary year begins in mid-July.

The Nepalese year is 365 days long, same as in the West, with 12 months ranging in length from 29 to 32 days.

These calendar months starting mid-April are called *Baisakh* (31 days), *Jesth* (31 days), *Asadh* (32 days), *Srawan* (32 days), *Bhadra* (31 days), *Ashwin* (30 days), *Kartik* (30 days), *Marga* (29 days), *Poush* (30 days), *Magha* (29 days), *Falgun* (30 days), and *Chaitra* (30 days).

The number of days in a month in a Nepalese calendar is never constant as it is dependant on solar movement.

The seven days of the week have been named according to the planets. They are: *Aityabar* (Sunday), the sun's day; *Somabar* (Monday), the moon's day; *Mangalbar* (Tuesday), Mars' day; *Budhabar* (Wednesday), Mercury's day; *Brihapatibar* or *Bihibar* (Thursday), Jupiter's day or the day of the Lord; *Sukrabar* (Friday), Venus' day; and *Shanisharbar* or *Shanibar* (Saturday), Saturn's day.

CLIMATE

From the eternal snow of the higher peaks to the tropical expanses of the lowlands, Nepal enjoys an extreme variety of climates. Altitudes and exposure to sun and rain are the most influential factors.

Sitting at an elevation of about 1,350 meters (4,400 feet), the Kathmandu Valley knows three seasons. The cold season from October to March is the best time to visit the country.

The night time temperatures may drop nearly to freezing point, but the sun warms the atmosphere by day, so that the morning hours see the mercury climb from 10°C to 25°C (50°F-77°F).

The sky is generally clear and bright; the air is dry and warm. Nippy mornings and evenings are invigorating. In the winter there is frequently an early-morning mist – a result of the rapid heating of the cold night air. October and February are particularly pleasant.

The weather is noticeably warmer in the Pokhara valley, where temperatures rise to 30°C (86°F) at midday in the lower altitude.

In April, May and early June the weather becomes hot and stuffy, with occasional evening thunderstorms.

Nature is in full bloom but the brightly coloured landscapes are often shrouded in heat mist. Daily temperatures in Kathmandu fluctuate between 11°C and 28°C (52°F and 83°F) in April and between 19°C and 30°C (66°F and 86°F) in June, with maximum temperatures of 36°C (97°F).

By the end of June the monsoon arrives, heralded by pre-monsoon rains which normally start in May. The rainy season lasts three months, during which time the Himalaya usually remains out of sight though the rains create some spectacular lighting effects. Violent downpours create some flooding but it is still possible to visit the Kathmandu Valley. Trekking stops with the proliferation of leeches *(jugas)*, and the lowlands are sometimes cut off by swollen rivers and occasional landslides.

The monsoon ends around mid-September. Autumn brings clearer skies, cooler nights and a symphony of brown and gold to the land.

CULTURE & CUSTOMS

What is a foreigner? By definition he or she is wealthy. Think how many bags of rice the place ticket that got you to Kathmandu is worth. The postulate of foreign wealth has been deeply ingrained in Nepalese minds.

CHARITY

Its consequences can be a bit unsettling for the visitor; the corollary is that the Nepalese should try to get a little of that wealth. Foreigners have often been extremely generous with sweets, goods, clothing and cash. As a result, a little blackmail is not unusual from porters and guides on mountain treks for those who go it alone. One often gets requests for free medicine, or encounters beggars in the tourist-trodden parts of the Kathmandu Valley.

Children frequently chant the magic words "Rupee! Paisa!" with palms extended. It is mostly a game. Ignore them and they will smile and romp away. Should they insist, grown-ups will shout and scatter them, for there is pride in the Nepalese be in the valley or in the hills.

On occasion, rowdy crowds of unruly children will throng you. Take care of your belongings, make sure your bag is zipped up, your camera equipment secure. Mostly they will annoy you by popping up between your camera and the statues you want to photograph. Let them be; children can give a sense of proportion to a picture. Ask a friend to distract them. Or else give up, or pretend to, until they are busy somewhere else.

One can go about almost everywhere in complete confidence. Women can walk on their own without being bothered.

RELIGION & SUPERSTITION

A source of bad feeling may arise if you are asked not to enter a certain precinct or not to photograph a shrine. Comply with good grace. The reasons for enforcing a taboo are as evident to the local people as they are obscure to you.

Nobody will ask you to forgo your own values and standards as long as you don't expect them to be followed by everybody. Respect and open-mindedness are essential. The apparent familiarity with which the Nepalese behave towards idols should be no invitation for you to imitate them by riding on statues or other such nonsense.

The Nepalese understand that Western values are different from theirs. Even if they are shocked or stunned by your behaviour, they will explain it as primitive barbarianism, and will not pursue the matter as long as they don't think the gods are offended.

In Nepal, superstition and religion merge and diverge until they become indistinguishable. But the beliefs, whether stemming from religious dogma or pure superstition, are deep-rooted and ever-present. It would be impossible to fully comprehend and adapt to the implications of these beliefs without becoming a thorough initiate of the regions, customs, traditions and rituals of the Nepalese people. However, an attempt is made here to list some important ones which, if you remember and heed, will help to establish a congenial rapport between the Nepalese and yourself.

First of all, know and accept the fact that you are a foreigner and therefore ritually "polluted." Thus some seemingly innocent act on your part, which could have been tolerated of a Nepalese, might have unpleasant repercussions.

Stepping over the feet or the body of a person rather than walking around him is not done. Never make the mistake of offering to share "polluted" food, that is food that you have tasted, bitten into or even touched with your used fork or spoon.

Lack of toilet paper has led to the customs (which has eventually become a ritual) of using water and the left hand to cleanse oneself after going to the toilet. Therefore nothing should be accepted, and especially not offered, with the left hand only. If you do offer or accept anything then do so with both hands, if this is practical or certainly using your right hand. This will please your Sherpa, or some Nepali whom you have met, very much. Using both hands to give or receive signifies that you honour the offering and the recipient or giver.

You will notice that most Nepalese take off their shoes before they enter a house or a room. It would not be practical to suggest that you unlace and take off your hiking boots or shoes every time you enter a village house. It would be helpful, however is you were to avoid entering a house unless you wished to spend some time in it – to eat a meal or drink some tea, for example.

The kitchen area or the cooking and eating area are to be treated with the utmost of respect. On no account should you go into the kitchen or cooking and eating areas with you shoes on. You should avoid intruding into these areas at all unless you are specifically invited there – remember the hearth in a home is sacred.

Nepalese often eat squatting on the ground. Do

not stand in front of a person who is eating, because your feet will be directly in front of his plate of food. If there is something you have to tell him, it is wiser to squat or sit by his side.

TIPPING

Tipping has become a habit in hotels and restaurants patronised by foreigners. A hotel waiter or porter will expect a one to two rupee tip. Taxi drivers need not always be tipped but when they have been especially helpful, about 10 percent of the fare is in order. A 10 percent tip is also customary in Westernised restaurants. Travel and trekking guides are customarily tipped much more.

Elsewhere, please do yourself and the country a favour and refrain from tipping.

WEIGHTS & MEASURES

Nepalese use the decimal system, but for specific purposes stick to traditional measures. As elsewhere in the Indian sub-continent, they count in *lakh* (unit of 100,000) and *crore* (unit of 10 million). Heights are usually measured in meters, but sometimes also in feet. (One foot equals 0.305 meters; one meter equals 3.28 feet). Distances are counted in kilometers.

Weights are measured in kilos (kilograms) with the following exceptions:

For rice and other cereals, milk and sugar; one *mana* equals a little less that half a liter; one *paathi*, about ¾ liters, contains eight *manas*; 160 *manas* equal 20 *paathis* equal one *muri*, about 75 liters.

For vegetables and fruits; one *pau* equals 200 grams; one *ser* equals four *paus*, or one kilogram; one *dharni* equals three *sers*, or 2.4 kilograms.

For all metals; one *tola* is equal to 11.66 grams.

For precious stones; one carat equals 0.2 grams.

The term *muthi* means "handful," whether it be of vegetables or firewood.

ELECTRICITY

Major towns in Nepal have been electrified using 220-volts alternating current, though some fluctuation is usual. When using a computer, or other sensitive electrical equipment, it is essential to use a voltage stabiliser. On festive occasions, Kathmandu is ablaze with lights at night. A few large hotels have their own power generators, as there are frequent power cuts. The rural electrification programme has a long way to go before it can phase out the poetry of candles and firesides. A small flashlight is useful.

BUSINESS HOURS

Government offices are open from 10 a.m. to 5 p.m. Sunday through Thursday for most of the year and close early at 3 p.m. on Fridays. They close an hour earlier during the winter months mid November to mid February. Banks open at 10 a.m. and close at 2 p.m. except Friday when they close at 12 noon.

Saturday is the rest day in Nepal, Sunday being a full working day for offices and banks. Only embassies and international organisations take a two-day weekend; they are generally open 9 or 9.30 a.m. to 5 or 5.30 p.m. during the rest of the week.

Shops, some of which remain open on Saturdays and holidays, seldom open before 10 a.m. but do not usually close until 7 or 8 p.m.

HOLIDAYS & FESTIVALS

Festivals are so much part of life in Nepal that they have been listed in detail, with descriptions as to how and where they are celebrated, in the feature section.

Festival dates vary from year to year because of the difference between the calenders and as many are determined only after complex astrological calculations. It is often difficult to know in advance when celebrations will take place, as the uncertainty is considered part of the mystique. Rely on local knowledge after you arrive in Kathmandu as the festival grapevine works well at short notice.

The Nepalese are usually happy to allow you to share in their festivities but it is wise to remain respectful and keep some distance. Remember they are predominantly religious in character, even though they can often get quite rowdy and crowded.

RELIGIOUS SERVICES

Roman Catholic church services are held at 9.00 a.m. on Sunday mornings and 5.30 p.m. Sunday evenings at St. Xavier's College in Jawalakhel, tel: 521050 and at 5.30 p.m. on Saturdays at the Annapurna Hotel tel: 221711.

Protestant services are held 9.30 a.m. on Sundays at the Lincoln School, Rabi Bhawan tel: 270603. For Jewish services contact the Israeli Embassy tel: 411811. For Moslems the main mosques are in Durbar Marg.

COMMUNICATIONS

MEDIA

Newspapers and Magazines: There are several newspapers published in English in Kathmandu, as well as dozens in Nepali. They are somewhat controlled, although Nepali dailies and weeklies express various shades of opinion. In English, the *Rising Nepal* has a wider coverage of foreign news than the more parochial *Motherland*. The outspoken *Independent* comes out every Wednesday. Of the magazines published in Nepal, look for the useful *Nepal Traveller* and the excellent, environmental *Himal* magazine.

The *International Herald Tribune* can be found at newsstands and hotels – it arrives one day late. Also available are *Time*, *Newsweek*, *The Far East Economic Review*, *Asiaweek*, and *India Today* among others. There are few daily foreign news publications to be found in Nepal, except Indian newspapers which arrive on the morning flights.

RADIO & TELEVISION

Two news bulletins in English are broadcast by Radio Nepal daily at 8 a.m. and 8 p.m. Bring a shortwave radio if you are addicted to international news.

Television arrived in Nepal early in 1986. Nepal Television presents several hours of programmes daily and they have plans for future expansion.

The news in English is broadcast on Nepal Television every evening at 9.40 p.m. Of the international stations, CNN news is broadcast daily at 7.30 p.m.and BBC World Service Television at 8.20 p.m. Check the programmes daily in the *Rising Nepal*.

POSTAL SERVICES

The **General Post Office** in Kathmandu has two sections located close to one another at the junction of Kanti Path and Kicha-Pokhari Road. They are open 10 a.m. to 5 p.m. daily except Saturdays and holidays, and close at 4 p.m. during the winter months.

Buy stamps, send letters or receive them through the Poste Restante at the General Post Office. Ensure the stamps on letters and post cards are franked in front of your eyes. Main hotels will usually handle mail and this is certainly the easiest way.

If you use Poste Restante ask your correspondents to either mention only your family name on the envelope, or to write it with a big initial.

The so-called **Foreign Post Office** next door deals only with parcels sent or received from abroad. Avoid sending or receiving any during your stay.

TELEPHONE & TELEFAX

The **Telecommunications Office** in Tripureshwar deals with telephone calls and telexes. Its cable service is available only during government working hours nearby at the **Central Telegraph Office**.

International telephone connections are now excellent and direct dial overseas is available in many hotels. Note the Nepal country code is 977, the Kathmandu area code is 1, and Pokhara area code is 61. The earth satellite station was installed by the British in 1982.

For assistance dial 186 for the international operator. Dial 187 for calls to India, 180 for internal trunk calls and 197 for enquiries.

Telefax is found in Nepal in the larger hotels and more progressive offices. Ask your travel agent or hotel if a public service is available.

EMERGENCIES

MEDICAL SERVICES

Doctors and Hospitals: For serious problems, there are doctors attached to the big hotels, the American-staffed CIWEC Clinic, Baluwatar tel: 410983, and the Nepali-staffed Nepal International Clinic, Naxal tel: 412842. Some Kathmandu hospitals do have English-speaking staff but are not up to international standards and where feasible foreign visitors are advised to get to the excellent facilities in Bangkok. For accidents and emergencies, the hospitals are:

Bir Hospital, Kanti Path, Kathmandu (in front of the Tundhikhel parade ground), Tel: 221119, 221988

Patan Hospital, Lagankhel, Patan (run by the United Mission to Nepal), Tel: 521034, 521048, 522286, 522278

It's just a little more different than staying at home.

At the Shangri-La, you are looked after by warm, polite and friendly people. Though there may be butterflies on your tea cup, there'll be lots of smiles all over the place-and if the laughter is too loud, don't expect any apologies. It's the one place you'll never be another room number.

SHANGRI~LA
K A T H M A N D U
NEPAL
Your private paradise

GPO Box 655, Lazimpat, Kathmandu Nepal
Tel: 412999, Telex: 2276 HOSANG NP, Facsimile 977-1-414184

Ask for it every day, everywhere you go.

Wherever you're going in the world, a copy of the International Herald Tribune is waiting for you. Circulated in 164 countries, on 70 airlines and in hundreds of quality hotels worldwide, the IHT brings you a view of the world that is concise, balanced and distinctly multinational in flavor. And you can get it six days a week, even when you're traveling.

Herald INTERNATIONAL Tribune

Published With The New York Times and The Washington Post

7th Floor, Malaysia Bldg, 50 Gloucester Road, Hong Kong
Tel.: (852) 861 0616. Fax: (852) 861 3073. Telex: 61170

Come to the Everest
Come to the Best

*It's no coincidence
that Everest rhymes
with best. We've got the best possible
standards of luxury in Nepal. The best rooms.
The best restaurants. The best bars.
The best service.*

The Everest Hotel

Baneswor, P.O. Box 659, Kathmandu, Nepal
Tel 220567 Fax 977-1-226088 Tlx 2260 HOTEVS NP

For the discerning traveller

For reservation contact us directly, your travel agent or Utell International

Teaching Hospital , Maharajgunj, Tel: 412303, 412404, 412505, 412808.

PHARMACIES

Most medicines that you will require during your visit are readily and cheaply available in Kathmandu without prescription. Do not rely on the pharmacists but ask for medical assistance when making a diagnosis. Look out for the well known brand names manufactured under licence in India but check the label carefully as contents may be different from those you are familiar with back home.

Pharmacies can be found in all the major towns of Nepal. For trekkers or those venturing off the beaten track be sure you have what you need with you before you leave Kathmandu.

KEY TELEPHONE NUMBERS

It is useful for the traveller to have some essential telephone numbers that might prove handy in the event of an emergency.

Service	Dialing Direct
Police Emergency	226999
	226998
Red Cross Ambulance	228094
Bir Hospital	221119
	221988
Patan Hospital	521034
	521048
Teaching Hospital	412303
	412404
	412505
	412808
CIWEC Clinic	410983
Nepal International Clinic	412842
Fire Brigade	221177
Telephone Enquiry	197
International Operator	186
Operator for India	187
Internal Trunk Calls	180
Telephone Maintenance	198

GETTING AROUND

MAPS

The green map of Nepal and the orange street map of Kathmandu published by Himalayan Booksellers will complement the maps found in this *Insight Guide*.

Regional trekking maps are also available, though most are not entirely reliable. The best are those prepared by Erwin Schneider, even though they cover only eastern Nepal and the Kathmandu Valley. National Geographic publishes a spectacular map of the Everest region. The ACAP (Annapurna Conservation Area Project) publishes the best map of the western region. *Apa Maps, Nepal* covers the country from Dhaulagiri to the eastern border.

FROM THE AIRPORT

If you are not being met by your travel agent, take a meter taxi that is normally available. The taxi ride should not cost more than Rs. 80 by the meter. Taxis usually can accommodate only two or three passengers.

For travel from Tribhuvan Airport to Kathmandu, a bus service is provided by RNAC and Indian Airlines. When travelling from Kathmandu to the airport, buses depart from the RNAC building at the beginning of New Road.

DOMESTIC TRAVEL

By Air: Flying is the best way of moving around fast in Nepal although domestic schedules are subject to last minute changes. Royal Nepal Airlines Corporation (RNAC), the national airline, has a monopoly on domestic flights and runs an extensive network using a fleet of Twin Otters, assisted by Avro 748s and Pilatus Porters on some routes.

The airline spider-web spreads from Kathmandu to the west (Bajura, Baitadi, Chaurjahari, Dang, Darchula, Dhanghari, Dolpa, Doti, Jumla, Mahendranagar, Nepalgunj, Silgari, Simikot, Surkhet, Tikapur); to the center (Baglung, Bhairawa, Bharatpur, Jomosom, Manang, Meghauly, Pokhara, Simra); and to the east (Bhadrapur, Bhojpur, Biratnagar, Janakpur, Lukla, Lamidanda, Phaplu, Rajbiraj, Ramechhap, Rumjatar, Taplejung and Tumlingtar).

In addition to Kathmandu, local "feeder" flights are scheduled out of Nepalgung, Pokhara and

Biratnagar. Details can be obtained from RNAC, New Road tel: 220757.

On certain tourist routes there are two fares; one fare for foreigners and a lower one for Nepalese and Indian nationals.

A Boeing or Avro takes visitors on a daily one-hour Mountain Flight leaving Kathmandu in the morning to fly east along the Himalaya for a view of Mount Everest. At US$94 it is a worthwhile trip.

There is a Rs. 30 airport tax on many domestic flights. Contrary to RNAC's generous international service, in-flight service is confined to boiled sweets and cotton-wool. There are no toilet facilities on Twin Otters or Pilatus Porters.

It is essential to book ahead, especially to distant destinations where only the smaller aircraft operate. There are cancellation fees of 10 percent if you cancel 24 hours in advance, 33 percent if less than 24 hours in advance and 100 percent if you fail to show up without informing the airline. If the flight is cancelled due to bad weather or other causes, your fare is refunded.

Small planes can occasionally be chartered, but these are expensive and difficult to secure, due to lack of availability. It is advisable to book through a travel agent. Helicopters can be chartered in addition to emergency rescues from the Royal Nepal Army, though are expensive. Alouettes cost US$ 750 per hour and Pumas US$1,700 per hour but check as rates fluctuate.

You will need to produce a trekking permit at Tribhuvan Airport on departure from Kathmandu to a trekking area. Always carry your passport (or a photocopy showing your visa) or trekking permit when travelling in Nepal, as there are occasional police checkpoints on all roads.

ROAD LINKS

In this mountainous country with deep valleys etched between peaks and ranges, roads are vital for bringing together the various communities. But until Nepal started opening to the outer world in the early 1950s, the kingdom had nothing except village trails and mountain paths. Cross-country trading was generally a tortuous affair measured in weeks and months. Since the 1950s, there have been major efforts to construct roads, many of them built with foreign aid. None were more active than Nepal's big-brotherly neighbours, India and China who were both prompted by obvious strategic considerations. There are six major road links:

The **Tribhuvan Raj Path**, linking Kathmandu with Raxaul at the Indian border 200 kilometers (124 miles) away, was opened in 1956 and built with Indian assistance.

The **Arniko Highway** or **Chinese Road** leads to the Tibetan border at Kodari. Some 110 kilometers (68 miles) long, it periodically suffers bad landslides, though it is normally possible to reach the border providing you walk across bad stretches. Check local

conditions before undertaking a trip.

Chinese engineers also helped to build the **Prithvi Raj Marg** in 1973 which covers the 200 kilometers (124 miles) between Kathmandu and Pokhara. There are two extensions to the Pokhara road: Dumre to Gorkha and Mugling to Narayanghat. In 1970 Indian engineers completed the 188 kilometer (117 mile) extension on from Pokhara to Sonauli on the Indian border south of Bhairawa; called the **Siddhartha Raj Marg**.

The most ambitious road is the result of the cooperation of the Soviet Union, the United States, Britain and India; the **Mahendra Raj Marg**. Popularly known as the **East-West Highway** this 1,000-kilometer (621-mile) lowland thoroughfare is part of the fabled Pan-Asian Highway linking the Bosphorus with the Far East. It has been completed up to the Karnali River, west of Nepalgunj.

China built the 32-kilometer **Ring Road** around Kathmandu and Chinese technicians have also installed a trolley-bus service between Kathmandu and Bhaktapur.

East of Kathmandu the Swiss-built highway from **Lamosangu to Jiri** stretches 110 kilometers (68 miles) and was completed in 1985. Now that the major road links have been established, locally built roads are slowly but surely creeping deeper into the mountains. Scars can be seen on the hills around the Kathmandu Valley and the road north from **Trisuli Bazaar** now stretches past **Dunche** into the Langtang National Park.

During the rainy season whole portions of existing roads are damaged and must be repaired. Maintenance on some roads is slow and it is best to inquire locally before setting off on a long-distance road trip.

PUBLIC TRANSPORT

All roads are plied by local bus services, with express coaches on the main routes. A bus ride in Nepal is a bumpy, noisy, smelly and slow affair that nevertheless can be fun. Some of these antediluvian beasts are mere sheet-metal boxes on wheels, but they eventually arrive at their destinations, even if passengers have to occasionally alight on the steepest climbs. No matter what, they are a cheap way of going about inside and outside of the Kathmandu Valley. They allow for a long, close look at the local folk inside the bus, if not always at the scenery outside.

BUSES

There are minibuses on the same routes as the public busses and coaches. They are less crowded, a bit faster and also slightly more expensive.

Please book one day ahead for the long-distance buses. The main bus station in Kathmandu is on the east side of the Tundhikhel parade ground, down from Durbar Marg. Minibuses start from near the

Post Office and those bound for Pokhara leave from near the Bhimsen Tower. In Pokhara, the bus terminal is close to the Post Office.

SCOOTERS

Within Kathmandu the three-wheeled public scooters can carry up to six passengers, always plying the same route and starting from Rani Pokhari. Also available are the black and yellow metered *tempos* which can be privately hired.

RICKSHAWS

These gaudily painted, slow moving, honking rickshaws are part of the Kathmandu city scene. They are large tricycles with two seats in the back covered by a hood; a man pedals up front. Whatever the driver may demand, a ride in town should not cost more than Rs.20, on average Rs.5 per kilometer. Make sure the driver understands where you are going and the price is settled before you start. Remember rickshaws should not cost more than taxis!

Keeping control of these vehicles on Kathmandu's narrow streets is quite a feat and it is not recommended to swap places with the driver.

TAXIS

Taxis are available to go most places within the Kathmandu Valley. They have black registration plates with white numbers whereas private cars have white numbers on red plates. Make sure their meters are working. Due to the rising gasoline costs, be prepared to pay a small surcharge. A short ride within the city will cost from Rs.15-30. To hire a taxi for half a day or a day trip within Kathmandu, negotiate a price before starting; do not pay more than Rs. 600 per day, gasoline included.

PRIVATE TRANSPORT

More reliable are private cars hired from any hotel or travel agency. They usually cost between US$50 - US$60 for the whole day but they are more comfortable and less likely to break down. The driver will wait until you have done your sightseeing and drivers normally speak at least a little English. A tip at the trip's conclusion will be welcome, but it is not mandatory, and should not be more than Rs. 100. A car can hold three or four people; a metered taxi usually cannot hold more than two.

CAR RENTAL

Avis is represented in Nepal by Yeti Travels and Hertz by Gorkha Travels, both located in Durbar Marg. It is not advisable to hire self-drive cars as roads can be treacherous and cars with drivers are no more expensive.

BICYCLES

Bicycling is one of the best ways of exploring the town. Many shops in the old part of Kathmandu and in Thamel have Indian and Chinese bicycles for hire at Rs.15 for the whole day. There is no deposit necessary; your hotel is enough. Make sure the bell works as, along with the brakes, this is the most important part of your bicycle as you will need it to weave through the throngs. Lights are supposedly compulsory after dark but a flashlight will suffice.

MOUNTAIN BIKES

The new mountain bikes are particularly suited to the back roads of the Kathmandu Valley and further afield. These can be rented from Thamel by the day for Rs. 60. Also rewarding are the escorted mountain bike trips lasting from one to 12 days arranged by Himalayan Mountain Bikes (c/o Sagarmatha Trekking, P. O. Box 2236, Kathmandu Tel: 225875 Telex: 2375 Fax: 416870).

MOTORBIKES

It is possible to hire Japanese motorbikes by the hour or by the day, but these are noisy and polluting and hardly suitable for the quiet stillness of the Valley.

ON FOOT

Be prepared to do a lot of walking. Taxis and cars can only take you limited distances. Apart from a few well-trodden spots, most of the interesting sites have to be reached on foot. Nepalese do not count distance by kilometers or miles, but by the number of walking hours involved for the duration of a journey. In the hills this is translated simply into the number of days.

There is no need to compete with their often brisk pace. A leisurely stroll amid the rice and mustard fields, through villages and across ridges and valleys is certainly the best way to "absorb" the Valley, its people, their culture and way of life.

Do not hesitate to venture off the tourist track. You can expect to be safe wherever you wander. Moreover, you will find the people to be even more friendly than you thought. Then you will have the pleasure of discovering this beautiful land and its people for yourself. See *Insight Pocket Guide Biking & Hiking in the Kathmandu Valley* for detailed routes and expert advice.

WHERE TO STAY

HOTELS & LODGES

Nepal has, in the last decade, seen a mushrooming of world class hotels. Facilities outside the Kathmandu Valley have also vastly improved. During the spring and fall seasons, the better hotels operate at near-full capacity so it is best to book well in advance.

Most hotels in Kathmandu, offer a choice of packages: bed and breakfast (CP); bed, breakfast and one other meal (MAP) and full board (AP). Rates listed below are for room only (EP) unless otherwise indicated and are valid in 1992. Add 10 percent to these quotes for service charge and between 12-15 percent for government tax, depending on the star rating as indicated in the following list of hotels. Those marked (*) have no official rating but have been listed according to their facilities.

There are plenty of less glamorous but decent hotels in Kathmandu to suit everyone's fancies and finances. At the bottom of the scale, there are a number of modest hotels between US$5 and US$15 a night depending on facilities; toilets and showers may or may not be communal and heating is extra. These are mostly located in the Thamel district of old Kathmandu.

Outside the Valley prices are for room only except where specified. The list includes only hotels and lodges that have reservations offices in Kathmandu. On the popular trekking trails, most villages offer small lodges or tea shops, usually with minimal facilities, dormitory accommodation (only a few offer single and double rooms) and simple food.

KATHMANDU

FIVE-STAR

Annapurna (140 rooms) Durbar Marg; Tel: 221711, 223602; Tlx: 2205; Fax: 225236. US$105 (single) US$115 (double). Managed by the Taj Group from India, central, swimming and tennis facilities.

Everest (162 rooms) Baneswar; Tel: 220614, 224960; Tlx: 2260; Fax: 226088. US$115 (single) US$125 (double). 5 minutes from the airport, swimming, tennis, health facilities, business center. 180° view of Himalayas.

Soaltee Oberoi (300 rooms) Tahachal; Tel: 272550-5; Tlx: 2203; Fax: 272205. US$125 (single) US$135 (double). 10 suites and seven Regal suites. 15 minutes from city center, casino, swimming, tennis, health club, beauty parlour. Recently refurbished.

Yak & Yeti (231 rooms) Durbar Marg, Tel: 411436, 228803; Tlx: 2237; Fax: 227782. US$110 (single) US$120 (double). Two penthouse suites, central, swimming, tennis, shopping. Recently extended.

FOUR-STAR

Dwarika's Kathmandu Village* Battisputali, Tel: 470770, 473725; Tlx: 2239; Fax: 225131. US$57 (single) US$74 (double). Bungalows with traditional woodcarving and antiques. Great charm though it is not central.

Himalaya (100 rooms) Kupondole, Tel: 523900-8 Tlx: 2566; US$94 (single) US$110 (double). Japanese-owned, swimming.

Kathmandu (120 rooms) Maharajgunj, Tel: 410786, 418494; Tlx: 2256; Fax: 416574. US$91 (single) US$109 (double). Friendly, caring personalised services.

Malla (75 rooms) Lekhnath Marg, Tel: 410320, 410966, 410968; Tlx: 2238; Fax: 418382. US$86 (single) US$102 (double). Near Royal Palace, lovely garden.

Shangrila* (80 rooms) Lazimpat, Tel: 412999, 410108; Tlx: 2276; Fax: 414184. US$80 (single) US$95 (double). Swimming, best beauty parlour, fine garden.

Shanker (135 rooms) Lazimpat, Tel: 412973, 410151; Tlx: 2230. US$88 (single) US$105 (double). Former Rana palace.

Sherpa (80 rooms) Durbar Marg, Tel: 227000, 227102; Tlx: 2223; Fax: 222026. US$85 (single) US$95 (double). Central, roof-terrace.

THREE-STAR

Crystal (50 rooms) New Road, Tel: 223397, 223611, 223636. US$40 (single) US$50 (double). Central, pleasant roof terrace.

Greenwich Village (20 rooms) Kopundole Heights, Tel: 521780, 522399; Tlx: 2406; Fax: 224237. US$40 (single) US$50 (double). Commanding panoramic views. More a homely experience than a hotel.

Narayani (88 rooms) Patan, Tel: 521711, 521712, 521408; Tlx: 2262; Fax: 521291. US$70 (single) US$85 (double). Swimming.

Hotel Kathmandu
- offers its unique
Nepalese architecture
& traditional culture

THE SECRET OF
OUR SUCCESS .....

We ensure that every client of ours enjoys the comforts, traditional hospitality and friendly caring services provided by our trained staff

Where things happen !

HOTEL
Kathmandu

P.O. Box: 11 MAHARAJGUNJ, KATHMANDU, NEPAL
TEL: 418494 (4 LINES)
TLX: 2256 HOKAT NP FAX: 977-1-416574
CABLE: HOKAT

Summit* (55 rooms) Kupondole Heights, Tel: 521894, 524694; Tlx: 2342; Fax: 523737. US$44 (single) US$50 (double). Good views, swimming, traditional style rooms.

Yellow Pagoda (57 rooms) Kantipath, Tel: 220392, 220337; Tlx: 2268. US$55 (single) US$65 (double). Central and refurbished.

TWO-STAR

Ambassador (35 rooms) Lazimpat, Tel: 410432, 414432; Tlx: 2321; Fax: 415432. US$15 (single) US$20 (double). Central.

Vajra (51 rooms) Bijeswari, Tel: 271545, 272719; Tlx: 2309; Fax: 271695. US$25 (single) US$27 (double). A cultural experience, rooftop bar, new garden extension.

Woodlands (125 rooms) Durbar Marg, Tel: 222683, 220123; Tlx: 2282; Fax: 225650. US$61 (single), US$73 (double). 2 suites, central.

ONE-STAR

Kathmandu Guest House (80 rooms) Thamel, Tel: 413632, 418733; Tlx: 2321. US$17 (single) US$20 (double). Most famous and central of the Thamel lodges.

Manaslu (28 rooms) Lazimpat, Tel: 410071, 413470 Tlx: 2447. US$20 (single) US$24 (double). Quiet and congenial.

Star (60 rooms) Thamel, Tel: 411004, 412100. US$7 (single) US$9 (double). Next to the Kathmandu Guest House.

Tibet Guest House (37 rooms) Chetrapati, Tel: 214383, 215893. US$14 (single) US$15 (double). Friendly.

Tridevi (30 rooms) Thamel, Tel: 416742, 412822. US$24 (single) US$28 (double). Clean, pleasant and convenient.

DHULIKHEL & THE VALLEY RIM

Dhulikhel Mountain Resort, Dhulikhel 011-61088, P.O. Box 3203, Durbar Marg, Kathmandu, Tel: 220031, 216930; Tlx: 2415. US$58 (single), US$60 (double). Perched high on a bluff past the village, Dhulikhel Mountain Resort offers good food and comfortable accommodation in bungalows with superb views of the mountains only one hour drive from Kathmandu.

Flora Hill, Nagarkot Tel: 226893, Chetrapati, Kathmandu , Tel: 223311 Tlx: 2321. US$34 (single) US$40 (double) . Modest accommodation.

Himalayan Heights, Hatiban, P.O. Box 1273, Maharajgunj, Tel: 221129, 290622. US$87 (single) US$129 (double) full board. Beautiful stone-built lodge two kilometers (one mile) above the Pharping road on the flanks of Champa Devi, commanding spectacular views across this historic corner to the Valley.

Himalayan Horizon Sun-N-Snow Hotel, Dhulikhel 011-61296, P.O. Box 1583, Kantipath, Kathmandu, Tel: 411696, 225092; Tlx: 2605. US$45 (single) US$50 (double). Just this side of the village, Nepali style building with modern comforts.

Taragaon, P.O.Box 507, Bodhnath, Kathmandu, Tel: 470409, 470634; Kakani Tel: 228222. US$13 (single) US$18 (double). Nagarkot Tel: 211008. US$13 (single) US$18 (double). Simple accommodation offered by this modest chain of hotels but spectacular views.

POKHARA

Hotels at Pokhara are either across the road from the airport or near Phewa Lake. While not famous for high quality lodging or food, they are generally comfortable. All the hotels listed boast splendid views of Fishtail and the Annapurna Massif.

Young travellers may prefer to join the back-packer crowd along the northern shore of Phewa Lake. A long string of lodges provide bed and breakfast for US$10 to US$15 a night. The general ambience and scenic surroundings are more pleasant than along the airport road, though less convenient. From here one can hire boats and dug-outs to travel on the lake.

Fishtail Lodge (50 rooms) , Tel: 061-20071. US$48 (single) US$66 (double). Generally considered the best hotel in town, great location, good local cultural show.

Dragon (20 rooms), Tel: 061-20052, 20391. US$25 (single) US$35 (double). Daily traditional dances.

Gurkha Lodge. For seclusion and peace by the lake. Four double rooms with bath at modest cost in a beautiful garden setting.

Hungry Eye (16 rooms), Tel: 061-20908. US$15 (single) US$20 (double). Lakeside hangout, ask for upstairs rooms, good restaurant with barbeques.

Kantipur Resort (15 rooms), Tel: 061-21226. US$20 (single) US$27 (double). Opposite Fishtail Lodge, good restaurant.

New Crystal (69 rooms), Tel: 061-20035/36. US$35 (single) US$51 (double). Near the airport.

Mount Annapurna (64 rooms), Tel: 061-20027, 20037. US$21 (single) US$30 (double) Tibetan murals and management, opposite the airport.

Tragopan (40 rooms), Tel: 061-20910. US$27 (single) US$35 (double). Newly built and friendly.

Tiger Mountain Lodge Pokhara. Scheduled to open 1993 on a hilltop 30 minutes from Pokhara overlooking the Annapurna ranges and the Pokhara valley, this local-styled village resort built by the Tiger Tops group promises a new dimension in places to stay. Swimming pool, saddle club. Details on request P.O. Box 242, Kathmandu Tel: 222706 Tlx: 2216 Fax: 414075.

ROYAL CHITWAN NATIONAL PARK

Listed here are those lodges who have been granted concessions to operate within the national park by the government. There is no system of star rating and most offer a package fully inclusive of meals and jungle excursions. All have reservations offices in Kathmandu who will also arrange transport, either by air or a five to six hour drive from the capital. Government taxes and national park entry fees are extra. The season is September to June, but many remain open during the monsoon.

There are a plethora of small lodges that have mushroomed on the edge of the park at **Saurah**, some of which have offices in Thamel. When visiting Royal Chitwan National Park on foot without trained naturalists, beware of rhinos which can be very dangerous for the unwary.

Chitwan Jungle Lodge, P.O. Box 1281, Durbar Marg, Kathmandu, Tel: 228918, 222679; Tlx: 2558. US$175 (single) US$250 (double) fully inclusive. Cost includes road transportation from Kathmandu, set in the middle of the park, east of Saurah.

Elephant Camp Hotel, P.O. Box 4729, Durbar Marg, Kathmandu, Tel: 223976, 222823; Tlx: 2576. US$85 (single) US$120 (double) all fully inclusive. On edge of the park at Saurah, the best of the non-concessionaires.

Gaida Wildlife Camp, P.O. Box 2056, Durbar Marg, Kathmandu, Tel: 220940, 220186; Tlx: 2659; Fax: 227425. US$128 (single) US$137 (double) fully inclusive. On the edge of the park at Saurah, accessible via Bharatpur airport or by road.

Island Jungle Resort, P.O. Box 2154, Durbar Marg, Kathmandu, Tel: 220162, 225615; Tlx: 2409 Fax: 223814. US$90 (single) US$120 (double) fully inclusive. Transportation from Kathmandu extra, located on Bandarjhola island.

Machan Wildlife Resort, P.O. Box 3140, Durbar Marg, Kathmandu, Tel: 225001, 227099; Tlx: 2409 Fax: 419749. US$234 (single) US$ 318 (double) fully inclusive. Cost includes transportation. Set in the eastern end of the park, charming chalet-style bungalows, small swimming pool and a separate tented camp.

Narayani Safari Hotel, P.O. Box 1357, Narayani Hotel, Patan, Tel: 525015; Tlx: 2262; Fax: 521291 US$30 (single) US$40 (double) room only. Located in the town of Bharatpur (Tel: 20130), air-conditioned, swimming and tennis. Narayani also operate **Ghadgai Camp** near Kasara for wildlife excursions US$110 (single) US$180 (double) fully inclusive.

Temple Tiger Wildlife Camp, P.O. Box 3968, Kantipath, Kathmandu, Tel: 221585, 225780; Tlx: 2637; Fax: 220178. US$300 (single) US$400 (double). Transportation extra, in the western end of the park.

Tiger Tops Jungle Lodge, P.O. Box 242, Durbar Marg, Kathmandu; Tel: 222706, 415659; Tlx: 2216; Fax: 414075. US$350 (single) US$500 (double) fully inclusive. Located in the heart of the park, 120 kilometers (75 miles) by air south-west of Kathmandu, this world famous lodge operates wildlife safaris from the comfort of 20 elegant tree-top rooms. Tiger Tops elephants, trained naturalists, boat trips, Landrover drives, jungle treks. There is also a spectacular Tented Camp set on a plateau overlooking grasslands and mountains for the more adventurous spirited, though the 12 safari tents with twin beds are no less comfortable. Superb service and food. Accessible with daily half-hour flights to Meghauly, the Tiger Tops airstrip, a five hour drive or a three day river trip with Himalayan River Exploration. Host of the annual World Elephant Polo Association championship.

Tiger Tops Tharu Safari Resort, P.O. Box 242, Durbar Marg, Kathmandu; Tel: 222706, 415659; Tlx: 2216; Fax: 414075. US$165 (single) US$220 (double) fully inclusive. Set on the edge of the park near the Narayani River, the Tharu Safari is 24 spacious rooms, with all modern comforts including adjoining bathrooms and ceiling fans, decorated in the style of the traditional tribal longhouses of the indigenous Tharu people. Facilities include a unique swimming pool, saddle club with horses and ponies to explore the local villages, bullock cart rides and elephant safaris. Nepali food and evening local dancing a speciality.

ROYAL BARDIYA NATIONAL PARK

Tiger Tops Karnali Lodge and Tented Camp, P.O. Box 242, Durbar Marg, Kathmandu, Tel: 222706, 415659, Tlx: 2216; Fax: 414075. US$120 (single)

US$240 (double) fully inclusive. For more remote wildlife adventures in far west Nepal, Tiger Tops operates the extremely comfortable **Karnali Lodge** on the edge of the forest, and **Karnali Tented Camp** on the banks of the great Karnali river. Access is four hours drive from the town of Nepalgunj with daily flights.

Elephant rides, Landrover drives, boat trips and walks are featured in the untouched and pristine area. Acknowledged as one of the best places in the sub-continent to see tigers in the wild, it is specially recommended for those who like to get off the beaten track. Adventurers will enjoy reaching Karnali via the four day Bheri River trip.

ROYAL SUKLA PHANTA WILDLIFE RESERVE

Silent Safari, P.O. Box 1679, Thamel, Kathmandu, Tel: 227236; Tlx: 2357; Fax: 225524. US$85 (single) US$130 (double) all fully inclusive. The only accommodation in this remote reserve is camps specially arranged for clients by Silent Safari. Book in advance. Flights to Mahendranagar or Dhanghari are extra.

SAGARMATHA NATIONAL PARK

Of the many small lodges and teashops in the Everest area, the best in Namche include the Khumbu Lodge, Thamserku Lodge and View Lodge. Listed here are only hotels that have reservations offices in Kathmandu.

Hotel Everest View, P.O. Box 283, Durbar Marg, Kathmandu; Tel: 224854, 223871; Tlx: 2233. US$175 (single) US$270 (double) fully inclusive. Fantastic views from one of the highest hotels in the world. 30 minutes walk from Syangboche airstrip which is serviced by Pilatus Porter flights operated by the hotel and Trans-Himalayan Tours. Oxygen in every room.

Hotel Sagarmatha, Lukla, P.O. Box 500, Kamaladi, Kathmandu, Tel: 222489, 220243; Tlx: 2419. US$15 (single) US$18 (double). 16 rooms with attached bath, operated by Sherpa Trekking Service.

The Sherpa Guide Lodges, P.O. Box 3776, Gairi Dhara, Tel: 415841, 416047; Tlx: 2558; Fax: 227919. Pleasant lodges spaced at day intervals between Jiri to Namche sold in a trekking package.

FOOD DIGEST

WHAT TO EAT

Despite centuries of isolation and, in some places, a very fertile soil, Nepal has failed to develop a distinctive style of cooking.

An exception is Newari cooking of the Valley which can be elaborate and spicy; but this is found only in private homes. Nepalese dishes are at best variations on Indian regional cuisine.

In most parts of Nepal, including the Kathmandu Valley, rice is the staple food. It is usually eaten boiled, supplemented with *dhal* (lentils), vegetables cooked with a few spices (notably ginger, garlic and chilies), and – in times of festivity – plenty of meat.

There is a predilection for enormous radishes which are sometimes made into delicious *achhar* (chutney). Hill people eat potatoes or *tsampa* – raw grain, usually barley, ground and eaten either dry or with milk, tea or water – as a compliment to or substitute for rice. *Chapatis* (flat bread) diversify the diet. Some castes eat pork. Goat, chicken and buffalo meat is available to all but beef is forbidden in this Hindu kingdom.

The Nepalis enjoy eating sweets and spicy snacks such as *jelebis* and *laddus*. These come in a variety of shapes and wrappings, not to mention ingredients and tastes. Fruit from the lowlands is found in Kathmandu and a wide variety of excellent vegetables. Buffalo milk is turned into clarified butter *(ghee)* or delicious curd sold in round earthenware pots. Curd *(dahi)* is a good buy but be sure to scrape off the top layer. Dairy products are rare elsewhere in Asia but fresh milk, butter and cheese are plentiful in Kathmandu. Excellent cheeses are available at the dairies in Thamel or the Nepal Dairy near Mahabouda, behind Bir Hospital, made under Swiss and Danish training.

Fresh bread, doughnuts and croissants are found in the bakeries of Durbar Marg, Lazimpat and Thamel. Most of the big hotels have bakeries and the Soaltee Oberoi has a delicatessen in their Al Fresco restaurant near the swimming pool.

Certain areas have developed regional dishes. The introduction of a potato crop in Sherpa country by the British revolutionised eating habits and it is now their major staple. Sherpas now survive on potatoes, eating them boiled or baked and dipped in salt and chilies. Delicious are the potato pancakes eaten with fresh cheese.

Tibetan cooking includes *thukpa* (thick soup with noodles) and *momos* (fried or steamed meat dumplings) and is widespread in the mountains and also available in the restaurants of Kathmandu.

WHERE TO EAT

Restaurants have vastly improved in the last few years. Prices are low by Western standards. Indian, Chinese, Tibetan, Japanese, and even Thai cuisine is found in Kathmandu, as well as a variety of European and Western menus. Large international hotels have three or four restaurants each, some of them excellent, though more expensive.

Outside of Kathmandu it is often difficult to find appealing food in the Valley, even for a snack. Travellers on day outings should carry their own food. Hotels will provide packed lunches or you may prefer to take a snack from one of the bakeries and fresh fruit and make-do for a midday picnic before repairing to the more substantial menus of Kathmandu. The restaurants below are open for lunch and dinner unless specified.

Al Fresco, Hotel Soaltee Oberoi, by the swimming pool, Tel: 272555. Delicious Italian specialities served in taverna surroundings.

Base Camp, Hotel Himalaya, Tel: 521887. Very pleasant coffee shop in cool white marble lobby overlooking the swimming pool and the Valley.

Bhancha Ghar (Nepali Kitchen), Kamaladi, Tel: 225172. Nepali food served in charming renovated old Newari house. Evening displays of handicraft-making and bar on the very top floor.

Chimney Restaurant, Hotel Yak & Yeti. Tel: 411436. Boris' original restaurant with a menu still reminiscent of Russian splendour. Central fireplace in a cosy setting with cramped tables. Open for dinner only.

Far Pavilion, Hotel Everest, Tel: 224960. A comfortable Indian dining experience with unrivalled views. Dinner only.

Fuji Restaurant, Kantipath, Tel: 225272. Good Japanese food in a converted Rana bungalow with a picturesque moat.

Ghar-e-Kabab, Hotel Annapurna, Durbar Marg, Tel: 221711. Wonderful tandoori and Indian cuisine accompanied by Indian *ghazals* music. Best to book as very popular.

Gorkha Palace, Keshar Mahal, Thamel, Tel: 417095. First floor Indian and European food in elegant copper and marble surroundings at moderate prices. Popular with residents, try the daily special and tandoori with *ghazals* music.

Gurkha Grill, Hotel Soaltee Oberoi, Tel: 272555. Most sophisticated restaurant in town offering smart Western food and dancing to a live band. Only open for dinner.

Himthai, Thamel, Tel: 419334. Thai cuisine in very congenial garden surroundings.

K.C.'s Restaurant, Thamel. A favourite hangout for aging hippies and world travellers. This is where the action is.

Kokonor, Hotel Shangrila, Tel: 410108. French elegance with good food, an interesting menu, pianist and a French pastry chef. For winter lunches, the Shangrila has the most attractive garden in town.

Kushi Fuji, Durbar Marg above Tiger Tops office Japanese food from an open counter with lunch and dinner specials.

Les Yeux, Thamel. Fun rooftop overlooking the action.

Mountain City Chinese Restaurant, Hotel Malla, Tel: 410320. Spicy Szechuan and Chinese cooking in pleasant surroundings.

Mike's Breakfast, Seto Durbar off Durbar Marg. Charming Rana cottage and garden offering huge breakfasts and lingering lunches (no dinner). Great value and great fun.

Nanglo Pub and Snack Bar, Durbar Marg, Tel: 223498. Cheap Western food and sandwiches served in the courtyard or on the roof.

Nirulas, Durbar Marg. Favourite with locals for pizzas and delicious icecream.

Pakizah, Hotel Kathmandu, Tel: 410786. Mughlai cuisine and an unusual menu accompanied by Indian music.

Rumdoodle, Thamel. Named after a climbing spoof, lively bar and restaurant.

Sun Kosi, Lal Durbar , Tel: 226520. Good selection of traditional Nepali and Tibetan food in pleasant surroundings.

Sanghamitra, Thamel, Tel: 411991. Vegetarian and soul food in pleasant garden. Try Boris' Rooms upstairs with evocative early photos and classic Russian menu.

Spam's Spot, Thamel. The closest place to an English pub in town with amusing menu.

Wong's Kitchen, Lazimpat. Good Chinese food served in unpretentious atmosphere.

DRINKING NOTES

The national drink, *chiya* (tea brewed together with milk, sugar and sometimes spices) is served in small glasses, scalding hot. Up in the mountains, the tea is mixed with yak-butter and salt and then churned Tibetan-style.

Another popular home-made mountain drink is *chhang*, a powerful sort of beer made with fermented barley, maize, rye or millet. *Arak* (potato alcohol) as well as *rakshi* (wheat or rice alcohol) are also consumed in great quantities among the locals.

Coca-cola and Pepsi is bottled in Kathmandu Valley, as is Sprite, Fanta and soda. Tonic is imported in cans. Excellent Nepal-brewed beer is widely available. Choose from Golden Eagle, Iceberg, Leo, Star and Tuborg. The classier Kathmandu establishments serve imported wine at prohibitive prices.

Good quality rum, gin and vodka are produced locally. If you are a whisky or brandy drinker, be warned against the local varieties and stick to the more familiar imports.

Things to Do

TREKKING

Anyone who is reasonably fit can trek, but the fitter you are, the more you will enjoy it.

PREPARATION & FITNESS

Do as much walking and exercise as possible in the weeks prior to your trek, to prepare for the effort that will be required of you in Nepal. Climbing up and down hills or stairs repeatedly are especially helpful.

A thorough medical check-up is recommended before you leave for Nepal. Inoculations against typhoid and paratyphoid, tetanus and meningitis should be on your list too. An injection of gamma globulin just before departure is the best protection against hepatitis, a serious and common complaint in this part of the world. Some of these shots cannot be given simultaneously with others so if you need them all, remember to start at least six weeks ahead of time.

Water contamination is a problem; do not drink from streams or tap water however pure they may look. On the trail all water should be well boiled or treated with iodine crystals, tincture or tablets. Tincture is available in Kathmandu pharmacies (four drops per liter; allow 20 minutes before drinking). Even chlorine is not effective against amoebic cysts.

Vegetables should not be eaten raw unless properly soaked in an iodine or potassium solution. Peel all fruits or similarly soak. Local food can become tedious for variety-oriented Western stomachs after a few days and sometimes Nepalese cooking oils can upset an unfamiliar digestive system. Bring your own high-energy goodies like chocolate, dried fruits and nuts, powdered drinks, herbal teas and spirits (whisky and brandy, though the local rum is also excellent) if you enjoy a sip on nippy evenings.

Minor ailments are to be expected. Being at high altitudes and around exotic bacteria puts a strain on the body so that cuts take longer to heal and colds or coughs drag on. On organised group treks, a collective medical kit is provided and the *sirdar* will occasionally have some knowledge of first aid. Some items might be in high demand, however, and it is best to bring you own first-aid kit. This should include:

Pain relief tablets with codeine (for high-altitude headaches)
Mild sleeping pills (for high-altitude insomnia)
Decongestant or preferred cold remedy
Throat lozenges or cough drops
Ophthalmic ointment or drops
A broad-spectrum antibiotic
Alcohol (for massaging feet to prevent blisters)
Blister pads or moleskin
Bandages and elastic plasters
Antiseptic and cotton
A good sun block
Lip salve (to prevent chapping)
Skin moisturizer
An ace bandage if you are prone to "trekker's knee" or have weak ankles
Pepto-Bismol
Handiwipes

Emergency evacuations are difficult to organise because of a scarcity of radio communications and lack of availability of helicopters. A rescue operation takes time and can start only when some guarantee of payment has been made. Medical insurance will cover such eventualities so check your policy before leaving. A good trekking agent can arrange rescues for its trekkers when necessary but individual trekkers have little chance of securing a helicopter.

Hiking in the hills is generally safe but it is advisable not to trek alone. Learning a bit of Nepali language will open many a door and helps when asking directions. Remember that farmers often have little concept of time and may unintentionally exaggerate by hours, either way. Trail directions should be repeatedly sought as each villager has their own version. Distance is always measured in hours, not kilometers which are irrelevant in such an up and down country.

When putting together a group of fellow trekkers, be sure to discuss each person's expectations for the trip in terms of hiking pace, rest days, special interests (photography, birds, fishing, cultural interactions, solitude, etc.) and whether it is the destination or the process of getting there which is most important. This should help assure a smooth, congenial trek.

Tea house or backpacking trekkers will find Stephan Bezruchka's *Guide to Trekking in Nepal* and Hugh Swift's *Trekking in Nepal, West Tibet and Bhutan* invaluable in planning a trek.

WHAT TO BRING

As you are going to walk four to eight hours a day, shoes are of paramount importance. They must be sturdy and comfortable with good tread on the soles; high tennis shoes or well-broken-in hiking boots will do. Most trekkers hike in sneakers in low altitude, though in snow at higher elevations or on rough and rocky terrain, good boots are essential. They must accommodate one or two layers of heavy wool or cotton (no nylon) socks, of which you should have a plentiful supply. Light tennis shoes or sneakers will help you relax in camp when the day's walking is over.

Many trekkers assume that it will be cold at all times, whereas many treks start low and it can be quite hot for a few days. For women, below-the-knee skirts are more comfortable than slacks; in deference to local sensibilities, neither shorts nor tight or revealing tops should be worn. Men should wear either hiking shorts or loosely fitting trousers. Cool cotton dresses and loose pants can be purchased in Kathmandu. For clothing, two light layers are better than a single thick one. If you get too hot, you can peel the top layer off. Thermal underwear can be useful in particularly cold months and at high altitudes. It is better to carry too many clothes than not enough. Drip dry fabrics are best.

When trekking with an organised group, you will normally be asked to fit all your gear in one duffel, to weigh no more than 15 kilos (about 35 lbs). You will carry only a day pack with your day-time essentials, such as camera, water bottle, rain gear, sweater or pile jacket, book or writing pad, binoculars and personal items. Your duffel should be tough, easily opened, lockable, packed in an organised fashion and generally no larger than about one meter by 15 inches. For a week's trek below 4,500 meters (14,500 feet), your equipment should include the following:

One to two pairs of loose woollen or corduroy trousers or skirts, plus a lighter version

One heavy and one light sweater or pile jacket

Three to four short-sleeve shirts or tee shirts

Two to three long sleeve wool, cotton or flannel shirts

Ski or thermal underwear (especially from November to February)

Four to five pairs of woollen socks with cotton liners

One pair of walking shoes or hiking boots

One pair tennis shoes (optional: rubber thongs)

Three or four bandanas, handy for a variety of needs

Four to six pairs underwear

One wool hat

A pair of gloves or mittens

A down jacket or padded anorak

A plastic raincoat shell and pants, or poncho

Sunglasses and a sun hat

Toilet gear (kept to a minimum)

One towel

Medical kit

Plastic water bottle, one quart or liter

A comfortable day pack (roughly 1,500 to 2,500 cubic inch capacity)

Photographic equipment

A down or warm synthetic-filled sleeping bag (rated to -5°C - 0°C, or 23°F - 32°F)

One thin layer of synthetic foam for mattress (usually your trek agent will provide a sleeping bag and mattress).

For women, a swimsuit or *loongi* (cotton cloth wrap) for bathing

For above 4,500 meters (14,700 feet) add one pair gaiters (rain pants can suffice) for walking through snow, glacier goggles, and boot protector (such as snow seal) unless boots are made of gortex.

You will also need a flashlight and spare batteries, a pocket knife with scissors, spare shoelaces, string, safety pins, a supply of toilet paper and small plastic bags to protect food, carry out trash or wrap wet or dirty clothes in, and several large ones to stuff sleeping bag and duffel contents into in case of rain. A notebook and pen doubles as a diary and bring a book or cards for the long evenings. An umbrella is handy for light showers and to shade the sun. Trekking maps of most areas, sporadically accurate, can be purchased at Kathmandu or Pokhara book stores.

Down jackets, trousers and much of this gear can be bought or rented from the trekking shops of Thamel and Chetrapati, though it is still best to arrive self-sufficient. If you are trekking alone, that is without the services of a trekking agency, you will need to add tents, food and cooking and eating utensils to this list.

Take the following special precautions:

— Ensure your trekking permit is in hand for the specific area in which you plan to trek before you leave Kathmandu. Trek permits require three passport photographs, are colour coded and available from the Department of Immigration at Keshar Mahal, Thamel, Kathmandu Tel: 412337. Trek permits are available in Pokhara but only for a limited time.

– If you are attempting a Trekking Peak (see page 231) your trek agent must get a Peak Permit from the Nepal Mountaineering Association in Naxal, Kathmandu Tel: 411525

– Carry your trekking permit in a plastic bag in your day pack. Don't leave it in your luggage as you are required to produce it during the day.

– Leave passport and valuables (jewellery, credit cards, extra money or travellers checks) in the hotel or trekking agents' safe. Carry a photo-copy of your passport or driver's license.

– Lock up your duffel with a small padlock to prevent pilferage or accidental losses.

– Your medical kit and toilet gear should be in separate plastic boxes with lids.

– Take US$50-100 worth of 5-100 rupee notes for minor expenses (bottled drinks, souvenirs, staff tips) along the way. It is customary, but strictly optional, for a trekking group to pool tip money for the trekking staff, generally dividing it according to relative pay scale, and even to pass on unneeded clothes, shoes or camping knick-knacks. As "thank you" or *dhanyabaad* is not commonly used in this culture, do not be surprised if the receiver merely accepts his or her prize and ducks away.

TREKKING TRAILS & TIMES

There are an overwhelming number of trekking trails to choose from in Nepal. Your choice depends upon the length of time you have available, the season, as well as your personal interests.

The following list, compiled by Mountain Travel Nepal (P.O. Box 170, Kathmandu Tel: 414508, 413019 Telex: 2216, Fax: 414075), will give you some guidelines. Consult the trekking section of this book and with your trek and travel agent as regions vary as to the time of year.

JANUARY - FEBRUARY

This is the best time of year for low-level walks at elevations up to 3,000 meters (about 10,000 feet) offering pleasant sunny days with clear skies and good mountain views. This is an excellent time to trek the old trade route between Kathmandu and Pokhara, visit the lower Lamjung Himal areas or trek in the valleys north of Gorkha.

Three good treks are recommended from Pokhara. The so-called Royal Trek follows the footsteps of the Prince of Wales for three or four days in the Gurung and Gurkha country north-east of the Pokhara valley. Great views of Annapurna, Machhapuchhre and Dhaulagiri are highlights of the Ghandruk-Ghorapani circuit trek. For those with more time, the 15-18 day Kali Gandaki trek to Jomosom and Muktinath is in excellent condition in the winter, although some snow is possible at Ghorapani.

North of Kathmandu, the Langtang and Helambu treks are both good, as long as you do not venture too high. You may meet some snow above the Sherpa villages of Tarkeghyang and Melamchigaun, but it should not hamper progress.

Khumbu is only for the hardy as temperatures are cold, but there is sensational scenery, few other trekkers, frozen waterfalls and snow in the higher elevations. Some delays on Lukla flights can be expected in the event of bad weather but this is good time to walk in from the road head at Jiri.

In late-February, spring arrives in Nepal and spring flowers and rhododendrons begin to bloom at the lower altitudes. Trek before mid-March if you want to beat the spring rush.

MARCH

Although spring has arrived in the Kathmandu Valley and at the lower levels, high altitude conditions can still be quite harsh. Do not plan on being able to cross high passes (5,000 meters or 16,400 feet) before mid-April.

March is a good time to start a long trek into Solu Khumbu from Jiri, although it is still a little early for Rolwaling. Further east, start mid-month on an excursion to the rhododendron forests of the Milke Danda ridge or for a botanical trek up the Arun river but not yet into Makalu Base Camp. Jugal is also rewarding for wilderness treks but expect spring flowers only late in the month.

All Langtang, Helambu and Pokhara-based treks are feasible, though some mountain haze may develop during the second half of the month. The Sanctuary may not be open until late March. The wide variety of wild flowers is a bonus. The Dhorpatan (from Tansen or Beni) and lower Dhaulagiri areas are a lovely alternative to the Annapurnas late in the month.

Out west, the valleys below Khaptad are pleasantly temperate and the *lekh's* rhododendrons are brilliant.

APRIL

In this high spring season, temperatures are warm in the lower altitudes and there is a likelihood of afternoon clouds and showers in most areas. But this is the best month for spring flowers and rhododendrons in the mountains and the favoured season for alpine treks and for climbing.

This is a superb month to spend high in the mountains around Manang and climbing is possible on Chulu and Pisang. After mid-April the Thorong La pass is usually open, critical to completing the classic Annapurna Circuit trek. Beware of avalanche danger in the Annapurna Sanctuary, though the Machhapuchhre base camp area is good for wildlife after the middle of the month.

For the adventurous, the high altitudes of the Dhaulagiri glacier region are at their best as is the rugged remote terrain of Manaslu and Dudh Pokhari.

This is an excellent time for treks to the higher altitudes, such as in east Nepal, to the Milke Danda ridge and alpine treks to the base camps of Kangchenjunga and Makalu.

This is one of the best times to visit the Khumbu, although the low-level walk in from Jiri can be disappointing due to increasing haze and heat. Now is the time for alpine and climbing treks to Rolwaling and the Hinku, Hongu and climbs of Island Peak and Mera.

Treks into the Jugal Himal are fairly tough but rewarding for the off-the-beaten-track adventurer. Spring flowers are beautiful. Between Helambu and Langtang, visits to the Gosainkund lakes are attractive. En route to Langtang, Trisuli Bazaar and Dunche are hot, but are worth enduring to reach the high altitude forests and wild flowers. A return via the Tirudanda or on to Gorkha enters seldom trekked highland areas.

Short treks of two to five days around the Kathmandu Valley are popular now as they are higher, therefore cooler, than short treks out of Pokhara.

In the far west of the country, Jumla-based treks to Rara Lake and Dolpo are logistically complex because of difficult access and food deficits in this remote region. The spectacular scenery rewards more persistent trekkers. Don't start a trek before late April or snow will bar the way.

MAY-JUNE

In these pre-monsoon months, there is haze and heat at all lower elevations and occasional heavy showers. If you are trekking, aim to get to the higher altitudes quickly. Some of the better areas at this time are Khumbu, flying in and out of Lukla, Rolwaling, Hongu, the Ganja La or Tilman's Col areas of Langtang and the Around Annapurna trek. Kathmandu Valley walks are pleasurable.

JULY-MID SEPTEMBER

Mad botanists and students of leeches will enjoy this monsoon time of year. Although not generally recommended for trekking, the terrain is lovely in the higher regions and rain-shadow areas, such as Muktinath, Manang and Langtang to a certain extent as well as Dolpo and the far west. Although rainfall may not be continuous and sunny days and mountain views do occur, trekkers must realize that rain, leeches and slippery paths and swollen rivers will hamper their progress. Various alpine wild flowers and plants are at their zenith at this time, spectacular in upper Khumbu.

MID SEPTEMBER-MID OCTOBER

The monsoon tails off about this time and the countryside is fresh and green. Lukla flights are not reliable until around 20th October so it is best to walk in and out of the Khumbu. When the mountains are free of clouds, the views are crystal clear though there are still a lot of showers at lower altitudes. Recommendations for trekking routes are much the same as for April and May, though high passes may be snowed over.

MID OCTOBER-MID NOVEMBER

This is the "high season" for trekking and with good reason. It is the classic time for high-altitude alpine and climbing treks and in general has the most reliable clear weather, although rain is not unheard of. The more popular routes are congested at this time; these include the Khumbu where the sheer weight of numbers create inevitable flight delays at Lukla. Even more crowded is the Pokhara region, especially the Kali Gandaki valley though weather-wise the Annapurna Sanctuary is at its best.

This is the time to get off-the-beaten-track and enjoy trips to east or west Nepal, Jugal Himal, Ganesh Himal and Tirudanda or routes between Pokhara and Kathmandu.

Throughout this autumn period there are many colourful religious festivals to ensure a good harvest in the fields.

MID NOVEMBER-DECEMBER

This period offers stable, winter weather as the rain and snow of true winter usually does not start in Nepal until mid-December. This period has the added advantage of avoiding the previous month's crowds. With crops harvested, the countryside lacks colour but the clarity of mountain views is superb and there is plenty of variety and pleasant walking conditions.

Low level and short treks up to about 3,700 meters (12,000 feet) are at their best at this time of year. The Pokhara region is ideal as are Helambu, Langtang and Gorkha.

The Khumbu is still good though getting colder and the Lukla flights more reliable than at the height of the season. Remember that most high passes cannot be safely crossed because of snow after the middle of December.

VALLEY PEAKS

There are three hills surrounding the Kathmandu Valley that provide worthwhile hikes for the energetic with spectacular views. The six-kilometer (four-mile) trail to the top of **Phulchoki** (2,762 meters, 9,062 feet) begins behind Godavari school and is particularly beautiful with the spring flowers. From Budhanilkantha, it is a four-hour climb to the top of **Shivapuri** (2,732 meters, 8,963 feet) with panoramic views of the Himalaya and the Kathmandu Valley. The summit of **Champa Devi** (2,278 meters, 7,474 feet) above Pharping in the south of the Valley, can be reached from above Hatiban in only two or three hours of climbing.

TREKKING TIPS

Whereas no one is likely to openly criticise you if you make a cultural *faux pas*, out of respect for the Nepalese, and to ensure a better rapport between you, your staff and the villagers, try to be sensitive to religious beliefs and local practices.

For example, on your trek you will come across stupas and *chortens* of various sizes and conditions. They are revered, regardless of their size, with great devotion and were built to pacify local demons, deities or the spirit of some dead person. It is inappropriate to sit or climb on *chortens* and they should be passed with the right shoulder in a clockwise direction. Lama's prayer wheels whirl prayers out in a clockwise direction. All circumambulations of temples, stupas and *chortens* must follow clockwise the revolution the earth and the universe.

In Buddhist areas you will see *mani* stones placed around *chortens* or stacked to make a *mani* wall. These flat stones are carved with inscriptions, prayers and supplications which have been artistically engraved with devotion. Though the temptation may be great, because of the beauty and small size of these stones, please do not take them for souvenirs. The removal of these religious *mani* stones from their place of offering is a sacrilege.

At some crossroads you may find bits and pieces of coloured cloth, a bamboo framework with threads woven into an intricate design, or dyed flour dumplings lying on the ground. Be careful not to touch these or step on them. These offerings are made to malignant demons and deities and should also be passed on the left.

Avoid touching a Nepali dressed all in white. His white cap, white clothes and non-leather shoes signify his state of mourning for a close family member.

Prayer flags may look old, ragged and torn but to the Nepalis and especially the Sherpas their significance in carrying prayers of supplication and gratitude never fades away.

Always ask permission and remove shoes before entering a temple or home. Leather should not be worn inside a Hindu temple.

Give and accept items with both hands (never with your left hand), signifying your honour at receiving or giving. Try to avoid eating with your left hand as well, for it is traditionally associated with personal cleansing.

Avoid stepping over a person's body or extended legs. When sitting on the floor, do not point your feet at another person or any sacred object.

Some people bring small gifts for children, meaning well but inadvertently causing a mini-riot when there is not enough to go around. Give such items to the schoolmaster for fair distribution.

Nudity, and public demonstration of physical affection are not accepted in this culture.

When looking for a toilet spot in the bush, be sure that you are not close to running water or to any holy relics such as prayer flags, mani walls or *gompas*. Burn and bury, or carry out all toilet paper. Carry all throw-aways to a rubbish pit or to camp where the staff can burn or bury it (but do not pollute the fire by feeding it trash while food is being cooked).

Help to minimise the burning of firewood in lodges by being adequately clothed so as not to rely on the fire's heat for keeping warm, by limiting hot showers heated with wood, and by combining orders for like food items with others.

There are many more customs, rituals and good habits that should be mentioned and discussed, but these few points will provide a general guide. (See Culture and Customs page 318).

ON TRAIL

A typical day, when trekking with an organised outfit, begins around 6 a.m. with a cup of tea or coffee. After packing, breakfast of porridge, eggs, toast or pancakes is served. Walking starts around 7-7.30 a.m. Late into the morning, trekkers halt for a substantial hot brunch or lunch, the cook having gone ahead to select the site and prepare the meal. As early as 3 or 4 p.m. the day's walking is over. Camp for the night is set up (usually with a toilet tent), dinner is cooked and served, and by 8 p.m. everyone is thinking of sleep.

You are free to walk at whatever pace you prefer. Fast or slow, there will always be a staff guide in front or behind you. You can hike alone or in a group, make endless stops to enjoy the scenery or chat with passing locals, take photographs or sip tea in a wayside shop.

If trekking independently, do not trek alone. Team up with other trekkers or hire a guide, preferably from a trekking agency rather than at the trailhead.

A few hints may help the daily routine and increase your enjoyment.

First and foremost, do not try too much too soon. Walk at your own pace, no matter what others may say. Watch the way the porters walk, slowly and steadily. Go uphill in short steps, feet flat on the ground, weight forward. Go downhill with your knees bent, using your thigh muscles. Rest as often as you feel like.

Drink as much liquid as you can to compensate for the sweaty hours under the sun; at high altitudes, this also helps your body to acclimatize. Shielding your head from the sun with a hat or umbrella, not only applying sun screen to your skin, helps prevent sun stroke, along with dehydration one of the most common ailments on the trail. Ensure that your feet are in good condition to walk. Do not wait until blisters develop to take care of your tender feet.

Be careful in the night as in certain areas thieves sometimes slit tents to steal cameras and other valuables. Keep your belongings close to you, well inside the tent and keep your tent closed when you are not in it.

Finally, add to your luggage a strong dose of patience, understanding and congenial curiosity for the values and ways of a world that is altogether different from, and at times, better organised than your own.

ALTITUDE SICKNESS

Anyone trekking above 2,500 meters (8,200 feet) may suffer from altitude sickness. Known as AMS or Acute Mountain Sickness it can ruin treks and should be treated seriously. Nearly half of those persons who have trekked to Everest base camp, for instance, suffer mild AMS and in some cases lives are endangered.

Dr. David Shlim, Medical Director of Himalayan Rescue Association and an expert on mountaineering medicine, has developed a three step approach to avoid death from altitude sickness:

– early recognition of the symptoms is very important

– never ascend with any symptoms

– descend only if symptoms are getting worse whilst resting at the same altitude

Even experienced mountaineers tend to forget that the Himalaya begin where other mountains ranges end. Everest base camp is some 1,000 meters (3,300 feet) higher than the summit of the Matterhorn. As altitude increases, especially above 3,000 meters (10,000 feet), the air becomes thinner, creating certain difficulties for the human body. This is especially true when one is sleeping above 3,700 meters (12,000 feet).

Youth, strength and fitness make no difference here. The only prevention is to give one's body time to adjust to high altitude. Those who go too high too fast are liable to be victims of Acute Mountain Sickness.

To minimize the pitfalls of AMS during your trek, heed the following advice:

Drink adequate fluids. At 4,300 meters (14,000 feet) for example, the body requires three to four litres of liquid a day, more if losing much sweat. At low altitudes, especially in the heat, try to drink at least two to three liters a day including soups and hot drinks.

Accept the fact you cannot go very high if your time is short.

Plan for "rest days" at about 3,700 meters (12,000 feet) and 4,300 meters (14,000 feet). This means sleeping at the same altitude for two nights. You can be as active as you wish during the day, and go as high as you like, but descend again to sleep.

Above 3,700 meters (12,000 feet), do not set up camp more than 450 meters (1,500 feet) higher in any one day, even if you feel fit enough to go higher.

Learn the symptoms of AMS and be alert for them. If you begin to suffer, do not go any higher

until the symptoms have disappeared. Often they will clear up within one or two days. Should any of the more serious symptoms appear, descend at once to a lower altitude. Even a descent of 300 meters (1,000 feet) will often make a difference.

SYMPTOMS & TREATMENT

There are three main types of AMS. Early mountain sickness is the first and acts as a warning. If it goes unheeded, it can progress to pulmonary edema (waterlogged lungs) or cerebral edema (waterlogged brain).

Early mountain sickness manifests itself in headache, nausea, loss of appetite, sleeplessness, fluid retention and swelling of the body. The cure is to climb no higher until the symptoms have disappeared.

Pulmonary edema is characterised by breathlessness, even whilst resting, and by a persistent cough accompanied by congestion in the chest.

Cerebral edema is less common. Its symptoms are extreme tiredness, vomiting, severe headache, difficulty in walking (as in drunken, uneven steps), disorientation, abnormal speech and behaviour, drowsiness and eventually unconsciousness.

Should any of these symptoms appear, victims must be carried to lower altitude immediately, either on a porter's back or on a yak or pony, and their trek abandoned. Do not delay descent for any reason and begin at night if necessary. Do not wait for helicopter or aircraft evacuation. The patient must be accompanied and may well not be capable of making correct decisions. You may need to insist that they descend, even if it is against their will.

Medicine is no substitute for descent. If a doctor is available, he may give medication and oxygen but even with treatment, the patient must go down.

RESCUE

Himalayan Rescue Association

The **Himalayan Rescue Association** (HRA) is a non-profit organisation which strives to prevent casualties in the Nepal Himalaya. The HRA runs Trekkers' Aid Posts at Pheriche in the Khumbu and at Manang in the Annapurnas. They are manned by doctors and equipped to treat and advise on AMS and other medical problems during the heavy trekking seasons of spring and fall.

The Himalayan Rescue Association has an office near the Kathmandu Guest House in Thamel where advice for trekkers is given between 11 a.m. and 5 p.m. daily except Saturdays tel: 418755.

As this is an entirely voluntary organization, donations are welcome to the HRA, P.O. Box 495, Kathmandu or channelled through your trekking agency. The HRA has no facilities to arrange helicopter evacuations which must be done through your trekking agent or embassy.

The HRA does not routinely recommend any

medicine for preventing AMS though there are two medicines which under certain circumstances are considered useful. Diamox (acetazolomide) is the safest for helping to cope with symptoms of mild AMS. The standard dose is 250 mg every 12 hours until symptoms are resolved. Dexamethasone is a powerful drug which can be useful in the treatment of cerebral edema. It should only be used under experienced supervision.

The HRA suggests the following additional precautions:

Do not go to high altitude if you have heart of lung disease. Check with your doctor if you have any doubts.

Do not expect everyone in your party to acclimatize at the same rate. It is possible that you will need to divide the party so that people who acclimatise more slowly will camp lower than others. Plan for this.

Take extra precautions when flying into high altitude STOL airstrips like Syangboche. Take two "rest days" before proceeding further.

RIVER TRIPS

Although a relatively new activity in Nepal, the better river-running outfits are well-equipped and have highly trained staff. Himalayan River Exploration (P.O. Box 242, Kathmandu tel: 418491 or 222706, telex: 2216; fax: 414075), the pioneers of the industry, provided the following advice:

River trips last from one to several days and your choice depends on the time available and where you are heading. White water varies as to the time of year as the rivers rise and fall dramatically during the season, depending on rainfall and snowmelt. As a general rule they are at their highest (and the white water at its biggest) during and after the June to September monsoon and drop to their lowest in February and March. By April the snowmelt in the mountains raises the water level.

Most popular is the three-day Trisuli or Seti river trips down to Royal Chitwan National Park from Kathmandu to Pokhara. More remote and adventurous is the four-day Bheri and Karnali river trip from above Nepalgunj to Royal Bardiya National Park. Most exciting of all is the huge rapids on the Sunkosi river in east Nepal, which takes 10 days to run.

What to Bring: In autumn (mid-September to mid-November) and spring (March to May) shorts and bathing suits, a sun hat, tee shirts, sneakers and a flashlight are all that is needed for a short trip. For early autumn and late spring bring a long sleeved shirt, light trousers, an umbrella (for shade and in case it rains) and plenty of sun block to protect you from the glare off the water. During winter (mid-November to February) in addition to the above bring a thick sweater, warm trousers, a down jacket and rain poncho. All the clothes you bring should not mind getting wet. For use in camp ensure you have a complete change of dry clothes and shoes.

A good river company will provide tents, sleeping bag and liner, foam mattress, towel and a rubber waterproof bag to stow your clothing. You will be given a life jacket and your guide will instruct you in its use. Safety must be taken very seriously on the remote big rivers of Nepal and should be a consideration when you choose your operator.

A waterproof "ammo can" is also provided to carry cameras, binoculars, sunglasses and personal items. This is clipped to the boat and is accessible during the day.

JUNGLE SAFARIS

Most wildlife operations in Chitwan and Bardiya supply basics as you would expect of any hotel, therefore only personal clothes are necessary.

Take casual, washable safari clothes in jungle colours – beige and green are the most suitable. Wear baggy shorts in the summer months but take long pants to protect legs from swishing tall grass whilst riding elephants. Sneakers are the most suitable footwear and jungle hats, mosquito repellent and sun cream are useful. The winter months are cold and morning mist makes it particularly chilly – sweaters and jackets are needed December to February. As a guideline, remember the Terai is about 1,200 meters (4,000 feet) lower in altitude than Kathmandu and so the weather is always several degrees warmer.

For those lodges that have swimming pools, don't forget your swimming gear. Tiger Tops has a retail outlet discreetly set in their elephant camp selling their specially designed range of tempting cotton jungle wear.

MOUNTAIN BIKING

– By Scott Diehl

What to Bring: Except for one or two mountain bike shops in Kathmandu, do not count on borrowing any specialised tools for on-the-road repairs. Self-sufficiency is essential within practical limits. Bring all the tools you will need for repairs and routine maintenance, including tire irons, a tube patch kit, an extra tube, a chain tool, a spoke wrench, allen keys and screwdrivers. Less frequently required components are cone wrenches, a headset wrench, a bottom bracket tool, a spanner, extra spokes, extra brake cables and pads, and an extra rear derailleur. And do not forget the obvious, like water bottles, a sturdy lock that can stretch around a fixed object, your helmet, gloves, a pump and definitely a bell.

Carrying Your Gear: Panniers are the preferred mode for carrying your gear while road riding in Nepal. Racks and panniers must be durable as many roads are rough and full of pot holes. Bring small padlocks to keep sticky fingers out of panniers. Riders taking to the trails may prefer to carry their equipment in a medium-sized, snug-fitting backpack, as panniers often hinder a bike's maneuverability on rugged terrain. Also, it is easier to carry a bike on your shoulder that isn't bulky with loaded panniers.

A "portager" is an essential piece of gear for carrying your bike which you will probably be doing frequently. The "portager" is a strap which mounts beneath the central bar and allows the bike to rest fairly comfortably on your shoulder. But on long, uphill totes, you may want to attach the bike to your backpack with nylon webbing to better distribute the weight.

Before leaving home, test your equipment thoroughly and take an extended ride on bumpy terrain fully loaded to make sure that the panniers and rack sit solidly, or that you can balance and manoeuvre easily wearing a loaded pack.

Bikers' Ethics: Be cautious at all times, on roads or trails, of other travellers: loaded porters and stock animals, women and children regularly ply the way and hardly expect to encounter a fast-coming bicyclist. Ring your bell habitually. Move to the inside when animals are passing to avoid being nudged off the trail. Stay on the roads and trails at all times, as off-road riding only contributes to Nepal's already serious soil erosion problems.

Dress modestly (for men long shorts are acceptable, always with a shirt; for women, loose pants or skirt to below the knee and an unrevealing top), and try to be tolerant of villagers' curiosity which is seldom with malice. In some parks and reserves, bicycle use is strictly prohibited. Check the rules before leaving Kathmandu.

NIGHTLIFE

CULTURAL SHOWS

By 10 p.m. Kathmandu is nearly asleep. The only life centers around some temples, Thamel and the big hotels. There are no nightclubs and no massage parlours.

The Soaltee Oberoi (Tel: 272555) offers dancing to a live band in the Gurkha Grill restaurant. The only action late in the evening is to be found in some bars in Thamel.

The best traditional dance performances are given nightly by the Everest Cultural Society at Annapurna Hotel (Tel: 221711) and by the New Himalchuli Dance Group at Shankar Hotel (Tel: 412975) in Lazimpat.

Most of the major hotels have dance and cultural shows staged in their restaurants. The Hotel Soaltee Oberoi (Tel: 272555) features Nepalese music and dancing every evening (except Tuesday) in the Himalchuli Restaurant. The Naachghar at the Hotel Yak & Yeti (Tel: 411436) has daily (except Wednesday) traditional dance performances and Mr Magdi on the piano before and after the show. The Shangrila hotel (Tel: 410108) feature Kala Kunj traditional dancing from Bhaktapur in their garden every Friday evening, with a buffet barbeque.

For excellent Indian classical music, go to the Ghar-e-Kabab restaurant in the Annapurna Hotel (Tel: 221711) in Durbar Marg. The Far Pavilion at the Everest (Tel: 220567) also has nightly ghazals and sitar music.

But the best show of all is the spectacular dancing amidst ancient squares and courtyards lit by countless oil lamps of Patan or Bhaktapur. This must be specially arranged in advance and is available for groups only – ask your travel agent for details.

MOVIES

Kathmandu has a few movie houses featuring mainly Indian tear-jerkers; Western visitors may enjoy the reactions of the audience more than the action on the screen. For Western films, check the programmes of the European and American cultural centers. Video is flourishing among more privileged Nepalis and video tapes, of mostly dubious quality, are widely available for rent.

GAMBLING

Casino Nepal is in the premises of the Soaltee Oberoi hotel. Here Indians toss small fortunes to the wind on baccarat, black jack, roulette and other games. The chit value is counted in Indian rupees or foreign exchange; no Nepalis are permitted entry. This is one of the very few international casinos between Malaysia and Suez.

If you decide to come, the casino will provide a free bus service back to your hotel and some complimentary play coupons for showing your incoming plane ticket stub within a week of arrival.

Out of a treasured past ...

... come living memories
of joyous occasions.

the legendary valley of Kathmandu there should be a
gendary hotel - it is the Yak & Yeti. A sumptuous
ilding and a splendid old Rana palace linked together
combine the special magic of tradition and
spitality with today's modern facilities. The decor is
re Nepalese, the atmosphere unforgettable.
mfort, care and service are built in with the brick and
e intricate Newari woodcarvings of the hotel.

e legendary Yak & Yeti offers three superb
staurants to the discerning traveller. Indulge in fine
ontinental cuisine with a Russian flair at the world
mous "Chimney" Restaurant, or adventure in
quisite Nepalese/Indian delicacies served under original
nburst Bohemian chandeliers in the century-old
latial theatre-restaurant "Naachghar". For a more casual
eal the "Sunrise" Cafe Restaurant, overlooking
athmandu's finest gardens has a menu everybody
grees upon.

e Business Centre will take care of secretarial and
formation requirements and provide an entire office at
ur disposal. In addition to the special room amenities
d personalised service the Yak & Yeti is the only
tel in Kathmandu to offer international direct dialling
lephones and close circuit TV with CNN news
annel in every room.

he legendary Yak & Yeti makes your visit
aforgettable.

HOTEL YAK & YETI

G.P.O. Box 1016, Durbar Marg, Kathmandu, Nepal Tel: 413999
Cable: YAKNYETI Telex: NP 2237/2683 YAKNYETI Facsimile: 977.1.227782

a hotel that's a legend

S O U T H   A S I A

*The Indian subcontinent encompasses some
of the most mysterious and culturally
independent countries in the world.* **Insight
Guide: South Asia** *gives a vivid
impression of the colourful kaleidoscope
and the mythic-mystical depth of India. See
Sri Lanka, jewel in the
Indian Ocean, the
Islamic nation of
Pakistan, the mountains of
Nepal, sandwiched between
India and China, the
extensive "rooftop world"
of Tibet and the special
travel experience
presented by Bhutan and
Bangladesh.
Or discover the unique wildlife and parks
of the region with* **Insight Guide: Indian
Wildlife**.

A P A
INSIGHT
GUIDES

SHOPPING

Kathmandu is a treasure trove for the shopper. Traders appear wherever tourists stray and merchants wait on temple steps. Wares are spread on every pavement but watch out for the junk, fake antiques and souvenir *khukris*. Peer into shops, take your pick or take your leave; try the next boutique or the next stall. There are good buys amongst the bewildering and dazzling array.

CLOTHING

– Clothes are good value and can be fun, from the lopsided *topis* (caps) to knitted sweaters, mittens and socks; from Tibetan dresses (*chubas*) that fasten at the side to men's Nepali cotton shirts buttoned diagonally across the chest. *Topis* come in two types; sombre black ones and multicolored variations. They are like ties, a must for all Nepalis visiting government offices, but with a difference – their asymmetric shape is said to be a replica of Mount Kailas, the most sacred mountain for Buddhists and Hindus.

– Nepalese cloth, red, black and orange, hand-blocked and checkered with dots or geometric designs, is worn by the women as blouses or shawls. It is also made into cotton quilts, covered on both sides with thin muslin, giving pastel overtones to the colours.

– Wool shawls in a variety of natural colours are a typical product of Nepal; made of the finest goat's wool called *pashmina*, they are extremely soft, warm and strong.

– Multicolored jackets and shoulder bags are made in bright cotton colours in large patchwork. More subtle are those made from the wool used for Tibetan *lamas'* robes and trimmed with striped cloth.

– Tee-shirts are available with a variety of imaginative printed and embroidered slogans, or with your personal message.

– Hand-blocked cotton fabrics are made into dresses, bedspreads, pillow covers by organizations supporting destitute or handicapped women and sold along with various weaving, hand-knit sweaters, and household and gift items at retail stores in Patan and Kathmandu.

FOLK ART OBJECTS

– Among the various Nepalese folk objects available and produced in Kathmandu is the national knife, the curved *khukri*, worn in a wooden or leather sheath at the belt and sometimes highly adorned with silver and gold. Make sure it comes complete with the two tiny blades for sharpening and cleaning.

– The *saranghi* is a small four-stringed viola cut from a single piece of wood and played with a horsehair bow by the *gaine*, the traditional wandering minstrels.

– Bamboo flutes sold by vendors who carry them as a huge "tree," make cheap and enchanting gifts.

– There are all kinds of hand-beaten copper and brass pots, jugs and jar, sold by their weight but rather heavy to carry home.

– Tibetan tea bowls made of a special wood and lined with silver and silver offering bowls, newly made and available in Bodhnath.

– Hand-made paper is beautifully block-printed or tie-dyed in a variety of designs by the women of Bhaktapur and sold as wrapping paper, cards and booklets.

– Intricately painted *thangkas* or religious scrolls mounted in silk are sold widely at a variety of prices. Look for the detail of the work and the amount of gold leaf used.

– Papier-mache dance masks are popular and puppet dolls made and sold by the people of Bhaktapur.

– Terracotta plant holders in the shapes of elephants, rhinoceros and temple-lions or plaques embossed with deities are hand-made in Thimi.

– Statuettes of Hindu and Buddhist deities are produced semi-industrially with the ancient "lost wax" process, a speciality of the people of Patan. Produced for export are metal filigree animals or Christmas decorations set with small pieces of coloured stones.

– Carpets, the hand-made production of which is flourishing with substantial exports specially made for Europe and the U.S., are excellent value. The ones in the shops, hand-made in private homes and factories, are in traditional Tibetan designs in either bright colours or more subtle "vegetable dyes," though all are in fact chemical colours. The density of knotting, straightness of lines and overall quality of workmanship influence the price of new carpets. The antique Tibetan carpets, with intricate motifs and beautiful colours, are available at substantially higher prices.

– Replicas of the lovely Newari woodcarvings seen on temples and 16th to 17th century homes can be purchased in handicraft emporiums or at wood-carvers' studios Bhaktapur.

ANTIQUES

Unless bought from a reputable antique gallery or certified by specialists, consider many "antique" pieces to have been made yesterday and pay accordingly. Tibetans and Nepalis will not willingly part with their jewels and adornments and, especially when you encounter people on the trail, it is impolite to pressure them to part with their personal heirlooms.

In addition to the beautiful old carpets which come in a number of sizes and types, most of the tempting antiques to buy are from Tibet. They include everything from old *thangkas*, carved and painted side-tables, metalwork from east Tibet and jewellery and trinkets made with turquoise, coral, amber, gold and silver. Prices are on a par with the world market and bargaining is expected.

BOOKSHOPS

Kathmandu has many bookshops with an excellent selection of books about Nepal, written in several languages and on a wide range of Asian subjects. The best shops include **Educational Enterprises** beneath a temple opposite Bir Hospital; **Himalayan Booksellers** with branches in Durbar Marg and Thamel;**Mandala Book Point** in Kantipath; **Pilgrim's Bookshop** deep in Thamel; and **Ratna Pustak Bhandar** off Bagh Bazaar near the French Cultural Center.

WHERE TO BUY

The best selection and the best prices are available in the Kathmandu Valley though you will find things to buy all over Nepal. As you sightsee in the Valley you will encounter many good shopping areas and as a general rule, if you see something you really like and the price is not too exorbitant, it is better to buy it than regret not being able to find anything similar! To get an idea of the variety of things that can be purchased, and of the relative qualities and prices, visits are suggested to:

– **Thamel**, the tourist area in the old part of Kathmandu which has a good selection of most things though the crowds may distract you.

– **Jawalakhel**, south of Patan, has a good selection of carpets. They can be seen being made in the **Tibetan refugee center** and are displayed in the many shops in the area. **Patan** itself is famous for the manufacture of jewellery and metalwork, still made by traditional methods.

– **Hastakala** (Handicrafts) is opposite the entrance to Himalaya Hotel. All the crafts on sale in this attractive shop run by UNICEF are made by disadvantaged groups under the auspices of the Nepal Women's Organization, the Mahaguthi and Bhaktapur Craft Printers. The **Mahaguthi** shops, one just down the hill in Patan and one in Durbar Marg have similar arrangements, as do the talented designers who run the private **Dhukuti**, on the same hill. **Pasal**, in an arcade off Durbar Marg, is especially clever for gifts with imaginative local and regional decorative items, household goods and toys.

– For antiques there are two reliable galleries on Durbar Marg with beautiful showrooms; **Tibet Ritual Art Gallery** is next to Tiger Tops and the **Potala Gallery** is on the first floor across from the Yak & Yeti gate.

The main shops in Kathmandu for imported articles are in New Road with supermarkets located in Thapatali and Lazimpat. Jewellers and shops selling handicrafts to tourists are centred around Durbar Marg and the big hotels but beware the many Indian Kashmiri shops if you are looking for something Nepali.

Remember when buying, antiques are forbidden for export if they are more than 100 years old. Certificates are required to prove their younger age if there is any doubt. Galleries will be happy to help you and it is recommend that you keep all receipts in case of queries regarding purchases when leaving the country.

SPORTS

PARTICIPANT

Sports as a pastime or occupation is an alien concept in Nepal. It has only recently been promoted into schools and the military. Football (soccer) and cricket have become popular while cycling, particularly mountain biking, and jogging are attracting some devotees.

Paradoxically, in Nepal commercial skiing is out of the question, though a few cross-country enthusiasts and mountaineering expeditions do try it. There are no ski-lifts, the steepness of the mountain slopes and the exceptionally high snow line (bringing with it attendant altitude problems) make skiing impractical.

However fishing, swimming, golf, tennis, squash and hockey can be enjoyed in and around Kathmandu though facilities are very limited. There are two nine-hole golf courses, both of whom welcome visitors; the **Royal Nepal Golf Club** is located near the airport and **Gorkana Safari Park** is on the Sankhu road past Bodhnath. Hotel guests and members can use the tennis courts and swimming pools of the Soaltee Oberoi, Yak & Yeti, Everest, Annapurna, Shangrila and Narayani hotels and for small entrance fees some allow drop-in day use.

If you want some exercise, the **Himalayan Hash House Harriers** welcome visitors to their men's run 5 p.m. every Monday and mixed family runs 5 p.m. every Thursday. Contact the Summit Hotel (Tel: 521894) for the weekly location.

Prudence is needed when bathing in mountain torrents because of swift, treacherous currents. The larger rivers in the Terai are safe but keep an eye out for the occasional crocodile.

Lowland rivers and valley lakes are often good fishing grounds. Besides the small fry, the two main catches are *asla*, a kind of trout, and the larger *mahseer* which grow to huge proportions. February, March, October and November are the fishing months. Permits are required in National Parks where the fish must be returned. Keen fishermen should bring their own tackle. Contact Tiger Tops (Durbar Marg, P.O.Box 242, Kathmandu tel: 220706 telex: 2216 fax: 414075) for information on fishing in the Karnali, Babai and Narayani rivers.

PHOTOGRAPHY

USEFUL TIPS

As the cost of photographic film is expensive in Nepal and can be purchased only in Kathmandu, you are advised to bring enough rolls for your personal use. Film can be reliably developed in Kathmandu, except for specialist transparencies such as Kodachrome, and enlargements made. Lotus Studios (Tel: 415396) have three convenient locations in the Lazimpat Plaza, Thamel and Durbar Marg. Photographic shops can supply batteries and effect camera repairs. Try Photo Concern in New Road (Tel: 223275).

Visitors should bear in mind that the range of consumer products and services do not match those in city centers in the West. Thus it is best to arrive in Nepal self-sufficient with regard to the photographic equipment that you need.

The keen photographer should bring along long telephoto as well as wide angled lenses as these will prove useful to capture the rich variety of wildlife and the awe-inspiring mountain landscape for which Nepal is famed. Fast film for the dark jungles is recommended, though 100 asa is suitable for most purposes.

When it comes to taking pictures of the Nepalese and their surroundings, tread gingerly. Be sensitive and bear in mind that religion and superstition play an integral part in Nepalese life. So do not simply click away at people, statues, shrines, buildings, trees, boulders etc. For what may appear to be innocuous may have deep spiritual significance for the locals. Seek permission whenever you are in doubt. It is always better to forgo a shot rather than risk offending your hosts.

LANGUAGE

NEPALI

There are as many tongues spoken in Nepal as there are races, and almost as many dialects as there are village communities. But just as centuries of inter-marriage have left the nation without a pure tribe or race, neither is there any pure language. Throughout history, the main languages have inter-mingled and influenced one another.

The official language, Nepali, is derived from Pahori, a language of northern India related to Hindi. Nepali and Hindi use the same writing system, called Devanagari. Nepali has also borrowed heavily from some local dialects as well as from Sanskrit, an ancient scholarly language which has survived (like Latin) as a religious medium. Nepali, Sanskrit and Newari – the language of the Newar people, predominant in the Kathmandu Valley – each has its own distinctive literary traditions. Newari, which uses three different alphabets, has the newer and more abundant literature.

In northern Nepal the Tibetan language – another traditional vehicle for religious teaching – remains widespread both in its pure, classical form and as derived dialects (including Sherpa and Thakali). In southern Nepal, the various people of the Terai speak their own Indo-European dialects. Three times more people speak Maithili, an eastern Terai dialect, than speak Newari, a reflection of the uneven distribution of population in Nepal.

English is widely spoken and understood in official and tourism-related circles. Most taxi drivers and merchants in the Kathmandu Valley have a working knowledge of English, as do most Sherpas. Elsewhere you may find it difficult to make yourself understood, although the younger generation is fast acquiring a smattering of English words.

We strongly recommend that you learn a few basic words and expressions. Like elsewhere, you will get big returns on this small investment in terms of hospitality, friendship and respect. Books that will

Sir Edmund Hillary

"I love the great cold mountains of the Himalaya – but it's the Sherpas that surround them with warmth and friendship."

For all of us, our image of Everest is indelibly coloured by the Sherpa people who live in the high Khumbu Valley. From my first encounter with the Sherpas in 1951, I developed a great respect for these people who lived so cheerfully in such formidable surroundings. My warm affection broadened to concern over their health and livelihood as I realized the difficulties they experienced in their harsh environment. So I set up the Himalayan Trust, and today it provides education and health care to hundreds of Sherpas.

Things were going smoothly when fate dealt us a heavy blow. In 1989, a fire destroyed the magnificent Thyangboche Monastery, shocking the Sherpa community and all those who had visited this revered site. We vowed to help and now I ask for your support. Please contribute towards the rebuilding of the monastery and to assist the Trust's on-going work. As a token of my appreciation, everyone who donates US$150 or more will receive a copy of 'Sagarmatha', a unique book of photographs on the Everest region. Each book will be personally signed by myself.

The pictures in 'Sagarmatha' (the Nepalese name for the highest mountain on earth) span several decades and were specially donated by my many mountaineering friends.

Please send your donation today and receive a book to treasure.

Please photocopy this form and return it with your donation of US$150 or more if you wish to receive a special copy of Sagarmatha. Your donation should be send (by crossed cheque made payable to The Himalayan Trust) direct by registered mail to The Himalayan Trust c/o Sir Edmund Hillary, 278A Remuera Road, Auckland 5, New Zealand. Funds can also be directly transferred to The Himalayan Trust Board, account number 0031716-00, Remuera Branch, Bank of New Zealand, Auckland, New Zealand. Please indicate "Sagarmatha Book Donation" with your contribution.

Yes, here is my donation to **The Himalayan Trust**

for US$ _____

(or equal currency)

Please send this book to me★/as my present to★

NAME: _____

ADDRESS: _____

_____

Name: _____

_____

Signature : _____

_____

Date: _____

★Please delete where necessary

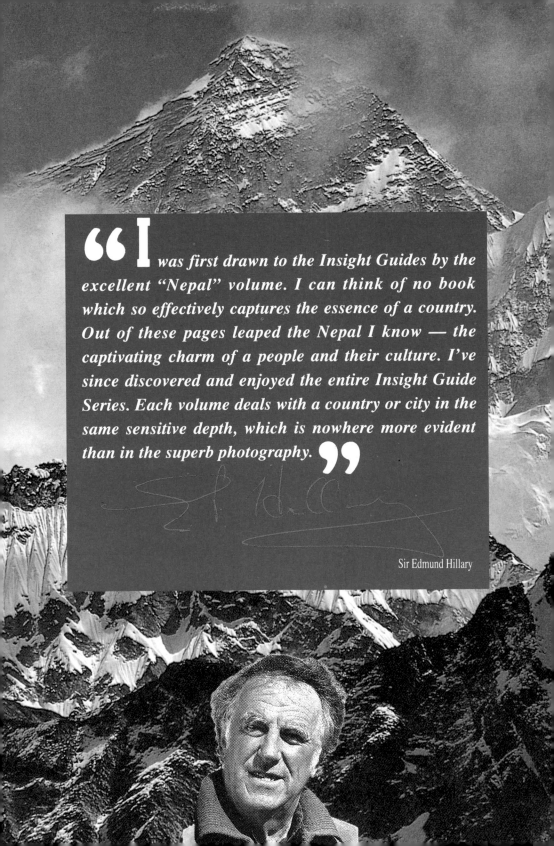

> **"I** *was first drawn to the Insight Guides by the excellent "Nepal" volume. I can think of no book which so effectively captures the essence of a country. Out of these pages leaped the Nepal I know — the captivating charm of a people and their culture. I've since discovered and enjoyed the entire Insight Guide Series. Each volume deals with a country or city in the same sensitive depth, which is nowhere more evident than in the superb photography."*

Sir Edmund Hillary

help you are B*asic Course in Spoken Nepali, Introduction to Nepali, Nepali Phrase Book* all available in Kathmandu bookshops.

FURTHER READING

GENERAL

Bernstein, Jeremy. *The Wildest Dreams of Kew: A Profile of Nepal.* New York: Simon and Schuster, 1970. Personal travelogue.

Choegyal, Lisa. *Insight Pocket Guide: Nepal.* Apa Publications, 1992. Useful and concise suggestions for a short stay.

Fleming, Robert and Linda. *Kathmandu Valley.* Tokyo, Kodansha Int'l, 1978.

Frank, Keitmar. *Dreamland Nepal.* New Delhi; S. Chand, 1978. Photographic book.

Gurung Harka. *Maps of Nepal.* Bangkok: White Orchid, 1983.

Gurung, Harka. *Vignettes of Nepal.* Kathmandu: Sajha Prakashan, 1980.

Haas, Ernst. *Himalayan Pilgrimage.* New York: Viking Press, 1978. Nice photographic book.

Hagen, Toni. *Nepal: The Kingdom in the Himalayas.* Berne: Kummerly and Frey, 1961. Second edition, 1971. Geographical study with many photos and tropical maps. Still one of the best books by one of the first persons to travel widely in the country.

His Majesty's Government of Nepal. *Nepal.* Kathmandu: Ministry of Industry and Commerce, Department of Tourism, 1974. Pictorial survey.

Hoag, Kathrine. *Exploring Mysterious Kathmandu.* Avalok, 1978, City guide.

Kelly, Thomas L. *Kathmandu City on the Edge of the World.* Author Patricia Roberts, photos by Thomas Kelly. A beautiful illustrated book on the Kathmandu Valley. It takes you through Kathmandu's historical layers and festivals.

Kelly, Thomas L. *Hidden Himalayas.* Author Carroll Dunham, photoas by Thomas Kelly. Documents the cycles of the seasons in Humla, the remote far northwest corner of Nepal.

Matthiessen, Peter. *The Snow Leopard.* London: Chatto and Windus, 1979. Journal of a journey to Dolpo.

Murphy, Dervla. *The Waiting Land: A Spell in Nepal.* London: John Murray, 1967, Travelogue.

Peissel, Michel. *Tiger for Breakfast.* London: Hodder 1966. The story of Kathmandu's legendary Boris Lissanevitch.

Ragam, V.R. *Pilgrim's Travel Guide: The Himalayan Region.* Gunter: 1963.

Raj, Prakash A. *Kathmandu and the Kingdom of Nepal.* South Yarra, Vic., Australia: Lonely Planet, 1980. A pocket guide.

Rieffel, Robert. *Nepal: Namaste.* Kathmandu: Sahayagi Prakashan, 1978. A thorough guidebook.

Shah, Rishikesh. *An Introduction to Nepal.* Kathmandu: Ratna Pustak Bhandar, 1976.

Suyin, Han. *The Mountain is Young.* London: Jonathan Cape, 1958. Novel set in Nepal of the 1950s.

HISTORICAL

Fisher, Margaret W. *The Political History of Nepal.* Berkeley: University of California, Institute of International Studies, 1960.

Hamilton, Francis. *An Account of the Kingdom of Nepal and the Territories Annexed to This Dominion by House of Gurkha.* Edinburgh: Archibold Constable and Co., 1819. Early history of the Himalayan region.

Hodgson, Brain H. *Essays on the Languages, Literature, and Religion of Nepal and Tibet;* (and further papers on the geography, ethnology, and commerce of the countries). London: Trubner and Co., 1974. Re-printed by Bibliotheca Himalayica, New Delhi.

Hooker, Sir Joseph Dalton. *Himalayan Journals.* London: Ward, Lock, Bowden and Co., 1891.

Hopkirk, Peter. *Trespassers on the Roof of the World. The Race to Lhasa.* Oxford University Press, 1982. Historical accounts of the early adventurers trying to enter Lhasa.

Kirkpatrick, Col. F. *An Account of the Kingdom of Nepal.* London: 1800, Reprinted by Bibliotheca Himalayica, New Delhi, 1969.

Landon, Percival. *Nepal.* Two volumes. London: Constable, 1928. Reprinted by Bibliotheca Himalayica, New Delhi. Popular historical account survives as the best overall early summary.

Oldfield, Henry Ambrose. *Views of Nepal, 1851-1864.* Kathmandu: Ratna Pustak Bhandar, 1975. Book filled with sketches and paintings.

Oldfield, Henry Ambrose. *Sketches from Nipal. Historical and Descriptive* (with anecdotes of court life and wild sports of the country in the time of Maharaja Jang Bahadur, G.C.B., to which is added an essay on Nepalese Buddhism and illustrations of religious monuments, architecture, and scenery from the author's own drawings). Two vols., London: W.H. Allen, 1880. Reprinted by Bibliotheca Himalayica, New Delhi.

Rana, Padma Jung Bahadur. *Life of Maharaja Sir Jung Bahadur of Nepal.* Allahabad, India: Pioneer Press: 1909. Biography and description of 19th century palace life.

Regmi, D.R. *Ancient Nepal.* Third Edition. Calcutta: Firma K.L. Mukopadhyaya, 1969. Detailed historiography to 740 from Nepalese religious viewpoint.

Regmi, D.R. *Medieval Nepal.* Three volumes. Calcutta: Firma K.L. Mukhopadhyaya, 1965. Definitive historiography covering period 740 to 1768, plus source material.

Regmi, D.R. *Modern Nepal: Rise and Growth in the Eighteenth Century.* Calcutta: Firma K.L. Mukhopadhyaya, 1961.

Stiller, Ludwig F. *The Rise of the House of Gorkha.* New Delhi: Manjustri, 1973.

Wright, Daniel, editor. *Vamsavali: History of Nepal* with an introductory sketch of the country and people of Nepal. Translated from the Parbatiya by Munshi Shew Shunker Singh and Pandit Shri Gunanand. Cambridge: University Press, 1877. Second edition, Calcutta: Susil Gupta, 1958. Thorough and reliable early history.

PEOPLE, ART & CULTURE

Anderson, Mary M. *Festivals of Nepal.* London: George Allen and Unwin, 1971.

Aran, Lydia, *The Art of Nepal.* Kathmandu: Shahayogi Prakashan, 1978. Mostly about the Kathmandu Valley with an accent on religion.

Baidya, Karunakar. *Teach Yourself Nepali.* Kathmandu: Ratna Pustak Bhandar, 1982.

Bista, Dor Bahadur. *People of Nepal.* Kathmandu: Ratna Pustak Bhandar, 1982.

Brown, Percy, *Picturesque Nepal.* London: Adam and Charles Black, 1912.

Deep, Dhruba Krishna. *The Nepal Festivals.* Kathmandu: Ratna Pustak Bhandar, 1982.

Fisher, James F. *Trans-Himalayan Traders: Economy, Society and Culture in Northwest Nepal.* Berkeley: University of California 1986. An anthropological study of the people of Dolpo.

Furer-Haimendorf, Christoph von. *The Inter-Relation of Castle and Ethnic Groups in Nepal.* London: University of London, 1957.

Furer-Haimendorf, Christoph von. *The Sherpas of Nepal; Buddhist Highlanders.* Berkeley and Los Angeles: University of California Press, 1964. Intensive study of Sherpa society.

Gajurel, C.L. and Vaidya, K.K. *Traditional Arts and Crafts of Nepal.* New Delhi: S. Chand, 1984.

Haaland, Ane. *Bhaktapur: A Town Changing.* Bhaktapur Development Project, 1982.

Höfer, Hans.*Cityguide: Kathmandu Valley.* Apa Publicaions, 1990. Best authoritative, in-depth guide to the Valley.

Hosken, Fran P. *The Kathmandu Valley Towns: A Record of Life and Change in Nepal.* New York: Weatherhill, 1974. Pictorial survey.

Indra. *Joys of Nepalese Cooking.* New Delhi: 1982.

Jerstad, Luther G. *Mani-Rimdu: Sherpa Dance Drama.* Calcutta: International Book House, 1969.

Jest, Corneille. *Monuments of Northern Nepal.* Paris: UNESCO, 1981.

Kansakar, N.H. *Nepali Kitchens.* Kathmandu: 1978.

Korn, Wolfgang. *The Traditional Architecture of the Kathmandu Valley.* Kathmandu: Ratna Pustak Bhandar, 1977. Limited edition with many diagrams.

Kramrisch, Stella. *The Art of Nepal.* New York: 1964.

Kuloy, Hallvard Kare. *Tibetan Rugs.* Bangkok: White Orchid Press, 1982. Nicely illustrated paperback with little information.

Lall, Kesar. *Lore and Legend of Nepal.* Kathmandu: Ratna Pustak Bhandar, 1976.

Lall, Kesar. *Nepalese Customs and Manners.* Kathmandu: Ratna Pustak Bhandar, 1976.

Macdonald, A.W., and Anne Vergati Stahl. *Newar Art.* New Delhi: Vikas, 1979.

McDougal, Charles. *The Kulunge Rai: A Study in Kinship and Marriages Exchange.* Kathmandu: Ratna Pustak Bhandar, 1979.

Messerschmidt, Donald A. *The Gurungs of Nepal.* Warminister: Aris & Phillips, 1976. A standard work of this large group of people.

Nepali, Gopal Singh. *The Newars.* Bombay: United Asia Publications, 1965. Subtitled: "An Ethno-Sociological Study of a Himalayan Community."

Pal, Pratapaditya. Nepal: *Where the Gods Are Young.* Asia House Exhibition, 1975.

Prusha, Carl. *Kathmandu Valley: The Preservation of Physical Environment and Cultural Heritage. A Protective Inventory.* Two volumes. Vienna: Anton Schroll, 1975. Prepared by His Majesty's Government of Nepal in collaboration with UNESCO and the United Nations.

Rubel, Mary. *The Gods of Nepal.* Kathmandu: Bhimratna Harsharatna, 1971.

Singh, Madanjeet. *Himalayan Arts.* London: UNESCO, 1968.

Snellgrove, David L. *Buddhist Himalaya.* Oxford: Bruno Cassirer, 1957. Excellent survey.

Vaidya, Karunaka. *Folk Tales of Nepal.* Kathmandu: Ratna Pustak Bhandar, 1980.

NATURAL HISTORY

Eckholm, Erik P. *Losing Ground.* New York: W.W. Norton, 1976. Nepal in the context of deforestation and world food prospects.

Fleming, R.L. Sr., R.L. Fleming Jr. and L.S. Bangdel. *Birds of Nepal.* Kathmandu: Avalok, 1979. Definitive work with good illustrations.

Gurung, K.K. *Heart of the Jungle: the Wildlife of Chitwan, Nepal.* London: Andre Deutsch and Tiger Tops, 1983. In-depth survey of the fauna of Royal Chitwan National Park with lovely drawings by the author.

Hillard, Darla. *Vanishing Tracks: Four Years Among the Snow Leopards of Nepal.* New York: Arbor House, 1989. A charming study of life in the western Himalaya with zoologist Rodney Jackson.

Inskipp, Carol and Tim. *A Guide to the Birds of Nepal.* Dover. New Hampshire: Tanager Books, 1985.

Inskipp, Carol. *A Birdwatcher's Guide to Nepal.*

England: Bird Watchers Guides, 1988.

Ives, Jack D & Messerli, Bruno. *The Himalayan Dilemma, Reconciling Development and Conservation.* London: Routledge, 1989. Important examination of today's problems.

Manandhar, N.P. *Medicinal Plants of Nepal Himalaya.* Kathmandu: Ratna Pustak Bhandar, 1980.

McDougal, Charles. *The Face of the Tiger.* London: Rivington Books and Andre Deutsch, 1977. The classic work on the Bengal tiger, by the director of Tiger Tops.

Mierow, D., and T.B. Shrestha. *Wild Animals of Nepal.* Kathmandu: 1974

Mierow, D., and T.B. Shrestha. *Himalayan Flowers and Trees.* Kathmandu: Saha-yogi Prakashan, 1978. Good handbook.

Mishra, Hemanta R. and Jeffries, Margaret. *Royal Chitwan National Park: Wildlife Heritage of Nepal.* Seattle, The Mountaineers 1991. Comprehensive and useful guide.

Polunin, Oleg and Stainton, Adam. *Concise Flowers of the Himalaya.* New Delhi: Oxford University Press, 1987. A much-needed standard work.

Smith, Colin. *Butterflies of Nepal (Central Himalaya).* Bangkok: Teopress, 1989.

Shrestha, T.B. *Development Ecology of the Arun Basin* Kathmandu: ICIMOD 1989.

Stainton, J.D.A. *Forests of Nepal.* London: Murray, 1972. Standard work on the flora of Nepal.

Storrs, Adrian & Jimmy. *Enjoy Trees: A simple guide to some of the shrubs found in Nepal.* Kathmandu: Shahayogi Press, 1987.

Tuting, Ludmilla and Dixit, Kunda. *BIKAS-BINAS/ Development-Destruction? The Change of Life and Environment of the Himalaya.* Munich: Geobuch, 1986.

Valli, Eric and Summers, Diane. *Honey Hunters of Nepal.* USA: Harry N. Abrams, 1988.

MOUNTAIN TREKKING

Armington, Stan. *Trekking in the Himalayas.* South Yarra. Vic., Australia: Lonely Planet, 1979. Survey and guide to trekking.

Bezruschka, Stephen. *Trekking in Nepal: A Traveller's Guide.* Seattle: The Mountaineers, 1991. One of the best books on the subject.

Bezruschka, Stephen. *The Pocket Doctor: Your Ticket to Good Health While Travelling.* Seattle: The Mountaineers 1988. Useful pocket book, never travel without.

Bonington, Chris. *Annapurna South Face.* London: Cassell, 1971.

Bonington, Chris. *Everest South West Face.* London: Hodder and Stoughton, 1973.

Bonington, Chris. *Everest the Hard Way.* London: Hodder and Stoughton, 1979.

Brook, Elaine and Donnelly, Julie. *The Windhorse.* London: Jonathan Cape, 1986. A blind English girl is taken trekking in Nepal.

Coburn, Broughton. *Nepali Aama: Portrait of a*

Nepalese Hill Woman. Santa Barbara, California: Ross Erikson, 1982.

Downs, Hugh. *Rhythms of a Himalayan Village.* New York: Harper & Row, 1980.

Fantin, Mario. *Mani Rimdu Nepal.* Singapore: Toppan, 1976

Fantin, Mario. *Sherpa Himalaya Nepal,* Bologne, Italy: Arti Grafiche, 1978.

Giambrone, James. *Insight Pocket Guide: Biking and Hiking in the Kathmandu Valley.* Apa Publications, 1992. First book on mountain biking and hiking routes for enthusiasts.

Hackett, Peter. *Mountain Sickness.* American Alpine Club.

Herzog, Maurice. *Annapurna: First Conquest of an 8,000-Meter Peak (26,493 Feet).* New York: E.P. Dutton, 1953.

Hillary, Edmund. *High Adventure.* New York: E.P. Dutton, 1955.

Hillary, Edmund. *School House in the Clouds.* Garden City, N.Y.: Doubleday, 1964. Account of the1963 climbing expedition as well the assistance rendered to Sherpa communities.

Hillary, Edmund and Desmond Doig. *High in the Thin Cold Air: The Story of the Himalayan Expedition Led by Sir Edmund Hillary.* Garden City, New York: Doubleday, 1962.

Hillary, Edmund and George Lowe. *East of Everest: An Account of the New Zealand Alpine Club Himalayan Expedition to the Barun Valley in 1954.* New York: E.P. Dutton, 1956.

Hillary, Edmund. *Sagarmatha.* Apa Publications, 1992. Incomparable collection of unusual and historical photos of Everest donated as a fundraiser for the Himalayan Trust.

Hornbein, Thomas F. *Everest, the West Ridge,* San Francisco: Sierra Club, 1965.

Houston, Charles S. *Going Higher: The Story of Man and Altitude.* Boston: Little Brown 1987.

Hunt, John. *The Ascent of Everest.* London: Hodder and Stoughton, 1953. Also *The Conquest of Everest.* New York: E.P. Dutton, 1954.

Hunt, John. *The Conquest of Himalayas.* New York: E.P. Dutton, 1954.

Hunt, John. *Our Everest Adventure: The Pictorial History from Kathmandu to the Summit.* New York: E.P. Dutton, 1954.

Iozawa, Tomoya. *Trekking in the Himalayas.* Tokyo: Yama-Kei, 1980. Excellent maps.

Izzard, Ralph. *The Abominable Snowman Adventure.* London: Hodder and Stoughton, 1955. Also Garden City, New York: Doubleday, 1955. Account of a solo journey from Kathmandu to Everest, chasing the Hunt expedition.

Izzard, Ralph. *An Innocent on Everest.* New York: E.P. Dutton, 1954. Laso London: Hodder and Stoughton, 1955 Account of a solo journey from Kathmandu to Everest, chasing the Hunt expedition.

Jeffries, Margaret and Clarbrough, Margaret. *Sagarmatha, Mother of the Universe: The Story of*

Mount Everest National Park. Auckland: Cobb/ Horwood, 1986. Most useful guide to the Khumbu.

Jones, Mike, *Canoeing Down Everest.* New Delhi: Vikas, 1979.

Kaplan, Amy R. and Keller, Michael. *The Nepal Trekker's Handbook.* Mustang Publishing Co. Inc 1989. Concise, witty and enjoyable book about how to organise your trek and what to expect.

Kazami, Takehide. *The Himalayas.* Tokyo: Kodansha International, 1973.

McCallum, John D. *Everest Diary*; (based on the personal diary of Lute Jerstad, one of the first five Americans to conquer Mount Everest). New York; Fallet, 1966.

Messner, Reinhold. *Everest: Expedition to the Ultimate.* London: Kaye and Ward, 1979.

Nakano, Toru. *Trekking in Nepal.* Union City, California: Heian International Inc., 1985. Translated from Japanese.

Nicholson, Nigel. *The Himalayas.* New York: Time-Life Books, 1978. Part of the "World's Wild Places" series.

O'Connor, Bill. *The Trekking Peaks of Nepal.* Seattle: Cloudcap Press, 1989 and England: Crowood Press. Excellent detailed guide with useful maps.

Peissel, Michel. *Mustang, the Forbidden Kingdom: Exploring a Lost Himalayan Land.* New York: E.P. Dutton, 1967. Trekking travelogue.

Rowell, Galen. *Many People Come, Looking, Looking.* Seattle: The Mountaineers. 1980. Personal trekking travelogue with good photographs.

Schaller, George B. *Stones of Silence.* London: Andre Deutsch, 1980. Report of a naturalist's survey in Dolpo.

Shirakawa, Yoshikazu. *Himalayas.* Tokyo: Shogakukan, 1976. Also New York: Harry N. Abrams, 1977. Beautiful photographic book.

Steele, Peter. *Medical Handbook for Mountaineers.* London: Constable, 1988.

Swift, Hugh. *Trekking in Nepal, West Tibet and Bhutan.* San Francisco: Sierra Club, 1989. Good general route information.

Tenzing Norgay and James Ramsey Ullman. *Man of Everest:* The Autobiography of Tenzing. London: George G. Harrap, 1955. Also *Tiger of the Snows.* New York: G.P. Putnam's Sons, 1955.

Tilman, W. *Nepal Himalaya.* Cambridge: Cambridge University Press. 1952. Mountaineer's reports of attacks on high peaks.

Tucci, Giusepee. *Journey to Mustag.* Translated from Italian by Diana Fussel. Kathmandu: Ratna Pustak Bhandar, 1982.

Ullman, James Ramsey. *Americans on Everest: The Official Account Led by Norman G. Dyhrenfurth.* New York: J.B. Lippincott, 1964.

Ullman, James Ramsey. *Kingdom of Adventure: Everest.* New York: E.P. Dutton, 1947.

Unsworth, Walt. *Everest.* London: Allen Lane, 1981. Best history written of world's highest peak.

Waddell, L.A. *Among the Himalayas.* Westminister England: Archibold Constable and Co., 1899. Concerns one mountaineer's travelogue.

Wilkerson, James. *A Medicine for Mountaineering.* Seattle: The Mountaineers, 1985.

USEFUL ADDRESSES

ROYAL NEPALESE MISSIONS OVERSEAS

Australia, Consulate, Suite 23, 2nd Floor, 18-20 Bank Place, Melbourne, Victoria 3000; Tel: 03 602 1271

P.O. Box 1097, Toowong 4066, Brisbane; Tel: 07 378 0124

4th Floor, Airways House, 195 Adelaide Terrace, Perth, Western Australia 6004; Tel: 09 221 1207

Bangladesh , Embassy, United Nations Road, Road No 2, Baridhara, Diplomatic Enclave, Dhaka; Tel: 601890, 602091, 601790

Belgium, Consulate, 149 Lamorinierstraat, B-2018 Antwerpen; Tel: 03 230 8800

Burma (Union of Myanmar), Embassy, 16 Natmauk Yeiktha, P.O. Box 84, Rangoon; Tel: 50633

Canada, Consulate, 310 Dupont Street, Toronto, Ontario M5 RIV9; Tel: 416 968 7252

China, Embassy, No 1, Sanlitun Xiliujie, Beijing; Tel: 5321795

Consulate, Norbulingka Road 13, Lhasa, Tibet Autonomous Region; Tel: 22880

Denmark, Consulate, 2 Teglgardsstr, DK-1452 Copenhagen K; Tel: 01 143175

Egypt, Embassy, 9 Tiba Street, Dokki, Cairo; Tel: 704447, 3603426

Finland, Nepalese Consulate General, Erottaja 11 A 14, P.O.B. 198, FI-00131 Helsinki; Tel: 6802225, Fax: 6801024

France, Embassy, 45 bis rue des Acacias, 75017 Paris; Tel: 462224867

Consulates: 7 bis Allee des Soupirs, 31000 Toulouse Tel: 61 329122

105 rue Jeanne d'Arc, Rouen; Tel: 35 98 62 14

Germany, Embassy, Im Hag 15, D-5300 Bonn 2; Tel: 0228 343097, 343099
Consulates: Flinschstrasse 63, P.O. Box 600880, 6000 Frankfurt am Main 60; Tel: 069 40871
Landsberger Strasse 191, D-8000 Munchen 21; Tel: 089 570 4406
Handwerkstr 5-7, D-7000 Stuttgart 80 (Vaihingen); Tel: 0711 7864614
Uhlandstr 171/172, 1000 Berlin 15; Tel: 030 8814049, 8814040

Greece, Consulate, 8 Herodotou Str, GR-106 75 Athens; Tel: 01 7214116

Hong Kong, Liaison Office, HQ Brigade of Gurkhas The Prince of Wales Building, HMS Tamar, British Forces Post Office 1; Tel: 852 8633255

India, Embassy, Barakhamba Road, New Delhi 110001; Tel: 3329969, 3327361, 3328191
Consulate: 19 Woodlands, Sterndale Road, Alipore, Calcutta 700027; Tel: 452024, 459027, 454293

Ital, Consulate, Piazzale Medaglie d'Oro 20, 00136 Rome; Tel: 348176, 342055

Japa, Embassy, 14-9 Todoroki 7-chome, Setagaya-Ku, Tokyo 158; Tel: 03 705 558, 705 559

Korea, Consulate, 541 Namdaemoonnro, Jung-Gu, Seoul 100; Tel: 778 3183, 22 9992

Lebanon, Consulate, c/o President of Lebanese Red Cross, Rue Spears, Beirut; Tel: 386690

Mexico, Consulate, No 24 Jardines de Sam Mateo, Naucalpan, Estado de Mexico

Netherlands, Prinsengracht 687 (Gelderland Building), 1017 JV Amsterdam; Tel: 020 241580

Norway, Consulate, Haakon Viis Gt 5, P.O. Box 1384 VIKA, 0116 Oslo; Tel: 02 414743

Pakistan, Embassy, House No 506, Street No 84, Attaturk Avenue, Ramna G-6/4, Islamabad; Tel: 823642, 823754
Consulate: 419 4th Floor, Qamar House, M.A. Jinnah Road, Karachi 2; Tel: 200979, 201113

Phillipines, Consulate, 1136-1138 United Nations Avenue, Paco, 2803 Manila; Tel: 589393, 588855

Saudi Arabia, Embassy, Khazan St near Prince Musaed Palace, P.O. Box 94384, Riyadh 11693; Tel: 4024758, 4036433, 4039482

Spain, Consulate, Mallorca 194 Pral 2A, 08036 Barcelona, Tel: 343 3231323

Sri Lanka, 5th Floor, Vision House, 52 Galle Road, Colombo 4; Tel: 583536, 502139

Sweden, Consulate, Eriksbergsgatanis, S-114 30 Stockholm

Switzerland, Consulate, Asylstrasse 81, 8030 Zurich; Tel: 01 475993

Thailand, Embassy, 189 Sukhamvit 71 Road, Bangkok 10110; Tel: 391 7240, 390 2280

Turkey, Consulate, Y.K.B. Ishani Valikonagi Cad 4/4, Nisantas, Istanbul

U.S.S.R., Embassy, 2nd Neopalimovshy Perulok 14/7 Moscow; Tel: 2447356, 2419311

U.K., Embassy, 12A Kensington Palace Gardens, London W8 4QU; Tel: 071 229 1594, 071 229 6231

United Nations, Permanent Mission, 820 Second Avenue, Suite 202, New York, New York 10017, U.S.A.
1 rue Frederic Amiel, 1203 Geneva, Switzerland

U.S.A , Embassy, 2131 Leroy Place N.W., Washington D.C. 20008; Tel: 202 667 4550, 202 667 4551, 202 667 4552
Consulates: 1500 Lake Shore Drive, Chicago, Illinois 60610
Heidelberg College, Tiffin, Ohio 44883; Tel: 419 448 2202
909 Montgomery Street, Suite 400, San Francisco, California 94133; Tel: 415 434 1111
16250 Dallas Parkway, Suite 110, Dallas, Texas 75248; Tel: 214 931 1212
212 15th Street N.E.; Atlanta, Georgia 30309; Tel: 404 892 8152

FOREIGN MISSIONS

Australia, Bhat Bhateni	411578
Bangladesh, Naxal	414943
Burma, Pulchowk	521788
China, Baluwatar	411740
Egypt, Pulchowk	521844
France, Lazimpat	412332
Denmark, Baluwater	413010
Germany, Ganeshwar	412786
India, Lainchaur	410900
Israel, Lazimpat	411811
Italy, Baluwatar	412743
Japan, Pani Pokhari	414083
Korea (North), Patan	521084
Korea (South), Tahachal	211172
Pakistan, Pani Pokhari	410565
Russia, Baluwatar	412155
Thailand, Thapathali	213910
United Kingdom, Lainchaur	410583
USA, Pani Pokhari	411179

INTERNATIONAL ORGANISATIONS

American Express, Durbar Marg	226172
British Council, Kantipath	221305
French Cultural Center, Bagh Bazaar	224326
Goethe Institute, Sundhara	220528
International Monetary Fund	411977
United Nations, Pulchowk	523200
US AID, Kalimati	270144
US Information Service, New Road	223893
Visa, c/o Nepal Grindlays Bank	228473
World Bank, Kantipath	226792

AIRLINES

Air France, Durbar Marg	223339
Air India, Kantipath	211730
Bangladesh Biman, Durbar Marg	222544
British Airways, Durbar Marg	222266
Cathay Pacific, Kantipath	226765
CAAC, Kamaladi	411302
Dragon Air, Durbar Marg	227064
Druk Air, Durbar Marg	225166
Indian Airlines, Durbar Marg	223053
Japan Airlines, Durbar Marg	222838
Lufthansa, Durbar Marg	223052
Northwest Airlines, Lekhnath Marg	418387
Pakistan International, Durbar Marg	223102
Royal Nepal Airlines, New Road	220757
Singapore Airlines, Durbar Marg	220759
Swissair, Durbar Marg	222452
Thai International, Durbar Marg	225084
Trans World Airlines, Kamaladi	411725

TRAVEL AGENCIES & OPERATORS

Adventure Travel Nepal, Lazimpath	415995
Annapurna Travels, Durbar Marg	223940
Everest Express, Durbar Marg	220759
Gurkha Travels, Durbar Marg	224896
Himalayan Travels, Durbar Marg	226011
Himalayan Mountain Bikes, Kantipath	225875
Kathmandu Travels & Tours, Gangapath	222985
Lama Excursions, Durbar Marg	220186
Machan Wildlife Resort, Durbar Marg	225001
Malla Travels, Malla Hotel	410635
Marco Polo, Kamal Pokhari	414192
Natraj Tours & Travels	222014
President Travels, Durbar Marg	220245
Shankar Travel, Shankar Hotel	411465
Tibet Travels & Tours, Thamel	410303
Tiger Tops, Durbar Marg	222706
World Travels, Durbar Marg	227810
Yeti Travels, Durbar Marg	221234

TREKKING AGENCIES

Above the Clouds Trekking, Thamel	416923
Adventure Nepal Trekking, Keshar Mahal	412508
Ama Dablam Trekking, Lazimpat	410219
Asian Trekking, Keshar Mahal	412821
Cho-Oyu Trekking, Lazimpat	418890
Guides For All Seasons, Gairi Dhara	415841
Himalayan Adventures, Lazimpat	411477
Himalayan Journeys, Kantipath	226138
Himalayan Rover Trek, Naxal	412667
International Trekkers, Durbar Marg	220594
Journeys Mountaineering & Trekking	225969
Malla Treks, Lekhnath Marg	418389
Mountain Travel Nepal, Lazimpat	414508
Natraj Trekking, Kantipath	226644
Nepal Himal, Baluwatar	419796
Nepal Trekking, Thamel	214681
Sherpa Cooperative Trekking, Durbar Marg	224068
Sherpa Trekking Service, Kamaladi	222489
Trans Himalayan Trekking, Durbar Marg	223854
Yangrima Trekking, Kantipath	225608

RIVER TRIPS OPERATORS

Great Himalayan Rivers, Kantipath	216913
Himalayan Adventure, Pani Pokhari	414344
Himalayan Encounters, Thamel	417426
Himalayan River Adventure, Lazimpat	410219
Himalayan River Exploration	418491
Himalayan White Waters, Thamel	225371
Journeys Whitewater Rafting, Kantipath	225969
White Magic Nepal, Thamel	226885
Wild Waters, Pani Pokhari	410561

ART/PHOTO CREDITS

GLOSSARY

A

akha - A traditional place where religious dancing is taught.

Ananda - The Buddha's chief disciple.

Ananta - A huge snake whose coils created Vishnu's bed.

Annapurna - The goddess of abundance; one aspect of Devi.

arak - A whisky fermented from potatoes or grain.

Asadh - The third month of the Nepalese year (June-July).

Ashta Matrikas - The eight mother goddesses said to attend on Shiva or Skanda.

Ashta Nag - Eight serpent deities who guard the cardinal directions and (if worshipped) keep evil spirits away.

Ashwin - The sixth month of the Nepalese year (September-October).

asla - A freshwater mountain trout.

Avalokiteshwara - A *bodhisattva* regarded as the god of mercy in Mahayana Buddhist tradition, and as the compassionate Machhendra in Nepal.

avatar - An incarnation of a deity on earth.

B

bahal - A two-storey Buddhist monastery enclosing a courtyard.

bahil - A Buddhist monastery, smaller and simpler than a bahal.

Baisakh - The first month of the Nepalese year (April-May).

Bajra Jogini - A Tantric goddess.

bajracharya - A Newar caste of Buddhist priests.

Balarama - The brother of Krishna.

Balkumari - A consort of Bhairav.

beyul - A hidden valley, sacred in ancient Tibetan texts.

bhaati - An inn or tea shop, especially those of the Thakali people.

bhaat - Cooked rice, also refers to a meal (of rice).

Bhadrakali - A Tantric goddess and consort of Bhairav.

Bhadra - The fifth month of the Nepalese year (August-September).

Bhagavad-Gita - The most important Hindu religious scripture, in which the god Krishna spells out the importance of duty. It is contained in the *Mahabharata*.

Bhairav - The god Shiva in his most terrifying form.

bharad - A reverential title.

bharal - Blue sheep.

Bhimsen - A deity worshipped for his strength and courage.

bhot - High, arid valleys in the Tibetan border region.

bodhi (also *bo*) - The pipal tree under which Gautama Buddha achieved enlightenment, and any tree so worshipped.

bodhisattva - In Mahayana tradition, a person who has attained the enlightened level of Buddhahood, but chose to remain on earth to teach until others are enlightened.

Bonpo - A follower of the Bon faith.

Bon - The pre-Buddhist religion of Tibet, incorporating animism and sorcery.

brahman - The highest of Hindu castes, originally that of priests.

Brahma - In Hindu mythology, the revered god of creation.

Brahmanism - Ancient Indian religion, predecessor of modern Hinduism and Buddhism.

C

Chaitra - The 12th and last month of the Nepalese year (March-April).

chaitya - A small stupa, sometimes containing a Buddhist relic, but usually holding *mantras* or holy scriptures.

chakra - A round weapon, one of the four objects held by Vishnu.

chapati - A type of bread made from wheat flour.

chapa - A small house annexed to a temple, in which feasts are held and rituals performed.

chautara - A tree-shaded stone wall resting place.

chhang - A potent mountain beer of fermented grain, usually barley but sometimes maize, rye or millet.

chhetri - The Hindu warrior caste, second in status only to brahmans.

chhura - Beaten rice.

chitrakar - A Newar caste of artists.

chiya - Nepalese tea, brewed together with milk, sugar and spices.

chorten - A small Buddhist shrine on high mountain regions.

chowk - A palace or public courtyard.

chuba - A Tibetan or Sherpa robe, man's or woman's.

crore - A unit of counting equal to 10 million.

D-F

dabur - An urban roadside square, used for religous dancing during festivals and as a market place at other times.

Dalai Lama - The reincarnate high priest of Tibetan Buddhism and political leader of Tibetans around the world.

damais - A caste of tailors who form makeshift bands to play religious music for weddings and other occasions.

damiyen - A traditional stringed instrument, similar to a ukulele.

danphe - The colorful impeyan pheasant, national bird of Nepal.

Dattatraya - A syncretistic deity variously worshipped as an incarnation of Vishnu, a teacher of Shiva, or a cousin of the Buddha.

Devi (or **Maha Devi**) - "The great goddess." Shiva's *shakti* in her many forms.

dhal - A lentil "soup."

dhami - A soothsayer and sorcerer; also, the priest of a temple, especially a priest claiming occult powers.

dharmasala - A public rest house for travelers and pilgrims.

Dharma - Buddhist doctrine. Literally, "the path."

dharni - A weight measure equal to three *sers*, or about three kilograms.

dhoti - A loose loincloth.

dhyana - Meditation.

dighur - A Thakali system whereby a group of people pools its money to annually support one of its members in a chosen financial venture.

digi - A place of congregation and prayer.

doko - A basket, often carried on the head by means of a strap.

dorje - A ritual scepter or thunderbolt, symbol of the

Absolute to Tantric Buddhists. (Also *vajra*)

dungidara - A stone water spout.

dun - Valleys of the Inner Terai.

Durga - Shiva's *shakti* in one of her most awesome forms.

dwarapala - a door guardian.

dwarmul - The main gate of a building.

dyochhen - A house enshrining protective Tantric deities. Used for common worship.

dzopkyo - A hybrid bull, the cross between a yak and a cow.

dzu-tch - According to Sherpas, a type of yeti that is about eight feet tall and eats cattle.

dzum - a hybrid cow, the cross between a yak and a cow.

ek - The number one, a symbol of unity.

Falgun - The 11th month of the Nepalese year (February-March).

G-H

gaine - A wandering, begging minstrel.

gajur - An often-ornate, bell-shaped finial crowning a *bahal*.

Ganesh - The elephant-headed son of Shiva and Parvati. He is worshipped as the god of good luck and the remover of obstacles.

Ganga - A Hindu goddess.

Garuda - A mythical eagle, half-human. The vehicle of Vishnu.

Gautama Buddha - The historical Buddha, born in Lumbini in the 6th Century B.C.

gelugpa - a Tibetan sect.

ghada - A type of club, one of the weapons of Vishnu and a Tantric symbol.

ghanta - A symbolic Tantric bell, the female counterpart of the *vajra*.

ghat - A riverside platform for bathing and cremation.

ghee - Clarified butter.

gompa - Tibetan Buddhist monastery.

gopala - A cowherd.

gopis - Cowherd girls; specifically those who cavorted with Krishna in a famous Hindu legend.

Gorakhnath - Historically, an 11th-Century yogi who founded a Shairite cult; now popularly regarded as an incarnation of Shiva.

granthakut - A tall, pointed brick and-plaster shrine supported by a one story stone base.

guthibar - The members of a buthi; also, a group of families with the same ancestry.

guthi - A communal Newar brotherhood serving the purpose of mutual support for members and their extended families.

Hanuman - A deified monkey, Hero of the *Ramayana epic,* he is believed to bring success to armies.

hapa - A bamboo rice-measuring device made only in Pyangaon.

Harisiddhi - A fierce Tantric goddess.

harmika - The eyes on a stupa, placed to face the four cardinal directions.

himal - Snowy peak or range.

hiti - A water conduit; a bath or tank with water spouts.

hookah - A water pipe through which tobacco or hashish is smoked.

I-J

impeyan - Nepal's national bird, a species of pheasant.

Indra - God of rain/rainfall; the chief deity of Brahminism.

jadun - A large vessel for drinking water at public places.

Jagannath - Krishna, worshipped as "Lord of the World."

Jamuna - A Hindu goddess who rides a tortoise.

janti - The groom's party at a wedding.

jarun - A raised stone water tank with carved spouts.

jatra - Festival.

Jaya Varahi - Vishnu's *shakti* in his incarnation as a boar.

jelebi - A sweet Nepali snack.

Jesth - The second month of the Nepalese year (May-June).

jhaad - Traditional rice beer.

jhankri - A shaman or sorcerer.

Jhankrism - Traditional animism, incorporating occult practices.

jhya - Carved window.

jogini - A mystical goddess.

juga - leech.

jyapu - Newar farmer caste.

K

kalashi - A pot.

Kali - Shiva's *shakti* in her most terrifying form.

kapok - The silk cotton tree.

karma - The cause-and-effect chain of actions, good and bad, from one life to the next.

Kartik - The seventh month of the Nepalese year (October-November).

kata - A ceremonial scarf presented to high Tibetan Buddhist figures.

khat - An enclosed wooden shrine, similar in appearance to the portable shrines carried during processions.

khola - River or stream.

khukri - A traditional knife, long and curved, best known as the weapon of Gurkha soldiers.

kot - small hilltop fortress.

Krishna - The eighth incarnation of Vishnu, heavily worshipped for his activities on earth.

kshepu - A snake-eating figure often depicted on temple *toranas*.

kumari - A young virgin regarded as a living goddess in Kathmandu Valley towns.

kunda - A recessed water tank fed by underground springs.

L

laddu - A sweet Nepali snack.

lakhe - Masked dancing.

lakh - A unit of counting equal to 100,000.

Lakshmi - The goddess of wealth and consort of Vishnu.

laligurans - Rhododendron, Nepal's national flower.

lama - A Tibetan Buddhist priest.

la - Mountain pass.

lingum (pl.*lingas*) - A symbolic male phallus, generally associated with Shiva.

Lokeshwar - "Lord of the World," a form of Avalokiteshwara to Buddhists and of Shiva to Hindus.

M

Machhendra - The guardian god of the Kathmandu Valley, guarantor of rain and plenty. The deity is also a popular interpretation of Avalokiteshwara or Lokeshwar and is enshrined as the Rato (Red) Machhendra in Patan and the Seto (White) Machhendra in Kathmandu.

Magha - The 10th month of the Nepalese year (January-February).

Mahabharata - An important Hindu epic.

Mahabharat Lekh - A range of hills between the Himalayas and the Terai.

maharishi - Literally, "great teacher."

Mahayana - The form of Buddhism prevalent in East Asia, Tibet and Nepal.

Maitreya - The future Buddha.

makara - A mythical crocodile, often depicted on *toranas*.

mali - A Newar caste of gardeners.

mana - A measure for rice and cereals, milk and sugar, containing a little less than half a liter.

mandala - A sacred diagram envisioned by Tibetan Buddhists as an aid to meditation.

mandap - A roofless Tantric shrine made of brick or wood.

mani - A Tibetan Buddhist prayer inscribed in rock in high mountain areas.

Majushri - The legendary Buddhist patriarch of the Kathmandu Valley, now often regarded as the god of learning.

mantra - Sacred syllables chanted during meditation by Buddhists.

Marga - The eighth month of the Nepalese year (November-December).

mahseer - A large freshwater fish highly prized in Nepal.

math - A Hindu priest's house.

migyu - Tibetan name for the yeti.

mih-tch - According to Sherpas, a hostile, man-sized, ape-like yeti.

momos - Tibetan stuffed pastas, somewhat like ravioli.

mudra - A symbolic hand posture or gesture often employed during religious prayer and meditation.

munja - The sacred thread worn by brahman and chhetri males from the time of puberty.

muri - A dry measure equal to about 75 liters. It contains precisely 20 *paathis* or 160 *manas*.

muthi - A measure equal to "a handful."

N

naamlo - A woven rope headstrap with which porters carry the doko (basket).

naga - Snake, especially a legendary or a deified serpent.

nak - Female yak.

namaste - A very common word of greeting, often translated as: "I salute all divine qualities in you."

Nandi - A bull, Shiva's vehicle and a symbol of fecundity.

nanglo - A cane tray.

nani - A type of *bahal* containing a large courtyard surrounded by residences, also including a Buddhist shrine.

Narayan - Vishnu represented as the creator of life. A lotus from Narayan's navel issued Brahma.

Narsingh - Vishnu's incarnation as a lion.

nath - Literally, "Place."

nirvana - Extinction of self, the goal of Buddhist meditation.

Nriteshwar - The god of dance.

P

paathi - A dry measure equal to eight *manas*, about 3® liters.

padma - The lotus flower.

pahar - The heavily eroded central zone of hills and valleys between the Himalayas and the Mahabharat Lekh.

panchayat - A government system of elected councils at local, regional and national levels.

Parvati - Shiva's consort, displaying both serene and fearful aspects.

pashmina - A shawl or blanket made of fine goat's wool.

Pashupati - Shiva in his aspect as "Lord of the Beasts." Symbolized by the *lingum*, he is believed to bring fecundity.

pasni - A Hindu rice-feeding ceremony conducted for seven-month-old babies, and repeated for old people of 77 years, seven months.

patasi - A sari-like dress, especially popular in Bhaktapur.

path - A small raised platform which provides shelter for travelers on important routes and intersections.

pathi - A liquid measurement, slightly less than one gallon.

patuka - A waistcloth in which to carry small objects and even babies.

pau - A measure for vegetables and fruit, equal to 250 grams.

paubha - Traditional Newari painting, usually religious in motif.

pith - An open shrine dedicated to a Tantric goddess.

pokhari - A large pond or lake.

Poush - The ninth month of the Nepalese year (December-January).

preta - A spirit of the dead.

puja - Ritual offerings to the gods.

pukhu - A pond.

punya - Merit earned through actions and religous devotion.

puri - Town.

R

rakshi - A homemade wheat or rice liquor.

Rama - The seventh incarnation of Vishnu. A prince, hero of the *Ramayana* epic.

Ramayana - The most widely known Hindu legend, in which Rama, with the aid of Hanuman and Garuda, rescues his wife, Sita, from the demon king Rawana.

Rawana - the anti-hero of the *Ramayana*.

rikhi doro - A golden thread which Shiva devotees tie around their wrists to ward off evil and disease.

rimpoche - The abbot of a Tibetan Buddhist monastery (*gompa*).

Rudrayani - A Kathmandu Valley nature goddess. Also known as Shekali Mai.

S

sadhu - A Hindu mendicant.

sajha - Cooperative, organized in the 1970s to deal with inequalities in land sharing.

sal - A strong timber tree of the lower slopes of Himalayan foothills.

sankha - The conch shell, one of the four symbols held by Vishnu. It is widely used in Hindu temples and shrines during prayer.

sanyasin - A religious ascetic who has renounced his ties to society.

saranghi - A small, four-stringed viola shaped from a single piece of wood and played with a horsehair bow.

Saraswati - Brahma's consort, worshipped in Nepal as the Hindu goddess of learning.

satal - A pilgrim's house.

ser - A unit of weight equal to four *paus*, or about one kilogram.

serow - A wild Himalayan antelope.

shakti (often cap.) - Shiva's consort, literally, power the dynamic element in the male-female relationship, and the female aspect of the Tantric Absolute.

shaligram - A black ammonite fossil regarded as sacred by Vishnu devotees.

shandula - A mythical bird, a griffin.

shikhara - A brick or stone temple of geometrical shape with a tall central spire.

Shitala Mai - A former ogress who became a protector of

children, worshipped at Swayambhunath.

Shiva - The most awesome of Hindu gods. He destroys all things, good as well as evil, allowing new creation to take shape.

shrestha - A Newar caste.

sirdar - A guide, usually a Sherpa, who leads trekking groups.

sindur - A votive mixture made of red dust combined with mustard oil.

Sita - Rama's wife, heroine of the *Ramayana* epic. She is worshipped in Janakpur, her legendary birthplace.

Skanda - The Hindu god of war.

Srawan - The fourth month of the Nepalese year (July-August).

stupa - A bell-shaped relic chamber.

sudra - Lowest of the Hindu castes, commonly thought to have descended from Brahma's feet.

sundhara - A fountain with a golden spout.

Surjya - The sun god, often identified with Vishnu.

suttee - Former Indian practice of immolating widows on their husbands' funeral pyres.

T-U

tabla - A traditional hand drum.

tahr - A wild Himalayan goat.

Taleju Bhawani - The Nepalese goddess, originally a South Indian deity; an aspect of Devi.

tal - lake

Tara - Historically a Nepalese princess, now deified by Buddhists and Hindus.

Terai - The Nepalese lowland region.

Thakuri - high Hindu caste.

thangka - A religious scroll painting.

thelma - According to Sherpas, a small, reddish, ape-like yeti.

thukba - A thick Tibetan soup.

tika - A colorful vermilion powder applied by Hindus to the forehead, between the eyes, as a symbol of the presence of the divine.

tola - A metal measure equal to 11.5 grams.

tole - A street.

topi - The formal, traditional Nepali cap.

torana - A decorative carved crest suspended over the door of a sanctum, with the figure of the enshrined deity at its center.

trisul - The trident, chief symbol of the god Shiva.

tsampa - Raw grain, sometimes eaten dry, usually ground and mixed with milk, tea or water. A traditional mountain food.

tulku - In Tibetan Buddhism, a religious figure regarded as a reincarnation of a great *lama* of the past.

tulsi - A sacred basil plant.

tunal - The carved strut of a temple.

tympanum - A decorative crest beneath the triangular peak of a roof.

Uma - Shiva's consort in one of her many aspects.

Upanishads - Early Brahministic religious texts; speculations on Vedic thought.

V

aisya - The "middle-class" caste of merchants and farmers.

vajra (also *dorje*) - In Tantric Buddhism, a ritual thunderbolt or curved scepter symbolizing the Absolute. It also represents power and male energy.

varahi - A god incarnated as a boar.

Vedas - The earliest Brahministic religious verses, dating from the second millennium B.C. They define a polytheistic faith.

vedica - A sacrificial altar.

vihara - A Buddhist monastery, encompassing *a bahal* and *a bahil.*

Vikrantha (also Vamana) - Vishnu in his fifth incarnation, as a dwarf.

Vishnu - One of the Hindu trinity, a god who preserves life and the world itself. In Nepal, he is most commonly represented as Narayan.

W-Z

yab-yum - Tantric erotica, a symbol of unity and oneness.

yeh-tch - The Sherpa name for the yeti; literally, "man of the rocky places."

yeti - A mythical anthropoid of Nepal's highest elevations, often referred to in the West as "The Abominable Snowman."

yoni - A hole in a stone, said to symbolise the female sexual aspect. Usually seen together with a *lingum.*

zamindari - A system of absentee landlordism, officially abolished in 1955 but still perpetuated in some regions.

INDEX

giant catfish, 131
Godavari Kunda, 233
Gokarna Aunshi (Father's Day), 114, 231
Gokarna Mahadev, 231, 236
Gokarna Safari Park, 236
Gokarna, 114
Gokyo Valley, 107, 297
Golden Gate, 211, 217
gompas, 80, 181, 225, 250, 279
   Kyangjin Gompa, 240
   Nage Gompa, 240
   Shey Gompa, 312
   Sing Gompa, 262
Gondwanaland, 31
Goodfellow, Basil (mountaineer), 153
Gopalas, 61
Gopinath Mandir, 207
Gorakhnath Cave, 226
Gorakhnath Shikhara, 231
Gorakhnath, 98
Gorkha, 51, 52, 61, 79, 91, 201, 216, 257
Gosainkund Lake, 262
Gosainkund, 113, 260
Gregory, Alf (mountaineer), 148, 152
Griffin, Lindsay (mountaineer), 149
Gurkha (soldiers), 63, 84, 91-92
Gurla Mandhata, 64
Gurung (people), 53, 84, 85, 91, 260, 269, 284
gurwas (priests), 86
guthi, 79

H

H. M. The King's Birthday, 114
Habeler, Peter (mountaineer), 169, 173, 178, 183
hang-gliding, 127
Hanuman Dhoka,111, 114, 310
Hanuman Durbar, 206, 207
Hanuman, 100
Hanumante River, 216
Haribodhini Ekadasi, 114
Harpan Khola, 282
helicopter skiing, 127
Herzog, Maurice (mountaineer), 162, 163, 253, 281
Hillary, Sir Edmund, 26, 68, 107, 129, 163, 169, 170, 178, 253
Himachuli, 51, 166, 257, 260, 269, 276, 282
Himalaya, 23, 31, 32, 33, 49, 51, 54, 57, 61, 63, 123, 162, 185
Himalayan Mountain Bikes, 125
Himalayan Pilgrimage, 312
Himalayan River Exploration, 124, 129
Himalayan Trust, 178, 292
Hinduism, 23, 25, 83, 97, 98, 99, 111
Hiunchuli, 147, 153, 154
Holi, 111
Hongu Basin, 295
hookah (pipe), 260
Hornbein, Tom (mountaineer), 169
Hotel Elephant Camp, 136
Houston, Charles (mountaineer), 163
Howard-Bury, Colonel C. K., 106
Hsuan Chang (Chinese pilgrim), 61
Humla, 53
Hunt, John (mountaineer), 106, 163

I-J

Ichangu Narayan, 114, 228, 241
Imanishi, Toshio (mountaineer), 166
Imja River, 148
India, 25, 54
Indra, 114
Indrajatra, 114, 204
Irvine, Andrew (mountaineer), 170
Isherwood (mountaineer), 155
Island Jungle Resort, 136
Island Peak, 147, 148, 295
Jackson, John (mountaineer), 165
Janai Purnima, 113, 213
Janakpur, 114
Jawalakhel, 214
Jaya Ranjit Malla, 217
Jayasthiti Malla, 61, 98, 201
jhankris, 80, 83, 104, 284
Jhobang, 282
Joechler, Sepp (mountaineer), 164
Jorsale, 293
Jugal, 152
Jumla, 309
Jung Bahadur Rana, 63, 91, 201, 208

K

Kabeli Khola, 304
Kagyudpa (Red Hats), 102
Kailas, 50, 97
Kala Pattar, 295
Kali Gandaki, 39, 42, 64, 66, 67, 83, 84, 114, 119, 129, 153, 186, 276, 281, 308
Kali, 103, 231
Kangchenjunga, 23, 26, 56, 64, 123, 158, 162, 164, 165, 178, 183, 262, 302
Kantipath (King's Way), 203, 209
karma, 100
Karnali river system, 37, 44, 131
Kartik, 114
Kasara Durbar, 136
Kashmir, 50, 63, 131
Kasthamandap (House of Wood), 201, 205, 206, 220
Kathmandu (capital), 26, 52, 61, 65, 66, 79, 112, 114, 127, 163, 170, 195, 201, 206, 259
Kathmandu Valley, 23, 25, 34, 50, 51, 55, 61, 63, 67, 79, 91, 101, 119, 121, 127, 153, 195
Kathmandu Zoo, 214
Kato, Yasuo (mountaineer), 169
Kawaguchi, Ekai (mountaineer), 67
Keshar Mahal, 209
Khasas, 91
Khel Tole, 208
Khirong La, 65, 66
khukri, 80, 92, 232, 302
Khumbila, 293
Khumbu, 148, 149, 159, 163, 180, 291, 295
Khumjung, 180
King Birendra Bir Bikram Shah Dev, 26, 68, 204
King Bupathindra Malla, 217, 219
King Mahendra Trust for Nature Conservation, 44
King Mahendra, 68, 208
King Manadeva, 210
King Narendradev, 98
King Prithvi Narayan Shah, 25, 26, 52, 61, 63, 91, 201, 206, 215, 257
King Songtsengampo, 101

V-Z

A
B
D
E
F
G
H
I
J
a
b
c
d
f
g
h
i
j
k
l

A P A
INSIGHT
GUIDES

ARE GOING PLACES:

Asia & Pacific
East Asia
South Asia
South East Asian Wildlife
South East Asia
★ Marine Life
Australia
Great Barrier Reef
Melbourne
★★ Sydney
★ Bhutan
Burma/Myanmar
China
Beijing
India
Calcutta
Delhi, Jaipur, Agra
India's Western Himalaya
Indian Wildlife
★ New Delhi
Rajasthan
South India
Indonesia
★★ Bali
★ Bali Bird Walks
Java
★ Jakarta
★ Yogyakarta
Korea
Japan
Tokyo
Malaysia
★ Kuala Lumpur
★ Malacca
★ Penang
★★ Nepal
Kathmandu
Kathmandu Bikes & Hikes
New Zealand
Pakistan
Philippines
★ Sikkim
★★ Singapore
Sri Lanka
Taiwan

Thailand
★★ Bangkok
★ Chiang Mai
★ Phuket
★ Tibet
Turkey
★★ Istanbul
Turkish Coast
★ Turquoise Coast
Vietnam

Africa
East African Wildlife
South Africa
Egypt
Cairo
The Nile
Israel
Jerusalem
Kenya
Morocco
Namibia
The Gambia & Senegal
Tunisia
Yemen

Europe
Austria
★★ Vienna
Belgium
Brussels
Channel Islands
Continental Europe
Cyprus
Czechoslovakia
★★ Prague
Denmark
Eastern Europe
Finland
France
★★ Alsace
★★ Brittany
★★ Cote d'Azur
★★ Loire Valley
★★ Paris

Provence
Germany
★★ Berlin
Cologne
Düsseldorf
Frankfurt
Hamburg
★★ Munich
The Rhine
Great Britain
Edinburg
Glasgow
★★ Ireland
★★ London
Oxford
Scotland
Wales
Greece
★★ Athens
★★ Crete
★ Rhodes
Greek Islands
Hungary
★★ Budapest
Iceland
Italy
Florence
★★ Rome
★★ Sardinia
★★ Tuscany
Umbria
★★ Venice
Netherlands
Amsterdam
Norway
Poland
Portugal
★★ Lisbon
Madeira
Spain
★★ Barcelona
★ Costa Blanca
★ Costa Brava
★ Costa del Sol/Marbella
Catalonia

Gran Canaria
★ Ibiza
Madrid
Mallorca & Ibiza
★ Mallorca
★ Seville
Southern Spain
Tenerife
Sweden
Switzerland
(Ex) USSR
Moscow
St. Petersburg
Waterways of Europe
Yugoslavia
★ Yugoslavia's Adriatic
Coast

The Americas
Bermuda
Canada
Montreal
Caribbean
Bahamas
Barbados
Jamaica
Trinidad & Tobago
Puerto Rico
Costa Rica
Mexico
Mexico City
South America
Argentina
Amazon Wildlife
Brazil
Buenos Aires
Chile
Ecuador
Peru
Rio

USA/Crossing America
Alaska
American Southwest
Boston
California
Chicago
Florida
Hawaii
Los Angeles
Miami
Native America
New England
New Orleans
★★ New York City
New York State
Northern California
Pacific Northwest
★★ San Francisco
Southern California
Texas
The Rockies
Washington D.C.

★★ Also available as
Insight Pocket Guide

★ Available as Insight
Pocket Guide only

फिर मिलेंगे!

See You Soon! In India

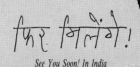